# THE MANCHESTER SCHOOL

Max Gluckman, Derbyshire, England, 1964

# THE MANCHESTER SCHOOL
## Practice and Ethnographic Praxis in Anthropology

*Edited by*

T. M. S. Evens and Don Handelman

*Berghahn Books*
NEW YORK • OXFORD
www.berghahnbooks.com

First published in 2006 by

**Berghahn Books**

www.berghahnbooks.com

© 2006, 2008 Berghahn Books
Reprinted in 2008

**Library of Congress Cataloging-in-Publication Data**

The Manchester School : practice and ethnographic praxis in anthropology /
    edited by T. M. S. Evens and Don Handelman.
        p. cm.
    Includes bibliographical references and index.
    ISBN 1-84545-282-8 (pbk. : alk. paper)
    1. Ethnology—Methodology. 2. Ethnology—Case studies.
    3. Ethnology—Study and teaching (Higher). 4. University of Manchester.
School of Social Anthropology. I. Evens, T. M. S. II. Handelman, Don.

GN345.M354 2006
305.8001—dc22

                                                                    2006025962

**British Library Cataloguing in Publication Data**

A catalogue record for this book is available from the British Library.

Printed in the United States on acid-free paper

The editors and publisher gratefully acknowledge the right to reproduce the articles
by Max Gluckman and Clyde Mitchell:

Gluckman, Max. 1961. "Ethnographic Data in British Social Anthropology."
*Sociological Review* 9, no. 1: 5–17.

Mitchell, J. Clyde. 1956. "Case and Situation Analysis." *Sociological Review* 31:
187–211.

Used by permission of the *Sociological Review*.

*Cover images*:

Max Gluckman and the Dover Street Building that housed the Department of Social
Anthropology and Sociology. Courtesy of the University of Manchester Archives.

Max Gluckman, Derbyshire, England, 1964. Photo by Terry Evens.

*To the memory of Max Gluckman and to all those whose work and research contributed directly to the creation of that powerful presence in social anthropology that came to be called the Manchester School*

# CONTENTS

# PROLOGUE

One way of thinking about the effects of the Malinowskian revolution in anthropological fieldwork during the first half of the twentieth century is to understand that it resulted in an enormous accumulation of fieldwork materials as anthropologists moved their easily portable method into all orbits of the globe for extended periods. Intensive fieldwork generated awareness and knowledge of social and cultural complexities hitherto unknown. This amassing of field data spawned problems of information processing in the production of knowledge, problems to which two major responses, both functionalist, arose in emerging British social anthropology. One tended to maximize this richly detailed information as ethnographic description. This response, that of Malinowski and his acolytes, used a crude functionalism to order and present large amounts of field material. The other response, that of Radcliffe-Brown and his followers, employed a more systemic and theoretically sophisticated functionalism to abstract from the field materials principles of social structure, thus allowing the anthropologist to exclude appreciably the materials themselves from the published ethnography.

During the 1940s and 1950s, a third perspective emerged, one that methodically valued both the theorizing and the ethnographic presentation of fieldwork materials. The materials were theorized by ever keeping them in view and combing ever so closely through the emergent and, by way of context and locale, constantly changing events, situations, and relationships registered therein. Through the work of Max Gluckman and his colleagues, the anthropology of the Manchester School shaped the extended-case method and situational analysis—the themes of this volume—into a version of what much later in the discipline came to be known as practice theory. Manchester anthropology practiced ethnography and analysis dialectically, so that each comes into existence primarily by way of the other. Such an analytical ethnography loses sight of neither the complexities of social life through time nor the importance of theorizing these. In Manchester School anthropology, fieldwork materials and conceptualization shape and use one another, producing recurrent epistemological surprise and, correlatively, inventing an anthropology not only *of* but also *as* practice.

The Manchester School had profound influence on British social anthropology and elsewhere. Yet by the 1970s, the approach had lost ground to vulgar claims that it was merely a remnant of structural-functionalism and its colonialist roots. By the 1980s, the impact on anthropology of approaches keyed to representation and reliance on text and media served to erode and blunt the significance of intensive and lengthy fieldwork in open social fields, helping further to eclipse Manchester School anthropology.

The present volume had its origins in a workshop on the extended-case method that we organized for the Biennial Conference of the European Association of Social Anthropologists in 2002. With no little irony, we regard the present time as auspicious for the reappearance of the Manchester School orientation to practice. It is our impression that more than a few anthropologists are awakening to forces that have undercut fieldwork anthropology, and that there is again something of a desire to ground ethnographic analysis ruthlessly through intimate scrutiny of field data rather than primarily in ideology, poetics, or theory per se. Perhaps this volume will contribute to this revival.

*T.E. and D.H., Chapel Hill and Jerusalem, July 2006*

# INTRODUCTION
## The Ethnographic Praxis of the Theory of Practice

*T. M. S. Evens and Don Handelman*

The ethnographic extended-case method, also known as situational analysis, was a diagnostic of the Manchester School of Social Anthropology—and today it remains an ethnographic practice of remarkable relevance and promise. Originated by Max Gluckman, the method was intended to use case material in a highly original way. Instead of citing examples from ethnography in apt illustration of general ethnographic and analytical statements, as was common in the discipline, Gluckman proposed to turn this relationship between case and statement on its head: the idea was to arrive at the general through the dynamic particularity of the case. Rather than a prop, the case became in effect the first step of ethnographic analysis. Underlying this methodological reversal, though, was a theoretical pursuit pertaining to an enveloping, indeed a suffocating, problem endemic to structural functionalism and implicating a social ontology radically different from this dominant paradigm.

As a young man in South Africa, Gluckman had studied law in university; he also was known throughout his career to have a certain affinity with psychoanalytical thought. Given the critical centrality of the notion of case in these two fields of study, using cases in a way essential to advancing his own discipline—ethnographic research—might well have had an intuitive appeal to Gluckman. At any rate, he grasped and shaped the case method in relation to the problem of "the on-going process of social life" (1965: 177), a problem with which he and his peers were inescapably confronted.

Gluckman's basic anthropological training was in structural functionalism, via, pre-eminently, Radcliffe-Brown's rendering of Durkheim. Plainly, the vital thesis of this paradigm—that the explanation of a social phenomenon is a matter of determining its function in reproducing the social structure in its current form—tended to picture society in terms of stability and equilibrium. This thesis recognized social process, yet only insofar as process was reducible to, and so in the service of, social stasis. In turn, the thesis created an undesirable, though virtual, constituent problem of the paradigm—to wit, the problem of how to explain social process that not only failed to contribute to the preservation of the status quo but also contravened or disrupted it. 'Disruptive' process of this kind loomed all too visible as intensive ethnographic fieldwork became the rule in social anthropology.

Gluckman's peers addressed this problem in a variety of ways, including the notable examples of Nadel's (1957) and Firth's (1961) psychologistic introduction of individual choice as the means by which to account for this kind of intrinsically generative process. In their psychologism they were inspired by their mentor, Bronislaw Malinowski. Gluckman, though influenced by Malinowski's ethnographic empiricism (a focused attention on how people actually behaved), was not taken with his psychologism. Moreover, Gluckman was disinclined by his strong Durkheimian persuasion to reduce social process to individual choice. Instead, influenced by an ardent commitment to empirical investigation and a deep and abiding interest in social conflict, Gluckman hit on the idea of scrutinizing particular situations of conflict as complexes of connected incidents that were occurring in the field, in order to isolate and identify the actual mechanisms underlying the development of the conflict.

The idea was to take the actors and their roles in any particular incident and trace these self-same actors through other incidents, in this way linking the varied incidents to one another and identifying the actual mechanisms (as logically distinct from the normative principles) operating in the relevant social order. So instead of trying to resolve the problem of process through theory alone (as, e.g., in Nadel's and Firth's theoretical recourse to the ontological dualism of the individual and society), Gluckman latched onto the idea of empirically isolating and identifying the social mechanisms that constituted process as such. He did this by analyzing conflicts ("trouble cases," as he named them) in their concrete emergence or as extending over a range of situations.

The development of the extended-case method stemmed most immediately from this constitutional incapacity of structural functionalism to address the issue of social process, as just described. As a 'method', it was above all intended as a means to overcome this incapacity and thereby to save the structural-functionalist paradigm. The method was designed to force the paradigm to confront the empirical realities of social process and their contribution to the state of the social order, thus rescuing structural functionalism from what seemed a fatal flaw. Yet this turn to social process *as process* probably did more to undermine structural functionalism than to save it, ultimately proving the flaw in question to be fatal and thereby promoting a shift in paradigms. It is in this connection that the extended-case method or situational analysis most emphatically warrants revisiting today, in the context of current anthropology.

The method enjoys a very practical ethnographic advantage in that first and foremost it requires attention to ethnographic detail. This gives the fieldworker a clear and specific empirical focus, without pre-judging this focus theoretically or ideologically. So, too, in light of the resulting case narrative, this attention to detail helps greatly to organize the writing up of the mire of data that field research typically produces. Nonetheless, the current principal relevance of situational analysis is not practical but instead emphatically theoretical, taking off from the implicit direction that this so-called method gave to the shift away from the structural-functionalist paradigm.

To perceive this, it is necessary to stress that the development of the method had a condition even deeper than, though closely related to, the ever-pressing need to remedy the constitutional weakness of structural functionalism's inability to recognize social process. This condition was so theoretically atmospheric that its contribution in the forging of the extended-case method was obscured, perhaps even to Gluckman. We have in mind Gluckman's broad and distinctive focus on political conflict and, more abstractly, on contradiction as key to social order and process.[1] Whether in his pioneering work on the anthropology of law or his more general analyses of tribal social orders, he was inclined to see conflict as the counter-intuitive optic through which to discern the essential character of any social order and, correlatively, to grasp this character in terms of basic principles that are at variance with one another. In this connection Gluckman had been powerfully influenced by Evans-Pritchard's stupendous analysis of how among the Nuer conflicting loyalties and crosscutting ties brought about order without government (or as Evans-Pritchard otherwise put it, "ordered anarchy"). But the force of Gluckman's views on conflict and social order is distinctly dialectical and as such, notwithstanding his admiration of Evans-Pritchard and his Durkheimian bent, most likely finds its essential philosophical spirit in the Marxian tradition. Though he made little direct reference to it in his work, his familiarity with Marxian tradition (not to mention his left-wing political sympathies) may not be doubted.

The trump role of situational analysis as a theoretical Trojan horse, as well as its especial significance and promise for current anthropology, pivots just here, pointing to Gluckman's deep, underlying attraction to the question of conflict and to the logic of dialectic. By "situation"—though there is no reason to think that he fully intended to restrict the rubric so—Gluckman primarily had in mind situations of conflict. And because he was given to understand conflict in terms of dialectic, this paralogical outlook informed (even if not by explicit design) situational analysis. Accordingly, the extended-case method worked not only to expose structural functionalism's principal inadequacy, but also to intimate the possibility of a paradigm in place of structural functionalism: the extended case bore the seeds of another way of looking at the social altogether, in which the social was pre-eminently a matter of *practice*.

In devising the extended-case study as a method for empirically ascertaining the actual mechanisms of social process, Gluckman was in effect engaging the Hegelo-Marxian dialectical conundrum of theory and practice. He was shifting the ethnographic focus from the normative to actual practice. Instead of trying to understand social life as a function of its ideal principles and formal rules, and so its theoretical self-presentation, Gluckman moved to understand social life in terms of its lived, concrete reality. Broadly speaking, this move is logically identical to Bourdieu's (as Bourdieu himself sensed[2]), when the late French anthropologist turned away from structuralism, in which actual conduct is grasped as a realization of an intellectual formation, to a theory of practice, in which people are seen to act according to the particulars of the situation in which they find themselves. These particulars are essentially exigent and contingent matters (historical, experiential, instrumental, socio-cultural, natural, and so forth). Normative principles bear on these matters but do so by virtue of not only their meaning in the abstract but also the demands of the situation. In other words, in practice these principles are deconstructed and reconstructed according to the momentary and the ephemeral, that is, the pre-eminently improvisatory flow of circumstance—in short, process as such.

In order to denote the unification of theory and practice, the Hegelo-Marxian tradition used the rubric *praxis*. But the exact nature of this unification was not uniformly agreed upon, since different interpretations within the tradition varied significantly as to the relative priority given to the two extremes in relation to each other. In this connection, Gluckman's take remains of considerable interest, even though as an anthropologist of his times he was in no position to see clairvoyantly its potential. As a Durkheimian, he remained interested in identifying the social structural principles from which social action was thought to issue. However, because he was also disposed to see these principles as contradictories, he injected into structural-functionalist orthodoxy a dynamic that implicitly admitted to the possibility of change as such.

It is true that in his well-known distinction between rebellion and revolution, Gluckman laid explanatory emphasis on his (ingenious) functionalist thesis on how rebellion served to reinforce the existing social structure, thereby avoiding fundamental transformation (see, e.g., 1963: intro. and chap. 3; see also 1959). Nonetheless, with his explicit attention to the possibility of revolutionary change, Gluckman implicated the more fundamental sense of process, the sense in which this notion, even when the actual dynamic seems archly conservative, ultimately denotes becoming. Yet, given that in his functionalist argument about rebellion he understood action especially by reference to principle, the picture of praxis he projected there was, as Marx might have said, still too theoretical. Nevertheless, even this theory of rebellion was dialectical and acknowledged the clash of fundamental structural principles. What Gluckman failed to do, though, was to ask why basic structural principles, whatever their particular content, *always* find themselves at variance with one another. Had he done so, he might have given more radically a certain primacy to process over structure in the dialectic, and therewith abandoned structural functionalism altogether.

Though all praxis entails the shaping of practice by human consciousness, in the end, the latter can exist only on condition of practice. Put another way, though theory will have its day, practice always exceeds and surprises even the best-laid plans and most practicable ideals. Practice generates its own emergent properties, altering itself. However, it is not the case that practice is simply disruptive of or opposed to theory. This is a dualistic preconception (one perhaps going back to Aristotle, who held that theoretical and practical knowledge are mutually exclusive) that, given structural functionalism's normativist bias, plagued those anthropologists of Gluckman's day who endeavored to treat the question of practice. Instead, it is necessary to acknowledge that practice is intrinsically more than—indeed (in, ironically, a Dumontian sense) encompassing of—theory. With this acknowledgement, it becomes possible to make empirically unassailable sense of the idea of the unification of theory and practice, by construing it in terms of an open rather than closed dialectic, a unity that denotes allness, not oneness.

This picture of practice as enjoying the final word in regard to theory is implicated by situational analysis, and this is why the latter already amounts to a theory of practice. Considered as a theory of practice, situational analysis is anthropologically distinctive. To see this, it is helpful to return to our example of Firth and Nadel. By introducing the factor of individual choice into structural functionalism, these scholars too were intimating a theory of practice. Doubtless, they were no more *acutely* aware of this than was Gluckman with respect to his development of situational analysis. But the difference between the resulting theories of practice highlights a striking feature of Gluckman's. Firth's and Nadel's respective turns in the direction of practice depended on the received Western dualism of the individual and society and therefore were wholly theoretical. However, Gluckman's offering was critically more than a matter of theory—it was also a way of empirically determining the actual mechanisms of practice in any particular case. This is why, despite its gravid theoretical content, it was explicitly referred to as a method. In point of fact, situational analysis is at once a practice for empirically investigating practice and an implicit theory of practice, and therefore it promises an ethnographic unification of theory and practice. Even Bourdieu, to whom current anthropology owes its only theoretically elaborated logic of practice, and who so richly produced an 'outline' of a theory of practice, did not create an ethnographic praxis of a theory of practice.[3] Situational analysis became a way of theorizing practice as it was practiced, and so the embrace of practice and its theorizing inched toward praxis.

Our point is not of course that the extended-case method constituted a fleshed-out theory. Rather, our point is that by virtue of its make-up as a developed ethnographic procedure for investigating practice through theoretical situationalism, the extended-case method holds noteworthy, untapped potential for the anthropological turn to practice. In other words, the very practice of situational analysis produces, procedurally, a theory of practice, one that, given its situationalism, comprehends praxis (including ethnographic praxis) as an ongoing, open-ended dialectic, rather than a completed synthesis. Bear in mind that the very idea of situation, considered existentially, presumes not only a predicament but also an agential capacity on the part of the situated (with their different subjectivities) to negotiate the predicament by praxis. That is to say, the 'obstructions' constituting the predicament suppose an agent capacitated to cope with them by practical conduct mediated through choice or meaningful purpose—a free agent, whose freedom is always dynamically relative to his or her situatedness.

## The Manchester School—Deceptively Disappeared?

What happened to situational analysis and the extended-case method? Where did they disappear to? Were we to ask graduate students and younger faculty at major American departments of anthropology whether they knew anything substantive about this approach, our educated guess is that nearly all would reply that they did not. In anthropologies smitten with vocabularies of practice, more effort is expended on theorizing practice as an end in itself than on the practice of practice in doing ethnography, theorizing as the ethnography progresses. Since the heyday of the Manchester School, both the theorizing of theory and the theorizing of practice have taken over more and more space in anthropology at the expense of the kinds of detailed ethnographies that enabled the fruitful formulations of situational analyses and extended cases. In discussions of practice, Mancunian situational analysis is simply absent, an absence correlative with the degree to which it has become all too easy to invoke the idea of practice rhetorically, with no substantive employment to speak of.

In 1966, Max Gluckman (1968) delivered a plenary address to the American Anthropological Association, as did Fredrik Barth (1967). Barth's address, in which he spoke of his variety of economistic methodological individualism in relation to the study of social change, was greeted with enthusiasm. Gluckman's flopped, and he returned to Manchester, disheartened. His lecture introduced the concept of 'structural duration'—the period that enables an institution to go through many of its regular alterations or changes that make it as it is, that can only be witnessed through time, and that constitute the cultural and social fullness of that institution (see Handelman, this volume). In earlier Manchester thinking, situational analysis had expanded temporally into the extended case. In this lecture, Gluckman implicitly argued that macro dynamics could become evident only if they were followed through time. In effect, he was asserting that because the extended case depended on the study of practice through time, the method of extended-case studies led to a macro anthropology grounded in practice.

Coming out of Bourdieu, practice theory became big in the United States. We mention briefly two renowned American anthropologists who have adopted practice theory. Marshall Sahlins, now one of the leading American rhetoricians of practice theory, developed the idea of the structure of the conjuncture— the extension of the concomitants of a historical event through time and their temporal structuring through the practice of cultural premises and knowledge of the parties to the event (see Sahlins 1985). Sahlins's ideas resonate with those of Gluckman. Yet nowhere does Sahlins acknowledge the existence of the Manchester School. This absence continues to come through strongly in one of Sahlins's most recent works, subtitled "How Microhistories Become Macrohistories and Vice Versa" (2005).

Another prominent case in point is that of Sherry Ortner. Ortner (2005) touts the theorizing of the actor, and through this the discovery of the subject, as if both had been scarce in anthropology. Her major route of theorizing the actor (as an agential and feeling subject) takes us through practice theory via Bourdieu, Giddens, Sahlins, and her own work, as well as through Clifford Geertz's understanding of the subject as existentially complex, "a being who feels and thinks and reflects, who makes and seeks meaning" (Ortner 2005: 33). Do the scholars she mentions *both* theorize practice and practice practice? In the main, they certainly do the former. The Manchester School, whose adherents (Victor Turner and Clyde Mitchell, among others) practiced practice in many of their analyses, is totally absent from her discussion. She holds up Geertz's interpretation of the Balinese cockfight and Richard Sennett's interviews with American workers under disorienting conditions of late-capitalist workplaces as prime examples of the practice of subjectivities. In both examples, though, practice is reduced to narrative, indeed, to representation. It is in relation to the cockfight that Geertz coined his celebratory phrase—a story that Balinese tell themselves about themselves—thereby reducing ritual practice to the said of a story,[4] while for Sennett it is crucial that in late-capitalist regimens people regain the capacity "to narrate their lives in a coherent and meaningful way" (Ortner 2005: 44). But the saying always exceeds the said, however coherent, meaningful, and efficacious the latter, and practice is primarily in the saying.[5]

Where did situational analysis and the extended-case study disappear to? We are not speaking here, after all, of an obscure theoretical innovation tucked away in a plodding third-grade university. Certainly, American anthropology disavowed Manchester anthropology, even as US anthropologists cried out their commitment to anthropologies that valued life as it is lived and therefore practiced. In this regard, the huge impact of Victor Turner on American anthropology bears scrutiny. Turner was, after all, a stellar representative of the Manchester School, and his brilliant work on ritual reflects nothing if not the turn of his teacher, Gluckman, to processualism. Yet Turner's social anthropology was assimilated to American cultural anthropology without regard to the fact that he realized his symbolic analyses ethnographically through the use of social dramas, a distinct variant of situational analysis and the extended-case method (see Kapferer, this volume).

American anthropology (in its multiplicities) is crucial here, for it is the dominant power in the anthropological world, by dint of sheer numbers and departments; by the weightiness of the wealth of its universities, foundations, other granting agencies, and fellowships; by its control of major journals and presses whose editorial perspectives are first and foremost American; and by the fluidity of its capital in buying foreign scholars of note. This dominance, perhaps overwhelming, is bound to breed the arrogance of power applied to intellect, and engenders the belief that any approach worth something, and its practitioners and ideas, will already be in or will come to the United States. The general response of world anthropologies to this academic colonizing of the globe is to align themselves as provinces or satellites. American anthropologists are seldom sufficiently subjective and reflexive enough to recognize the consequences and vicissitudes of US domination of global anthropology.

Has the Manchester anthropology we discuss survived? The answer is yes, here and there, in different forms and variants, as the contributions to this volume attest. The last substantive overview of the approach was that of the late Kingsley Garbett in his Malinowski Memorial Lecture of 1970 (Garbett 1970).[6] Bruce Kapferer brought the approach to Adelaide University, where it was influential for some time. Myron Aronoff (1977), Emanuel Marx (1976), Shlomo Deshen (1970), and Moshe Shokeid (1971) took the approach to

Israel, where it played a role in the founding of anthropology in Israeli universities. Even in the United States, the approach was, by design, at least introduced by Terry Evens in a collection he co-edited with James Peacock (1990).[7] Resonances of the approach appear in northern Europe, particularly Scandinavia (witness the contributions to this volume in the section on extended-case studies). Situational analysis and the extended case strongly influenced how anthropologists in Britain came to do field research in British locations (well before such studies became legitimate in the United States, apart from the study of 'minorities'). Ronnie Frankenberg's *Village on the Border* (1957), done with Gluckman's strong encouragement, marked the beginning of a seminal shift into the anthropological study of rural Britain (see Cohen 2005). So, too, Gluckman encouraged the use of the approach in the study of British industry, for example, in the innovative studies of Cunnison (1966) and Lupton (1963), even as other British anthropologists, especially those at Oxford and Cambridge, insisted that such studies simply were not anthropology.[8] Is the disappearance of the Manchester School deceptive? The answer is open.

The implications and advantages of situational analysis and the extended-case method are manifold, extending to matters of ethnographic observation and analysis, to situational flow between the local and the global, to the ontological nature of social life, to reflexive and activist anthropology, and more. Some of these are discussed in various of the essays collected here, and all remain to be explored further in connection with the continuing, substantial promise of the Manchester case-study method and its practice. The last collection to feature the Manchester School case-study method, edited by Bill Epstein (1967), appeared over 35 years ago, and we have gathered the present collection to further convey the promise of which we speak. To initiate this collection we reprint two articles, one by Max Gluckman, from the period during which the Manchester case-study method was consolidated, and one by Clyde Mitchell, a retrospective look at the social-scientific legitimacy of the approach. We briefly discuss these contributions in the preface to section 1. Apart from these reprints, the essays collected here, though they overlap some in their foci, are organized in three topical sections—theory, history, and case analysis—each of which is prefaced with a brief editorial commentary. We thought it appropriate to leave the last word, the coda, to Bruce Kapferer.

We are grateful to Caroline Baggaley of *Sociological Review*, for her efforts in securing permission for us to reprint Max Gluckman's (1961) and Clyde Mitchell's (1983) articles; Jean Mitchell, for granting us permission to use her late husband's article; Vivian Berghahn, for her editorial encouragement and efficient assistance; Shawn Kendrick, whose excellence as copyeditor is, in our experience, without parallel; and Timothy Elfenbein, for giving his time and intelligence to construct the index. We would like to acknowledge the sorrowful passing of Kingsley Garbett, who, in his capacity as managing editor of *Social Analysis*, gently nudged us along in the editorial process. We wish also to acknowledge the sad loss of Marian Kempny, Björn Lindgren, and Karin Norman's husband, Johan, all three well before their time.

## Notes

1. Naturally, we were aware of Gluckman's propensity, which he makes plain in his essay, "Ethnographic Data in British Social Anthropology" (1961), to see case studies as crucial for analyzing instances of social conflict. But it was Kapferer's insightful description (his essay, this volume) of the fundamental nature of the extended-case study method that moved us here to our own account of the specific contribution of Gluckman's abiding interest in social conflict to the development of situational analysis.
2. In *Outline of a Theory of Practice*, Bourdieu comments on situational analysis as follows (1977: 26): "[A]nthropologists who appeal to 'context' or 'situation' in order ... to 'correct' what strikes them as unreal and abstract in the structuralist model are in fact still trapped in the logic of the theoretical model which they are rightly trying to supersede. The method known as 'situational analysis' [and here Bourdieu cites Gluckman 1961], which consists of 'observing people in a variety of social situations' in order to determine 'the way in which individuals are able to exercise choices within the limits of a specified social structure', remains locked within the framework of the rule and the exception, which Leach (often invoked by the exponents of 'situational analysis') spells out clearly: 'I postulate that structural systems in which all avenues of social action are narrowly institutionalized are impossible. In all viable systems, there must be an area where the individual is free to make choices so as to manipulate the system to his advantage.' In accepting as obligatory alternatives the model and the situation, the structure and the individual variations, one condemns oneself simply to take the diametrically opposite course to the structuralist abstraction which subsumes variations—regarded as simple variants—into the structure ... [This] leads one to regress to the pre-structuralist stage of the individual and his choices, and to miss the very principle of the structuralist error." What is off target about Bourdieu's (decidedly astute) observation that despite their efforts these anthropologists remained "trapped" in the theory they found wanting is that he assimilates Gluckman's "situational analysis" to Leach's (and thus Firth's and Nadel's) Malinowskian individualistic approaches to the problem. But what we wish to bring out by this quotation from Bourdieu's classic text is that in bothering to distinguish his position from Gluckman's, Bourdieu plainly reveals that he sees well enough the kinship between his own theoretical turn toward practice and Gluckman's. In point of fact, he goes on to note (ibid.: 202n37) that the analyses of Jaap van Velsen, a student of both Gluckman and Clyde Mitchell, "are essentially consistent with my own analysis of the strategic uses made of kin relations" (adding parenthetically, "which I wrote before [van Velsen's] *The Politics of Kinship* came to my notice").
3. In an appreciative but radical critique, Evens (1999) argues that at bottom Bourdieu's attempt to transcend the dualism of subject and object falls prey to reductionism. If Gluckman's attempt at praxis was too theoretical, then Bourdieu's is too practical. Bourdieu's theory of practice is keyed to what he speaks of as "generalized materialism," by which he means that beyond sheerly material advantage there is augmentation of social being—in effect, symbolic advantage. But as Evens puts it (ibid.: 27n23), because "Bourdieu's concept of the symbolic remains epiphenomenal," it also "remains ontologically ill-equipped to do justice to the surpassing reality of the meaningful side of social existence." In other words, in respect of human practice, which constitutes an essential tension, "materialism, even when it is generalized, is not enough" (ibid.: 30).
4. Handelman (1994: 345) maintains that "Geertz has authored or advertised many memorable phrases: 'models of ... models for,' 'thick description,' 'from the natives' point of view,' 'blurred genres,' and others. These are catchy—something like scholarly jingles, erudite slogans, scholastic pop tunes ... as I read these phrasings (hum them? chant them? recite them?), their project is not that of concept formation nor of theory-building ... [but rather] refractions of an attitude, a point of view, a subtle sensibility." The reader is invited to pair the Balinese cockfight with Clyde Mitchell's situational analysis of the Kalela dance (1956) in which, rather than enclosing culture in text, Mitchell

    tackled social dynamics as emergent, open-ended formations in mining towns on the Zambian Copperbelt.

5. Regarding her study of her high-school class of 1958, Ortner (2003: 297–298) writes: "The general theoretical framework behind this structure of inquiry and exposition is so-called practice theory, which I mostly leave implicit in the course of the book." The first part of the book situates the study socially and historically in the 1950s. The second part asks what the graduates of the class of 1958 did with themselves and their lives after graduation. The second part is based primarily on interviews. Just how this constitutes "practice" is left up to the reader.

6. Richard Werbner (1984) later did an overview of the approach, but specifically with reference to south-central Africa.

7. The collection comprises a half-dozen extended-case studies on the topic of transcendence and social movements. The studies, based on intensive fieldwork, and all but one by students of Evens and Peacock, were executed, as dictated by the project's blueprint, in accordance with "Max Gluckman's case study method" and are "developed primarily as dynamic, descriptive aids to the discernment of the particular social horizons or limits over and against which the cases unfold, and lend themselves to interpretation in terms of existential tensions" (Evens and Peacock 1990: intro.). The collection appeared as a book supplement of a sociological research annual, of which the series editor was Craig Calhoun (who—a not irrelevant consideration in the present connection—did an MA in social anthropology at Manchester and then a DPhil in sociology at Oxford University, under the supervision of Clyde Mitchell). Regretfully, the vehicle of publication proved obscure, at least in respect of anthropologists who might have taken notice, and the book is still not easy to find.

8. Lupton and Cunnison were among the founders of the Manchester Business School, perhaps the best in Britain (Bruce Kapferer, personal communication).

## References

Aronoff, Myron J. 1977. *Power and Ritual in the Israel Labor Party.* Assen: Van Gorcum.

Barth, Fredrik. 1967. "On the Study of Social Change." *American Anthropologist* 69: 661–669.

Bourdieu, Pierre. 1977. *Outline of a Theory of Practice.* Cambridge: Cambridge University Press.

Cohen, Anthony P. 2005. "*Village on the Border*, Anthropology at the Crossroads: The Significance of a Classic British Ethnography." *Sociological Review* 53: 603–620.

Cunnison, Sheila. 1966. *Wages and Work Allocation.* London: Tavistock.

Deshen, Shlomo. 1970. *Immigrant Voters in Israel.* Manchester: Manchester University Press.

Epstein, A. L., ed. 1967. *The Craft of Social Anthropology.* London: Social Science Paperbacks in association with Tavistock Publications.

Evens, T. M. S. 1999. "Bourdieu and the Logic of Practice: Is All Giving Indian-Giving or Is 'Generalized Materialism' Not Enough?" *Sociological Theory* 17: 3–31.

Evens, T. M. S., and James Peacock, eds. 1990. *Transcendence in Society: Case Studies.* Supplement 1 of *Comparative Social Research.* Series editor: Craig Calhoun. Greenwich, CT: JAI Press.

Firth, Raymond. 1961. *Elements of Social Organization.* London: Watts & Co.

Frankenberg, Ronald. 1957. *Village on the Border.* London: Cohen & West.

Garbett, Kingsley. 1970. "The Analysis of Social Situations." *Man* 5 (n.s.): 214–227.

Gluckman, Max. 1959. *Custom and Conflict in Africa.* Glencoe, IL: Free Press.

_____. 1961. "Ethnographic Data in British Social Anthropology." *Sociological Review* 9, no. 1: 5–17.

_____. 1963. *Order and Rebellion in Tribal Africa.* London: Cohen & West.

_____. 1965. *Politics, Law and Ritual in Tribal Society.* Oxford: Basil Blackwell.

_____. 1968. "The Utility of the Equilibrium Model in the Study of Social Change." *American Anthropologist* 70: 219–237.

Handelman, Don. 1994. "Critiques of Anthropology: Literary Turns, Slippery Bends." *Poetics Today* 15: 341–381.

Lupton, Tom. 1963. *On the Shop Floor: Two Studies of Work Organization and Output*. London: Pergamon.

Marx, Emanuel. 1976. *The Social Context of Violent Behavior*. London: Routledge & Kegan Paul.

Mitchell, J. Clyde. 1956. *The Kalela Dance*. Manchester: Manchester University Press.

_____. 1983. "Case and Situation Analysis." *Sociological Review* 31: 187–211.

Nadel, S. F. 1957. *The Theory of Social Structure*. Glencoe, IL: Free Press.

Ortner, Sherry B. 2003. *New Jersey Dreaming: Capital, Culture and the Class of '58*. Durham, NC: Duke University Press.

_____. 2005. "Subjectivity and Cultural Critique." *Anthropological Theory* 5: 31–52.

Sahlins, Marshall. 1985. *Islands of History*. Chicago: University of Chicago Press.

_____. 2005. "Structural Work: How Microhistories Become Macrohistories and Vice Versa." *Anthropological Theory* 5: 5–30.

Shokeid, Moshe. 1971. *The Dual Heritage*. Manchester: Manchester University Press.

Werbner, Richard. 1984. "The Manchester School in South-Central Africa." *Annual Review of Anthropology* 13: 157–185.

# Ethnographic Data in British Social Anthropology*

*Max Gluckman*

In this paper I discuss changes in the use of ethnographic field data in social anthropological analyses in Britain. I begin with two caveats. First, I do not in any way imply that the developments I discuss represent the only fruitful new methods of analysis in the subject: social anthropology, like all sciences, has to proceed by exploiting many theories and lines of analysis. Secondly, because of limitation of space, I cannot touch on many of the influences which have produced this particular development, or on the stimulating work of scholars in countries of Europe other than Britain, in America, and elsewhere. My purpose is to deal with Britain alone.

Modern British anthropology was dominated for many years by Bronislaw Malinowski and A. R. Radcliffe-Brown. Radcliffe-Brown supplied the more fruitful theoretical approach, though British anthropologists have proceeded far beyond the point he reached. Yet I regard Malinowski as the real father of modern British anthropology. Theory is but one side of a science: the other equally important side is the type of data which are subjected to theoretical analysis. Here Malinowski produced a revolutionary change in the subject, though scholars in other countries were working on the same lines as he. Malinowski's long residence in the Trobriands and the fact that he worked through the Trobriand language enabled him to make observations on social life which were quite different in quality from the observations made by the casual travellers who had passed through colonial countries, and even from those made by missionaries and administrators working among particular colonial peoples. The change in the nature of his data had a profound effect on his own thinking, and hence on the subject. I can illustrate this briefly by comparing two of his books with a work which is still a great classic of ethnography, Henri A. Junod's *The Life*

* This paper was originally read at the International Congress held at Stresa in 1959.

Notes for this article are located on page 22.

*of a South African Tribe*, about the Tsonga of Mozambique. In this book, in his description of the life-cycle of a man, Junod devotes 151 pages to the ceremonies through which a man passes from before birth (including, the pregnancy taboos observed by his mother), until after death, and including his career as an ancestral spirit. Against these 151 pages on 'ritual', Junod has five pages on growing up and seven pages on mature age and old age. Of course we gain information on secular activity from other sections of the book; but these too are overloaded with accounts of ritual. We can set against Junod's allocation of space, his descriptions of what he thought important, Malinowski's two books *Sex and Repression in Savage Society* and *The Sexual Life of Savages*. These books are full of detailed information on how boys and girls grow up, their relations with their kin, the relations between spouses, etc.; and unlike Junod, Malinowski did not write descriptions at the level of culture, custom, ritual and belief. He dealt with how people grew up in a society of particular culture, and used and rebelled against that culture. The difference in the types of data and analysis provided by Malinowski and Junod is most striking if we remember that Junod was greatly influenced by the theoretical anthropologists in the metropolitan countries, particularly by the French school of Durkheim, but also by Van Gennep, Frazer and Tylor. His development through the twenty odd years he lived among the Tsonga is exhibited if we compare his *Les Ba-Ronga* written in 1898, with *The Life of a South African Tribe*, first published in 1913.

I would go so far as to say that the type of data collected by Malinowski broke anthropology completely away, on its one side as a science, from its own line of ancestry, though this continued to influence its interests and its theoretical preoccupations. Malinowski's data were akin to the raw material of the novelist, the playwright, the biographer and autobiographer, all drawing directly on social life, rather than to the facts which the theoretical anthropologists of the nineteenth and early twentieth century had available to them. For these facts on which Durkheim, Tylor, Frazer, even Maine and Morgan, had worked, were the superficial observations collected, largely through interpreters, of people making unco-ordinated observations on tribal life. Even the Haddon Expedition in 1898, and later Rivers among the Todas, Seligman among the Veddahs, and finally Radcliffe-Brown among Andamanese and Australians, lacked the depth, complexity, and comprehensiveness of Malinowski's descriptions.

Malinowski explicitly discussed the difference between his data and those used by his predecessors. Indeed, in some respects he fought and won one important battle, during which he raised ethnographic fieldwork itself to a professional art. This battle was to establish that primitive life and primitive institutions were more complex, far more complex, than earlier theorists had thought. I need not here elaborate this point. Malinowski's personal tragedy was that he continued to fight this same battle, after he had won it, against his successors, the pupils whom he himself had trained to collect data similar to his data; and that he was so involved in correcting the erroneous simple opinions of specialists in other social disciplines about primitive society, that he learnt little from these disciplines. He is not the first great scientist to become trapped in his own first burst of originality; but this story lies outside my present analysis. I have cited Malinowski's outstanding contribution in the form of his providing a sociological microscope, to put more recent developments into historical perspective.

In his introduction to his first book, *The Argonauts of the Western Pacific*, Malinowski called for three types of evidence: the delineation of the organization of the tribe and the anatomy of its culture through concrete statistical documentation; the description of the imponderabilia of actual life; and the collection of documents of native mentality. He summed up a lot of these facts as 'cases', which must be continually cited to validate all general statements. In this paper, I discuss a change in the use of 'cases'. Of course, in the actual books written by Malinowski and his successors, the methods are not as simple as my statements of them; nevertheless these methods exhibit a general similarity, which I call the 'method of apt illustration'.

Malinowski and the next 'generation' of anthropologists, in which I include myself, used so-called 'cases' in two ways. We made a large number of observations on how our subjects actually behaved, we collected genealogies and censuses, made diagrams of villages and gardens, listened to cases and quarrels, obtained commentaries on all these incidents, collected texts from informants about customs and rituals, and discovered their answers to 'cases stated'. Out of this vast mass of data we analysed a general outline of the culture, or the social system, according to our main theoretical bent. We then used the apt and appropriate case to illustrate specific customs, principles of organization, social relationships, etc. Each case was selected for its appropriateness at a particular point in the argument; and cases coming close together in the argument might be derived from the actions or words of quite different groups or individuals. There was no regularly established connection between the series of incidents in cases cited at different points in the analysis, though when incidents affecting the same persons at different points were used, careful anthropologists made cross-references. I cite an example where this was not done from Barton's *The Kalingas*. Early in the book we are told that under hunting laws a pig belongs primarily to the village whose dogs started the pig. This is illustrated with a case in which while hunters of Village A were pursuing a pig, dogs and hunters from Village B killed it. When Village A claimed the pig, Village B asserted that their dogs had started the pig, a fight ensued, and several men were killed. Many pages later, in an illustration of land tenure law, we learn that these two villages were at feud over a piece of land. It thus appears as if Village B's failure to comply with the hunting law was part of the total process of relations between the villages; and the case cited under hunting law falls into quite different perspective. I have used this example because it is the simplest known to me of a general methodological weakness in a whole series of books, including my own. I have not space to cite more complex examples from other works.

In this example, the method of apt illustration is adequate if we are interested in outlining the customs and the culture, even the social morphology, of Kalinga society: clearly it is inadequate if we are trying to analyse the total process of Kalinga social life.

Anthropologists of my generation also used 'cases' in a slightly different way. They sometimes described a case first, and then extracted the general rule of custom or social relationship from it. Clearly the more complex the case, the more could be extracted from it. A simple example is Malinowski's analysis of the use of language in Trobriand fishing. More complex examples are provided by Fortes's analysis of a collective fishing ceremony[1] and of the great harvest festivals of the Tallensi.[2] I myself used a complex series of events, principally the ceremonial opening of a newly built bridge, to illustrate the extent to which Zulu and Whites were involved in a single social system, and to demolish Malinowski's attack on Fortes and Schapera for adopting this viewpoint.[3] We called these complex events social situations, and we used the actions of individuals and groups within these situations to exhibit the morphology of the social structure. But it was still the social morphology that we were aiming to present.

Let me say at once that I believe this to have been an important stage in the development of social anthropology, and of our knowledge of the tribal peoples. Faced with an enormous variety of ecological relations, of forms of grouping, and of culture, we had to provide a systematic morphology of the forms of tribal society; and in doing this, we have developed the monographic analysis to a high peak of excellence. The monographs of this period are outstanding advances on anything previously written about tribal peoples, and they have illuminated in general theoretical terms a whole series of problems in political science, economics, law, family and kinship relations, ritual and magic. But there is as little doubt that the younger anthropologists whom we have taught since the war have found weaknesses in our method. They still ask for more case material, as Malinowski did in his introduction to the *Argonauts*. My contention is that they are asking for quite a different kind of case material.

This demand for case material is marked, for example, in Freedman's penetrating analysis, from published sources including the books of Western-trained Chinese anthropologists, of the lineage in South-Eastern China.[4] It occurs in M. G. Smith's critical survey[5] of the analyses of lineage systems which made such advances from the time when Evans-Pritchard, Firth and Fortes first established our knowledge of these. Clearly one good case can illuminate the working of a social system in a way that a series of morphological statements cannot achieve. Evans-Pritchard was unfortunately unable to give a single case of the waging or settlement of a feud, in detail, among the Nuer; Colson's analysis of such a case among the Northern Rhodesian Tonga[6] throws considerable light on the Nuer social system.

But even Colson's analysis here of the settlement of a single actual case of homicide in a feuding society does not provide the kind of analysis which exhibits the fullest use of the case-method. This new kind of analysis treats each case as a stage in an on-going process of social relations between specific persons and groups in a social system and culture. The refusal of one Kalinga village to recognize hunting law is related to a continuing state of feud with another village, possibly arising out of a dispute over land, possibly itself involved in a systematic state of feud. Colson, it is true, was concerned in the limits of an article to show the kind of mechanisms, inherent in Tonga culture, which tended to effect a settlement after homicide, and I am unfairly using her here to illustrate my methodological point—which is that a full analysis would continue to trace the relations within the specific groups involved back in time, and then forward if possible. For I consider that the most fruitful use of cases consists in taking a series of specific incidents affecting the same persons or groups, through a long period of time, and showing how these incidents, these cases, are related to the development and change of social relations among these persons and groups, acting within the framework of their social system and culture. Where this method has been applied to monographs using the method of apt illustration, quite a different picture of a social system emerges—a more complex, less rigid, less highly interconnected picture. Freedman's analysis of the S.E. China lineage depends on thus putting together facts about persons which are scattered throughout his original sources. Worsley[7] by thus putting together the individually cited instances in Fortes' analyses of the Tallensi, has given a differently weighted, and in my opinion more penetrating, analysis of that society. Singh in an unpublished thesis on the political organizations of the *kula* ring[8] has similarly gathered together incidents cited as individual illustrations in Malinowski's *corpus* on the Trobriands and Fortune's book on the Dobu to give us much deeper understanding. He shows, for example, that a Trobriander does not help his son in the *kula* merely out of paternal affection: for *kula* relationships are only one of the types of relationships in Trobriand society which separate the individual from the corporate group of the matri-lineage. These individual links become associated with other lines of descent than the corporate one of matriliny: hence father and son are linked with the *kula*. This immediately reminds us of how Fortes showed for the Tallensi that in the reverse process it is matriliny which distinguishes the individual within the patrilineage, and a male's first individual emergence as a property-holder is associated with gifts from his mother's brother.

I am arguing that if we are going to penetrate more deeply into the actual process by which persons and groups live together with a social system, under a culture, we have to employ a series of connected cases occurring within the same area of social life. I believe that this will greatly alter our view of the working of some institutions, and deepen our understanding of the significance of all custom. It will enable the subject of social anthropology to cope with what Malinowski dismissed as accidental quarrels and individual differences of temperament; it will bring to the monographic analysis some of the penetration which Freud brought to the study of human personality, and some of the depth which many find in the novel, but not in the scientific analysis. The test of this method lies in its application to work already done, and I have cited published studies by younger anthropologists which make it clear that the method survives this test. In my own department, we have applied the method to a whole series of works by senior anthropologists, and always we have found that we came out with more understanding, and above all with more problems demanding further data from the field and further analysis. It is a measure of the skill of these senior anthropologists that they provide the data allowing this re-analysis of their work. I am one of them, so I introduce my final examples with a critique of my own work, *The Judicial Process among the Barotse of Northern Rhodesia*. I can take this book as a good example of my generation's work, because my reviews allow me to do so. I set out in that book to analyse the modes of thought of Barotse judges in deciding case, and to relate those modes of thought to the economic and general social backgrounds of Barotse life. When I had finished the book, I realized that I had made an important contribution on the problem I had tackled, but I felt dissatisfied as a sociologist with the book as a whole. I felt that I was on the verge of important sociological discoveries, but was not making them. It is now clear to me that though I had woven my analysis out of many cases, some quoted at great length, I had in fact used each case as an isolated incident coming before a court. Yet each case was obviously but an incident in a long process of social relations, with its roots deep in the past; and often the protagonists in the case would be living together again, and their interaction would be affected by the court's decision. I had not studied that process of social life; and in my opinion here lies the next step in deepening our understanding of law and morality—the intensive study of the judicial process in a limited area of social life, if you like Malinowski's analysis of *Crime and Custom in Savage Society* concentrated in detail on one Trobriand village.

Yet, as I have suggested earlier, perhaps my own type of analysis of the judicial process was necessary before we could make the further sociological step. This is certainly suggested by the research which has followed on Evan-Pritchard's analysis of *Witchcraft, Oracles and Magic among the Azande*. Here too Evans-Pritchard was interested in modes of thought, in relation to their economic and social background. He made clear to us that witchcraft explained the particularity of misfortunes, and not their whole causes: they answered the question *why* an individual suffered a particular misfortune at a particular time and place, and not *how* the misfortune occurred. He went on to relate this *why* to the sufferer's personal relations with his fellows, for beliefs in witchcraft as a philosophy of morals say that envy, spite, malice, and other ignoble feelings set witchcraft at work. He sketched the way that in Azande society certain types of social relations are likely to produce accusations of witchcraft, while these are excluded from the agnatic vengeance-group even though presumably this is full of hostile feelings. Finally he analysed with telling detail the relation of witchcraft beliefs to the use of oracles and magic, and the rôle of witchdoctors, and he showed how the whole system of beliefs and practices appears to conform with reality and is insulated against contradicting evidence. This analysis was a remarkable advance on anything previously done in social anthropology: it has been confirmed by all later research, and has influenced the writings of scholars outside anthropology, notably Polanyi's work on the philosophy of knowledge.

Anthropologists in other tribes have followed up the lines of enquiry opened by Evans-Pritchard in various ways: thus Nadel[9] has contrasted the different forms of witchcraft belief in four societies, and Monica Wilson[10] these forms in two societies, and they have related these variations to the general systems of the societies concerned. Another fruitful advance has been in developing

Evans-Pritchard's exhibition that the problem of *who* accuses *whom* lies at the core of the sociological problem, and that this involves considering the types of social relations within which accusations are common, and those from which accusations are excluded. The Kriges discussed this contrast more explicitly than Evans-Pritchard for the Lovedu of the Transvaal, and tried to put the problem in statistical form. For the purposes of my present argument, however, the significant change occurs in Mitchell's study of *The Yao Village*. So good was Evans-Pritchard's analysis of the way in which beliefs in witchcraft, the use of oracles, and the use of magic, worked as a system, that Mitchell is able to clear this intricate problem out of the way with the bald statement: 'I assume his [Evans-Pritchard's] analysis in my discussion.' This frees Mitchell to proceed more deeply into the sociology of accusations, and after discussing types of accusation, his argument reaches its climax in an eight-page record of the manner in which accusations of witchcraft operated through six years in the personal and sectional relations of a single Yao village. We learn that individuals act on their own, combine with different allies according to changing pressures, seek one divination after another, to further their ambitions and satisfy their sense of rightness. Mitchell's employment of this data is the first example I know in British anthropology of the new use of the extended-case method; and it develops greatly our understanding of the rôle of accusations in the social life of an African village. It was followed up by an important article analysing the varying significance of different types of accusation among the neighbouring Cewa, written by Marwick,[11] who acknowledges the use of Mitchell's analysis before it was published. Monica Wilson has developed this and similar points for the Nyakyusa, but the method, in my opinion, is up to the present shown at its best in Turner's study of the Ndembu of Northern Rhodesia.[12] In this analysis, after presenting a general outline of Ndembu social morphology, Turner proceeds to analyse the development of social and personal relations within a limited number of villages, and particularly in one village; and he shows how a great variety of custom and belief, including patterns of witchcraft accusations, divinations of ancestral wrath, etc., operate in the repetitiveness of pattern and the changes occurring within Ndembu villages. The analysis is of course too long to quote, but anyone who, has studied the book carefully will see in it a significant advance, both theoretically, and in making use of the richness of ethnographic data.[13]

Many difficult problems inevitably arise from this use of the extended-case method, and I have not space to discuss them. Indeed, I do not yet see clear-cut answers to problems such as the reliability of data on the past collected from interested parties, data which will have to be used since the anthropologist's period in the field is limited in time. I can only say here that I believe that ordinary historical caution can be applied; and since the method is clearly fruitful, these problems must be faced and overcome, and not cited to obstruct the development of the method. I can touch briefly on the problem of the typicality for a society of the area of social life selected for analysis in this way. In the first place, the use of the extended case does not do away with the need for the outline of social morphology, on which Malinowski insisted, and this may have to be illustrated by apt examples. But here the increasing use of statistics, in more refined form, by anthropologists provides an important safeguard. Firth, Fortes, and Schapera, among my generation, made considerable use of numerical statements; but in recent years quantitative analysis, developing into proper statistical analysis, has been much further developed. Here again Mitchell in *The Yao Village*, and in his studies of Central African towns,[14] has set new standards, together with Barnes[15] and Colson[16] (an American who worked in British territory for some years); and younger anthropologists like Freeman, Freedman, Watson, Turner and Gulliver, have followed their lead. This type of analysis gives some control over typicality; but it may well be that we shall have to abandon the concept of a society altogether, and speak of 'social fields', a likelihood stressed in the work of Fortes, Nadel and Leach. Here again I am not sure by any means what answer will be given.

I have cited one example of a general trend of development, which is exhibited also in other works, such as those of Gulliver on the Turkana[17] and Stenning on the Fulani.[18] The examples I have taken are all of studies of domestic and village life: but I believe the same trend appears in studies of tribal political systems. Here instead of getting morphological analyses of the structure of political relations in a tribe, set out with apt illustrations, anthropologists are beginning to set their analyses of this structure in an extended analysis of actual history—the extended case on a large scale. Examples are Evans-Pritchard's work on the Sanusi,[19] Barnes on the Ngoni,[20] Southall on the Alur,[21] Fallers on the Soga,[22] Watson on the Mambwe,[23] and my own work on the Zulu. Epstein shows the same trend in urban studies.[24] This work appears to me to forecast a new approach to problems of social change, as shown in how Watson handles in detail Mambwe reaction to the then proposed Federation of the Rhodesias and Nyasaland, as against the general statements on modern politics of earlier anthropologists. It does not mean that anthropology is becoming history.

I have outlined what appears to me to be an important change in the use of ethnographic data in the sociological type of anthropology practised in Britain. I consider it a most fruitful development; and I suggest that a similar development, in the detailed analysis of individuals, is creeping into and will be significant in cultural and psychological (personality) anthropology. As far as sociological anthropology is concerned, I believe that this new method of presenting facts, statistically and by extended cases, will not only require the development of new field techniques, but that it will also enable us to cope better with certain developments on the theoretical side of the science. I have space only to touch on these. First, the view of a kind of consistent system which was the framework of analysis of Radcliffe-Brown has steadily ceased to be held by his successors. The works of Evans-Pritchard and Fortes markedly stressed the existence of cleavage, fission, conflict, etc., as inherent in social systems. Our whole view of a social system became less rigid and integrated: Leach[25] has argued that we did not go far enough. Nowadays the anthropologist accepts 'conflict' as an integral part of even stable social systems: I have outlined some of these ideas in my broadcast lectures on *Custom and Conflict in Africa*. I state baldly that the problems which are emerging, and which involve the basic problems of the endurance, stability, and different types of change in a social system existing in space-time, can only be tackled through the use of the extended-case method. Simmel's treatment of conflict, with the use of the method of apt illustration, despite its high value, has basic weaknesses that emphasize my whole argument.

Secondly, there is another trend in sociological anthropology which also requires the new method for its full development. It is becoming apparent that it is increasingly unsatisfactory to pursue monographic and comparative analyses depending on gross concepts such as agnation or matriliny. We see that these concepts cover complex clusters of rights and duties, which operate with varying weight in different situations. This type of analysis is being developed by Peters on the Bedouin of Cyrenaica.[26] The significance of the varying weight of the elements in these clusters can only be elaborated through the analysis of a series of connected situations, and not by apt illustrations. This applies also, for example, to the type of problem set in the recent Cambridge University symposium on the developmental cycle of domestic groups, as was demonstrated by Worsley in his revaluation of Fortes' earlier work.

Looking back on the course of anthropology, in the light of these developments, you will not be surprised that I find Malinowski's *Crime and Custom in Savage Society*, with all its jurisprudential weaknesses, to be the most striking of his books. I have often criticised Malinowski for his theoretical weaknesses: so I feel it just that I end this essay by paying tribute to his great contribution to our methods of getting facts, and thus changing the nature of our facts. He made theoretical contributions besides this: but by developing our methods, he made our new science, and he still points the way to both ethnographic and theoretical advances. We are, I believe, going into a much less tidy era of research, with the concepts of society and structure and culture very much under critical examination. As we appreciate more fully that culture is in fact to some extent a hotch-potch, and that customs and values are independent of one another, discrepant, conflicting, contradictory, we shall have to evolve concepts to deal with social life which are less rigid, and which can cope with lack of interdependence as well as the existence of interdependence, with the haphazard as well as the systematic. As we stand now on the brink of this advance, I feel that it is important we continue to develop the monographic analysis as still the core of our science, even though continual comparative analysis is an essential check. But with the change in monographic analysis, there will have to be a change in the manner of comparisons. I plead also that anthropologists will have again to accustom themselves to welcoming great ethnographic detail, including descriptions and analyses of extended cases, as in the 20's and 30's we welcomed the rich detail of Malinowski's books. I believe it is fatal to become, like Leach, 'bored with ethnographic fact'.

*University of Manchester*

# Notes

1. M. Fortes: 'Communal fishing and fishing magic in the Northern Territories of the Gold Coast,' *J.R.A.I.*, lxvii, 1937.
2. M. Fortes: 'Ritual festivals and social cohesion in the hinterland of the Gold Coast,' *American Anthropologist*, xxxviii, 4, 1936.
3. M. Gluckman: *Analysis of a Social Situation in Modern Zululand*, Rhodes-Livingstone Paper No. 28, Manchester University Press, 1958, reprinted from *Bantu Studies* 1940 and *African Studies* 1942.
4. M. Freedman: *Lineage Organization in Southeastern China*, London School of Economics Monographs in Social Anthropology No. 18, 1958.
5. M. G. Smith: 'Government and politics in lineage systems,' *J.R.A.I.*, lxxxvii, 1957.
6. E. Colson: 'Social control and vengeance in Plateau Tonga society,' *Africa*, xxiii, 1953.
7. P. M. Worsley: 'The kinship system of the Tallensi: a revaluation,' *J.R.A.I.*, lxxxvi, 1956.
8. *Political Organizations of the Kula Ring*, Manchester University Press (in press).
9. S. F. Nadel: Chapter VI in *Nupe Religion*, Routledge and Kegan Paul, 1954; S. F. Nadel: 'Witchcraft in four African societies: an essay in comparison,' *American Anthropologist*, liv, 1952.
10. M. Wilson: 'Witch beliefs and social structure,' *American Journal of Sociology*, lvi, 1951.
11. M. G. Marwick: 'The social context of Cewa witch beliefs,' *Africa*, xxii, 1952.
12. V. W. Turner: *Schism and Continuity in an African Society: A Study of Ndembu Village Life*, Manchester University Press, 1957.
13. J. A. Barnes: 'Social anthropology in theory and practice: inaugural lecture at Sydney University,' *Arts, the Proceedings of the Sydney University Arts Association*, i, 1958. In this lecture, Barnes discusses the same development as I do.
14. J. C. Mitchell: *The Kalela Dance*, Rhodes-Livingstone Paper No. 27, Manchester University Press, 1957; J. C. Mitchell: 'Urbanization, detribalization, and stabilization in Southern Africa: a problem of definition and measurement.' Working paper prepared for the Abijan Conference on the social impact of industrialization and urban conditions in Africa, 1954; etc.
15. J. A. Barnes: *Marriage in a Changing Society*, Rhodes-Livingstone Paper No. 20, 1951; J. A. Barnes: 'Measures of divorce frequency in simple societies,' *J.R.A.I.*, lxxix, 1951.
16. E. Colson: 'The intensive study of small sample communities,' in R. Spencer (Editor): *Method and Perspective in Anthropology*, University of Minnesota Press, 1954.
17. P. Gulliver: *Family Herds*, Oxford University Press, 1957.
18. D. Stenning: *Pastoral Nomads*, Oxford University Press, 1959.
19. E. E. Evans-Pritchard: *The Sanusi of Cyrenaica*, Clarendon Press, 1949.
20. J. A. Barnes: *Politics in a Changing Society*, Oxford University Press, 1954.
21. A. W. Southall: *Alur Society*, Heffers, 1956.
22. L. A. Fallers: *Bantu Bureaucracy*, Heffers, 1956.
23. W. Watson: *Tribal Cohesion in a Money Economy*, Manchester University Press, 1958.
24. A. L. Epstein: *Politics in an Urban African Community*, Manchester University Press, 1958.
25. E. R. Leach: *Political Systems of Highland Burma*, Bell (University of London), 1954.
26. E. L. Peters: 'The proliferation of lineage segments among the Bedouin of Cyrenaica,' *J.R.A.I.*, lxxx, 1960.
27. E. R. Leach: *op. cit.*, p. vii (cited in R. Firth's Foreword).

# CASE AND SITUATION ANALYSIS[1]

*J. Clyde Mitchell*

> Clearly one good case can illuminate the working of a social system in a way that a series of morphological statements cannot achieve. (Gluckman 1961: 9)

## Introduction

The current division between those sociologists who prefer to rely on survey techniques and quantitative analysis in the prosecution of their art as against those who prefer to rely on observation and verbal types of analysis has had a long history. Just over fifty years ago—in the late 1930s in fact—the division manifested itself in a lively debate in some of the journals about the validity of statistical methods of enquiry on the one hand as against what were called 'case studies'.[2]

Textbooks on sociological methods of research published before say 1955 such as Young 1939 (226–54) or Goode and Hatt 1952 (313–40) invariably included a chapter on case studies but since then the topic seems to have lost its appeal, since while non-quantitative procedures such as participant observation receive extensive treatment the issue of the role of case studies as such seems to have disappeared. The change in emphasis is dramatically reflected in the general index of the *American Journal of Sociology* which had its origin in Chicago from which the most important case studies first emerged and which carried the account of the debate in its pages. The Cumulative Index at 1950 contained sixteen references to case studies and case histories.[3] The most recent reference is to Oscar Lewis's discussion of the detailed studies of families in 1950. After that the entry for case studies disappears from the index! A paper on case studies appeared in *Social Forces* at about the same time (Foreman 1948). Since then it appears to have faded from sociological discussion but it has survived in education research (see Simons 1980).

---

Notes for this article begin on page 40.

This eclipse of interest in case studies as a method of sociological analysis is partly due to the vast expansion of quantitative techniques stimulated by the wide availability of computers which has broken the back of formerly extremely time-consuming processing of large sets of survey data. Hand in hand with the steady strides in the sophistication of statistical techniques a theory of sampling soundly based on probability mathematics has grown up so that the survey analyst has available an extensive armamentarium of procedures and techniques all resting on firm epistemological grounds.

The foundation of statistical inference from samples representative of a wider population has now become commonplace knowledge and most first year students in the social sciences are made familiar with such notions as 'a representative sample', 'sampling error', 'biased and unbiased estimates' and similar ideas developed to express the logic of making inferences about a larger population from a considerably smaller sample.

In the course of this development the epistemology of the case study seems to have been neglected with a corresponding confusion about the degree to which those who either by force of circumstances or by deliberate choice find themselves engaged in case studies. The consequence is that we find criticism of their findings to the effect that these findings are invalid because they are based on only one case.[4] This confusion of procedures of statistical inference with those appropriate to case studies is indexed particularly by the challenge frequently addressed to those who have chosen to pursue the deviant path of case studies: 'How do you know that the case you have chosen is typical?'

I shall argue that this question betrays a confusion between the procedures appropriate to making inferences from statistical data and those appropriate to the study of an idiosyncratic combination of elements or events which constitute a 'case'. It is my purpose to establish what these differences are and thereby one hopes to provide guidelines for the use of case studies in social investigation and theory building.[5]

## The Case Study in Social Anthropology

The method of case studies is, of course, general and has been extensively used, for example, in political science and in sociology. But more than in other social sciences, perhaps, each fieldworker who presents a study of some 'people' or another in a social anthropological monograph is in fact doing a case study. Possibly because quantitative techniques do not play so central a role in social anthropology as in sociology there has been more discussion of the method of case study in anthropology. One of the earliest general statements about the role of case studies by Barnes in 1958 drew a contrast between the formal method of institutional analysis and the complexity of the 'Russian novel' approach through case studies (Barnes 1958). In 1960 he described the case-history approach as a 'distinctive feature' of presentday social anthropology (Barnes 1960: 201).

Each people an anthropologist studies may be looked upon as displaying a unique combination of cultural characteristics. But the anthropologist sets out to interpret some aspect of the way of life of this people by using an approach which an anthropologist studying some quite different people may also employ. In short nearly the whole of the respectable body of anthropological theory has been built up over the years from a large number of separate case studies from which the anthropologists have been prepared to draw inferences and to formulate propositions about the nature of social and cultural phenomena in general. What appears not to be so widely discussed in anthropology, however, is the epistemological basis upon which these generalisations have been made and it is to this question that I wish to turn with its implication for the role of case studies in the development of theories in general whether in social anthropology or not.

A more focused statement appeared in 1961 when Max Gluckman discussed the history and use of case material in anthropological analysis (Gluckman 1961). In it he drew the important distinctions among what he called 'apt illustrations', 'social situations' and 'extended case studies', the implications of which I return to later [see p. 28 below]. The basic problem in the use of case material in theoretical analysis, however, is that of the extent to which the analyst is justified in generalising from a single instance of an event which may be—and probably is—unique. This problem is normally presented as that of the 'typicality' of the case which is used to support some theoretical analysis. A typical case implies that the particular set of events selected for report is similar in *relevant* characteristics to other cases of the same type.

Gluckman was well aware of this since he raises the question in the following terms: 'I can touch only briefly on the problem of typicality for a society of the area of social life selected for analysis in this way. In the first place the use of the extended case does not do away with the need for the outline of social morphology, on which Malinowski insisted and this may have to be illustrated by apt examples. But here the increasing use of statistics, in more refined form, by anthropologists provides an important safeguard' (Gluckman 1961: 14).

He argues in effect that a specification of the general wider context in which the events of the case are located must be based on other analytical techniques. Typicality, therefore, in his argument pertains to the social morphology rather than to the case, which may only be an apt illustration of it. Similarly the use of statistical analysis as a counter-measure to the untypicality of the case material also implies the use of methods other than the case study as a basis to assure typicality. Gluckman does not develop these points which remain peripheral issues to his argument as a whole so that the crucial issue of the basis upon which the case analyst may extrapolate from his material is left unanswered.

In another important discussion of case analysis van Velsen 1967 once again addressed the problem of the typicality of the case chosen for analysis. His essay is concerned with a variant of case analysis, that is, with situational analysis, and his main purpose is to redress the imbalance he saw in the over-emphasis on structuralist types of analysis in anthropology at that time. He argues instead for a greater emphasis on the optative approach in

which the choice-taking of actors is given due weight as against the concentration on the institutional framework within which the actors were operating. Analysis of this kind requires a very detailed and intimate familiarity
by the observer of the behaviour and cognitive orientations of the actors in
the events being described. The restriction on the coverage such detailed
investigation requires necessarily imposes limitations on the extent to which
the observer is able to describe the whole 'culture' or whole 'society' of the
people being studied. These restrictions, van Velsen argues, raise 'the question of the typicality of the anthropologist's analysis' (1967: 145). Van Velsen
resolves this question by arguing that the object of the analysis is not in fact
'culture' or 'society' of which the events studied might be considered samples but rather social processes which may be abstracted from the course of
events analysed.

At this point, I feel, van Velsen stops short of making the essential point
about the basis of making inferences from case material: that the extrapolation
is in fact based on the validity of the analysis rather than the representativeness
of the events. This is a point to which we will need to return but before doing
so it is necessary to specify more exactly the sort of material implied by the
terms 'social situation' or 'case'.

## Specification of the Case Study

The term 'case study' may refer to several very different epistemological entities and it is necessary at the outset to specify the particular meaning I am
attributing to it here.

In its most basic form a case study may refer to the basic descriptive material
an observer has assembled by whatever means available about some particular
phenomenon or set of events. The case material here is simply the content of
the observer's field notes prior to any deliberate analysis or selection for presentation in some analysis. Similar in character are the case records developed
by practitioners in some field of action—physicians, clinical psychologists,
psychiatrists, social workers, probation officers and the like. Normally these
practitioners are trained in the art of systematically recording information
which may be germane for their practical action.

Both of these types of 'case study' may become the basis of the rather more
specific means I shall be attributing to the terms here, that is, as material from
which some theoretical principles are to be inferred. Some writers like Madge
(1953: 100) are mainly concerned with the material of this kind so that the
problem then becomes the procedure upon which data may be extracted from
material of this kind for theoretical purposes.

But throughout what follows I shall be assuming that the 'case study' refers
to an observer's data; i.e. the documentation of some particular phenomenon
or set of events which has been assembled with the explicit end in view of
drawing theoretical conclusions from it.[6] The focus of the case study may be
a single individual as in the life-history approach or it may be a set of actors

engaged in a sequence of activities either over a restricted or over an extended period of time. What is important is not the content of the case study as such but the use to which the data are put to support theoretical conclusions.

In what way then does a case study differ from any other way of assembling systematic information about social phenomena for research purposes? Goode and Hatt, the authors of one of the few textbooks on sociological methods which discusses case studies, describe the case study as 'a way of organizing social data so as to preserve the *unitary character of the social object being studied*'. They go on:

> Expressed somewhat differently, it is an approach which views any social unit as a whole. Almost always this means of approach includes the development of that unit, which may be a person, a family or other social group, a set of relationships or processes (such as a family crisis, adjustment to disease, friendship formation, ethnic invasion of a neighbourhood etc.) or even an entire culture. (1952: 331, original italics)

They contrast this with the 'survey' type of analysis in which the person is replaced by the trait as the unit of analysis. The wholeness 'characterising' the case study, they point out, is determined by the extent to which the analyst has assembled enough information about the object of study to provide sufficient specification of the research purpose in mind.[7] As they point out, 'The case study attempting to organize the data around the unit of growth, or group structure, or individual life pattern, does force the researcher to think in these terms rather than fall back on trait analysis alone' (Goode and Hatt 1952: 339).

But Goode and Hatt in this early—and relatively rare—discussion of the use of case studies in sociological research overlook two crucial features of the case study which bear directly on the main topic of this paper, that is, the basis of extrapolation or of inference from case studies. In the first instance Goode and Hatt assume without demur that the *only* way of extrapolating from data is on the basis of a statistically representative sample and they spend a good deal of space pointing to the problems of securing representative cases for subsequent statistical analysis. The second point is that while they emphasise the 'wholeness' of the case they appear to be unaware that each individual case is influenced by circumstances which the researcher may wish to control for in the analysis. All cases, as van Velsen (1967: 146) and Garbett (1970: 217) point out so clearly, are located within some wider context[s] which in turn impose constraints on the actions of the protagonists in the case study. These contexts constitute a panoply of *ceteris paribus* conditions which the analyst will need to allow for in some way.

With this background in mind we may now turn to a specification of what we imply by the term 'case' or the cognate tern 'social situation'. As a working definition we may characterise a case study as a detailed examination of an event (or series of related events) which the analyst believes exhibits (or exhibit) the operation of some identified general theoretical principle.

The important point here is the phrase 'the operation of some general theoretical principle' since a narrative account of some event or a series of related events does not in itself constitute a case study in the sense in which I am using the notion here. A case study is essentially heuristic; it reflects in the events portrayed features which may be construed as a manifestation of some general abstract theoretical principle.

Material derived from cases or from social situations however may be used analytically in different ways and it is to this question that we now turn.

## Types of Case Study

It was one of the merits of Gluckman's early (1961) essay in which he discussed case studies that it drew a sharp distinction between 'apt illustrations', 'social situations' and 'case studies', and how they may be used in theoretical analysis. These types of case phenomena may be viewed as falling along a continuum of increasing complexity.

(i) Near one limit—the simple end—would fall what Gluckman called 'the apt illustration' (1961: 7). The apt illustration is normally a description of some fairly simple event or occurrence in which the operation of some general principle is clearly illustrated. An anthropologist may, for example, describe how he had noticed a man step off a path to conceal himself as his mother-in-law approached, and use this account to illustrate the operation in daily life of mother-in-law/son-in-law avoidance. The particular event is sequestrated from all other ongoing events either connected with the behaviour among other in-laws or from other events going on at the same time in the vicinity. The use of case material in this way is, as Gluckman's terminology indicates, merely illustrative. A *sine qua non* is that the observer must be convinced of its typicality to be able to use it as an illustration.

(ii) Considerably more complex is the analysis of a social situation. A social situation is a collocation of events which the analyst is able to construe as connected with one another and which take place in a relatively restricted time span.[8] The classic example of a social situation used as an analytical tool is Gluckman's description and analysis of the official opening of a newly-built bridge in Zululand in 1935 (1958). In the analysis of a social situation some restricted and limited (bounded) set of events is analysed so as to reveal the way in which general principles of social organisation manifest themselves in some particular specified context. The official opening of the bridge brings together representatives of different sectors of the population in Zululand, Blacks and Whites, Christians and pagans, officials and citizens, Zulu nobles and commoners, and Gluckman shows how their behaviour leading up to, during and following the opening of the bridge reflects the structure of South African society with all its alliances and cleavages at the time when the study was done. The analysis of social situations has become a significant example of case analysis and has been discussed particularly by van Velsen (1967) and Garbett (1970).

(iii) At the complex end of the continuum is the extended case study. This is a further elaboration of the basic study of case material for it deals with a sequence of events sometimes over quite a long period, where the same actors are involved in a series of situations in which their structural positions must continually be re-specified and the flow of actors through different social positions specified. The particular significance of the extended case study is that since it traces the events in which the same set of main actors in the case study are involved over a relatively long period, the processual aspect is given particular emphasis. The extended case study enables the analyst to trace how events chain on to one another and how therefore events are necessarily linked to one another through time. I used this procedure in a study of the social structure of a people in Malawi (Mitchell 1956: 86ff.). In the first four chapters of the book I set out the general features of morphology of social life of the people. In this section in order to locate the operation of the general features of morphology, as for example the struggle for status among village headmen, I use case material as apt illustrations.

Subsequently I move to an analysis of the process whereby the villages grow and break up. For this purpose I make use of several case studies, including one which is in fact an extended case. The events described started some eight years before I was in the field and continued while I was in the field—and no doubt continued after I left it. The circumstances revolve around the daily incidents, the squabbles and altercations, the births and deaths, all of which the protagonists relate to their position in the general matrilineal kinship structure of the village, in which witchcraft accusations, marriage arrangements, village moots and even physical assaults are involved. These events in juxtaposition with one another provide us with an analytical prism through which the basic principles of matrilineal kinship located in the context of local politics may be refracted into relatively clearcut terms.

The extended case is similar to, but broader than, the 'social dramas' which Turner (1957) used in his analysis of Ndembu social life. Social dramas are accounts of a series of crises in the daily life of the people during which, as Turner expresses it,

> The social drama is a limited area of transparency on the otherwise opaque surface of regular, uneventful social life. Through it we are enabled to observe the crucial principles of social structure in their operation and their relative dominance at successive points in time. (1957: 93)

The rationale upon which the distinction among 'apt illustration', 'social situations' and 'extended cases' [is] differentiated is not immediately explicit in Gluckman's presentation. While the three types of case material are all used to support theoretical statements as against the distinction between 'clinical' and 'theoretical' case studies referred to earlier, the distinction between 'apt illustration' and 'social situations' is clearly one of the degree of complexity of the events described, the distinction between 'social situations' and 'extended cases' is partly one of even more complexity, but it is also one of the duration of time spanning the events described. Complexity and duration are obviously linked since events covering a longer time period are likely to reflect changes and adjustments as well as simple patterns of relationships.

For this reason the classification of case studies suggested by Eckstein (1975: 94–123) is perhaps more instructive. Eckstein distinguishes five categories of case study which highlight the way in which they may be used as a contribution to theoretical thinking.

These five ways of using case material are as follows:

(i) *Configurative-idiographic studies* [are case studies] in which the material is largely descriptive and reflects the particular concatenation of circumstances surrounding the events in a way which, while [it] may provide insights into the relationships among the component elements in the case, [does] not easily lead to direct general theoretical interpretations.

(ii) *Disciplined-configurative studies,* as their name implies, are still configurations or patterns of elements, but the observer does not look upon these as unique or 'idiographic'. Instead, the analyst seeks to interpret the patterns in terms of general theoretical postulates. Eckstein writes:

> The chain of enquiry in disciplined-configurative studies runs from comparatively tested theory to case interpretations and thence, perhaps, via *ad hoc* additions, newly discovered puzzles, and systematised prudence, to new candidate theories. Case study is thus tied to theoretical inquiry—but only partially, where theories apply or can be envisioned; passively, in the main, as a receptacle for putting theories to work; and fortuitously as a catalytic element in the unfolding of theoretical knowledge. (Eckstein 1975: 100)

However, Eckstein goes on to point out that

> The application of theories in case interpretation, although rarely discussed, is not at all a simple process, even leaving aside the question of how valid theory is to be developed. Such applications only yield valid interpretations if the theories permit strict deductions to be made and the interpretations of the case are shown to be logically compelled by the theories. (Eckstein 1975: 103)

He argues that the major utility of attempted disciplined case interpretation is that it 'forces one to state theories more rigorously than might otherwise be done—provided that the application is truly "disciplined" i.e. designed to show that valid theory compels a particular case interpretation and rules out others' (Eckstein 1975: 103).

(iii) *Heuristic case studies* are distinguished from configurative-idiographic and disciplined-configurative studies in that they are deliberately chosen in order to develop theory. As Eckstein phrases it, the heuristic case study is

> deliberately used to stimulate the imagination towards discerning important general problems and possible theoretical solutions.... Such studies, unlike configurative-idiographic ones, tie directly into theory building, and therefore are less concerned with overall concrete configurations than with potentially generalisable relations between aspects of them: they also tie into theory building less passively and fortuitously than does disciplined-configurative study, because the potentially generalisable relations do not just turn up but are deliberately sought out. (Eckstein 1975: 104)

(iv) *Plausibility probes* are case studies used specifically to test interpretative paradigms which have been established either by previous case studies or by other procedures. Eckstein writes:

> In essence plausibility probes involve attempts to determine whether potential validity may reasonably be considered great enough to warrant the pains and costs of testing, which are almost always considerable, but especially so if broad, painstaking comparative studies are undertaken. (Eckstein 1975: 108)

Plausibility probes may be undertaken after heuristic case studies have been successfully concluded. They may constitute part of a series of case studies devoted to the expansion and development of an interpretative schema or theoretical formulation relative to phenomena represented by the case. As Eckstein points out, 'The essential point for us that as empirical plausibility probes, case studies are often as serviceable, as or more so, than comparative ones—and nearly always a great deal cheaper' (1975: 110). Plausibility probes are used, then, as a preliminary test of theoretical formulations previously established by some other procedures, before a rigorous test by formal procedures.

(v) *Crucial case studies* are, as the name suggests, similar to the crucial experiment in the natural sciences, and offer the circumstances which enable the analyst to reject some theoretical proposition or, which amounts to the same thing, to support it when the circumstances appear to be loaded against it. The selection of the case is clearly difficult: the assumption is that enough will be known about the phenomenon *a priori* to enable the analyst to recognise its particular significance for the way in which the proposition has been formulated. A detailed study of the case will then enable the analyst to relate events to the theoretical proposition.

Throughout this discussion the role of theory and of theorising in the use of case material is of paramount importance and it is this feature which provides the means through which the fundamental problem in case studies may be approached: the basis upon which general inferences may be drawn from them.

## Inference and Extrapolation from Case Studies[9]

However clearly the basic principles are reflected in some particular case material the crucial question upon which there is much misgiving is that of the extent to which the analyst is justified in making generalisations from that particular case to all instances of that type. In ordinary English usage there is a strong connotation that the word 'case' implies a chance or haphazard occurrence.[10] This connotation is carried over into more technical and sociological language in the form of implying that a case history or case material refers to one 'case' and is therefore unique or is a particularity. If this is true then how can unique material form the basis of inference about some process in general?

That case material may so be used is apparent since as previously mentioned, most social anthropological and a good deal of sociological theorising has been founded upon case studies. The difficulty arises, I conjecture, out of the common assumption that the only valid basis of inference is that which has been developed in relation to statistical analysis. In the procedure considerable care is taken to select a sample from some parent population in such a way that no bias is introduced to the sample. The implication of the notion of 'no bias' is that the examples in the sample are not selected in a way which would reflect inaccurately the characteristics of the parent population. The procedures for achieving this are varied, the most straightforward of which is the simple random sample. The assumption behind this procedure is that if the instances for inclusion in the sample are selected in a way which excludes any possibility of biased selection then the characteristics of the sample will reflect those of the parent population within some range of certainty which may be estimated using the assumptions of probability theory. By this procedure the sample is typical of the parent population or in more common terminology it is a 'representative sample'.

The logic in this procedure is that the incidence and in fact the coincidence of characteristics in the sample reflect within the range of sampling error the incidence or coincidence of the characteristics of the parent population. Inferences are made about the parent population from the characteristics in the sample population so that dependence on a 'representative' sample is, of course, vital.

In so far as the descriptive features of the sample (and therefore of the parent population) are concerned, the validity of the inference is probably sound. The distribution of age of a representative sample drawn from a parent population probably reflects reasonably accurately—given sampling errors—the distribution of ages within that population. A difficulty arises however when the relationship *between* characteristics is considered. In the sample analysed a relationship—a correlation—in fact may be noted between say age and the probability of being married. In terms of the canons of statistical inference the analyst may assume that the same relationship exists between the same characteristics in the parent population. Note, however, that the inference from the sample in relation to the parent population is simply about the concomitant variation of two characteristics. The analyst must go beyond the sample and resort to theoretical thinking to link those characteristics together—in terms for example of an appreciation of normal life-cycle processes in the instance of age and marriage. The relationship between the characteristics may be validated by other types of observation and encapsulated in the values of the people concerned The inference about the *logical* relationship between the two characteristics is not based upon the representatives of the sample and therefore upon its typicality, but rather upon the plausibility or upon the logicality of the nexus between the two characteristics.

The point is well illustrated in another context by Lykken (1970) who, for purposes other than those I have in mind, quotes a finding reported by Sapolsky, who records the responses of respondents with or without dietetic disorders to Rorschach ink-blots. Sapolsky found that among sixty-two respondents some identified the ink-blots as a frog and some did not but that there was an appreciable tendency for those with dietetic disorders to react to the blot in terms of a 'frog' response and for those without these disorders not to do so. In fact some 61 per cent of those with dietetic disorders reacted with the 'frog' response to the ink-blots whereas only 16 per cent of those without dietetic disorders responded with a 'frog' response. If we are able to assume that the sample of respondents is in fact representative of the population at large we would estimate from the chi-square statistic that a sample with a departure of this extent from the state where the frog response is distributed equally among those with and those without dietetic disorders would arise by chance sampling errors in less than one occasion in 1000 samples.

We may be reasonably confident therefore that the relationship between a respondent's interpreting the ink-blot as a frog and also having a dietetic disorder seems unlikely to have arisen purely by chance and we rely on statistical inference to assert this. But the explanation that Sapolsky advanced for this association was according to Lykken 'an unconscious belief in the cloacal theory of birth' which involves notions of oral impregnation and anal parturition. The excretary [sic] and reproductive canals of the frog are—they constitute the cloaca—common and this biological fact presumably provides the rationale for the belief. 'Since patients should be inclined to manifest eating disorders: compulsive eating in the case of those who wish to get pregnant and anorexia in those who do not.... such patients should also be inclined to see cloacal animals such as frogs on the Rorschach' (Lykken 1970: 267). Lykken then asked twenty of his colleagues, many of them clinicians, about the hypothesis. As Lykken reports it, their reaction before they were given the experimental results was 'I don't believe it', and after they were given the experimental results it was 'I still don't believe it' (Lykken 1970: 268).

The issue raised here is essentially that of the relationship between the theory linking the interpretation of the Rorschach ink-blots with dietary disorders. While the clinical psychologists may well have accepted that more people with dietary disorders saw the blots as frogs than those without, they could not accept the *explanation* of the relationship between the two characteristics the original author chose to link to one another.

The distinction is that of the commonly accepted distinction between what has been called statistical inference on the one hand or scientific or causal inference on the other (see Henkel and Morrison 1970 *passim*). Statistical inference is the process by which the analyst draws conclusions about the existence of two or more characteristics in some wider population from some sample of that population to which the observer has access. Scientific or causal—or perhaps more appropriately—logical inference, is the process by which the analyst draws conclusions about the essential linkage between two or more characteristics in terms of some systematic explanatory schema—some set of theoretical propositions. In analytical thinking based on quantitative procedures *both* types of inference proceed *pari passu* but there has been some tendency to elide logical inferences with the logic of statistical inference: that the postulated *logical* connection among features in a sample may be assumed to exist in some parent population simply because the features may be inferred to *coexist* in that population. This is the point that Lykken was making about

Sapolsky's study of the frog response among people with dietary disorders. By contrast I argue that the process of inference from case studies is only logical or causal and cannot be statistical and that extrapolability from any one case study to like situations in general is based only on logical inference. We infer that the features present in the case study will be related in a wider population not because the case is representative but because our analysis is unassailable. The emphasis on case studies used to relate theoretically relevant characteristics reflected in the case to one another in a logically coherent way. Analytically sound studies using statistical procedures are of course doing the same thing but two very different inferential processes are involved in them: logical inference is epistemologically quite independent of statistical inference.

## Enumerative and Analytical Induction

This distinction between logical and statistical inference is related to the notions of enumerative and analytical induction introduced to sociology by Znaniecki as long ago as 1934. Znaniecki, a vehement opponent of the vogue for quantitative studies which were becoming popular at the time of his writing, contrasts the two modes of inference. Enumerative induction in his view exists in the form either of simple enumeration in which the characteristics of a class of phenomena are established simply by listing them, or in the more elaborate form of statistical induction in which probability theory is involved. In the simple form, he argues, enumerative induction has 'continued to be used with very little change, in ethical and political works from antiquity, down to present times, whenever an author not satisfied with deducing rules of conduct from principles accepted *a priori* attempts to base this view on experience and observation' (Znaniecki 1934: 221). He describes its general principles as

> an attempt to discover some final truths about a certain class of empirical data, circumscribed in advance, by studying a number of cases belonging to this class. Originally and fundamentally, the truths sought for are to be characters common to all data of the given class and only to these. (Znaniecki 1934: 222)

This implies identification of a class of phenomena by some identifiable but not necessarily essential characteristics and then examining a set of instances of this class to identify those features of the instance that define that class. By contrast,

> in analytical induction certain particular objects are determined by intensive study, and the problem is to define the logical classes which they represent. No definition of the class precedes in analytical induction the selection of data to be studied as representatives of this class. The analysis of data is all done before any general formulations; and if well done, there is nothing more of importance to be learned about the class which these data represent by any subsequent investigation of more data of the same class. (Znaniecki 1934: 249)

Znaniecki goes on to say:

It may be said that analytical induction ends where enumerative induction begins; and if well conducted leaves no really soluble problems for the latter. With such a radical difference in logical problematisation, the logical procedure should naturally differ widely. While both forms of induction tend to reach general and abstract truths concerning particular and concrete data, enumerative induction abstracts by generalisation, whereas analytical induction generalises by abstracting. The former looks in many cases for characters that are similar and abstracts them conceptually because of their generality, presuming that they must be essential to each particular case; the latter abstracts from the given concrete case characters that are essential to it and generalises them, presuming that insofar as essential, they must be similar in many cases. (Znaniecki 1934: 250–251)

The process of analytical induction proceeds according to Znaniecki not by developing a self-sufficient theory from one instance well analysed, for he criticises Durkheim's analysis of religion based on Australian totemism (Znaniecki 1934: 237), but rather by examining cases so selected as to illuminate formerly obscure aspects of the general theory.

Znaniecki's discussion of the significance of exceptions and how they may be made to 'prove the rule' (Znaniecki 1934: 305–6) appears to contradict his austere statement quoted earlier to the effect that 'if well done there is nothing more of importance to be learned about the class which these data represent by any subsequent investigation of more data of the same class'. But we should distinguish here between the *principles* of analytical induction and its *practice*. The intention behind analytical induction is to specify the necessary connections among a set of theoretically significant elements manifested in some body of empirical data. But in practice any one set of data is likely to manifest only some of the elements whose explication would contribute to a cogent theoretical interpretation of the processes involved. An indeterminate number of strategically selected sets of events would need to be examined, therefore, before the state of complete knowledge that Znaniecki refers to can be approached.

This issue was specifically recognised by Znaniecki for after developing the point about the establishment of complete knowledge from only one instance he goes on to say:

Of course the inductive scientist continuously goes on investigating objects or processes already defined and classified even though he does not doubt the validity of his former definition, for there is always something to learn about individual data: concrete reality as we have said is an inexhaustible source of new knowledge. (Znaniecki 1934: 250)

But he goes on to specify that the new knowledge he refers to is not a mere supplement to pre-existing knowledge but rather an extension of *theoretical* knowledge.

Robinson (1951, 1952) subsequently in a criticism of Znaniecki's ideas distinguished between analytic induction as a research procedure, as a method of causal analysis and as a method of proof. Any of these epistemologically disjunct implications might be conveyed by the term. The main burden of Robinson's argument, however, is that there is no essential contradiction between analytical induction and enumerative induction on the grounds that by its procedures analytical induction isolates the *necessary* circumstances for the manifestation of some phenomenon but does not in itself establish *sufficient* conditions. Analytic induction, Robinson argues, enables the analyst to 'establish the conditions without which the phenomenon would not appear' (Robinson 1951: 815), whereas enumerative induction, as exemplified by statistical procedures, establishes sufficient conditions for the phenomenon to occur. His argument is based on the premise that analytical induction as exemplified by case studies examines only instances in which the phenomenon under investigation in fact occurs, whereas statistical procedures ideally would also take into account those occasions when the phenomenon does not occur. This, he argues, allows the analyst to establish sufficient conditions as distinct from necessary conditions for the phenomenon to occur. He goes on to argue that as a practical as against a logical procedure there is little difference between enumerative and analytical induction since practitioners of the art of analytical induction indirectly study cases in which the phenomenon in which they are interested does not occur. Radcliffe-Brown, it is said, was interested in totemism. In order to understand it more fully therefore he elected to study the Andamanese islanders amongst whom there was no totemism. The point is that if an analyst is working with some conception of the general role of totemism in a social system then an examination of the operation of the social system in which totemism does not occur ought to enable the analyst to some assessment of the *absence* of totemism. The essential point is the one which Robinson makes: 'The success of analytical induction in producing complete explanation is due to its procedure, to its systematisation of the method of the working hypothesis and not to its logical structure' (1951: 816).

In reality no case study can be presented in isolation from the corpus of empirical information and theoretical postulates against which it has significance. The point is well made by Kaplan who quotes Hartmann in relation to clinical observation in psychiatry: 'Every single clinical "case" represents, for research hundreds of data of *observed regularities* and in hundreds of respects' (Kaplan 1964: 117, original italics). The single case becomes significant only when set against the accumulated experience and knowledge that the analyst brings to it. In other words the extent to which generalisation may be made from case studies depends upon the adequacy of the underlying theory and the whole corpus of related knowledge of which the case is analysed rather than on the particular instance itself.

## The Significance of the Atypical Case

This consideration justifies the selection of the case for study (or for exposition) in terms of its explanatory power rather than for its typicality. Formally any set of events deemed to reflect the abstract characteristics that the observer wishes to use in analysis may be used. Since the analyst's purpose is to demonstrate how general explanatory principles manifest themselves in the course of some ongoing set of events the particular set of events is in itself a subsidiary consideration.

There is absolutely no advantage in going to a great deal of trouble to find a 'typical' case: concern with this issue reflects a confusion of enumerative and analytic modes of induction. For general purposes any set of events will serve the purpose of the analyst if the theoretical base is sufficiently well developed to enable the analyst to identify within these events the operation of the general principles incorporated in the theory.

There is, however, a strategic advantage in choosing particular sets of events for study or for exposition. It frequently occurs that the way in which general explanatory principles may be used in practice is most clearly demonstrated in those instances where the concatenation of events is so idiosyncratic as to throw into sharp relief the principles underlying them.[11] The point is analogous to the crucial role that untoward events have played in the elucidation of unexpected connection in the natural sciences. A dramatic example is provided by the veterinary scientist W. I. B. Beveridge who describes how in 1889 a laboratory assistant chanced to notice that flies had congregated around the urine of a dog from which the pancreas had been removed. A test showed sugar in the urine thus leading to the establishment of the connection between the pancreas and diabetes[12] (Beveridge 1950: 28). So in the social sciences an illuminating case may make theoretical connections apparent which were formerly obscure.

It is of course obvious that the significant case is only so because the analyst is able to perceive the illuminating contradictions in the material. But the contradictions only become significant because of the observer's familiarity with current theoretical formulations in terms of which the contradictions are articulated. This highlights the point made earlier that the presentation of a case study is significant only in terms of some body of analytical theory. Pasteur's aphorism is highly apposite: 'Where observation is concerned chance favours only the prepared mind' (Oxford Dictionary of Quotations 1979: 369).

## The Case in Its Context

The characteristic uniqueness of each case is largely due to the fact that the particular events described in the case are usually presented in the first instance at a fairly low level of abstraction. The observer provides a detailed account of who the *dramatis personae* were, what they did and how they reacted to the events (and their social relationships) in which they were involved. The particularities of the context, of the situation and of the actors, then, are important features of case studies.

It is this particularity of case studies which has been the basis of what I consider to be ill-founded criticism of the use of case studies as a basis for generalisation. But of course in interpreting the events in any particular case theoretically the analyst must suppress some of the complexity in the events and state the logical connexions among some of the features which are germane to the interpretation. This process of abstraction and the suppression of contextually irrelevant features has led Ralph Turner to a critique of the process of analytical induction. Turner sees analytical induction primarily as a procedure for establishing the necessary and essential features that characterise the phenomenon or class of events under consideration, that is, as a definitional procedure. These necessary and essential features, however, are usually part and parcel of some coherent and cogent theoretical explanatory system so that analytical induction necessarily involves what Turner calls 'causal closure', that is, that the procedure must produce causally self-contained systems. This implies that an explanation of events based on analytical induction relates typically to a limited set of events restricted in the sense that the events must of necessity be explicable in terms of the explanatory rubric that informed the analysis. In these circumstances, Turner argues, the 'causal prime mover' must be outside the set of events being considered, or in his words, 'the system is not capable of activation from within but only by factors coming from outside the system' (1953: 609). It is for this reason that predictions from an analysis based on case study techniques tend to be *theoretical* rather than *empirical*. External factors, or *intrusive* factors as Turner calls them, always influence the events in a case study but can only be included in the theoretical explanation by their incorporation into the case as one of the essential and necessary characteristics.

But it is not essential that events located, from the analyst's point of view, outside the events with which the case is concerned and which need to be taken account of in the explication of the case material, need be treated in the same detail as the events in the case itself. The problem of isolating events intellectually from seamless reality in order to facilitate their analysis in terms of some explanatory system was discussed at some length by Gluckman and his colleagues (Gluckman (Ed.) 1964). One of the points Gluckman makes is that it is perfectly justifiable for the analyst to operate with a simplified account of the context within which the case is located provided that the impact of the features of that context on the events being considered in the analysis are incorporated rigorously into the analysis.

All cases are necessarily contextualised and generalisations made from case studies must therefore be qualified with a *ceteris paribus* condition. It is incumbent on the observer to provide readers with a minimal account of the context to enable them to judge for themselves the validity of treating other things as equal in that instance.

The very particularity of the case study, located as it is in some setting, however, can be turned to good advantages; it can provide the opportunity to demonstrate the positive role of exceptions to generalisation as a means of deepening our understanding of social processes. It is only under specified conditions that a clear and simple formulation of the operative principles underlying a social process can be stated. But the very circumstances of the case study make a strict imposition of a *ceteris paribus* condition impracticable. The analyst may therefore take account of the unique circumstances surrounding the event in the case being analysed in order to show [that] these circumstances obscure the simple and direct way in which the general principles should be operating. Because of the intimate knowledge of the relationships in the particular circumstances which connect the events in the case, the analyst might be able to show how the general principles being examined manifest themselves in changed form.

The contextual features surrounding the case are in effect held constant by a process of logical analysis. It is in this sense that Znaniecki remarks:

> Wherever, thus, an exception can be explained, that is, can be proved only apparent, not real, we gain not only a confirmation of our previous knowledge but also new knowledge: we discover the limits within which our causal processes occur or find some other causal process and thus determine the range of validity of our law or validate some other law.... it is not the exception that matters, but our attitude towards it: if we refuse to submit to it, but go on analysing our data, it is a factor of scientific discovery, whereas if we passively accept it, it is a check on further progress. (Znaniecki 1934: 306)

The case study, because of the observer's intimate knowledge of the connections linking the complex set of circumstances surrounding the events in the case and because of the observer's knowledge of the linkages among the events in the case, provides the optimum conditions in which the general principles may be shown to manifest themselves even when obscured by confounding side effects.

## Conclusion

The argument that has been advanced here, then, is that case studies of whatever form are a reliable and respectable procedure of social analysis and that much criticism of their reliability and validity has been based on a misconception of the basis upon which the analyst may justifiably extrapolate from an individual case study to the social process in general. A good deal of the confusion has arisen because of a failure to appreciate that the rationale of extrapolation from a statistical sample to a parent universe involves two very different and even unconnected inferential processes—that of statistical inference which makes a statement about the confidence we may have that the surface relationships observed in our sample will in fact occur in the parent population, and that of logical or scientific inference which makes a statement about the confidence we may have that the theoretically necessary or logical connection among the features observed in the sample pertain also to the parent population.

In case studies statistical inference is not invoked at all. Instead the inferential process turns exclusively on the theoretically necessary linkages among the features in the case study. The validity of the extrapolation depends not on the typicality or representativeness of the case but upon the cogency of the theoretical reasoning.

In terms of this argument case studies may be used analytically—as against ethnographically—only if they are embedded in an appropriate theoretical framework. The rich detail which emerges from the intimate knowledge the analyst must acquire in a case study if it is well conducted provides the optimum conditions for the acquisition of those illuminating insights which make formerly opaque connections suddenly pellucid.

Nuffield College, Oxford

Received 23 February 1982
Accepted 10 May 1982

## Notes

1. This paper has been in draft form for some time. I am grateful to the following who have provided me with bibliographical references or valuable comments: David Boswell, Robert Burgess, Jean Edwards, Barry Glassner, Les Green, Sheldon Himmelfarb, Elinor Kelly, Chris Pickvance, Dave Reason, Ralph Ruddock, Sue Smith, Rory Williams; seminar groups at Adelaide, Durham and Oxford and two anonymous referees. Unfortunately I have not been able to take all of their suggestions into account.
2. Prior to the development of the social survey in the 1930s case studies seemed to feature regularly in sociological research (see bibliography in Young 1939: 569–72) and there were several useful discussions of the method e.g. Cooley (1930). Znaniecki writing in 1934 (246–8) reflects this division very clearly and lists a number of contemporary works that have used the case approach. Znaniecki points out that at that time the model for sociological case studies [was based on] the clinical methods [of] psychiatry, particularly since the spread of psychoanalysis, but also [those of] social work. He lists several sociological studies which had used case studies analytically most of them part of the 'ethnographic' wing of the Chicago school such as works by Thomas, Cooley, Shaw, Park and Burgess. He also, however, drew attention to the division of opinion between those using case methods and those using survey methods. Articles bearing on the debate are Burgess 1927, 1945, Eldridge 1935, Hotelling and Sorokin 1943, Jocher 1928, Jonassen 1949, Lewis 1950, Queen 1928, Sarbin 1943, Shaw 1927 and Waller 1935.
3. The references to case studies were Waller 1935, Eldridge 1935, Hotelling 1943, Sarbin 1943, Burgess 1945, Komarovsky and Waller 1945 and Lewis 1950.
4. As for example in Ashton's review of Blackburn, R. M. and Mann, M.: *The Working Class in the Labour Market* in *The Sociological Review* (1980) 28: 433–4. Ashton's point, however, that Blackburn and Mann fail effectively to establish the *ceteris paribus* conditions of their generalisation is valid.
5. Recently Hamilton, working in the field of educational studies, has yet again drawn the contrast between case studies and survey analysis and concludes that 'the assumptions of case study research and survey analysis stand in mutual opposition' (1980: 90). My own argument, however, is that in the end the oppositions are more apparent than real.
6. [Cf.] '[the case study] attempts to arrive at a comprehensive understanding of the group under study. At the same time the case study also attempts to develop more general theoretical statements about the regularities in social structure and process' (Becker 1968: 233).
7. Goode and Hatt go on to discuss other features that distinguish case studies from other research procedures such as the breadth of data, the levels of data, the identification of types and profiles and the significance of the developmental aspects of the case.
8. Garbett (1970: 215) defines a social situation as a temporarily and spatially bounded series of events abstracted by the observer from the ongoing flow of social life.

9. Stake (1980) provides one of the few discussions of the nature of generalisations from case studies and from survey findings but his emphasis is on the quality of the generalisations rather than on the basis upon which they are achieved.
10. Captured by the Shorter Oxford English Dictionary phrase 'an event or occurrence, hap or chance'. The word 'hap' is defined in the same dictionary as 'a chance accident or occurrence'.
11. Lindesmith in his comments on Robinson's paper phrases the same point in terms of discovering the case that *disproves* the rule. He writes: 'There is no point to the random selection of cases when this is obviously not the most efficient manner of seeking evidence' (1952: 492).
12. Beveridge heads the chapter in which he discusses the role of chance in making important theoretical connections in physiology with a quote from Charles Nicolle: 'Chance favours only those who know how to court her.'

# References

Barnes, J. A. (1958), Social anthropology: theory and practice: inaugural lecture at Sydney University, in *Arts: the Proceedings of the Sydney University Arts Association.*
Barnes, J. A. (1960), 'Intensive studies of small communities', in *Meanjin: A Quarterly of Literative Art Discussion* 19: 201–3.
Becker, H. S. (1968), 'Social observation and case studies', in Sills, David L. (ed.) *International Encyclopedia of the Social Sciences,* New York: The Macmillan Company and the Free Press: vol. 11: 232–8.
Beveridge, W. I. B. (1950), *The Art of Scientific Investigation,* London: Heinemann.
Burgess, E. W. (1927), 'Statistics and case studies as methods of sociological research', *Sociology and Social Research* 12: 103–20.
Burgess, T. W. (1945), 'Sociological research methods', *American Journal of Sociology* 50: 474–82.
Chassan, J. B. (1960), 'Statistical inference and the single case in clinical design', *Psychiatry* 23: 173–84.
Cooley, C. H. (1930), 'The case study of small institutions as a method of research', in *Sociological Theory and Social Research,* New York, Henry Holt & Co: 313–22.
Eckstein, H. (1975), 'Case study and theory in political science', in Greenstein, F. and Polsby, N. (eds), The *Handbook of Political Science: Strategies of Inquiry,* London: Addison-Wesley: vol. 7: 79–137.
Eldridge, S. (1935), 'Textbooks, Teachers and Students', *American Journal of Sociology* 40: 637–45.
Foreman, Paul (1948) 'The theory of case studies', *Social Forces* 26: 408–19.
Garbett, G. Kingsley (1970), 'The analysis of social situations', *Man* 5: 214–27.
Gluckman, M. (1958), *The Analysis of a Social Situation in Modern Zululand,* Rhodes-Livingstone Paper no. 28, Manchester: Manchester University Press for Rhodes-Livingstone Institute.
Gluckman, M. (1961), 'Ethnographic Data in British social anthropology', *Sociological Review* 9: 5–17.
Gluckman, M. (ed.) (1964), *Closed Systems and Open Minds: The Limits of Naivety in Social Anthropology,* London: Oliver & Boyd.
Gluckman, M. (1967), 'Introduction' in Epstein, A. W. (ed.), *The Craft of Social Anthropology,* London: Tavistock: i–xxiv.
Goode, William J. and Hatt, Paul K. (1952), *Methods in Social Research,* New York: McGraw-Hill.
Hamilton, David (1980), 'Some contrasting assumptions about case study research and survey analysis', in Simon, H. (ed.), *Towards a Science of the Singular: Essays about Case*

*Study in Educational Research and Evaluation,* Care Occasional Publications no. 10, Norwich: Centre for Applied Research in Education: 78–92.

Henkel, R. E. and Morrison, D. E. (eds) (1970), *The Significance Test Controversy,* London: Butterworth.

Hotelling, H. and Sorokin, P. (1943), 'The prediction of personal adjustment: a symposium', *American Journal of Sociology* 48: 61–86.

Jocher, K. (1928), 'The case study method in social research', *Social Forces* 7: 512–15.

Jonassen, C. T. (1949), 'A re-evaluation and critique of the logic and some methods of Shaw and McKay', *American Sociological Review* 14: 608–14.

Kaplan, A. (1964), *The Conduct of Enquiry: Methodology for Behavioral Science,* San Francisco: Chandler.

Komarovsky, M. and Waller, W. (1945), 'Studies of the family', *American Journal of Sociology* 50: 443–51.

Lewis, Oscar (1950), 'An anthropological approach to family studies', *American Journal of Sociology* 55: 468–75.

Lindesmith, A. R. (1952), 'Comments on W. S. Robinson's "The logical structure of analytical induction"', *American Sociological Review* 17: 492–3.

Lykken, David (1970), 'Statistical significance in psychological research', in Henkel, R. E. and Morrison, D. E. (eds), *The Significance Test Controversy*: 267–279.

Madge, John (1953), *The Tools of Social Science,* London: Longmans, Green & Co.

Mitchell, J. Clyde (1956), *The Yao Village,* Manchester University Press for the Rhodes-Livingstone Institute.

Oxford (1979), The *Oxford Dictionary of Quotations,* 3rd edn, Oxford University Press.

Queen, S. (1928), 'Round table on the case study in sociological research', *Publications of the American Sociological Society*: 22.

Robinson, W. S. (1951), 'The logical structure of Analytical Induction', *American Sociological Review* 16: 812–18.

Robinson, W. S. (1952), 'Rejoinder to comments on "The logical structure of Analytical Induction"', *American Sociological Review* 17: 494.

Sarbin, T. R. (1943), 'A contribution to the study of actuarial and individual methods of prediction', *American Journal of Sociology* 48: 593–602.

Shaw, Clifford (1927), 'Case study method', *Publications of the American Sociological Society* 21: 149–57.

Simons, Helen (ed.) (1980), *Towards a Science of the Singular: Essays about Case Study in Education Research and Evaluation,* Care Occasional Publications no. 10, Norwich: Centre for Applied Research in Education.

Stake, Robert E. (1980), 'The case study method in social enquiry', in Simon, H. (ed.), *Towards a Science of the Singular: Essays about Case Study in Educational Research and Evaluation,* Care Occasional Publications no. 10, Norwich: Centre for Applied Research in Education: 64–75.

Turner, Ralph H. (1953), 'The quest for universals in sociological research', *American Sociological Review* 24: 605–11.

Turner, V. W. (1957), *Schism and Continuity in an African Society,* Manchester University Press for the Rhodes-Livingstone Institute.

van Velsen, J. (1967), 'The extended case method and situational analysis', in Epstein, A. L. (ed.), *The Craft of Social Anthropology,* London: Tavistock: 129–49.

Waller, Willard (1935), 'Insight and scientific method', *American Journal of Sociology* 40: 285–97.

Weinberg, S. Kirson (1952), 'Comment on W. S. Robinson's "The logical structure of analytical induction"', *American Sociological Review* 17: 493–4.

Young, Pauline (1939), 'The Case Study Method', in *Scientific Social Surveys and Research,* New York: Prentice Hall: ch. X, 226–54.

Znaniecki, Florian (1934), *The Method of Sociology,* New York: Rinehart.

# SECTION I

# THEORIZING EXTENDED CASES

# PREFACE
## Theorizing the Extended-Case Study Method

*T. M. S. Evens and Don Handelman*

The essays composing this section vary in their purport and approach, but nonetheless address in common a number of questions that cut across at least any two of the essays, thus exhibiting what Wittgenstein spoke of as family resemblance for the lot. These include the question of dualism, of the relation between the micro and macro realms of social life, of the differences among the variants of the Manchester case method, of the determination of the boundaries of a case, of the part played by conflict theory in the development of the extended-case method, of the importance of the creative or emergent moment in the unfolding of a case, of the nature of the logic involved in analyzing a case, and, above all, of the intimate connection between the social-scientific turn to process and the creation of the extended-case method.

For obvious reasons, it is only fitting that the reprints of Max Gluckman's 1961 article, "Ethnographic Data in British Social Anthropology," and J. Clyde Mitchell's 1983 article, "Case and Situation Analysis," should come before the various essays written for this volume. But the theoretical force and implications of these two articles are worth featuring and give a primus inter pares face to the family resemblance presented by the essays in this section bearing on theory.

In his article, Gluckman documents how, in British social anthropology, the (Malinowskian) emphasis on intensive field research shaped the ethnographic redirection from custom and morphology to the total "process of social life" and the need to rethink how to use ethnographic case material. In prescribing a shift in the usage of cases, from the method of 'apt illustration' to that of the 'extended case', the essay elucidates how this change of ethnographical method makes critical common cause with the implicit promise of a grand theoretical swing toward, in our terms, practice. It is remarkable to see, in an article first published at the front end of the second half of the twentieth century, the mainstay anthropological concepts—culture, society, structure, matriliny, agnation, and so on—already being overtly thrown open to doubt on the basis of a theoretical orientation, processualism, with which, in many ways, social science is still trying to come to terms.

Gluckman raises but does not closely tackle the question of the analytical validity of generalizing from a particular case to the social whole. An anthropologist/sociologist and a close associate of Gluckman, Mitchell, who played a major role in the development of the extended-case method (as well as in that of network analysis), takes up this epistemological question in his article. In an analytically rich, rigorous, and incisive discussion, he observes that the question takes its force from the misleading presumption that if the generalization from the case study is to be sound, the case must be deemed to be typical of the social order. Mitchell points out that this presumption is fundamentally misleading, for, unlike statistical inference, the emphasis in the case study is not on whether a characteristic of a particular case (say, the distribution of age) is representative of that characteristic in the population as a whole, but rather on the nature of the connection between different characteristics (say, between age and the probability of being married), a relationship that demands theoretical explication. In effect, Mitchell is arguing that justification of extrapolation from case studies is a matter not of typicality but rather of the creation and assessment of theoretical propositions about the way things hang together.

The shift toward process makes more than an epistemological question, though, for it also implicitly presupposes an ontological reassessment of the very nature of the social. Two of the essays presented here, by Evens and by Glaeser, directly confront the question of ontology qua ontology. In his exercise, Evens is basically concerned to extract the processual implications of situational analysis for social ontology. He argues that Cartesian dualism constitutes the ontological scaffolding for structural functionalism and that it is for reasons of this taken-for-granted ontology that Gluckman found it so difficult to seize fully the advantage of his awareness of the fundamental importance of process and break cleanly with structural functionalism. Evens's tack is to recommend an ontology that grasps in processualist terms what there is. He does so by drawing on certain notions in Heidegger's phenomenological philosophy. By defining being and the world as no less part and parcel of as distinct from each other, Heidegger's famous notion of 'being there' (*Dasein*) or 'being in the world' essentially displaces dualism. In addition, because being obtains thus only as a tensile phenomenon (always between what it is and what it is not), Heidegger's notion implicitly redefines being as process in the sense of becoming. Evens further observes that 'being in the world' is another way of talking about humans as innately 'situated', by which he means that they are constrained but that, paradoxically, the set of constraints always includes the constraint to act and react creatively and reflexively in the face of the basically open-ended character of social existence. From this gloss on the idea of 'situation' (implicit in 'situational analysis'), Evens is urging that in the accounting of social processes, anthropology needs always to bear in mind, in addition to causality and motivational elements, this singular and defining human condition of creative response, a condition that ontologically describes human social existence in terms of responsibility and in this sense as, at bottom, an ethical reality.

A sociologist with a keen professional interest in ethnography, Glaeser too sets out the makings of an ontology suitable to understanding social life in terms of process. The result is distinguished by its comprehensive scope and systematic conceptual exposition. The immediate object of his ontological exercise is to facilitate translating a theoretical interest, bearing on one or another social process, into a fitting, concrete ethnographic project. Glaeser's problem, then, is correlative to Mitchell's of the relevance of particular cases to sociological generalization—but rendered, in Glaeser's argument, as how to go about, in light of processualism, profitably selecting one's ethnographic site and case material. By blurring the boundaries between one social phenomenon and another, and by describing social life as open-ended, processualism complicates this problem anew.

Handelman's contribution focuses on the aleatory nature of situated existence and argues that extended casework amounts to 'micro-historical' research. In his 1961 essay, Gluckman specifically eschews the idea that, in studying particular cases in their extension, one is doing history. However, given that in construing situational analysis as history Handelman means to bring to the theoretical fore the innate temporality of extended cases, and that it is unlikely that in his comment about history Gluckman had in mind the technical notion of micro history, the founder of the Manchester School might well have been open to Handelman's usage. Using Goffman's concept of the encounter, Handelman keys his argument to interaction. His main point, though, is that the extended-case method can show how practice is practiced into existence, and, correlatively, since practice is open-ended, how extended cases constitute what he calls 'prospective' (in contra-distinction to 'retrospective') history: one simply cannot know what will happen next and just how the case will inform the macro realm of institutions. In effect, Handelman is arguing that in Walter Benjamin's aphorism of the Angel of History, as *the* angel of history, the Angel should look forward no less than back, and, in doing so, see the chaotic dynamics that the social is generating and entering into continuously. For Handelman, the brilliance of the practice of extended case is its joining together, and at times its potentiality to synthesize, social life, duration, scale, past-ness, futurity, and uncertainty, all as emergent process.

Finally, Kapferer presents an exceptionally rich, intimate, and comprehensive account of Manchester anthropology in connection with the development of the case study. His discussion of Gluckman's anticipation of so much that is now anthropologically current is particularly valuable, not only for its scrutiny of the Manchester School's theoretical framework and tradition but also, in view of the too often thoughtless presentism characterizing major trends in today's anthropology, for the discipline in general. Kapferer, who as a novice anthropologist enjoyed an appointment at the Rhodes-Livingstone Institute of Social Studies in British Central Africa at a time when the prolific research of that institute had been powerfully informed by Gluckman's directorship, brings out just how strongly political the anthropologists associated with the Manchester School were and how this political disposition gave critical impetus to the resulting anthropology. In this connection, Kapferer is inclined to see Gluckman's abiding interest in conflict as a programmatic component of the extended-case method rather than a tacitly impelling force toward its creation. But Kapferer is by no means wholly uncritical of the tradition and finds that there is room to build on the Manchester edifice. Hence, in a concluding discussion that aims to run between radical relativism and a kind of universalism, he argues that Gluckman was, for all his innovation, insufficiently open to the discursive practices characterizing the cases he studied and was therefore unable to allow these to inform his own discursive perspective of how the social works.

*Chapter 1*

# SOME ONTOLOGICAL IMPLICATIONS
# OF SITUATIONAL ANALYSIS

*T. M. S. Evens*

## I

Ever since I began teaching, over 30 years ago, I have been in the habit of advising students who either are going into the field or are writing up their field research to take recourse to the Manchester School case-study method. When doing so, I was not merely indulging an old school tie. Most immediately, I had in mind the very substantial practical advantages of an aid to finding observational foci in the field and to organizing the glut of data with which one is confronted upon return from field research. In addition, though, to introduce my theme, I always suspected in the back of my mind that this technique runs much deeper than the word 'method' ordinarily allows. I want to take this opportunity to explore this suspicion.

Gluckman himself thought that the method is more than procedural, suggesting that it had a certain theoretical weight. In his introduction to Bill

---

Notes for this chapter begin on page 61.

Epstein's (1979) edited volume on fieldwork techniques, *The Craft of Social Anthropology*, Gluckman, surely with the case-study method in mind, wrote of the contributors: "They are … able to discuss within a common framework modern fieldwork methods not simply as a set of techniques *per se*, but rather as tools for examining a number of problems that have come to interest them" (Gluckman 1979: xv). I believe he was trying to express that the case method is not merely a canonical way to collect data but that by its very nature it put in a fresh light certain theoretical problems then plaguing the discipline. Indeed, in the same piece Gluckman goes so far as to observe: "A new technique of observation may virtually create a new discipline" (ibid.: xvi). He asserts: "[W]e have tried in these essays to set techniques in the framework of theoretical problems, so that those who use the book may remind themselves of what they are aiming at when they collect their material" (ibid.: xv).

What, then, are these problems they were aiming at? By combing van Velsen's (1979) contribution ("The Extended-Case Method and Situational Analysis") to Epstein's collection, they can be set out summarily as a series of binarisms. To wit, using van Velsen's lexicon, they are problems of how to bring into account the individual, the diachronic, operation, the deviant, behavior, the irregular, and the exceptional or unique by contrast to, respectively, the group, the synchronic, structure, the normative, norm or principle, the normal, and the cyclical. The slant of the Manchester School was to refer all of these problems and their like to the thesis of norms in conflict, a dialectical theory central to Gluckman's anthropology. The thesis was propounded to remediate what was seen as a pronounced incapacity of the received Durkheimian picture of social order. The axial normativism of the Durkheimian picture seemed unable to admit of the empirical character of social life. Social phenomena that were perfectly ordinary but out of keeping with the normative ideal could not be projected onto the Durkheimian analytical screen. Yet these phenomena were brought into high empirical relief as a result of intensive field research. The case method, in its prescription to focus on incidents of conflict in particular, offered a way at once to document the actual empirical flow of social life and to save the Durkheimian picture by referring this flow to conflicting but nonetheless axiomatic principles of the social order. The argument was epitomized in Gluckman's ingenious contention that some kinds of conflict actually serve to maintain the social structure in its current, normative form.

In effect, the case method seemed to bring together, in an empirically compelling fashion, the general with the particular. Contrasting the method to the use of cases as 'apt illustration' set off this lesson in induction—extended cases were meant to be studied not simply to illustrate or exemplify the principles underlying the social order but to isolate and identify them in the course of their operation. The idea was, it might be said, to bring the social structure analytically to life.

It would be hard not to be struck by the salutary power of the Manchester case method in respect of the "framework of theoretical problems" just described, and occasioned by the infamous normative bias of structural functionalism. The method, particularly when 'extended', really did turn the analyst's gaze pointedly to the question of process. That said, though, given anthropological developments over the past three decades or so, and even more long-standing philosophical ones, it seems to me that the method has theoretical implications far more radical than Gluckman and company surmised when they first advanced its merits. The radical implications I have in mind are ontological.

# II

For all the fruitfulness of the thesis of basic norms in conflict, it left much to be desired. There is no need here to detail the shortcomings of the Manchester approach to the theoretical problems presented by the findings that fly in the face of the normativist paradigm. Suffice it to say that whereas this approach aimed still to preserve the paradigm by tweaking it, these problems necessarily arose *with* the paradigm: that is to say, they were not incidental to but constituent of it.

In order to found sociology as a scientific discipline, it was necessary to determine its object in substantive terms. If society were not construable as an entity in its own right, a reality as such (*sui generis*, as Durkheim was fond of saying), then society would in fact be simply reducible to the sum of its entitative parts. As we all know, Durkheim accomplished this task by showing that we do indeed experience society just as we experience natural phenomena—as part of the world as we find it, outside ourselves. As one physicist put it, you know something is real when, if you kick it, it kicks back. Durkheim demonstrated that society has just this kind of reciprocating kick. But when it came time to determine the nature of the integrity of this thing called society, Durkheim, ultimately at least, and with an insight that remains still to be turned to best account in the human sciences, alighted on the idea of 'moral adhesion'. In this view, society was an order held together by ends that were socially constructed rather than naturally determined, ones precisely not given in the physical order of things. But given this proposition—that the social is a moral order—what can be made of the claim to the substantive reality of society? Construed oxymoronically as an *ideal* reality, doesn't society once again become an abstraction of sorts and thereupon subject to reduction to the sum of its individual parts? And, then, doesn't the standing of the parts as patently behavioral and substantive essentially deny the reality of society as such, and in this sense constitute nothing less than an ever present threat to that reality's basis in fact, its authenticity?

My point is this. If society is conceived of as a moral order, then behavioral process *cannot but* be construed as an opposing phenomenon—*at least, not as long as the entitative is received as the defining nature of reality.* According to such a substantive ontological projection, a moral order is precisely what material behavior is not. This projection is epitomized in Descartes' ontology, whereby thinking stuff (*res cogitans*) and stuff extending in space (*res extensio*)—in other words, mind and body, spirit and matter—constitute an opposition that is immaculate, making what he called thinking stuff anything but *stuff*. I wager that this ontology is, as Martin Heidegger (1962: 133) said of it more than 70 years ago, "still the usual one today." Certainly, it is the one

Durkheim had to consider in order to found sociology as a science, and also the one on which his project, when conceived of as a disciplinary paradigm, ultimately foundered. In the task he set himself of demonstrating the reality of society, Durkheim presumed rather than questioned the Cartesian ontology. As a result, he was forced to vacillate, grasping society as a power that is, on the one hand, immanent (with a kick) and, on the other, transcendent. In the end, thus, he begged the question as to how the two sorts of power can co-exist.

The problem with which Gluckman and his students were faced—that is, the problem of how to bring into account process, with all that this entails—was part of the legacy of Durkheim's ontological presupposition. Gluckman's remediating idea of norms in conflict does not confront this presupposition but, like Hegel's revision of Kant, serves only (even if provocatively) to conceal its dualistic folly. Take any two basic norms that stand in a contradictory relationship to each other, and in the particular situation they are bound to collapse into a contest over which norm is the more normative and which is the more normatively amiss. This is because the norms themselves amount to nothing but prescriptions for addressing the chronic tension between behavior and ideal in the first place. Norms comport values and therefore present themselves as transcendent to and, accordingly, regulative of material behavior. When Mahatma Gandhi counseled the Indian populace to rise above the reciprocal economy of violence and turn the other cheek, he—in the conviction that at the end of the day value is more powerful than power itself—was promoting the creation of value as such. That is, he was fostering an end irreducible to (but by no means necessarily exclusive of) material account. At the bottom of every set of norms in conflict, then, is the essential tension between norm and behavior. Unhappily, the Cartesian ontology, still taken for granted in Gluckman's remediation of the Durkheimian project, pictures this tension as a matter of opposition alone, making it basically inconceivable that the two principles of the tension can actually obtain together.

It is my contention that the Manchester case method not only lends itself to the study of process in an analytical context keyed to normative design, as Gluckman proposed, but also tends to betray, with a singular acuity, the profoundly problematical nature of thinking of the reality of society in such dualistic terms in the first place. That is, the method intimates an understanding of reality other than the received one.

## III

As is well known, the Manchester case-study method manifested itself under different rubrics, each with a separate emphasis. Thus, whereas the 'extended-case study' underscores the focus on a series of connected incidents, Turner's 'social drama', favoring an aestheticism, features the *dramatic* form found in the process constituted by any such series. 'Situational analysis', the term preferred by van Velsen, highlights a notion employed by Gluckman in the title of his famous study (1958) of the ceremonial opening of a bridge in "modern Zululand"—the notion of 'social situation'. It is in connection with this notion that I can best bring out the nature of the ontological difference that interests me here.

The meaning of 'social situation' was largely taken for granted by the practitioners of the method and was thus not explored in any depth. I take it that in using this notion, two basic senses were intended. The first was that of an incident of serious or dramatic conflict—to use Gluckman's words, a "trouble case." This is the sense understood when, under sudden tense or fragile social circumstances, one might exclaim: "We've got a situation here!" The second sense is relative to social scale, such that the term 'situation' was used to describe particular incidents involving concrete interactants rather than social structure as such. This usage, distinguishing between an interactional or small-scale perspective and a morphological or large-scale perspective, tends thus to convey the dichotomous differentiation that marked the wrench in the Durkheimian works—the differentiation between actual practice and normative order.

In both of these senses of 'situation', what was critically understood was the operation of constraining social force: in respect of the 'trouble case', it was the force of norms in conflict that constrained, whereas the interactional event was determined by the force of the social structure at large, the 'large scale'. It was indeed such social constraint that described what it means to be 'situated'. In the main, the object of the exercise was to infer the character of this constraining or situating force from the concrete practice to which the force itself was presumed to somehow give rise.

But the contexts defined by conflicting norms and social structure, though of considerable sociological moment, hardly exhaust what it means to be situated. For instance, in themselves, neither context comprehends the aleatory nature of a particular situation, which nature is, I expect, ever implicit in the very idea of a case and must surely be counted as situating. This is the sense of situation focused by, say, the Chinese *Book of Changes* (*I Ching*), an oracle meant to divine coincidence (co-incidents) and attuned to time as (to use Jung's word) synchronicity. Or, to take an ethnographically more familiar instance, it is the sense of situation registered in the Zande's question when he asks not why the granary collapsed, but why it collapsed when he happened to be resting under it. However, I wish to feature still another aspect of situatedness.

There is implicit in the example of Azande witchcraft and of the *Book of Changes* a certain conception of human agency, one that is not registered firmly, if at all, in the picture of situatedness drawn by the structural-functional thesis of social constraint. Neither the *Book of Changes* nor Azande witchcraft makes any sense, even in its own terms, outside of the presumption that humans play a critically active role in—that they can do something about—what happens. These examples describe humans paradoxically as situated by constraint to resolve their own ends, that is, to participate in situating themselves. Both divination and witchcraft presuppose that the constraint to condition one's own situation, which is to say, one's own self, is a constant feature of every human situation.

Here, then, we have a constraint that constitutes a world-making freedom.

## IV

In his neologistic notions of *Dasein* and "Being-in-the-world," Martin Heidegger included, as a crucial component, this signal and profoundly paradoxical sense of constraint.[1] *Dasein*, Heidegger's word for human being, translates directly into English as 'to be there' or 'being there', the word 'there' indicating that there is no human being or being human that is not always already somewhere—in effect, situated. Outside of a particular context or certain kind of spatiality (a "there," a "worldhood"), one simply does not exist, that is, one *is not* or *cannot be*. The hyphenation "Being-in-the-world" is still another word for situated being. Like *Dasein*, it captures the fact, totally eclipsed by Cartesian dualism, that being and the world are in fact coeval, that they define each other from the start.

Cued by his concept of "authenticity," Heidegger distinguished between two senses of situation: *Lage* and *Situation*. Both senses bear critically on the constraint to be free, one in a positive way, the other in a negative way. Whereas *Lage* signifies one's submission to the prevailing or standard social definitions of the situation, definitions set by *Das man* or "the they," *Situation* describes one's breaking out of this socio-epistemological prison house to project one's "ownmost potentiality-for-Being." *Lage* implies, then, not that one has neglected to deploy one's freedom, but that one has used it in a way that arrests that very freedom. By contradistinction, *Situation* implies that, hearing the call of conscience, one has exercised one's freedom creatively and "resolutely," literally "authenticating" one's own self by taking advantage of the circumstantial openness characterizing any and every human situation. Inasmuch as every situation is no less fortuitous than culturally and institutionally conditioned, so it must also be indefinite or open.

Because Heidegger sees the *authentic* exercise of this peculiarly human freedom as an escape from the alienation and the gravity of "theyness," his approach highlights the question of this freedom in relation to situational analysis.[2] His notion of *Situation*, with its emphasis on individual authenticity, plainly hints at an implicit limitation of situational analysis as Gluckman and company practiced it. It suggests that the findings that served to frustrate the Durkheimian paradigm—all of which, in the very terms of that paradigm, may be anchored to the idea of the individual—should not be construed, solely from the perspective of a certain sociology, *as disagreeable*; instead, they betray a situational and positive constraint in their own right. And though this constraint, as I will show, does not lack for a social co-efficient, neither does it reduce to the usual suspects of normativity and social structure.

We must resist the temptation to conclude that if this constraint is not a matter of the normative and the structural, then it must be a question of self-interest and rational choice. Were we to do that, we would simply have recurred to the dualism between society and the individual in which structural functionalism and its opposition (various methodological individualisms, such as, e.g., transactional analysis and rational choice theory) were bemired. Alternatively, Heidegger's concept of authenticity suggests that the constraint in question is best viewed as a matter of a dynamic complementarity between, on the one hand, the openness of any situation and, on the other, the situated agent's response to that openness. Both terms of this complementarity bespeak singularity. The way in which any situation is open shares in the singular nature of the situation itself. It is tempting to conclude that the singularity of the agent's response is, likewise, a matter of the singularity of the agent, her nature as an 'individual'. But in the Heideggerian connection, this conclusion would be critically mistaken. The ordinary Western acceptation of 'the individual' describes a self the singularity of which is defined by immaculate distinction from the social. But the kind of agency at point here conveys, instead of sheer self-containment, selfhood that is intrinsically social or other to itself. Far from being self-contained, the resultant individual is always caught in the act of making itself as between self and other, and its singularity is thus described by a dynamic of betweenness. Though nonetheless real and consequential, this sort of moving selfhood may be described as a 'becoming other', an inherently non-institutional and fundamentally social motion and notion.[3]

At any rate, there is little doubt that Heidegger's concept of authenticity does not imply the dualistic rejection of the social per se, for at least three reasons.[4] First, authenticity dialectically depends, for its own possibility, on the quotidian existence of "theyness." It can arise only as a standing against or extrication from "the they." In fact, the entirety of Heidegger's project makes no sense apart from his thesis that our existence in this world is always and necessarily encumbered (in ways that include, of course, social, cultural, and historical constraint), a fundamental existential condition to which he gave the name "thrownness." Second, as Heidegger sees it, far from becoming asocial, authenticity makes it more likely that we will undertake our social obligations, for by grasping fully our own capacity for choice, we confront ourselves with precisely our responsibilities in relation to others. According to Heidegger's pivotal concept of "care," the heightened freedom of "authenticity" entails that, by contrast to its submersion in the everydayness of "the they," *Dasein* comes to grasp itself in terms of concern for others and the world.

There is yet a third reason why the constitutional opposition of "authenticity" to "theyness" does not define a dualism of individual and society. It is that, as was mentioned above, conformance to the humdrum sociality of "the they," no less than escape from it, entails the exercise of choice. Both authenticity and inauthenticity register choosing and therewith the individual.[5]

Nevertheless, there is a critical difference of constitution between an authentic and an inauthentic choice. By and large, choices to conform to a prevailing social definition of the situation represent the path of least resistance and tend to come so easily as to be taken thoughtlessly. This consideration, I surmise, is part of what Heidegger has in mind by inauthenticity, and it also informs, if only tacitly, the structural-functionalist presumption of the determining primacy of the social as over and against the individual. Indeed, there is a significant sense in which an innocent or unconsidered choice is no choice at all. The main point to see, though, is that the movement from inauthentic to authentic choice is not so much anti- or asocial as it is emancipatory and creative. This movement marks, in its own Heideggerian way, the tacit (ultimately Enlightenment) theme of liberation found in philosophical phenomenology from Husserl to Heidegger and beyond, including even thinkers such as Gramsci and Foucault. Indeed, today social scientists are in the habit of speaking of this kind of socially dominated and less-than-considered choice in terms of Foucauldian power or Gramscian hegemony, terms contrarily but implicitly loaded with the theme of liberation. But at least in Western thought, the theme is age old, going back to, for one primal scene, the Hebrew biblical tale in which, by virtue of a definitively incognizant but audacious choice amounting to an act of disobedience, Adam and Eve liberate or re-create themselves into consummate or self-conscious choosers and, correlatively, the world into their very own oyster. Such a world—a worldly world—opens every human situation, no matter how foregone or aleatory, to choice.

Once the notion of situation is put in this ontological light, situational analysis can be seen as especially capacitated to attend to the question of social forces, but in a way that represents social constraint not only as opposed to but also concordant with individuality. The hyphenation "Being-in-the-world" describes situated being as that being that situates itself in the face of its situatedness. It thus redefines the individual's autonomy—what, in the West, we are in the habit of equating with individuality as such—as fundamentally wedded to the individual's heteronomy.[6]

## V

At this juncture, I can take stock and address the question of what difference this phenomenological picture of situatedness makes to situational analysis. At least the following eight considerations apply.

1. The social no longer appears as primarily a matter of the normative, but rather of the norming, that is, the continuous constructing and deconstructing of norms. Even when social interactants are doing their level best to adhere to pre-existing norms, they are nonetheless necessarily engaged in both the construction and deconstruction of norms. This consideration does not mean that there is no longer any analytical need to attend to the social constraints of a situation; rather, it is necessary to do so in the context of a broader sociological objective—that of identifying the meaningful direction(s) the situation defines. At bottom, what the analyst is examining is movement, a movement that glides creatively within and between meanings, both old and new, thus making, breaking, and remaking norms.

2. If situational analysis brings the social structure to life, it does so by obliging the analyst to view the social structure, whatever its relative stability, as essentially an open dynamic. It entails that the situation must be grasped more fundamentally in its temporal openness than in its substantive definition and design. Put another way, it reminds the analyst that the substantivity of social structure is, though necessary and efficacious, if not exactly a fiction, at least both more and less than a thing. It thus moves beyond the dualism of structure

and process and the concomitant dualisms such as those van Velsen trots out, as cited above at the beginning of this chapter.

3. Situational analysis may be considered a precocious exercise in practice theory. As such, in line with Bourdieu's Marxian reading of practice, it cautions against intellectualism. By doing so, though, situational analysis is by no means falling in with the dualism of theory and practice. Instead, it is rejecting the assumption that all action is preceded by a theoretical blueprint in favor of the understanding that though practice is not simply a function of theory, it never lacks for an implicit theoretical co-efficient. In addition, by affording practice a certain primacy, situational analysis cautions against 'thingifying' social process.

4. The sense of situation proposed here, with its accent on openness, features essential ambiguity, the most dramatic, lived manifestation of which is conflict. Gluckman's idea of basic norms in conflict entails dispute that at bottom is irresolvable by appeal to the customary rules of logic and argumentation. Take, for example, conflict centering on the opposition between the rule of descent and the rule of residence among the Ndembu, as analyzed so splendidly by Victor Turner (1957). In light of this example, Gluckman's assumption of conflict included, if not distinctly at least implicitly, the idea of fundamental ambiguity. This sense of conflict evokes recent philosophies of difference that owe much to Heidegger's philosophical anthropology and its picture of human existence as self-identity perpetually suspended. Jean-François Lyotard's (1988) notion of *differend*, for instance, is indicative in this connection. *Differend* is Lyotard's usage for political difference in which the rules of disputation systematically disadvantage one of the opposing parties, producing a victim. In this way, a *differend* necessarily—at least when considered politically and ethically—calls into question the taken-for-granted rules or norms that serve peculiarly to distinguish a particular social setting. Lyotard's concept suggests, then, that even when a conflict has been resolved in favor of maintaining the current social structure, the relevant situation will nonetheless have exposed the normative order in some measure as conventional rather than necessary and, accordingly, will have opened the door to the possibility of deconstruction.

5. As movement, the social is seen no longer as occurring in time but as directly identifiable with time. The relevant kind of time is not in the first place the routine temporality we tend to sum up in the terminological triad of past, present, and future. Such temporality is predicated on a dualism of being and time, as if being were not itself time but simply obtained in or through time (one is *in* the present and *has* a past and a future). However, when social existence is construed in terms of the uniquely human capacity of self-transcending in the face of a fateful and finite world in which one finds oneself and into which one has been thrown, then that existence is time pure and simple, for it does not describe a fixed entity but instead a movement of becoming in which what *is* is always ahead of and never caught up with itself. Put in existential terms, this dynamic image portrays anticipating. Indeed, such existence might usefully be regarded as essentially messianic in nature, as long as it is understood that the

critical condition of this messianism is the failure of the messiah ever truly to materialize. This kind of existence—meaningful existence—is found, then, in the act of protention. To invoke Samuel Beckett's play on the logical absurdity of such an existence, we are always waiting for Godot. As a result, both past and present are existentially meaningful only by virtue of futurity or projection, and no matter what direction(s) it defines, a situation has to be grasped in terms of not only its apparent constraints but also its essential openness. Analytically, then, it is necessary to attend not only to the situational possibilities elected but also to the ones foregone, and thus to acknowledge the fact that interactants are, in their very determinateness, also determining.

6. To grasp a social situation primarily in view of its temporal process entails ultimate focus not on the fixed and explicit principles of the social order but on the tacit ones, the principles that are chiefly lived rather than predicated categorically. Put differently, such principles are found in the saying instead of the said. Because they are implicit and bodily, they run deep and are greatly efficacious. Bourdieu's famous concept of the habitus comes to mind here. But given its overriding emphasis on power, Bourdieu's concept does too little to bring out the other critical aspect of these principles. I have in mind the representative way in which they remain—for reasons of precisely the same nature that makes them so forceful and resistant to change—peculiarly open and dynamic. Inasmuch as they receive their basic articulation from embodiment, they lack rigorous conceptual definition. Granted this condition, whereby they go unfixed cognitively in their routine social context, it stands to reason that they are especially vulnerable to improvisation and creative transmogrification. Indeed, we might construe them as registering the movement of becoming that the social is in fact. Put another way, because they can be determined only ambiguously in conceptual language (a consideration that the analyst must bear in mind when conceiving of them), they are in this sense always on the move or 'becoming other', and therefore constitute categorial lenses with which we can see through to the social movement as such, its directionalities, potentialities, and ambiguities.

7. Situational analysis entails a reflexive ethnography, one critically attuned to the issue of the ethnographer's authority. Inasmuch as by virtue of her ethnographic task the analyst is herself a feature of the situational field she is studying, then by definition she is engaged in situating herself in relation to her subject matter. This is scarcely to say that she no longer need attend to the ethnographic facts (they remain her essential objective), but that she bears a measure of responsibility for defining these facts and the situation she is considering. It sharply attests to the power of situational analysis to rethink social theory that in his discussion of the case-study method, Gluckman (1979: xxii–xxiii), anticipating the so-called new ethnography, took up at some length the matter of the ethnographer's need to become aware of how her own involvement in the social situation helps to shape her analysis.

8. Situational analysis renders all social situations as a question of responsibility as well as constraint. Given that constraint is essential to the definition of a situation, any situation is—as has been the theme of so much recent anthropology—a

question of power. But inasmuch as any situation is determined by interactants who retain the capacity of choice in some measure, a situation remains always significantly open. Therefore, in an ultimate sense, each and every situation is ethical before it is political. Take, for example, the dire circumstances of, say, a concentration camp, where the capacity of choice is so limited that the only real choice available may be between bare life and no life at all. Though in a deep sense such a choice is no choice at all, in another it marks the defining condition of humanity. For the patent inhumanity of the choice marks the possibility of choice as such—only human beings have the choice to conduct themselves inhumanly.

## VI

As I suspected, Gluckman was right to intuit that the case-study method promised much more than a canonical way of doing ethnographic research. In connection with this intuition, I want to conclude by invoking one last distinction of Heidegger's, this time between the "present-to-hand" and the "ready-to-hand." What is present-to-hand entails an objective or abstract perspective, one in which the observer tries to position herself as detached from the observed. It is, then, the perspective of the scientist and the theoretician. In critical contrast, the ready-to-hand implies the practically engaged perspective of, say, the painter or sculptor. Here, there is no ideal of objective detachment but rather of seeing things in their lived potential. This angle of perspective—to show things not as objective and identical to themselves but in their transformative nature—leads away from the Cartesian ontology toward a radically different sense of reality, including social reality. By contrast to the present-to-hand, which, for reasons of its abstraction, lends itself to precise linguistic conceptualization, the ready-to-hand can be shown but not said. Precisely because it is a matter of openness, lived potential cannot be fixed with words but rather must be grasped in its very movement.

Situational analysis may be perceived if not to constitute at least to aspire to a marriage of these two kinds of observation. It means to produce a scientific picture of social life but to do so by showing this life as it is lived. It confronts us with the social dynamic itself, that consummate aspect of social reality which ultimately cannot be captured by the said, at least not with the terminological fixity of logical logic and rational language. Though it contains much in the way of explanatory power, situational analysis is also fundamentally descriptive. It is a mode of showing as well as saying, such that what it says illumines what is there, but at the same time— because what is there is open and in this sense not exactly there—implicates itself as less than true to what is there. Even in a case study, we continue to look through a terminological screen, the analyst's, and not directly at the happening itself. Nevertheless, this particular terminological screen is special, for, like a novel, it tends to focus process rather than essence. In the end, although it explains events, it also directly shows them in their becoming, a becoming in which the analyst participates in virtue of her ethnographic authority. Gluckman certainly sensed this feature of situational analysis, as he held that the method would bring to monography "some of the depth that many find in the novel but not in scientific analysis" (1979: xix–xx). He also maintained that the method would yield "some of the penetration which Freud brought to the study of human personality" (ibid.). Here, I suggest, in line with my juxtaposition of description to explanation, that the sense of Gluckman's insight goes toward dynamics as such. By invoking the "penetration" of psychoanalysis, Gluckman probably had in mind unconscious motivation and depth psychology. But I would urge that instead of viewing the unconscious as a set of submerged stimuli attaching to a self, it is better regarded in terms of self-interpretations so bodily, basic, and implicit that they are indistinguishable from the self in its current (but always imperfect) form. As such, they do not so much incite the self to action as describe it in its meaningful motion, its becoming other. The penetration and depth of which Gluckman speaks, then, appear to envision an anthropology in which humans can be seen not simply as determinate functions of a social order but as a meaningful social dynamic, the principal constituents of which are situated beings who are condemned to make and remake themselves unceasingly, for life and for a living.

Like the sculptor's raw, unworked material, situational analysis, as a vehicle of anthropological research, steers its users to certain visions of what there is. By expanding on the very idea of a situation, I have argued that situational analysis impels us to a picture of social reality different in fundamental respects from the Durkheimian one. In this picture, the binarisms of the individual and society, behavior and norm, change and stasis, and the like are reconstrued and relativized as torsions of the social regarded primarily as movement, a general dynamic. This picture of social reality makes a powerful difference. For one thing, it raises the question of whether we can have an institution that pays heed to this dynamic by remaining genuinely open to it. Or is it the case that any institution so capacitated must amount simply to the imaginary and to a contradiction in terms? By virtue of their powerful defense mechanisms, social institutions as we know them certainly acknowledge this non-dualistic dynamic—but only negatively, in opposition to it.

This question aside, though, given the phenomenological conception of what it means to be situated, situational analysis brings into focus the paralogical way in which humans come to terms with the ineluctable but vital gap between words and what they stand for. It draws attention to the paradoxical constraint on humans to create their own worlds in the face of the worlds in which they already find themselves. Instead of a sheer opposition, this constraint expresses itself as a crossing of word and world, a logic-defying dynamic and (if ever there was one) a magical act, in virtue of which human existence continuously conjures itself up. With this emphasis on basic ambiguity, situational analysis can help to liberate us from the instrumentally prodigious but ultimately unhinged and misguided dualist presumption that we can be observers without taking part in the observed, for the act of observation, which too proceeds in terms of terms, cannot but be an element of the chiastic movement under observation. Situational analysis can thus grant us, in our role as professional observers, a novel objective distance from our subject matter. Ironically, this distance is afforded us by the insight that when it is conceived of in the absolute, as perfectible, distance between the observer and observed is a self-defeating impossibility. The challenge, then, is to take advantage of this insight to determine better the ethnographic facts of the matter, neither turning them into things, as our predecessors were predisposed to do, nor vitiating the defining empirical and analytical purpose of anthropological inquiry, recasting it as primarily ideology, as many of our contemporaries are prone to do.

## Acknowledgments

I am grateful to Bruce Kapferer and Ananta Giri for their remarks upon the delivery of this essay at the EASA meetings in Copenhagen. I must also thank Don Handelman for his thoughtful reading of the penultimate draft.

---

Terry Evens is Professor of Anthropology at the University of North Carolina at Chapel Hill, where he has taught since 1971. He has held visiting appointments at the University of Chicago, the Ecoles des Hautes Etudes en Sciences Sociales, the University of Calcutta, and Asmara University, Eritrea. He has done intensive field research in an Israeli kibbutz, and is author of *Two Kinds of Rationality: Kibbutz Democracy and Generational Conflict* (1995) and co-editor of the collection *Transcendence in Society: Case Studies* (1990). His book *Anthropology as Ethics: Nondualism and the Conduct of Sacrifice* is forthcoming with Berghahn Books. His essays have appeared in a variety of journals and edited collections. Drawn especially to social theory and phenomenology, he has sought from the beginnings of his professional career to isolate, identify, and critically explore the philosophical underpinnings of empirical anthropology.

## Notes

1. The relevant text here is, of course, Heidegger's masterpiece, *Being and Time* (1962).
2. In order to bring into relief this peculiar human condition—of being situated to situate ourselves—I do not have to appeal to Heidegger's tortured profundities. Merleau-Ponty, for instance, another celebrated phenomenologist, also made much of this paradoxical human constraint. He wrote (1962: xix; italics in original): "Because we are in the world, we are *condemned to meaning.*" In other words, the very idea of situatedness entails a meaningful world. Non-humans can find themselves in situations no more than they can enjoy history as such. Hence, Merleau-Ponty links his striking thesis (of condemnation to meaning) to the consideration that we are creatures of history, his way of asserting that we make meaning of whatever happens—no matter how it happens—by giving it a name. Considered in terms of his philosophy as a whole, he is proposing that the world is always already pregnant with meaning, to the birth of which humans serve, peculiarly and creatively, in the role of midwife. Put forthrightly, humans are the representative

manifestation of this wondrous capacity to create meaning, for to say that we are *in* the world implies that, although we are always *of* the world, we also enjoy, as does any part from the whole in which it finds itself, a certain relative distinction or distance *from* it. One way of measuring this distance is as a "slackening of the intentional threads that attach us to the world" (ibid.: xiii)—in effect, as a freedom characterizing all human situatedness. To express this freedom is to bridge the distance or to make history. Another way of measuring this distance, still in keeping with Merleau-Ponty's broad thematics, is in terms of 'ambiguity', such that the world is basically ambiguous and therefore wants the imposition of meaning. The joining of this want amounts to the human activity of setting ends—that is, making meaning. Overall, Merleau-Ponty describes humans and the world as an irreformable duo, the exceptional dynamic of which he pictures as self-mediation, whereby something negates itself in order to realize or transcend itself.

3. The concept of 'becoming other' is due to Gilles Deleuze and Felix Guattari (1987: chap. 10).

4. For this point I rely heavily on George Steiner's (1978) strongly appreciative critique of Heidegger, which explicates why Heidegger's notion of *das Man* may not be taken as anti-social. Of the plethora of books interpreting Heidegger's philosophy, Steiner's little book is distinguished at once by its depth of interpretation and exceptional clarity.

5. I am reminded here of Sally Moore's (1975) disquisition on the overall anthropological problem presently at issue, the problem of the discrepancy between the normative order and actual practice. For in it she elucidates—what at the time was largely obscured by the terms of the debate—that the normative as well as the deviant, manipulative, exceptional, etc. is a product of individuals making choices.

6. In this connection, though he patently rejects the Cartesian dualism besetting Durkheim's grasp of the reality of the social, Heidegger exhibits common cause with the great French sociologist. *Dasein* highlights autonomy as man's distinctive feature. But with theological import and conviction, Heidegger took this to mean that man was specially charged with the care of being. He held that insofar as man failed to use his freedom to guard and watch over Being as such—a failure Heidegger attributed unequivocally to modern society and its characteristic emphasis on technological power and control—far from all that he can be, man was being perilously less than himself. One is reminded here of the Marxian concept of alienation in industrial society as well as of Durkheim's concern with anomie under conditions of modernity. Underlying all this, ironically even in respect of Marx and Engels, lurks something of a reactionary sentiment. In Heidegger's case, this sentiment fostered a romantic embrace of the Nazi Party and its gruesome utopian vision. Much has been made of Heidegger's brief fling with Nazism and its implications for his philosophy. However, for my purpose of using his philosophical ideas to explore what it means to be situated, this important and interesting debate has little if any direct bearing. One thoughtful, informed, and substantial account of this important and interesting issue is John Caputo's *Demythologizing Heidegger* (1993).

# References

Caputo, John D. 1993. *Demythologizing Heidegger*. Bloomington: Indiana University Press.

Deleuze, Gilles, and Felix Guattari. 1987. *A Thousand Plateaus: Capitalism and Schizophrenia*. Trans. Brian Massumi. Minneapolis: University of Minnesota Press.

Epstein, A. L., ed. 1979. *The Craft of Social Anthropology*. Oxford: Pergamon Press. (Reprinted from the 1978 Hindustan Publishing Corporation edition.)

Gluckman, Max. 1958. *Analysis of a Social Situation in Modern Zululand*. Manchester: Manchester University Press for Rhodes-Livingstone Institute.

_____. 1979. "Introduction." Pp. xv–xxiv in Epstein 1979.

Heidegger, Martin. 1962. *Being and Time*. Trans. John Macquarrie and Edward Robinson. Oxford: Basil Blackwell.

Lyotard, Jean-François. 1988. *The Differend: Phrases in Dispute*. Minneapolis: University of Minnesota Press.

Merleau-Ponty, Maurice. 1962. *Phenomenology of Perception*. Trans. Colin Smith. London: Routledge & Kegan Paul.

Moore, Sally Falk. 1975. "Epilogue: Uncertainties in Situations, Indeterminacies in Culture." Pp. 210–239 in *Symbol and Politics in Communal Ideology: Cases and Questions*, ed. Sally Falk Moore and Barbara G. Meyerhoff. Ithaca: Cornell University Press.

Steiner, George. 1978. *Martin Heidegger*. New York: Penguin Books.

Turner, Victor W. 1957. *Schism and Continuity in an African Society: A Study of Ndembu Village Life*. Manchester: Manchester University Press.

Van Velsen, Jaap. 1979. "The Extended-Case Method and Situational Analysis." Pp. 129–149 in Epstein 1979.

*Chapter 2*

# AN ONTOLOGY FOR THE ETHNOGRAPHIC ANALYSIS OF SOCIAL PROCESSES
## Extending the Extended-Case Method

*Andreas Glaeser*

Imagine that we wanted to study a particular social process in contemporary social settings. How could we translate such an interest into an ethnographic project among a concrete set of people located in a particular space and time? What kind of a theoretical imagination of process would be useful in guiding this research? How could we use such engagements to systematically develop theory? How could we go about identifying field sites that are equally responsive to both our substantive and theoretical interests? Wherein lie the specific advantages and problems of ethnography for the study of process in contemporary societies? In this chapter, I will develop the contours of an answer to these guiding questions by proposing an ontology of social processes that is Weberian in its focus on action, Meadian in its constitutive constructivism, and network theoretic in its emphasis on the importance of relationship patterns, while imagining processes to be the very stuff of social life.

An essay about process and ethnography must not fail to consider the work of Max Gluckman, who has contributed significantly to what might be called the 'processual turn' in the social sciences. Gluckman inspired the first wave of ethnographers who viewed processes rather than a bounded set of people as the proper object of their investigation. Seen from today's perspective, his exhortations to focus on process (see, e.g., Gluckman 1967) have a visionary touch, positively unsettling the mainstream of their time. For Gluckman wrote in the heyday of both structure-functionalism and structuralism, each enchanted with systems metaphors borrowed from biology, engineering cybernetics, and linguistics. Of course, it is not the case that structuralists or structure-functionalists were completely disinterested in processes. However, their attention was focused on processes of proper systems functioning and beyond that on disequilibration (often conceived as external shock) and subsequent re-equilibration. Neither structuralists nor structure-functionalists were looking to understand processes of genesis, slow change, and disintegration in historically contingent circumstances, and this is precisely what interested Gluckman. Given that structuralist and structure-functionalist thinking always proceeded from and ended in structure, it is perhaps not surprising that it all too quickly fell into a reification of structure and thus into a fallacy so aptly analyzed by Whitehead (1979: 7) as "misplaced concreteness."

Moreover, structuralists and structure-functionalists operated explicitly or implicitly with a notion of totality (the 'systems level'), a notion that was as alien to Gluckman as it was to Weber simply because neither believed that such knowledge was humanly attainable.[1] Gluckman, much like Elias, that other processualist out of synch with the zeitgeist, refused to conceive of processes as *systemic* (i.e., in the context of systems' operations), even though he conceived of them as *systematic* (i.e., as the consequence of ordering action) in historically contingent circumstances.

Gluckman has probably become most recognized for his original conceptualization and advocacy of an ethnographic practice, which got branded in his name as the "extended-case method" (see Gluckman 1961, 1967; cf. Burawoy 1998, 2000). And it is of course precisely the question of how to uncover the systematicity of unsystemic, historically contingent processes that he urged himself and his associates to answer. Yet the processualism that transpires from Gluckman's work is neither a worked-out body of theory nor a bounded methodology, but rather, to use a metaphor from the world of software engineering, an 'open platform' to which many people inspired by him have later contributed significant pieces.

Building on previous reflections about how to employ ethnography systematically to develop theory (see Glaeser 2000: esp. 12–24), I too hope to contribute to this by now venerable platform. I will begin quite abstractly by proposing an ontology[2] of social processes that undergirds a theoretical perspective that might be called 'consequent processualism'. I undertake this step for several reasons. First, the ontology of social processes allows me to transcend a number of dichotomized concepts that have for a long time now organized (and troubled) the division of labor in the social sciences. Chief among these are the distinctions between subject and object; agency-structure, event-structure, micro-macro and culture-social structure; and, last but not least, the traditional versus the modern. Ethnography as a research practice has overwhelmingly been associated with the respective first term in these pairings. Not only did this association have serious consequences for the politics of method in the social sciences, which turned ethnography into something of a low-status pursuit, but, more importantly, it impoverished the sociological imagination of the social sciences as a whole.[3] I will then show how consequent processualism has been able to transcend these organizing dichotomies while retaining what was analytically useful about them. In a next step I will use the ontology developed here to evaluate critically the assumptions underlying the ethnographic practices of classical Malinowskian and Chicago School work, and I will show how subsequent Gluckmanian (and more generally Mancunian) ethnographic innovations, as well as the emergence of historical ethnography and the reflexive ethnography of the last two decades, have systematically led in the direction proposed here. Finally, I will show how consequent processualism can be used to think systematically about theory development and field-site choice, which are closely associated issues for the analysis of social life for which significant portions of the relevant contexts are fragmented and spatially and temporally removed.

## Ontology: Imagining Social Life as Process

I would like to begin the development of an ontology of social processes at a level of social imagination that is not only very congenial to Gluckman's own, but is today, after the convergence of several theoretical and methodological approaches on this point, perhaps already a commonplace, at least among social scientists working ethnographically and/or historically.[4] I propose to imagine social life as an incredibly dense thicket of partially independent and partially interacting social processes. What, then, are processes?

### Action-Reaction-Effect Sequences

A good starting point may lie in the observation that the big questions in the social sciences typically inquire about the why and how of developments. Thus, we ask, for example, "How did capitalism or the nation-state emerge?" "How do revolutions begin, succeed, or fail?" "What was the impact of colonialism on the subjectivities of the colonized?" "How do natural scientists construct knowledge?" The very formulation of these questions suggests that, conceptually, we tend to think of processes as changes to 'something' (a form of economic organization, of governance, etc.) in which the process manifests itself. I call these 'somethings' social formations, because they come into being as *effects* of interconnected reactions to antecedent actions.[5] The spark of social creation is, as Weber clearly recognized with his very definition of sociology, active attunement to the actions of others.

At this point, it might be helpful to illustrate social formation through action-reaction-effect sequences with a handful of paradigmatic cases that are central to the history of social thought. The first is Durkheim's ([1893] 1997) analysis of the emergence of social bonds between people either in shared ritual attunement or in the interdependence of regular exchange. The second is George Herbert Mead's (1934) analysis of the constitution of the self in the "conversation of significant symbols" between two individuals. For Mead, the self as the fundamental capacity of human reflexivity is the effect of the internalization of communications with other human beings. The third case is Wittgenstein's (1984) argument that human beings cannot follow a rule individually, that rule-following is instead always the result of interactions within a larger interpretative community.[6] From Wittgenstein's understanding of speaking as a form of action among other actions grew, finally, the fourth case, which consists in what speech act theorists call performative utterances. In speech act theory, marriage, for example, comes into being as the effect of the exchange of mutual vows (Austin 1962; Searle 1969, 1992). Marriage, and social formations like it, originates in the perlocutionary force, that is, the effect of utterances understood as actions. The point of all of these examples is that something new comes into social life through action-reaction-effect chains. Whether this is an intentional or unintentional creation is secondary—both happen.

Social formations have a number of peculiar ontological characteristics. First, their ultimate material substrate consists of actions and reactions and thus human bodies. The existence of social formations is therefore always rooted in concrete spatio-temporal locations. Second, they transcend every concrete action-reaction pair, however, by pointing backwards and sideways to other action-reaction pairs with similar effects and forward to the future, creating the expectation that there will be additional such pairs with comparable effect. Third, chiefly because our memories systematically become faint in the course of time and because expectations need to be met eventually if they are to maintain their forward-pointing thrust, social formations achieve significant duration and stability exclusively through *continued* action-reaction sequences.[7]

Although ritual is an important source for the maintenance of social formations, it is by no means the only or even the most important one. The fourth characteristic of social formations is that they can be, and very often are, maintained as the effect of *diverse* sets of action-reaction sequences. An individual self, for example, is maintained in communicative interactions not only with the original care-givers but with pretty much everyone with whom this person converses, as well as in every act of performed reflexivity. In everyday life, marriage is reproduced through rather diverse sets of interactions not only within the couple but also between either partner, or both partners, and outsiders. This in turn points to the fact that individual selves and individual marriages depend on the rooting of social formations such as 'self' and 'marriage' in the interactions of a set of interconnected people with whom the self and the couple in question might come to interact. Only then can strangers face each other with the expectation to 'have a self' and 'to be married'. The technical term for this distributed rooting of social formations in interaction is 'institutionalization', which is the fifth ontological characteristic of social formations. It is through institutionalization that social formations acquire their peculiar object-like character (cf. Berger and Luckmann 1966). We rightly perceive that social formations are not dependent on our individual actions. They face all of us individually as independent, objective entities, even though we all together keep reproducing them through our reactions to other people's actions. At that point, we tend to forget that social formations are in fact made and remade in interaction by all of us together. If we want to stop reproducing them, we face the problem of collective action.

Analytically it is useful to distinguish four categories of social formations: *people* (including their agency, desires, hopes, and fantasies), their *relationships* with one another, the *cultural forms* they use to navigate the world (practices, symbolic and emotive forms, values, and styles), and the *material environment* they build.[8] Among these social formations, people are primus inter pares, insofar as human bodies are the key material substrate of all the other social formations.[9] In every other respect, all four categories mutually constitute each other through people's actions. Human bodies become people only in interactions within relationships (e.g., to parents, siblings, and friends), situated in a built environment (e.g., nourished and sheltered), and in use of cultural forms (e.g., ideas of what a good life is about). Relationships in turn are made by people in use of cultural forms (e.g., ideas and norms about friendship) and the built environment (e.g., spaces where people can meet), and so forth.[10]

As actors, people are not only the effects and thus objects of processes but also their primus inter pares subjects. Of course, relationships, cultural forms, and the built environment are co-stars in the (sometimes rather boring) drama of process. It is through us lending them life that they in a sense become co-actors. This, I believe, is why we have such an ambiguous relationship toward them. On the one hand, we seem to possess the 'other' social formations totally; they belong to us as our creatures, our tools. Yet even slight changes in use (e.g., an extra amount of reflexivity) reveal how 'other' they are, and we begin instead to feel possessed by them. This is the fascination, power, and horror of masks—the celebration of technology as a savior and its condemnation as a corruptor. It is the deep, ongoing resonance we feel for Frankenstein and 'his' (or should I say 'the') monster.[11] In his theory of commodity fetishism, Marx (1960, chap. 1) has, paradigmatically for the social sciences, worked out the process of objectification for that part of the built environment that he called commodities. However, objectification is something that affects all social formations through institutionalization. Persons can become objectified as exalted majesties, stars, or saints; cultural forms can become objectified as truth in positivistic science and in everyday life; social relations can become objectified as biological ones; the built environment can become objectified as nature *tout court*.

It may seem that the fact that persons, relations, cultural forms, and the built environment all play the roles of both objects and subjects constitutes a classical paradox because that which is made seems to make itself. However, this is no Münchhausenesque tale in which a rider is pulling himself out of the swamp by the tail of his wig. The reason is simply that the roles of subject and object are *distributed* over a large number of actors in all four categories, which means that we all are subjects and objects—not primarily of ourselves but of each other. No subject is completely his or her own object; otherwise, he or she would not be a participant in society. Object and subject are thus but names for accents of attention. They indicate directions in which we turn our gaze in the investigation of the temporality of process.[12] Looking forward, we see subjects acting; looking backward, we see objects being made.[13]

People are the primus inter pares subjects of processes in a dual sense. They bring actions into being, and they connect in these actions as *reactions* many actions of others that thus have a common effect. And they do so by utilizing other social formations. The point here is to see actions not only—and perhaps not even primarily—as origins, as expressions of sovereign decision making, but as nodes connecting an often diverse set of other people's actions performed at various times and in different contexts, such that these obtain a common thrust in a particular action as reaction. Seen from this perspective, an actor is less a source than a collector and transformer producing actions out of confluences. The confluences from which actors can produce their actions are contingent on opportunity. Their situational trajectory puts them 'in the reach' of some actions to which they could or must react, while it provides them with particular relations, cultural forms, and built environments. How much these actions are the result of poiesis, of creative play with influences, rather than mere habit or other quasi-automatic forms of reaction, is, as we know from Simmel (1992) and like-minded theorists, a matter of the plurality and polysemy of relations. And as we know from advances in cultural theory in the last two decades, it is also a matter of the plurality and polysemy of cultural forms and the built environment.[14] Agency is neither just there (gracing a sovereign subject) nor just absent (leaving a mere object); instead, building on an innate potential, it is constructed, augmented, or diminished within the flow of process (see, e.g., Bieri 2001).

The following example may illustrate how the various elements of the ontology I have presented here hang together. It may also show how repeated action-reaction-effect sequences interweave both similar and different processes into a coordinated field. A price hike for a particular fashion item (the changing object) may occur because a vendor in Los Angeles who is facing a rise of orders from certain buyers (two large department store chains) over a given time period might feel tempted to increase the price of the item in question. What helps the vendor to make this (more or less conscious) decision are the lessons she had once learned in business school in Philadelphia, her shareholders' expectations to maximize the value of their stock, her sense that her competitors in Tokyo and Milan are on the way to making similar moves for similar reasons, alongside her own desire to squeeze the last buck out of her business operations, now that she has, for her mother's sake, forfeited a life in the arts for one in business. Here the vendor connects the actions of dispersed (but not necessarily independent) buyers, of shareholders, of teachers, of her mother, etc., into a unified reaction. Note how the actions she is reacting to have taken place not only in a variety of locations but at different times as well. Her reaction in a sense makes simultaneous the non-simultaneous and local the non-local. It presents the non-present and thus connects the at least seemingly non-connected. Other vendors may follow suit so that there is indeed a general pattern of price increases for the particular good under consideration here.

The department stores themselves may have reacted to the consumers' novel demand, which may again be seen as reactions to other people's actions, such as the flaunting of this particular fashion item by people who present themselves as fashion avant-gardists in public places. The latter's entrepreneurship may in turn be a reaction to their realization that other people's ability to create a following had eroded their peculiar fashion advantage, a marked difference they had acquired in the previous round of fashion differentiation. The ideas for how to differentiate themselves were perhaps coming from the latest Parisian prêt-à-porter shows in which they have of course not participated but the photographs of which they have seen in fashion magazines.[15] These shows in turn may have been keyed to some 'retro' theme (styles associated with a particular decennium and recognizable thanks to family photo albums, the movies, and television). And again, the end-buyers react and thereby connect actions in disparate times and places that have an effect through these purchases.

This example shows quite nicely how processes dovetail. On the one hand, the same action can be part and parcel of a variety of processes constituting different social formations. For example, the purchase of a particular fashion item is, reconfirmed by the admiring glances of others, an aspect of the identity-formation process of that person, the confirmation of a particular ideology of what it is to dress tastefully, as well as part of the price-hike process. Similarly, a manager's decision to raise the price of the same item may be a move in asserting a particular identity of the firm in the business world (the vendor as price leader), a reconfirmation of the cultural forms absorbed in business school, a signaling to the board that suspicions of indecisive management are indeed not warranted, and so forth. On the other hand, this example also shows how various strands of the same kind of process (distinction through fashion) can be interwoven to furnish another (price hike). In this way, social life comes together as that incredibly dense thicket of partially independent and partially interacting social processes that I have defined above.

## Socialities and Processual Dynamics

As soon as somebody reacts to the actions of another, a relationship is initiated. These relationships can take many different qualitative forms, or socialities, which deeply influence subsequent reactions to the other's actions. In fact, the very same action can call forth startlingly different reactions, depending on the sociality invoked between actor and reactor at the point of reaction. Just imagine how differently people react to a particular critique depending on who utters it. For that very reason, actors have a key interest in trying to persuade potential reactors that their relationship is actually characterized by a particular quality that promises a more favorable reaction. Rhetoricians have long known that the particular quality of a relationship is formed socially.

Accordingly, in order to understand the dynamics of process, it is absolutely key to consider the socialities involved. Scholars of society have been keenly aware of this; thus, their models frequently center around assumptions concerning prevalent socialities. Hobbes, for example, understood the relationships between human beings as fundamentally competitive, entailing dangers of violence. These could only be mastered, he argued, through balancing relationships of submission and domination of each and every citizen with the Leviathan. For Smith, too, the basic relationships between humans were competitive. In contra-distinction to Hobbes, however, Smith argued that competition leads through the division of labor to cooperation.

During the nineteenth century, the argument shifted from universalistic assumptions about socialities to universalistic assumptions about the development of socialities that themselves came to be seen as temporally variant. The process of 'modernization' was widely understood as a movement from 'traditional', that is, authoritarian, and hierarchical (kinship, caste, estate, guild) relationships to 'modern', at least nominally voluntary, and egalitarian contractual relationships. More recently, Foucault (1978) has argued similarly for dominant forms of sociality in relation to changing regimes of power that correspond for him to changing forms of subjectification. What such totalizing claims about sociality miss is the fact that social life is characterized by the co-existence of a wide variety of socialities that can stand in interesting systematic relationships to each other.[16] It is also important to see that socialities are situationally articulated. They can change from one instant to the next, thus widely affecting how actions are answered. Finally, several ambiguous and possibly even contradictory socialities can be at play in one and the same action-reaction link.

## Webs of Effect Flows and Social Networks

I have already explained above how the interlinking of various action-reaction chains can lead to the bundling of their effects in such a way that the social formation thus constituted becomes objectified as an institution. It is important, therefore, to understand how such interrelationships come about. For these purposes, the literature on social networks appears to be a logical starting point; indeed, contemporary network theory has valuable insights to contribute to the present project. However, the consequent processualism argued here also reveals fundamental limitations of current network approaches.

What contemporary social scientists mean when they speak of networks is a stable, ordered set of relationships that structure particular kinds of interactions. A number of scholars pioneering the network concept—most notably, perhaps, Clyde Mitchell, A. L. Epstein, and J. A. Barnes—were in close conversation with Gluckman and indeed seem to have owed their mutual acquaintance to what appears to be a Gluckman-centered network.[17] The network literature has thus received many inspirations form Gluckman. The form in which the network concept has taken shape in the perimeter of the Manchester School and in which it has also moved into the very core of American sociology pays acute attention to the formal patterning of social relationships and the effects that such patterning has on the processes that take place within networks. Two distinctions are particularly fruitful here because they focus on how relationship patterns support different kinds of processes.[18] The first is the differentiation according to the *strength* of linkages.[19] Research building on this distinction, a simple and for some contexts congenial criterion for different forms of sociality (cf. Granovetter 1983), has shown how, for example, a particular search process (e.g., finding a new job in industrial societies) can depend not so much on 'strong' ties, such as friendships and relations with close kin, but on a wider net of 'weak' ties, such as acquaintances. What is central to analyses based on this distinction is that the distribution of particular kinds of information in particular social contexts does not typically require the shelter of intimate relations.

The other key distinction brought to the foreground in formal network analysis (e.g., Burt 1992; Granovetter 1973, 1983) is the one between different types of *positions* within a network. What this literature distinguishes primarily are positions with ideoiosyncratic relationship patterns (my relations are unlike yours) from others within densely clustered (or clique-like) relationships in which participants share a large number of key relationships with each other (the people with whom I entertain relations are likely to maintain relations with each other as well).[20] The internal processes of clusters of strong ties have been linked systematically to group cohesion (e.g., Festinger, Schachter, and Back 1950; Homans 1992; Mitchell 1969; for an overview, see Moscovici 1985) and the production of agreement, while the more 'individual' positions outside of clusters have been systematically linked with innovation (e.g., Burt 1980), competitive dynamics (e.g., Burt 1992), and the rapid spread of information (e.g., Epstein 1969, in response to Gluckman 1963). Of course, these distinctions are only a beginning. With an eye on what I have just referred to as sociality of human beings, it seems to me we need much more research on how other kinds of qualitative differences in relationships support different kinds of processual dynamics as well as substantive network interaction. And yet the outcome of this research is very important: the patterning of the relationships has a significant impact on the process dynamics.

Ironically, the network literature, which grew out of an acute dissatisfaction with structure-functionalism (e.g., Mitchell 1973), has in the end remained firmly structuralist (and the more so as it has taken the path to quantification) by effectively treating networks as exogenously given. From the perspective of the consequent processualism I have begun to outline, the literature overlooks how networks themselves are social formations (i.e., associations of relations) that get constituted through the webbed flow of people's action-reaction sequences, in use of cultural forms and the built environment. One could also say that the current network literature does not pay attention to how processes within networks and network-constituting processes emerge from the same actions. It thus also ignores that there are a number of other processes involving people, cultural forms, the built environment, and relations outside of the network that are necessary to maintain it. The dominant approaches to networks have yet another shortcoming, however, in predominantly imagining relationships on a personal, extended face-to-face model, which disregards the importance of reaction to actions far removed in time and space, a key phenomenon of social life in contemporary societies.

## The Projective Articulation of Actions across Time and Space

Most actions we undertake are reactions not just in the sense that traditional micro-sociological research has conceived of them: as answers to questions or chess moves upon chess moves. Instead, actions and reactions can be far removed in space and time and must be understood in a framework that departs decisively from the face-to-face model we usually think of first when we hear the term 'social relation'.[21] The implication is that the relevant context of a particular action is by no means evident. In fact, any particular action can be a reaction to any number of other people's actions in a diverse set of far-away places and distant times. The fashion item price hike mentioned above contains some examples in this respect.

Since all actions are embodied, they are *necessarily* local in time and space. If actions produce an effect on people beyond the proximate time-space coordinates in which they are performed—Schütz's "world in immediate reach" (Schütz and Luckmann 1984)—some effects of this action need to be taken from the here and now and projected and articulated in the there and then. This is accomplished by intermediary processes for which I propose the umbrella term 'projective articulations'.[22] Thus, projective articulations enable action-reaction-effect sequences that could not take place at all in their absence, or at least not in this form. As processes, projective articulations involve persons, cultural forms, the built environment, and relationships that are different from those drawn upon for the original act. To stay with the fashion example above, the consumer admiring himself in a recently purchased fashion item reacts to the projected articulation of the myriad actions effectively embodied in the production, marketing, and distribution of that item. The fashion designer raising the prices for these items reacts to the projected articulation of demand, the changes of which become discernible in accounting procedures, and so on.[23]

In the course of projected articulations, the locally registered effect of the actions gets converted into a transportable form and may be articulated elsewhere in yet another form. A locally delivered political speech may first be taped and then transcribed to be printed and distributed in a newspaper. Sometimes the projected articulation of the local effect of an action preserves some iconicity with the original action. This is the case, for example, with 'live' transmission of voices and images.[24] While it may be rather obvious then that what gets projected originates in an action, the awareness of the projection itself as enabled by action vanishes into the background. The more the projective articulation loses an iconic relation with the original action, the more it can be forgotten that it is indeed someone's local action that one is reacting to. This is most clearly the case for social formations industrially produced and traded today.[25] How we react to them as projectively articulated actions is in part contingent on how, to which degree, and with what involvement of imagination we make clear to ourselves that social formations are indeed projective articulations of actions that are made available by yet another set of actions. People react differently to a product (think of beef after BSE or of Oriental rugs) depending on how aware they are of the kinds of actions bundled up in the product that reaches them. Creating this transparency is what consumer advocacy is in part about. Since a certain degree of non-awareness is key to the functioning of projective articulations, however, because we would otherwise experience acute informational overload, the question is not so much whether this does create (commodity) fetishism, but what its effect is under particular kinds of circumstances. This includes the question as to what kinds of processes particular kinds of fetishisms enable or undermine.[26]

Certain areas of research have crystallized around particular forms of projective articulations of action effects. There is a well-established body of literature about the mass media, for example, and a fast-growing literature on social-memory practices (cf. Olick and Robbins 1998), as well as an increasing interest in the ways that the center of organizations, states included, render their periphery legible (e.g., Porter 1995). Unfortunately, the focus of these literatures has been on these techniques per se, not on how they enable other processes. Only more recently have scholars begun systematically to leverage an understanding of specific forms of projective articulations into the analysis of a diverse set of social processes that are enabled by them. What begins to take shape here is the insight that the use of new forms of projective articulations of action also produces novel forms of particular socialities precisely because they enable new action-reaction-effect linkages—that is, new forms of social processes. The agenda-setting book in this respect is Anderson's *Imagined Communities* (1983), which argues that print capitalism, in conjunction with rising literacy rates, has enabled the emergence of new ways to live and imagine the social.[27]

The very notion of projective articulation suggests, then, that we need to rethink what it is that constitutes a social relation or, more precisely, a whole web of such relations. We have relationships with all people, alive or dead, known to us or unknown, whose actions we somehow react to with our own actions. Projective articulations vastly increase the number of relations in which an individual stands. In social contexts that are permeated with numerous forms of projective articulations, the sheer number and complexity of relations through which people are processually connected to each other become literally unfathomable. For a social scientist attempting to study processes, this is a dizzying, if not utterly nauseating, vista.

## Further Notes on Time-Honored Dichotomies

Viewing social life as a dense thicket of processes in the way that I have out-lined it here transcends some of the major dichotomies that have galvanized some of the theoretical debates in the social sciences since World War II as either-or choices that have profoundly influenced the division of labor in the social sciences. Individually, the points I will make about these dichotomies have all been made before, yet I want to point out again that these dichotomies all disappear *together* within a consequent processualism of the kind I have outlined, because they are all the consequence of particular reifications that the kind of processualism I have introduced in this essay avoids. The subject-object dichotomy is *au fond* the consequence of reifying extra-socially (by God or nature) constituted actors capable of sovereign choice. Entities capable of such choices are seen as subjects, those that lack this capability as objects. In the classical formulation, subject and object characteristics are distributed over different classes of social formations. From what I have said so far, it should be clear that the dichotomy cannot be overcome by reduction to either end. By contrast, consequent processualism sees object and subject not as things but as accents of perspectives within processes.

The structure-event dichotomy owes its existence to the Platonic reifica-tion of structures as the 'really real' of which events are only instantiations. The dichotomy effectively makes a distinction between a temporal and an extra-temporal domain. There is an overreaction to the claim of morphological primacy in the affirmation of super-fluidity in processes of infinite semiosis, endless difference, and so on. What gets lost in this view is that the differ-ence in the rate of change in various processes is significant. This, however, is precisely the point emphasized by consequent processualism. It acknowledges that there are action-reaction sequences that lead to the maintenance of social formations, while others lead to their change. With different speeds in change, interrelated complexes of maintained formations look like structures in com-parison to changing ones.

Finally, there is the micro-macro dichotomy and its more recent cognates, lifeworld-system and local-global. The well-known problem with macro theo-retization is that it reifies collective actors and collective states that need to be conceived as constituted processually through the interaction of real persons in real locations at real times. There is the possibility, of course, that these processes are, first, so unifying as to make persons as members of collectivities interchangeable and, second, so stable that talk of them as entities could in fact be legitimate as a form of shorthand. Such macro entities could indeed be the effects of coordinated, reproduced action-reaction sequences. Yet this needs to be demonstrated rather than presupposed.

With this goal in mind, various authors have suggested programs to 'trans-late' the macro into the micro.[28] Yet such efforts are doomed to fail as long as the micro continues to be imagined on the face-to-face model without keen attention to the face-to-other-via-object or face-to-other-via-symbol relation-ships, that is, without a systematic consideration of projective articulations.

The problem with traditional micro theory is that it reifies the immediately adjacent context of interaction, which needless to say can in the absence of projective articulations never produce the kinds of phenomena that macro theorists are interested in. The issue, then, is one of specifying processes with due regard for projective articulations. Some actions produce only local effects; others, thanks to projective articulations, produce transtemporal and translocal ones. This does not mean that more encompassing social processes stretching across a wider swath of locations might not require action-projecting techniques that are different from those used in smaller-scale processes. Nor does it mean that such widely distributed processes could not have peculiar dynamics of their own.[29]

| Conceptual Dichotomies | Consequent Processualism |
| --- | --- |
| traditional-modern | Which kind of socialities are at play in what kind of network patterns? How are various socialities dependent on each other? How do socialities and network patterns shape the dynamics of process? |
| event-structure | Which processes maintain a social formation as selfsame? What is the relative clock speed of various processes in relationship to each other? |
| culture-structure | How do cultural forms (and other social formations) play into the instigation, maintenance, or change of social relations? How do patterns of relationship (and other social formations) influence the reproduction of cultural forms? |
| agency-structure | How does the situation of an actor within the reach of various confluences create possibilities for poetic play? How does the distribution of the maintenance of social formation over wider networks of actors lead to their objectification? |
| subject-object | How does a social process appear looking forward into the future? How has a particular social formation come to be what it is? |
| micro-macro | What is the role of projective articulations in any particular social process? |

Consequent processualism replaces traditional conceptual dichotomies that have structured the division of labor in the social sciences with analytical questions.

## Analysis: Studying Social Processes Empirically

The idea of social life as a set of partially independent and partially interacting social processes, imagined as a web of effect flows in which actions are the nodes and various socialities the 'docking points' at which particular relations get formed by reactions mediated by social formations, is utterly daunting. The pervasiveness of projective articulations seems to make that picture outright nauseating because they increase exponentially the possibilities for producing effects. As a result, the prospects of analysis seem to sink into the morass of endless possibilities of tracing action-reaction-effect linkages. In facing this web of social effects, from the dynamics of which emerge all social formations, every analysis may seem arbitrary. Thinly legitimized by shallow notions of emergence, macro theory has been the classical defense against this nauseating complexity. Macro theory insisted that it was possible to understand the seemingly chaotic to and fro of the beehive as the orderly interaction of collective entities (queens, workers, drones), which produce the collective states of the society. I have already argued why this move is highly problematic. How, then, has ethnography, macro theory's classic antipode, historically dealt with this nausea?

## From the Ethnography of Clusters to Reflexive Ethnography

There are in effect five background assumptions underpinning classical, 'first wave' ethnographic studies based on systematic participant observation in anthropology and sociology. Not all studies hold these assumptions to the same degree, of course, and some ethnographers (perhaps not by accident, in particular Znaniecki and Malinowski) maintain a fascination today precisely for having violated them in one way or the other. Nevertheless, I think these assumptions can be used to characterize conventions on method. The first is that the object of ethnography is to investigate the life of a group of people, its customs, and its traditions. Second, such groups as objects of study were typically conceived as self-constitutive in at least those aspects relevant to the ethnographic investigation. This means that all relevant interaction that could be observed was supposed to happen within that group. Third, the group was imagined in network terms as a cluster, that is, as a dense network of cross-cutting, redundant links, which could be projected onto a relatively clearly bounded location. Fourth, the group was conceived as a more or less selfsame structure, as a self-sustaining system. In the ecological jargon of the early Chicago School ethnographers, these groups occupied an 'ecological niche' (e.g., Park and Burgess 1984).

In other words, ethnographers laboring under classical assumptions considered it more or less possible to analyze their object by spending limited amounts of time in a rather clearly circumscribed area, even if this involved some adventurous travel over hundreds of miles of open sea, including encounters with similarly autonomous people, and even if it took a number of volumes to accomplish this task. Finally, since the group was thought of as self-constitutive, the ethnographer could treat him- or herself as a kind of alien, a member of another world who had no real influence on what was going on locally. Researchers and the people they studied could not possibly be conceived as entangled in the same action-reaction network. Structure-functionalism, as the predominant theoretical approach, and the methodology of an ethnography of the present in a clearly circumscribed locale were mutually reinforcing.[30] Structure-functionalist ethnography has avoided the nausea of thinking in terms of cascading effect flows by limiting the breadth of the web to a more manageable number of actors and by temporally folding the web onto itself.

The attack on the assumptions of classical ethnography in this sense came in several waves. The first big step was Max Gluckman's turn away from the ethnographic conventions of his own teachers (already adumbrated in Gluckman [1940] 1958). Gluckman and his school are associated with a number of innovations. The object of ethnography is no longer taken to be a clustered group but a process that gets instantiated by a particular set of people with relations stretching well beyond the confines of clusters. Rather than editing the colonial context out of the picture, it is clearly understood as part and parcel of what is going on (ibid.). To describe how a process ought to be studied, Gluckman (1961) adopts the term "extended-case method." In comparison to the more conventional use of cases to illustrate structural features of society, Gluckman (1967: xv) proposes to take "a series of specific incidents affecting the same persons or groups through a period of time, and showing how these incidents, these 'cases', are related to the development and changes of social relations among these persons and groups, acting within the framework of their social system and culture."

What distinguishes Gluckman and his collaborators as well is a clear understanding that adequate representations of 'total ways of life' are simply impossible. With the move to process comes the question of how the 'field' could be meaningfully delimited, since not even the restriction to particular substantively characterized processes offers clear-cut boundaries. This means that analysis would have to be carried out on a limited 'chunk' of a principally open web of effects that had to be justified somehow (Gluckman and Devons 1964).[31] It remained for Gluckman's friends and collaborators to devise more concrete frameworks within which to study and delimit process. Victor Turner (1974), for example, focuses on crises and their resolution. He sets "structure" and "anti-structure" into a dynamic relationship and follows the unfolding and resolution of conflict along the lines of guiding "root metaphors" and rituals. Process is for Turner not an even flow of happenings but rather an unfolding of events with a dramatic profile in which analytic focus is most suitably placed on culminating points. Instead of concentrating on the temporal *development* of process, Sally Falk Moore (1978) proposes to look at what she considers to be fairly universal: dialectically related *kinds* of processes.[32] She also argues that it is particularly fruitful to look at the constitution of relatively autonomous fields of social interaction and their mutual contextualization and delimitation. With the notion of "diagnostic events" (1987; this volume), she has also developed a concept that is, if you like, the commedia dell'arte counterpart to Turner's somewhat formalistic sequencing of drama. For Moore, diagnostic events elucidate *in nuce* the larger process under investigation because they reveal the tension and dynamic of what I have referred to above as action-reaction-effect patterns.[33]

The next big step was the appropriation of history into ethnography. This was very much in Gluckman's spirit, and several people on whom he has had a lasting impact have become driving forces in this move, criticizing the ethnography of the ethnographer's present, which in spite of its attention to process still had no means to take into account a longer if not a *longue durée* (e.g., Comaroff and Comaroff 1992; Moore 1986). Of course, historical anthropology was not only a Mancunian affair. Post-structuralist neo-Marxism was an equally vital force in this transition (e.g., Sahlins 1981; Wolf 1982). If the historical conditions for the emergence of a structure-functionalist, other-allochronizing (Fabian 1983) ethnography were at least in part due to colonialist nostalgia (Clifford 1988), then decolonization (a process, after all) is the historical canvas in front of which the turn toward processes and history takes place. Now colonialism had epochal bookmarks, and the imaginary past of a timeless tradition was at least one whole epoch removed. Moreover, colonial administrations had, needless to say, produced precisely the kinds of records that 'proper' historical methodology required to be exercised upon. In this context, it became all of a sudden also much clearer that the connections between colonizers and colonized were in an important sense not so unique after all, that it had always been important to study the relationships between various groups of people, no matter how isolated they might have appeared to the naive European eye, casting itself as 'discoverer' of countries and people.

With the advent of history in ethnography arrived also a new interest in issues of political economy that necessitated a view in which Third World locales were integrated into translocal political and economic processes. With this explicit recognition of the reality of pervasive projective articulations also came the awareness that cases needed to be extended not only in time, a movement that led into the archive, but also across space, which slowly triggered what would eventually be termed 'multi-sited ethnography' (e.g., Burawoy et al. 2000; Hannerz 2003; Marcus 1998). The consequence was that ethnographic practices had to become both temporally and spatially extended. What had once given ethnography its very identity as a research practice was now drawn into doubt as a possible impediment for good research results.[34]

The increasing awareness of pervasive projective articulations also furthered a reflexive mode that had to reconsider radically the role of the observer, including the power relations in which observers and the observed were entangled (e.g., Clifford and Marcus 1986). In other words, reflexive ethnography acknowledged the fact that ethnographers and their objects were part and parcel of a wider encompassing network that enabled ethnography as a practice. Consequently, it was also finally recognized that ethnography itself is indeed one particular way of producing projective articulations sustaining new sets of relationships, interlinking people in uncontrollable ways. This insight resulted in a virtual conundrum of new ethical problems in ethnographic practice (e.g., Shryock 2004) that have in turn produced a strategy for foreshortening the web of processual flows—dealing with the ethnographer-local partner interaction as the critical site of ethnographic knowledge production and an instance of globalization at work.

If you like, then, the history of ethnography can be written as slowly moving toward something like the social ontology I have presented in this essay.[35] The changes I have just described are the effect of an increasing understanding of the principal open-endedness of social life in every respect as well as a reflection on the conditions under which ethnographic knowledge is produced. Changes in these directions have also been facilitated by dramatically changing social circumstances that have rendered classical assumptions about boundedness, with increasing palpability, implausible. Thus, we have lost our 'defenses' against the nausea I have spoken about above. The crisis of ethnography over the last two decades is the crisis produced by an awareness of seemingly unfathomable interdependencies.[36]

## The Role of Theory

This nausea is productive, however. It reminds us with visceral force that (maybe contrary to our desires) we cannot tell it all. Thus, we need to think carefully which story we would want to parse out. A stringent limitation of perspective, together with a reflection on the rationale for it, is necessary. The reason to tell a tale is interest. That interest can attach itself to three different aspects of process. There is first its concrete embodiment in particular people, their actions in concrete time-space in all its singular curiosity.[37] The second is the social formation as the effect of process, its becoming, maintenance, or disintegration understood as a case standing for a class of phenomena. Finally, interest can attach itself to the patterns, principles, or regularities underlying the very dynamics of process. This is the realm of theory proper. In good social science research, all three levels of interest should be closely intertwined, simply because they are dependent on each other: principles of process dynamics and classes of objects can be studied only in concrete embodiment; a particular embodiment is studied and theories of process dynamics are developed in the hope that this project yields relevant insights for wider classes of phenomena; and without the development of an explicit understanding of process dynamics, all narrations of process ultimately remain unreflexive. The tension between the peculiarity of embodiment and the generality of theory is only apparent; in fact, they delimit each other. Yet this delimitation can come about only in comparison in which several parallel strands of action-reaction-effect sequences are compared with each other. And it is precisely through such comparisons that theoretization becomes a productive response to the nausea created by the infinity process. The search for principles itself can provide the tracing direction because there is little reason to trace processes along the beaten path of the well established or the haphazard.

Theory provides us with a notion of what kind of systematic action-reaction-effect linkages to expect. And we can see whether they hold up under particular circumstances. Thus, theory gives us clues for tracing processes; it moves our gaze in certain directions. The search can move either forward from action-reaction chains to formations or backward from formations to the action chains that constitute them. In the first case, the question is which formations (persons, relationships, cultural forms, the built environment) these action-reaction chains constitute to a significant degree and which ones of those are interesting. The debates about globalization reveal in an instant how this movement from apparent actions (e.g., movements of people, goods, ideas, capital) to their effect on a formation is anything but trivial. Under which circumstances (cross-links with other processes) do these movements strengthen or weaken the nation-state? In the second case, the trick is to define an object well enough to get a clear sense of what kind of action chains are critical to constitute it. Again, this is in many interesting cases anything but trivial. What kind of action-reaction sequences and their interlinkages have been historically decisive in sustaining the papacy in any given period? In reality, we have to alternate between both of these tracing directions to juxtapose any particular logic of linking to the question of whether it alone can be credited with doing the trick. We have to experiment with various depths and breadths of action-reaction chains to see where systematic links begin to diffuse. We have to investigate which socialities in conjunction with which other formations produce these regularities and what it is that maintains them. In the end, we will have used existing theories to mine data, and we will use these data to alternate or replace theories until our data and our theory as emplotment schema combine into a satisfying story (cf. Abbott 2001; White 1973).[38]

Let us return one more time to the price-hike example. The social formation in question is indeed the movement of an index; the actions constituting it are price settings determined by individual actors. I hypothetically traced one vendor's price increase to a number of antecedent actions (parental demands, previous competitor actions, presentations of managerial and/or corporate identity, demand) that seem to be at play. To get a full understanding of the breadth of relevant actions to which an individual price increase is a reaction, to get a full understanding of the socialities, the cultural forms, the relations, and the built environment, is to define a case revealing the directions in which a theoretization might develop. Just imagine a psychodynamic theory of inflation or, somewhat less revolutionary, one that traces continuous price pressures to corporate governance arrangements or to managerial ideologies! Even if in this one instance the vendor's reaction to her mother's demands and the pressures of the board were as important as sustained changes in demand (the old Econ 101 story), it does not mean that next time they will be or that a competitor will follow similar action-reaction-effect paths. But if they do, through a number of comparative cases, we are onto something. Let us imagine for a moment that we had told an Econ 101 story as far as the object, the price hike, is concerned. Let us assume that what we would like to explain is persistent inflation, for which our example was just a case. Does the Econ 101 story make sense? Demand fluctuates, but prices seem to be more generally on the rise. So the story needs a bit more complexity. At this point we might want to follow some of the other leads we had and construct perhaps a Lacanian theory of inflation. But could we substantiate it?[39]

Here is another example. In my first book (Glaeser 2000) I tackled the following problem. Soon after the reunification of Germany in October 1990, which proceeded under the assumption of an essential unity of the German people, many signs emerged suggesting that if there were not already two German identities, an eastern one and a western one, then they would emerge fairly soon. People began to talk about "walls in the minds of people" that had effectively replaced the Berlin Wall to describe misunderstandings and hostilities between easterners and westerners. The first challenge in terms of an analysis of process was to grasp 'identity' in such a way that it could be linked to actions performed by real people in real time and space. I chose a phenomenological understanding of identity as a momentary interpretation of self that proceeds through contextualization. But how do people *do* identity? What I saw in the field was that people continuously identified each other as easterners or westerners performatively in speech, gesture, habitus, and reference to objects, and I learned to take such identifications as building blocks of identity formation processes.

The next question concerned what it is that people are reacting to when they identify themselves or others in such ways. Contrary to expectations, life in East and West had produced significant cultural differences ranging from architectural styles and lexical variations to ways of managing work and the uses of time. People reacted with oppositional identifications to the perception of these differences. These identifications, which were in no way accommodating or even neutral, were heavily morally laden.

In this context it is important to understand that the very way in which the unification process was organized produced countless circumstances in which the state, with its bureaucratic techniques of projective articulations, identified easterners as deficient variants of westerners to which they were asked to assimilate themselves. And why was this policy pursued with such a vengeance? On the one hand, it became clear to me that the Cold War was yet being acted out in this way; on the other hand, it also became evident that this was still a reaction to Germany's Nazi past. A sociality was thus stipulated by a conundrum of historical memory and current policy in which easterners were related to westerners as students to teachers, as recipients of democracy to givers of democracy, as receivers of wealth to givers of wealth, producing oppositional identifications on a massive scale. If not torn apart by competition for ever scarcer jobs, easterners reacted to this by forming a community of sufferers that could reconfirm oppositional identifications. Likewise, westerners working in the East returned 'home' as often as they could, and they too huddled with each other, complaining about easterners' ungratefulness. Thus, friendship networks remained origin specific. The theoretical gain of this study was an analytic theory of identity construction processes that remains open to what identity is about by centering on the performance of acts of identification, their context sensitivity, and the specific modes in which they can be cast.

## Choosing Field Sites

Neither anthropological nor sociological ethnography developed with a systematic approach toward field-site choices. The disciplinary project was one of cataloguing human diversity that in comparison promised to shed light on the *condito humana* more generally. Moreover, assumptions about the systematicity and homogeneity of cultures made site strategies beyond the expediency of access irrelevant. The point was to get in *somewhere*; spatial and temporal homogeneity assumptions took care of the rest. The acknowledgment of the pervasive existence of projective articulation changes the situation dramatically. First, different locations may have different positions in networks of relations, and these need to be considered because they offer different perspectives on effect flows and interactions with other processes. Influenced by world systems theory, parts of such differences in network positions have been considered for a long time in the guise of center-periphery exchanges. Yet the center-periphery model is only one among many to consider here. The relatively smooth operation of (international) *lex mercatoria*, for example, can probably not be understood in this way.

Second, projective articulations regularly create a number of parallel action-reaction-effect strands. These will inevitably have distinct local flavors, and yet at first glance they might provide equivalent possibilities to study the kinds of processes we are interested in. However, even if they are subjected to comparable influences, these sites may differ vastly in what they can offer us in terms of the very observability of process. What we want to understand is why people act/react the way they do and what the effects of their reactions are on the formation. This means that contexts are particularly helpful in which people comment locally on each other's actions as reactions and where a diverse set of such commentaries is available. In the case of German unification, for example, I wanted a site where a number of identical easterners and westerners encountered each other on a daily basis, not only across hierarchical levels but also at the same level of hierarchy. This way I hoped to get more open conflict. Berlin, as the once divided and now unified city, seemed to offer more in this regard than any other place in the country. It was, after all, the only reunified city on German territory. I considered a number of organized environments—banks, cultural institutions, public administrations—and settled on the Berlin police for a number of reasons. The department had created a situation in which about half of the remaining former eastern People's Police officers were sent to the western part of the city and a similar number of western officers were sent east. Here was a quasi-experimental set-up, virtually unique in the entire country. These officers had to encounter each other's spaces, work with each other's equipment, and accomplish tasks together that involved many other people and social problems.

The Berlin police department was typical neither of post-unification police organizations nor of East-West encounters in state bureaucracies more generally. A good field site is not necessarily typical for contexts in which processes of particular kinds proceed. Instead, it needs to be productive in revealing action-reaction-effect linkages that may be going on elsewhere as well, if often less visibly so. Much like a play, a good field site is a theater of process that communicates through its particulars something more general. Artists may create the *besondere Allgemeine* (the particular general); we ethnographers need to go find it.

## Formal Organizations as Sites

Formal organizations offer a number of advantages as field sites. They are interesting for the ethnography of processes because they funnel—that is, gather and concentrate—a wide variety of actions toward a limited, interconnected set of people. Formal organizations projectively articulate action effects along a number of different dimensions. Typically, they bring people together from different families, diverse neighborhoods, and different socio-economic backgrounds, submitting them to related sets of disciplines, professional standards, and so on. If the organizations are large, they connect people across countries and continents and, through their very endurance, across time. Moreover, they enforce government policies among employees and mobilize their employees in response to the actions of other organizations. More importantly yet, projectively articulating action effects is typically what formal organizations are all about, no matter whether they are businesses, government agencies, parties, or movement headquarters. They collect and transmit information about what people do, think, or feel; they bring goods produced by some people to others who use them; they make available the money earned by some for investment by others; they force the orders issued by some on designated others, etc. In the name of efficiency, formal organizations are usually busily attempting to shape the identities of their employees as practitioners of particular crafts and as citizens or members of the collectivity. Accordingly, organizational life is saturated with memory practices small and large, ranging from learning from past experiences to improve operations to the establishment and dissemination of the history of the organization in the interests of positive emotive bonding. Formal organizations are in this sense enormous linking operations that incubate a diverse set of processes by connecting actions to reactions.

This role of formal organizations has proved to be essential for my first project. Easterners and westerners brought their home, neighborhood, and family lives into the organization in the form of countless stories in which vacations, illnesses, renovation projects, and large-scale acquisitions, as well as reminiscences of all sorts, played a significant part. At the same time, the police subjected them to the state's vision of what unification should look like. Westerners were encouraged to serve as models, furnishing easterners with knowledge about how things ought to be done. Easterners, in turn, were assimilated into new practices: they were scrutinized for deeds and affiliations deemed morally problematic, their qualifications were reassessed, and they were given a new rank and a new place. Thus, the police as a formal organization allowed me to show how the political process of unification was enacted on the ground, how the 'macro' that emerged from being a set of ideas developed by a limited number of people in some location was projected into the realm of everyday life. The local designation of policies became a mass ('macro') phenomenon through the projection of formal organizations such as the police, which in turn fueled the growing alienation between easterners and westerners.

But through its self-historicization, the police organization also made it easy to trace the perceived impact of the past, especially the overwhelming shadow of the Nazi past and, in its umbra, the peculiarly German interpretation of the Cold War as a continuing battle against totalitarianism. The hyper-self-consciously performed reaction of the state's political leadership to that Nazi past was in turn projected into the everyday minutiae of habitus, police station design, and typeface, yielding together an intricate semiotics of overcoming, which in turn formed a convenient benchmark to measure relative moral worth between easterners and westerners.

Locating fieldwork in formal organizations often also gives rise to an opportunity to follow the second strategy, that is, an investigation of the full circle from action over projective articulation to reception and reaction, to the reverse projective articulation of reaction effects, back to the original actor. Such feedback loops are very important because they can lead to process dampening or amplification. These loops are relatively easy to study as long as they are internal to the organization, for this often involves little more than fieldwork on hierarchically distinct layers. In the unification study, I researched how the police bureaucracy in Berlin was developing its policy to integrate eastern officers in response to the general unification treaty negotiated by both governments. I then studied how these were enforced, what effect this had on the officers so treated, and how they, through their performance, affected the Berlin police and its perception by a wider public. Studying feedback loops that transcend the perimeter of a formal organization is more difficult because one typically has to switch field sites.

## Conclusions

In settings where social life produces relatively few traces that would allow later generations to construct a rich understanding of what this life was about, ethnography understood as a documentary practice may make sense (even if there is no such thing as simple documentation), because this is a way of producing at least some signs that later generations may wish to interpret for their own gratification. After all, we are glad that Thucydides was around to tell us about the Peloponnesian Wars, notwithstanding his peculiar angle on things and his errors of fact. However, in settings in which more traces are produced than any later interpreter can possibly take in view anyway (and a large number of contemporary settings are of this kind), ethnography as documentary practice lessens dramatically in value because it produces just another set of signs in a sea of signs. In such contexts, ethnography has to choose between two alternative paths. It can develop into a systematic form of reporting that for the sake of efficient communication forfeits explicit reflection on its own emplotment. Alternatively, ethnography can become one of the ways in which social theory is produced, that is, one of the ways in which we develop languages of the social that help us to make sense of the world in which we live.

The partial social ontology that I have presented here suggests a number of broad areas for theory development. The first is sociality. More knowledge about the systematic connection between different kinds of socialities, their contextual invocation, their change through different network contexts, and their historical transformation would make significant contributions to a better understanding of the unfolding of social processes. The critical contribution would be a network analysis in which relations are seen not as an unqualified component of a structure but as a dynamic, qualitatively highly differentiated path through which action-reaction connections are not only enabled but shaped. The second major area of development is the link between social formations and their constituting actions. Better ideas about what kinds of often diverse action-reaction links sustain what kinds of formations in particular times and places would lead to a much improved analysis of institutional/cultural change. The third area—the ways in which cultural forms, relationships, and the material environment interact to produce reactions to actions—has, with the advent of practice theory, already experienced a significant boost. What would be desirable here is a better integration between approaches focusing on conscious reflection and those focusing on practices and emotions. In any event, we also need to study the temporal and spatial projective articulation of action effects, not just for their own sake but as component pieces of the processes they enable. The face-to-face needs a face-to-object and face-to-symbol extension through which these projective articulations interface with other processes. Thus we will learn how the past is in the present, how the translocal is in the local. For this to happen, the study of formal organizations—as the predominant purveyor of all kinds of projective articulations—needs to be seen less as a special field and more as an integral component of studying processes more generally.

For all this, ethnography should be the method of choice. No matter whether we trace our ethnographic ancestry to Gluckman, through Goffman to Mead, or through contemporary instantiations of practice theory to Marx, we are all processualists now. Ethnography must not lose depth; if anything, it may want to gain depth, for example, by retooling itself psychoanalytically. In this sense, we will want to continue to do cases—albeit ones that for the sake of achieving this depth need to be carefully delimited—theoretically. Starting with Gluckman and his collaborators and followers in anthropology and sociology, we have already gained considerable breadth, and we need to gain much more to capture fully the work of projective articulations. For some time we may help ourselves by carefully choosing our field sites, both in a single site and in two- to three-site mode, by strategically placing them within nodes that continue to mediate between the locally and temporally present and absent. In this context, we may also exploit more vigorously the potential of formal organizations as critical sites. In the medium run, however, we will have to learn to cooperate with each other. None of us will want to give up completely our cherished artisanal mode of production. Alas, we might have to shift to working in cooperatives.

## Acknowledgments

In one sense I owe this essay to the kind invitation of Terry Evens to participate in this volume. Yet in another, I owe it to my undergraduate and graduate students at the University of Chicago with whom I have wrestled over the question of how to define a productive ethnographic project. It is in conversations with them that some of the ideas expounded here have originated. The other part stems, needless to say, from the ontological and epistemological qualms about my own research. Many thanks go to Terry Evens, Sally Falk Moore, Michael Biggs, Daniel Cefai, Jeffrey Olick, and Gary Fine for comments on earlier drafts of this essay.

Andreas Glaeser is Associate Professor of Sociology at the University of Chicago. He is committed to developing social theory through ethnography. His first book, *Divided in Unity: Identity, Germany and the Berlin Police*, crafts a theory of identity-formation processes in dialogue with a narrative about why Germans have come to understand themselves in a culturally divided nation precisely at the moment when political unification succeeded. He is currently finishing his second book, *Political Epistemologies: The Secret Police, the Opposition and the End of East German Socialism*, which theorizes the emergence, maintenance and change of popular understandings of the state and politics in former East Germany.

## Notes

1. Of course, there were, interestingly, structure-functionalists who were also highly skeptical about the possibilities to create totalizing views of societies. This is, perhaps, the most fundamental difference between Parsons and Merton, the former never tiring in producing ever more comprehensive models of the totality 'society', thus setting forth what some have come to call 'grand social theory', the latter exhorting us equally tirelessly to stick with what he called 'theories of the middle range' (with all of the logical problems this entails for a functionalist).
2. By 'ontology', I do not mean the venerable philosophical quest for the ultimate constituents of the universe. Instead, I take it to be the art of making productive assumptions about such constituents and their linkages in a particular domain of life that will prove useful in guiding our research practices.
3. I will discuss how farther below, but here are two examples. For ethnographers, the danger of this division of labor has always been to focus on the temporally and spatially proximate context of field sites and, in a desire to go beyond it, to do in effect little more than speculatively overlay concrete observations with the 'larger picture' fashion speak of the moment. For macro theorists, the danger, in turn, has always been to wield a vocabulary of collective actors, which, deprived of an interactional imagination, quickly produced a shadow theater of abstract heroes.
4. Besides Gluckman's influence in ethnography, the turn to processes was energized by renewed interest in Meadian interactionism and Wittgensteinian pragmatism, as well as Peircean (as opposed to Saussurean) semiotics, and it was most forcefully propelled forward by ethnomethodology; the post-structuralisms of Derrida, Foucault, and Bourdieu; the historical turn in anthropology (e.g., Comaroff and Comaroff 1992; Moore 1986; Sahlins 1981; Wolf 1982); and historical sociology (e.g., Skocpol 1979; Tilly 1976; or more recently, Adams, Clemens, and Orloff 2005).
5. I think of actions here in the widest possible sense of 'doing', which includes habitual, non-reflexive behavior, unconsciously motivated actions such as parapraxes, and so forth. I speak hear of action-reaction sequences rather than of interaction because the latter term insinuates immediate feedback loops between both actors. However, as I will show farther below, this is by no means necessary.
6. In short, the reason is that without the input of other people, *believing* to follow a rule would be exactly the same as *following* a rule. Left to their own devices, individuals have no hard criterion by which to determine whether or not they follow a rule.
7. Our forgetfulness is therefore the fundamental source of something like social entropy.
8. I shall employ the term 'built environment' henceforth. I take it to encompass all human-converted nature, that is, the entirety of the material conditions of our lives, which includes the architectural spaces we live in as much as the food we consume and the

raw materials we convert into energy. I have taken the term from Bill Sewell (2005) precisely because it emphasizes nature that has been humanly acted upon (in contrast, for example, to 'material environment', which does not).

9. Even nature typically becomes a resource only through work, and it needs continued work to remain a resource. Fields need to be tended, machines repaired, clothes mended, and so on.

10. And to complete the circuit, cultural forms are reconstructed by people in relationships (e.g., through use in conversations) and within a built environment (e.g., with spatial features as a repository of social memories). A portion of the total physical environment is transformed by people in relationships (e.g., the division of labor in production) in use of cultural forms (ideas of the product or about humans' relationship to nature).

11. Fittingly for my argument, the scientist and the monster are more popularly known under the same name: Frankenstein. Shelly's name for the monster, Victor, is more or less forgotten.

12. This formulation does not solve the mind-body dualism in the way Terry Evens addresses it (e.g., 1995 and in this volume), but it makes it less of an issue in a Wittgensteinian sense.

13. This is in fact a generalization of what is indeed one of the great collective insights of the social sciences in the past century: the simultaneous made and making character of what I have called here social formations. In reconstructing a genealogy of this insight through its perhaps most prominent embodiments, the key inspirations of Marx's (1960, chap. 1) analysis of commodity fetishism and Hegel's (1986) master-slave dialectic need to be mentioned. Not least through the influence of Lukács (1969), we find early formulations of it in Mannheim ([1936] 1984), and then, revising Mannheim, in Berger and Luckmann (1966), through their emphasis on the dialectic of 'internalization and externalization'. We find it also in Bourdieu's (1977) notion of 'habitus' and Giddens's (1984) concept of 'structuration' wherein he also describes this peculiar aspect of social structures very aptly as 'duality', which is finally very fruitfully discussed by Bhaskar (1989). Related formulations can be found in Latour's (1987) poignant analysis of the Janus-headed nature of scientific theories which in development are written as hypothesis and in agreed settlement as facts. I am sure other examples could be added.

14. This means that our role as primus inter pares subjects of processes is contingent on being the object of processes. There is no action without anything to 'act on' and to 'act with'; we need to acquire language, knowledge, etc. Unfortunately, it is not true that we are always made the objects of processes because we are subjects capable of poiesis. In other words, there is the danger of objectification in which we are as (grammatical) objects only ever addressed as objects expected to produce nothing but necessary, predictable confluences.

15. It is conceivable, of course, that the price hike could be the outcome of a random walk. However, more likely than not, the unfolding of the process is far from random. If it were, social scientific inquiry would be pointless.

16. In some basic form, this dialectic between forms of sociality was obvious to Hobbes and Smith. However, what is needed is a much more thorough consideration of a wider multiplicity of socialities and their relationships within a particular historical context. For example, the contractual market relationship between a male laborer and his employer is to this day often contingent on a non-contractual relationship between the laborer and his wife. During the Industrial Revolution, the contractual relationship between this couple's children and their employers was likewise contingent on the non-contractual relationship between these children and their parents. Žižek (1997) has analyzed a number of such interdependencies with great verve.

17. Thus, Clyde Mitchell (1969) and his collaborators dedicate their collection, *Social Networks in Urban Situations: Analysis of Personal Relationships*, "To Max Gluckman— point-source of our network."

18. Actually, some network analysts (e.g., Burt 1980, 1992; Granovetter 1973, 1983) conflate the two, assuming implicitly that strong ties are always clustered and that weak ties are not. This, of course, is by no means the case.

19. In American sociology, this distinction was most widely disseminated by Granovetter (1973). Earlier contributions speak about the same characteristic as "intensity" (Mitchell 1969: 27f.) or "strength" (Reader 1964: 22).

20. There are a number of other terms in use to denote the same phenomenon. Bott (1957) speaks of "close-knit" and "loose-knit" networks. Barnes (1954) speaks of "small and large mesh" and has contributed to a formalization of this notion by developing it further into "density" (1969: 63). If cluster ties are strong, they are also often called "cliques" (Burt 1980: 79).

21. Schütz and Luckmann (1984) make some very interesting turns to break out of the face-to-face mode as the ur-model of interaction. Alas, in keeping with the character of the work as an outline of the structures of consciousness, their effort remains somewhat typological, designating whole classes of people according to the ways in which they are present to an actor. Yet it remains a real contribution that they have alerted us to the fact that people's knowledge of whom they could possibly affect under what kinds of circumstances may have a profound influence on how they experience the world and what they do.

22. I do not want call them 'mediations ' for the simple reason that this term is also used to describe the shaping of actions by cultural forms, relations, and the built environment. All actions are mediated in this sense. However, not all actions are projectively articulated.

23. To name a few more, the mass media produce such projective articulations, as do technologies of state or corporate legibility. Military and law enforcement capabilities projectively articulate power over long durations and across wide swaths of space. Telecommunication and transportation, social-memory practices, payment methods and other financing tools—all produce projective articulations.

24. Yet highly iconic, live projective articulations should not be confused with the local action, even where the latter was produced expressly to become projectively articulated. Anybody who has participated in videoconferences, to say nothing about such crude means as telephone conversations, can attest to the difference.

25. This is, of course, not the case for all produced objects. Those considered 'art' or at least 'traditional handicraft' continue to be expressly read as the effect of action, even if the conditions of the production of such action are often shrouded in myths of what 'artwork' or 'handicraft production' is like.

26. Someone who has regularly done interesting if not necessarily very systematic work along these lines is Slavoj Žižek (e.g., 1989, 1997).

27. Other, more recent exemplars are Dominic Boyer's (2005) analysis of journalism in the making of the German polity; Karin Knorr Cetina and Urs Bruegger's (2002) investigation of international currency dealer cultures emerging through interactions on networked trading screens; Sally Falk Moore's (2001) study of the imposition of conditionalities by donor countries on developments in sub-Saharan Africa by way of international organizations and agreements; Arvind Rajagopal's (2001) investigation of the role of television in the emergence of Hindu nationalism in India; and, finally, James Scott's (1998) splendid analysis of techniques of legibility in nation-state formation processes.

28. The misplaced concreteness inherent in most macro categories is well recognized and has led to various attempts in the social sciences to develop the macro from the micro (e.g., Coleman 1990; Collins 1981; Hechter 1983; Schelling 1978).

29. The "small world" phenomenon discussed, for example, by Watts (2003) is an excellent case in point. The small world problem wonders how it is possible that, for example, information (but also diseases) can spread rapidly throughout a social network even though the majority of relations people have tend to be cluster-like—or this is at least what network analysis like to assume. Projective articulations are assumed here (e.g., through the Internet) but not really thematized.

30. The blinders one has to use to legitimate ethnography under classical assumptions are then very similar to those one has to use to legitimate micro-sociological approaches. Both overlook the co-constitution of what goes on locally by what goes on in connected locations.

31. This problem is, of course, closely related to the issues of delimitation that historians have been arguing back and forth. It is the question of legitimate beginnings and endings (and, for example, the use of epochal markers in this respect), as well as of the legitimacy of 'special' histories (of gender relations, economic affairs, etc.).

32. Rooted in the study of "law," she makes an argument to trace ways in which people try to impose order ("regularization") in the face of others who try to take advantage of these orders through their necessary gaps, contradictions, and ambiguities to follow their own interests (situational "adjustment"). This approach becomes particularly useful if it is understood that the dialectic envisioned here is itself contingent on the mediation of particular cultural forms and the activation of particular socialities. From within studies of (organized) contestation, it is easily overlooked that contestation is in itself an achievement.

33. Turner's and Moore's emphasis on crisis as revelatory of process due to its foregrounding of expectations and local theories of 'how things happen' deeply resonates with the phenomenological emphasis on breach and repair (e.g., Garfinkel 1967; Goffman 1967), which makes a similar kind of argument for a still smaller scale (cf. Austin 1956–1957).

34. For a nice dramatization between Evans-Pritchard's advice on how to proceed and musings about his own recent multi-sited work, see Hannerz (2003).

35. That Gluckman's vision of moving to a study of processes has been born out is visible in a marked shift in emphasis of ethnographic titles from particular groups of people ("The Nuer," "The Polish Peasant in Europe and America"), localities ("Middletown"), or institutions ("The Hobo," "The Taxi-Dance Hall," "Nuer Religion") to the result or course of processes ("Distinction," "Facts and Fabrications," "The Poetics of Manhood"). Linguistically, this is reflected by the new prominence of a verb somewhere in the title, most notably verbs of production used in continuous form ("Manufacturing Consent," "Crafting Selves").

36. This awareness is the source of the injunction against 'violent' theoretization and is the font of strong moralization of ethnographic practices, which offers some guidance for navigating an endless web of processual flows with regard to the effect of one's own position in it and with the hope for betterment of the world.

37. Except for cases of 'celebrity embodiment', few people other than the researcher might share this interest. One way of producing celebrity status is the exoticization of that concrete embodiment as 'other'. In this case, it is often hard to decide when an interest in the variation of what it means to be human—a program associated most clearly with Ruth Benedict (1934) or Margaret Mead (1963)—gives way to sensationalism. Any exercise of ethnography as 'mirror' or 'cultural critique' is bound to overstate difference at the expense of similarity.

38. In this respect, our performed judgments are themselves reactions—to genre conventions enforced by journals and publishers, to past or ongoing differences with colleagues, to our admiration for others past and present.

39. The theory could be presented along the following lines: the burning desire stemming from inevitable misrecognition becomes symptomatic in wanting to have ever more, which is reflected in profit maximization behavior. Žižek (e.g., 1989) seems to have a jolly good time offering Lacan as an answer to the puzzles of humankind. Unfortunately he never follows through with an empirical analysis of process.

## References

Abbott, Andrew. 2001. *Time Matters*. Chicago: University of Chicago Press.

Adams, Julia, Elisabeth S. Clemens, and Ann Shola Orloff, eds. 2005. *Remaking Modernity: Politics, History, and Sociology*. Durham, NC: Duke University Press.

Anderson, Benedict. 1983. *Imagined Communities: Reflections on the Origin and Spread of Nationalism*. New York: Verso.

Austin, John L. 1956–1957. "A Plea for Excuses." *Proceedings of the Aristotelian Society* 57: 1–30.

———. 1962. *How to Do Things with Words*. Cambridge, MA: Harvard University Press.

Barnes, John A. 1954. *Politics in a Changing Society: A Political History of the Fort Jameson Ngoni*. Cape Town and New York: Oxford University Press for the Rhodes-Livingstone Institute.

———. 1969. "Networks and Political Process." Pp. 51–76 in Mitchell 1969.

Benedict, Ruth. 1934. *Patterns of Culture*. New York: Houghton Mifflin.

Berger, Peter, and Thomas Luckmann. 1966. *The Social Construction of Reality*. New York: Anchor Books.

Bhaskar, Roy. 1989. *The Possibility of Naturalism: A Philosophical Critique of the Contemporary Human Sciences*. New York: Harvester Wheatsheaf.

Bieri, Peter. 2001. *Das Handwerk der Freiheit: Über die Entdeckung des eigenen Willens*. Munich: Hanser.

Bourdieu, Pierre. 1977. *Outline of a Theory of Practice*. Cambridge: Cambridge University Press.

Bott, Elizabeth. 1957. *Family and Social Network*. London: Tavistock.

Boyer, Dominc. 2005. *Spirit and System*. Chicago: University of Chicago Press.

Burawoy, Michael. 1998. "The Extended Case Method." *Sociological Theory* 16, no. 1: 4–33.

———. 2000. "Introduction: Reaching for the Global." Pp. 1–40 in Burawoy et al. 2000.

Burawoy, Michael, et al. 2000. *Global Ethnography: Forces, Connections, and Imaginations in a Postmodern World*. Berkeley: University of California Press.

Burt, Ronald S. 1980. "Models of Network Structure." *Annual Review of Sociology* 6: 79–141.

———. 1992. *Structural Holes: The Social Structure of Competition*. Cambridge, MA: Harvard University Press.

Clifford, James. 1988. *The Predicament of Culture: Twentieth-Century Ethnography, Literature, and Art*. Cambridge, MA: Harvard University Press.

Clifford, James, and George Marcus. 1986. *Writing Culture: The Poetics and Politics of Ethnography*. Berkeley: University of California Press.

Coleman, James S. 1990. *Foundations of Social Theory*. Cambridge, MA: Harvard University Press.

Collins, Randall. 1981. "On the Microfoundations of Macrosociology." *American Journal of Sociology* 86, no. 5: 984–1014.

Comaroff, Jean, and John Comaroff. 1992. *Ethnography and the Historical Imagination*. Boulder: Westview Press.

Devons, Ely, and Max Gluckman. 1964. "Introduction" and "Conclusion: Modes and Consequences of Limiting a Field of Study." Pp. 13–19, 158–261 in *Closed Systems and Open Minds: The Limits of Naïvety in Social Anthropology*, ed. Max Gluckman. Chicago: Aldine.

Durkheim, Emile. [1893] 1997. *The Division of Labor in Society*. New York: Free Press.

Epstein, A. L., ed. 1967. *The Craft of Social Anthropology*. London: Tavistock.

———. 1969. "Gossip, Norms and Social Network." Pp. 117–127 in *Social Networks in Urban Situations*, ed. J. Clyde Mitchell. Manchester: Manchester University Press.

Evens, T. M. S. 1995. *Two Kinds of Rationality: Kibbutz Democracy and Generational Conflict*. Minneapolis: University of Minnesota Press.

Fabian, Johannes. 1983. *Time and the Other: How Anthropology Makes Its Object*. New York: Columbia University Press.

Festinger, Leon, Stanley Schachter, and Kurt W. Back. 1950. *Social Pressures in Informal Groups*. Stanford: Stanford University Press.

Foucault, Michel. 1978. *The History of Sexuality*. Vol. 1. New York: Vintage Books.

Garfinkel, Harold. 1967. *Studies in Ethnomethodology*. Englewood Cliffs, NJ: Prentice-Hall.

Giddens, Anthony. 1984. *The Constitution of Society: Outline of a Theory of Structuration*. Berkeley: University of California Press.

Glaeser, Andreas. 2000. *Divided in Unity: Identity, Germany, and the Berlin Police*. Chicago: University of Chicago Press.

Gluckman, Max. [1940] 1958. *Analysis of a Social Situation in Modern Zululand*. Manchester: Manchester University Press for Rhodes-Livingstone Institute.

_____. 1961. "Ethnographic Data in British Social Anthropology." *Sociological Review* 9, no. 1: 5–17.

_____. 1963. "Gossip and Scandal." *Current Anthropology* 4, no. 3: 307–316.

_____. 1967. "Introduction." Pp. xi–xx in Epstein 1967.

Goffman, Erving. 1967. *Interaction Ritual: Essays on Face-to-Face Behavior*. New York: Pantheon.

Granovetter, Mark. 1973. "The Strength of Weak Ties." *American Journal of Sociology* 78, no. 6: 1360–1380.

_____. 1983. "The Strength of Weak Ties: A Network Theory Revisited." *Sociological Theory* 1: 201–233.

Hannerz, Ulf. 2003. "Being There ... and There ... and There! Reflections on Multi-sited Ethnography." *Ethnography* 4, no. 2: 201–215.

Hechter, Michael, ed. 1983. *Microfoundations of Macrosociology*. Philadelphia: Temple University Press.

Hegel, Georg. 1986. *Phänomenologie des Geistes*. Frankfurt: Suhrkamp.

Homans, George. 1992. *The Human Group*. New Brunswick, NJ: Transaction Publishers.

Knorr Cetina, Karin D., and Urs Bruegger. 2002. "Global Microstructures: The Virtual Societies of Financial Markets." *American Journal of Sociology* 107, no. 4: 905–950.

Latour, Bruno. 1987. *Science in Action*. Cambridge, MA: Harvard University Press.

Lukács, Georg. 1969. *Geschichte und Klassenbewußtsein*. Neuwied: Luchterhand.

Mannheim, Karl. [1936] 1984. *Ideology and Utopia*. San Diego, CA: Harcourt.

Marcus, George E. 1998. *Ethnography through Thick and Thin*. Princeton: Princeton University Press.

Marx, Karl. 1960. *Das Kapital*. In *Marx Engels Werke*. Vols. 22–24. Berlin: Dietz Verlag.

Mead, George Herbert. 1934. *Mind, Self, and Society: From the Standpoint of a Social Behaviorist*. Ed. Charles Morris. Chicago: University of Chicago Press

Mead, Margaret. 1963. *Sex and Temperament in Three Primitive Societies*. New York: Morrow Quill Paperbacks.

Mitchell, J. Clyde. 1969. "The Concept and the Use of Social Networks." Pp. 1–50 in *Social Networks in Urban Situations*, ed. J. Clyde Mitchell. Manchester: Manchester University Press.

_____. 1973. "Networks, Norms and Institutions." Pp. 15–35 in *Network Analysis Studies in Human Interaction*, ed. Jeremy Boissevain and J. Clyde Mitchell. The Hague: Mouton.

Moore, Sally F. 1978. *Law as Process*. London: Routledge.

_____. 1986. *Social Facts and Fabrications: "Customary" Law on Kilimanjaro, 1880–1980*. Cambridge: Cambridge University Press.

_____. 1987. "Explaining the Present: Theoretical Dilemmas in Processual Ethnography." *American Ethnologist* 14, no. 4: 727–736.

_____. 2001. "The International Production of Authoritative Knowledge: The Case of Drought-Stricken West Africa." *Ethnography* 2, no. 2: 161–189.

Moscovici, Serge. 1985. "Social Influence and Conformity." Pp. 347–412 in *The Handbook of Social Psychology*, vol. 2, ed. G. Lindzey and E. Aronson. New York: Random House.

Olick, Jeffrey, and Joyce Robbins. 1998. "Social Memory Studies: From 'Collective Memory' to the Historical Sociology of Mnemonic Practices." *Annual Review of Sociology* 24: 105–140.

Park, Robert E., and Ernest W. Burgess. 1984. *The City*. Chicago: University of Chicago Press.

Porter, Theodore M. 1995. *Trust in Numbers: The Pursuit of Objectivity in Science and Public Life*. Princeton: Princeton University Press.

Rajagopal, Arvind. 2001. *Politics after Television: Religious Nationalism and the Reshaping of the Indian Public*. Cambridge: Cambridge University Press.

Reader, D. H. 1964. "Models In Social Change with Special Reference to Southern Africa." *African Studies* 23: 11–33.

Sahlins, Marshall. 1981. *Historical Metaphors and Mythical Realities*. Ann Arbor: University of Michigan Press.

Schelling, Thomas. 1978. *Micromotives and Macrobehavior*. New York: Norton.

Schütz, Alfred, and Thomas Luckmann. 1984. *Strukturen der Lebenswelt*. 2 vols. Frankfurt am Main: Suhrkamp.

Scott, James. 1998. *Seeing Like a State: How Certain Schemes to Improve the Human Condition Have Failed*. New Haven, CT: Yale University Press.

Searle, John. 1969. *Speech Acts: An Essay in the Philosophy of Language*. Cambridge: Cambridge University Press.

_____. 1992. *The Construction of Social Reality*. New York: Free Press.

Sewell, William H., Jr. 2005. *Logics of History*. Chicago: University of Chicago Press.

Shryock, Andrew, ed. 2004. *Off Stage/On Display*. Stanford: Stanford University Press.

Simmel, Georg. 1992. *Soziologie: Untersuchungen über die Formen der Vergesellschaftung*. Vol. 2 of *Gesamtausgabe*. Frankfurt am Main: Suhrkamp.

Skocpol, Theda. 1979. *States and Social Revolutions*. Cambridge: Cambridge University Press.

Tilly, Charles. 1976. *The Vendee: A Sociological Analysis of the Counterrevolution of 1793*. Cambridge, MA: Harvard University Press.

Turner, Victor. 1974. *Dramas, Fields and Metaphors: Symbolic Action in Human Society*. Ithaca, NY: Cornell University Press.

Watts, Duncan. 2003. *Small Worlds: The Dynamics of Networks between Order and Randomness*. Princeton: Princeton University Press.

White, Hayden. 1973. *Metahistory: The Historical Imagination in Nineteenth-Century Europe*. Baltimore: Johns Hopkins University Press.

Whitehead, Alfred North. 1979. *Process and Reality*. Corrected edition. Ed. David Ray Griffin and Donald Sherburne. New York: Free Press.

Wittgenstein, Ludwig. 1984. *Philosophische Untersuchungen*. Pp. 225–618 in *Werkausgabe*, vol. 1. Frankfurt am Main: Suhrkamp.

Wolf, Eric. 1982. *Europe and the People without History*. Berkeley: University of California Press.

Žižek, Slavoj. 1989. *The Sublime Object of Ideology*. London: Verso.

_____. 1997. *The Plague of Fantasies*. London: Verso.

*Chapter 3*

# THE EXTENDED CASE
## Interactional Foundations and Prospective Dimensions

*Don Handelman*

Follow your nose wherever it leads you.
— *Max Gluckman*

Life is what happens to you while you are making other plans.
— *William Gaddis*

I have used these epigraphs before, in writing of the Manchester extended-case method. Together, like no others, they shape Max Gluckman's sense that anthropological intuition is integral to good research, that a researcher can anticipate but never predict what may occur, and so that (in Gaddis's aphorism) the prospective (where we live most of our lives) is replete with indeterminacy and uncertainty.

Notes for this chapter begin on page 113.

Gluckman did not put it this way. His primary concern was to uncover how social relationships were linked together through great social institutions, their reproduction and change. Nonetheless, he told me on more than one occasion, "Follow your nose wherever it leads you." For the anthropologist, the ever-present implication in his adage was that only through following the social practices of persons would such linkages be unearthed empirically. Following one's nose is at the crux of what came to be called the extended-case method, a major contribution to the practice of anthropology, one pioneered by Max's work.

Yet so long as the extended case is perceived as a 'method', primarily as a way of gathering data, much of its epistemology for perceiving social actors, social relationships, and, through these, social institutions will stay in a minor key. The extended case needs to be theorized more in relation to the practices and organization of social life. This is much more than I can essay here. But I will argue for the value of thinking about the extended case in relation to interaction that underlies and informs many of the practices that contribute to the making of an extended case. I will argue further that the extended case is inherently processual, so that (in keeping with Gaddis's aphorism) it is continuously becoming what I call 'prospective history'. Therefore, the dynamics of the extended case, whether understood in more micro or more macro terms, are necessarily temporal. This point is obvious once made, yet then there is no longer any separation between the practice of social life and history, most immediately, micro history. Then, too, the extended case also becomes an anthropology of social order as it is becoming—of social order continuously emerging into phenomenal existence, with implications both for reproduction and change.

In the following section I emphasize the extended case as the capturing of emergence. I continue by shifting to face-to-face interaction, discussing the encounter and arguing further that much of extended cases are constituted through encounters, and that these have their own micro dynamics that influence how a case is shaped. In the section after, I discuss how the processuality of the extended case resonates with prospective history. The overall thrust of my argument is that a case, emerging from encounters, is intrinsically temporalizing, becoming prospective history on its way to intersecting with more macro domains, with social institutions. I conclude by returning to the extended case as time, taking up Gluckman's concept of structural duration.

## The Manchester Extended Case

No one has theorized the extended case in relation to the forming of social order. Its self-description as the extended-case method pinched off any desire to understand this way of thinking as an entry into ways of forming social order. Treating the extended case primarily as method and leaving it at that is overly reductionist. Though the extended case is the construction of the researcher, much of the data through which a case is constituted depends on practices of interaction that have their own forming qualities for micro-social order.[1] I call these forming qualities of interaction 'encounters'. Through the extended case, the practices of encounters and micro history are understood to follow from one another in real time. Therefore, there is no epistemological distinction between an anthropology grounded in the study of social practice and an anthropology that does history. The extended case demonstrates the artificiality of the distinction.

Gluckman's route toward the extended-case method took him from a structural functionalism that conceived of social order more as an organic system toward the openness of social fields. In his original formulation of Swazi "rituals of rebellion" (the Frazer Lecture of 1952), Gluckman still held to a central tenet of such organic functionalism—to wit, that the institutions of a system were necessary for its maintenance. Several years later, reflecting on this work, he commented, "I was still thinking in crude functionalist terms of institutions contributing to the maintenance of a rather rigidly conceived social structure" (Gluckman 1963: 20). He continued: "I now abandon altogether the type of organic analogy for a social system with which Radcliffe-Brown worked and which led me to speak of civil war [through rituals of rebellion] as being necessary to maintain the system. Social systems are not as nearly integrated as organic systems, and the processes working within them are not as cyclical or repetitive as are those in organic systems ... I think therefore much more in terms of series of social processes ... These are never perfectly adjusted; and hence processes do not cancel themselves out as in organic systems" (ibid.: 38–39).

Gluckman was developing a key insight into how social practice opened into understandings of social order. His intuition was to treat the very description of social life as a means to expand the scale of anthropological understanding, so that the ordering of the social life of institutions could be theorized through the analysis of particular events. The coming into social existence of an event was already, for the ethnographer, the onset of its analysis. Gluckman advocated beginning analysis with close observations of the practices of others as kinds of persons (in terms of role, status, ethnicity, and so forth) in relatively circumscribed events that he called "social situations" (Gluckman 1958: 9), yet following these persons as kinds back into the social structural arrangements from whence they appeared. In this way, the anthropologist would understand how general institutional arrangements produced the singularity of particular events by entering into these arrangements through these very events. In this way, too, Gluckman let the practices of others lead to and reveal conflicts in the disordering and ordering of their social life, without bounding off the discontinuities that were revealed. The study of social situation let social practice itself lead to some degree of closure (events began and ended, more or less), rather than letting this be dictated by assumptions about how society should be integrated. Situational analysis clashed with organic functionalism, though this was not evident immediately in Gluckman's work. Here I discuss briefly Gluckman's idea of situational analysis and its expansion by others into the extended-case study.

The crucial work in these conceptual developments is Gluckman's *Analysis of a Social Situation in Modern Zululand* (1958), based on fieldwork in 1935 and first published in two parts in 1940 and 1942. However much this lengthy essay has been discussed, the basics of its thinking must be foregrounded here.

Gluckman wrote as follows: "As a starting point for my analysis I describe a series of events as I recorded them on a single day. Social situations are a large part of the raw material of the anthropologist. They are the events he observes and from them and their inter-relationships he abstracts the social structure, relationships, institutions, etc., of that society. By them, and by new situations, he must check the validity of his generalizations ... I have deliberately chosen these particular events from my notebooks because they illustrate admirably the points I am at present trying to make, but I might equally well have selected many other events or cited day-to-day occurrences ... *I describe the events as I recorded them, instead of importing the form of the situation as I knew it from the whole structure of modern Zululand into my description*" (1958: 2; italics added).

Gluckman points intentionally to the closeness between the interactions he observed and the inscriptions in his field notes. Despite the inevitable ruptures and alienation between what is happening and what is inscribed, there is significant continuity between them. The social situation opens not a window, as in Geertzian usage, but axes of practice *in particular contexts*. Gluckman's perceptions crisscross and intertwine with the trajectories of practice of the social actors. These trajectories project in their varied ways toward horizons that for Gluckman indexed the social structure of modern Zululand at that time. Gluckman's reasoning is neither deductive nor inductive. Though he knows a lot about Zululand, he is not using this knowledge to predict trajectories of practice. So, too, he will not move lineally from trajectory to horizon, such that the former simply indexes the latter. By emphasizing the practice of social actors (though at that time the term 'practice' hardly existed, if at all, in anthropological usage), Gluckman was open to whatever happened in the social situation, open to surprise (in a more Peircean, abductive sense), and this too effected his understanding of how the social situation refracted social structure.[2]

The social situation he discusses was the opening of a bridge by the chief native commissioner, the event attended by the regent of Zululand, by European and Zulu officials, and by missionaries, chiefs, and tribesmen. Gluckman's description is sequential. I refer here to this sequence schematically. As the cars of the Europeans approached the bridge, they were directed by Zulu in full war dress. The Europeans gathered on one side of the bridge, the Zulu on the other. The regent joined the Zulu, the European commissioner, the whites. The clan songs of the Zulu warriors were hailed by the regent, a Christian, and hymn singing (during which the warriors removed their head gear), led by a missionary, opened the ceremony. Europeans and the regent gave speeches thanking one another. The commissioner gave the Zulu cattle to slaughter, so that they could pour the bile at the foot of the bridge to ensure safety and good fortune, and then cook and eat the meat. The Zulu warriors led the cars of the Europeans across the bridge to break the opening ribbon, after which the cars drove back to the European side. The Europeans retired to their shelter for tea and cakes, some of which the commissioner sent across the bridge to the regent. In turn, from amongst the Zulu, drinking beer and waiting for their meat to cook, the regent sent over four pots of brew. Though the Europeans left soon after, the Zulu gathered at the bridge for the rest of the day.

Here I offer aspects of Gluckman's analysis, and do not add my own. The bridge opening is a straightforward piece of ethnographic description from the viewpoint of the anthropologist. Gluckman does not use this social situation as a microcosm of colonial South Africa. Instead, close to the scale with that which occurred at the bridge, the situation offers social categories for analysis. Gluckman uses the categories of persons who gather together at the bridge and the ways in which they interact and juxtapose their behaviors as threads to follow further, beyond the situation, into the wider social order. In this way, he shows how these threads ravel and unravel in weaving a social fabric.

Above all, Gluckman stressed the impact of apartheid on the Europeans and the Zulu—the cleavage separating them was so much more powerful and far-reaching than the exchanges that linked them. He emphasized that this cleavage depended on the control of the Europeans over the Zulu, a domination ultimately based on force and repression. Gluckman's rendering of the structure of colonial Zululand is grounded in the practices of the people who constituted this ordering and who reproduced this through numerous social situations, of which the bridge opening was one.[3] Therefore, Gluckman (1958: 9) argued for comparisons between social situations in order to reveal more of the underlying structure. Bruce Kapferer (1987: 10) has commented that through his anti-reductionist stance, Gluckman "dramatically showed the whole in the process of its parts." Nonetheless, Gluckman's position was distant from issues of emergence through interaction and far no less from prospective history.

For that matter, to explain how the bridge opening was put together as it was, Gluckman did turn to time, but to the macro history of the Zulu peoples. Later on, thinking on time and history, he formulated the important idea of 'structural duration' (Gluckman 1968), which in my terms organized, in degrees, how emergence is formed through time. I return to this in the concluding section. As Chandra Jayawardena (1987: 33) pointed out, Gluckman's concept of the social situation is "a historical precipitate. It is the point of convergence of a series of processes, operating through time, which could have possibly taken other paths, but did not, and which brought a miscellany of customs and people to the opening of the bridge." Even so, this early vision of comparing social situations with one another was intended in a more static sense to expose the complexities of social structure. As Gluckman (1967: xiv) wrote: "[I]t was still social morphology that we were aiming to present."

The turn to micro time, to temporality more in scale with situational analysis, occurred when this kind of analysis was elaborated as the extended-case method (Gluckman 1961; van Velsen 1967). In his later understanding of the social situation, Gluckman argued vigorously that it was not to be understood simply as ethnographic description nor as what he termed "apt illustration," the appropriation of ethnographic examples rarely related to one another, in order to illustrate the appropriateness of arguments (Gluckman 1961: 7–8). The apt illustration, the most widely used way of supporting qualitative arguments, is used continually by modern (and post-modern) anthropologists, yet this technique merely buttresses and embellishes generalizations reached deductively or inductively. Inductively, deductively, researchers have already decided in advance where they want their discussion to go, and apt illustrations are chosen to support particular positions. However, the anthropologist who follows closely the social practices through which situations are constituted learns that their trajectories lead more in certain directions and less in others. Gluckman's commonsensical field research dictum with which I began—follow your nose wherever it leads you—meant that the lives people were practicing would emerge from the ethnographic materials. Even more so, it meant that initially there was little distance between ethnography and the concepts that grew out of ethnographic description. This did not mean a low level of abstraction but rather a tight relationship between social practice and the anthropologist's thinking through this in ever-broadening and deepening conceptual gyres. Like Peircean abduction, the Manchester approach encouraged creative and rigorous guesswork as a logic that introduced new ideas.

In studying social situations, it made excellent sense to take the additional step of following some of the same persons from one situation into others. In effect, each situation, each case coming into being, was treated as a segment or "a stage in an on-going process of social relations between specific persons and groups in a social system and culture ... the most fruitful use of cases consists in taking a series of specific incidents affecting the same persons or groups, through a long period of time, and showing how these incidents, these cases, are related to the development and change of social relations among these persons and groups" (Gluckman 1961: 9–10). Such social situations were treated as a series—emerging through time, invoking different contexts of social practice, creating variance in continuities and discontinuities, evoking inconsistencies in self-presentation—all the while staying close to "lived realities" (Kapferer 1987: 10), that is, close to the scale at which people in interaction, by themselves, shaped their own lives. As Gluckman (1961: 10) argued, through the extended-case method, social (and moral) order became more complex, less rigid, less integrated, more contradictory, more indeterminate (see Garbett 1970; Mitchell 1983; van Velsen 1967).

Gluckman stated bluntly that the concept of society, of relatively well-bounded, holistic social orders, might well have to be abandoned, perhaps in favor of more open "social fields" of practice (Gluckman 1961: 14), which could be pinched off only through arbitrary analytical closure. Further elaborations of situational analysis made it more actor and choice oriented (Kapferer 1972), connecting people and events through ego-centered social networks (Garbett 1970). The agency of individuals was given greater scope through time, just as this flexibility was constrained in emergent ways by the very kinds of interaction and social relationships that these individuals developed (Handelman 1977). With this perspective in mind, relationships among persons could not be understood as straightforwardly morphological or as unchanging through time. Field research now required the anthropologist to do analysis—explicitly, implicitly—with passing time, shifting space, foregrounded, backgrounded, but always very much present. The extended case, whether used in major or lesser ways, put change at the center of British anthropological endeavor, along with the recognition that actions, relationships, and social formations were only sometimes (perhaps rarely) anticipated by or predictable from initial conditions. Often they were not. Issues of uncertainty and indeterminacy in the practices of social life came more to the fore.

Nonetheless, Gluckman himself sought resolution in macro-historical explanation for the social open-endedness generated by situational analysis and the extended case, in what he referred to as "the extended case on a large [historical] scale" (1961: 14). He eschewed the theoretical possibility that micro domains of the social could generate more macro domains. In this respect, Gluckman remained a self-described 'institutionalist' whose concerns were with the constitution of broad normative order. In his view, interpersonal behavior derived still from hierarchical norms, strained through the customary directives of institutions. He thus stated uncompromisingly, "[A] theory of inter-personal relationships within small groups, or between individuals, cannot account for stabilized social institutions which persist for generations. The sum of the parts cannot account for the whole" (Devons and Gluckman 1964: 255), though whether "the whole" existed was open to question and critique. Something of Gluckman's position undoubtedly rubbed off onto Manchester anthropology. Though Manchester anthropologists collected and used materials that often were behavioral and interactional—the stuff of daily life—they rarely used these data to ask questions about face-to-face interaction, about interaction processes, and about how interaction generated the stuff of daily life out of which much of the social emerged, reproduced, changed. When they did address such problematics, it was through theories (such as exchange theory) that enabled them to summarize interactional processes speedily in order to move summarily to more macro matters (see Kapferer 1972). In this regard, Manchester anthropology did not address micro domains of the social or their formative capacities for organizing social life, capacities on which most of social life depends.

Nevertheless, apertures into micro domains were opened, however ambivalently. Thus, Gluckman (1968: 235) wrote: "[T]he separation of institutions from interaction is to a large extent an analytical distinction. For it is partly from action and interaction that we build up our abstract structure of institutions; and conversely, in studies of interaction, we are concerned with incapsulations from institutions. Somehow we must try to bring these different types of analyses together." This aperture, however, remained quite constricted: action and interaction remained incapsulations of institutions, while the substance of interaction derived from the latter. I will return to this problematic in discussing the encounter as the forming of interaction.

Situational analysis and the extended-case study were much more than a method as they shifted social anthropology toward more elastic and open-ended understandings of social analysis, in which the boundaries of study were more flexible and did not necessarily enclose and contain fixed social units.[4] Probably more so than any other approach in anthropology at the time (and likely more so than post-modern approaches), the extended case addressed the dynamics of practice and process. Although its adherents did not express themselves in this way, in my view the extended case analyzed how people practiced social order continuously coming into existence.[5] Once again, this is the issue of the ongoing emergence of social orders, their reproduction, their re-forming. Kwinter (2002: 10) refers to such dynamics (which he relates to the Deleuzian idea of virtuality) as morpho-genesis, the creation of form, the principle of a mobile ground of continuous production of the real. Therefore, argues Kwinter, morpho-genesis is a principle of perpetual instability and so of creation itself. However, Gluckman and the practitioners of the extended case were concerned explicitly with extending cases to the study of macro domains, to the ongoing macro genesis (with existing institutions as fundament and foundation) of social order.[6]

Here I will do the opposite, grounding the idea of case in dynamics of interaction. For this I turn to Erving Goffman and to my own thinking. Goffman is an epistolary figure here, but one teetering between the study of micro domains of interaction as relatively autonomous in their own right and his understanding that interaction reproduced social orders by invoking over and again their normative injunctions and constraints, with which persons played, maneuvered, strategized. I argue that the interactions that make up a good deal of extended-case materials should themselves be grounded in their own dynamics of the creation and emergence of micro form, and in the ways in which such forms effect the interactions that emerge within them, thereby effecting the case that these micro forms become part of.

## Encounter and Extended Case

Goffman's work had long been appreciated in Manchester; he was a friend of Gluckman's and a welcome guest in the department (see Sharrock 1999). Goffman was path-breaking in arguing that that which he called the "interaction order" was "a substantive domain in its own right … the warrant for this excision from social life must be the warrant for any analytical extraction: that the contained elements fit together more closely than with elements beyond the order" (Goffman 1983: 2). The interaction order is a face-to-face domain, a body-to-body starting point, a domain only loosely coupled with social structure. Yet by calling much of the interaction he studied 'interaction ritual', Goffman shut the door to interaction as a ground for morpho-genesis and turned interaction instead into a prominent mode by which social structure was reproduced in its range of variability (which is how Gluckman [1968: 235] understood interaction).[7]

Goffman (1983: 6) argued that one should try to identify this "naturalistically based [order] … the basic substantive units, the recurrent structures and their attendant processes." In my reading of his earlier work, the interaction order constitutes itself through encounters. In one of his clearest statements on the encounter, he writes: "An encounter provides a world for its participants but the character and stability of this world is intimately related to its selective relationship to the wider one. The naturalistic study of encounters, then, is more closely tied to studies of social structure on the one hand, and more separate from them, than one might at first imagine" (Goffman 1961: 80). Like the idea of the interaction order, that of the encounter emphasized some degrees of autonomy for the micro order of interaction.

I doubt that Goffman's claim for the autonomy of the interaction order was ever addressed in its own right. Perusing more recent responses to Goffman's thinking foregrounds further my proposal that the materials of the extended case are grounded in interaction, morpho-genesis, emergence. As I will discuss farther on, this was a pathway Gluckman chose not to take, though it is one forking path—to borrow from Borges (1998)—that the extended case opens into. At the interactionist extreme of these recent commentaries on Goffman is the sociologist Randall Collins. Collins (1987: 195) argues that the empirical "meets us only in the form of micro encounters," and that therefore "any macrostructure, no matter how large, consists only of the repeated experiences of large numbers of persons in time and space ... Macrostructure consists of nothing more than large numbers of micro encounters, repeated (or sometimes changing) ... it is at the micro level that the dynamics of any theory must be located." Here, "the true microunit is the encounter" (ibid.: 200). Nonetheless, in Collins's thinking, the encounter itself consists entirely of the individual contributions of its participants. Collins hardly considers the encounter as a structuring of emergence. Thus, the encounter itself does not acquire relative autonomy from its participants and is always reducible to the individuals who participate, that is, reducible to the acts of the participants as a series of actions in which each is added to the next.

As individuals practice encounters, they generate their own histories of participation. These histories of interaction Collins calls "interaction ritual chains" (2000: 29; 2004). Structure is a shorthand way of referring to patterns of the repetition of encounters through these chains of interaction (2000: 28). At the core of his argument is the claim that these encounters are ritual forms in a Durkheimian sense, binding together persons socially, emotionally. Interaction ritual qua Durkheimian ritual is the glue of everyday social life. For Collins, the interaction order has autonomy because all structure emerges empirically from repetitive interaction with its ritualistic capacities to invest successful human contacts with binding emotional energy.

P. M. Strong (1988) recognizes the autonomy of the interaction order, using the idea of encounter to discuss over 2,000 meetings between pediatricians and patients. He refers to some of Goffman's parameters for the encounter (rules of relevance and irrelevance, transformation rules), saying that its "little world" is "an extraordinarily robust structure capable of ignoring all kinds of routine trouble" (ibid.: 232). Nonetheless, he does not recognize the encounter itself as an emergent property of interaction, one generating its own structuration.

In contrast to these interactionists, anthropologist Eric Schwimmer (1990: 49, 53) argues that although the interaction order is an autonomous domain, its study cannot identify basic units of social organization (such as the encounter) because such units can be discovered only in how micro levels are coupled to macro levels. However, my sense is that the idea of encounter precisely counters such claims and thereby opens space for the discussion of the emergence of structuration within the interaction order, relatively independent from macro domains. Anthony Giddens (1988: 272), for his part, unsurprisingly maintains that nothing about macro levels can be inferred from micro levels. Moreover, Giddens insists that Goffman's understanding of interaction has much more to do with the reproduction of macro institutions than he acknowledges. Micro order derives from (incapsulates, in Gluckman's terms) and reproduces the macro.

My understanding of the interaction order argues for its autonomy on the grounds of this order's capacity to continuously reproduce and change itself through its own ongoing emergence. In this perspective, ongoing emergence happens primarily through the organizing medium of the encounter. In his early writing on the encounter, Goffman (1961: 19–29) implied that a focused gathering of two or more persons takes its shape by often unspoken and unrecognized rules: for keeping identities; for relating to subjects outside the gathering (rules of irrelevance); for enabling participants to actualize their resources inside the gathering (realized resources); and for guiding identities, subjects, and resources into the gathering while it is in progress (transformation rules).

Rules of irrelevance focus participants on what should be paid attention to during focused interaction. Realized resources are concerned with the allocation and verification of locally understood identities and roles. Transformation rules suggest the modifications that will occur when elements previously defined as irrelevant are given recognition within the encounter. Together, these rules describe what happens to any element selected to become a constituent of the internal order of the encounter. Together, too, these rules bound and bind (indeed, frame, as Goffman [1974] later used the idea) the encounter through its own interactive dynamics—what is going on inside the encounter is somehow different from what is going on outside the encounter, and this often is not due simply to a particular definition of the situation, nor to the imposition of normative difference.

I am insisting that encounters are emergent phenomena, developing through time from within themselves. This emergence might be an unfolding of what is expected and thus relatively closed from the outset, as in the case of formally defined, ritualistic encounters, or it might be quite open-ended. In both these instances (and in others), the very processes of interaction contain the potential to generate something other, something different, something unexpected, of smaller scale and consequence, of larger scale and consequence. Goffman frequently implied that the encounter (often referred to as a focused gathering) was a structure of interaction. However, I am stressing that the encounter itself is *structuring*: as interacting persons structure their encounter, so the emerging encounter organizes their interaction in keeping with the forming and forms of its emergence.[8] Encounters are formed through the interaction of their creators, but they also shape this interaction as it is occurring. Therefore, encounters in general simply are not reducible to the contributions—the particular life conditions, decisions, strategies, moves, emotions—of the participants.[9] The forming of interaction cannot be reduced to versions of methodological individualism—for my purposes here, interaction understood as the addition of discrete individual acts, each with its own individual intention—without destroying the idea of encounter.[10] However, I believe that it is our own cultural propensity (psychologistically, economistically) toward methodological individualism in understanding interaction that blocks perception of the more (momentary) self-organizing qualities of its social organization.

If my proposal is worth thinking on, even in a rudimentary way, then the encounter acquires the epistemological status of a naturally existing phenomenal form, one that can be called a unit of social organization. An encounter always begins to come into phenomenal existence from the moment two or more persons begin interacting. A 'folding' in a phenomenal world, one that has not been here a moment before, begins to take shape.[11] As interaction continues, the shaping of this fold emerges as it enfolds and subsumes the participants within their own interaction.[12] Emerging interaction encompasses itself, its folding shaping this interaction and the ways in which the participants appear within it. Used in this way, the fold is self-referential as it emerges. Becoming self-referential, the further it emerges in sustained fashion, the more the encounter evinces other qualities of at least minimal, though always transitory, self-organization. These qualities can be understood in terms of Goffman's rules of irrelevance, realized resources, and rules of transformation, all of which imply degrees of relative self-closure within an encounter.

Encounters differ in the degrees to which—despite their inbuilt transience—they develop interior complexity, the capacity to sustain interaction and to withstand rupture from within and without. That which may seem linear as a sequence of interactions—act or utterance after act or utterance—is curving within itself as it continues to emerge and develop. The interaction order consists of transient, often supra-individual encounters of shorter or lengthier duration, of lesser or greater self-resiliency, of weaker or more powerful capacities to carry information, instrumentality, feeling. The outcomes of encounters are continuously reproducing and changing the shape of any given interaction order, even if in tiny ways. The interaction order of encounters should therefore be understood as an ongoing process of phenomenal emergence.

None of what I am saying here contradicts the foundational logic of the extended case. To the contrary, all of this is in keeping with how extended cases come into existence, though from the analyst's perspective. Surprisingly, the more powerful extended-case analyses of social order changing as it is coming into existence—one thinks of Mitchell's (1959) study of the Kalela dance, Kapferer's (1972) study of a Zambian factory, and various works of Victor Turner—hardly point to its indeterminate emergence. The point is significant, given the relationship between encounter and extended case. The extended case follows directly from the idea of encounter and from that of emergence. Both are first and foremost the forming of temporality, and both emphasize emergence as the indeterminate actualizing of potentials for change (on repetition, see Deleuze 1994; on non-repetitive time, see Assad 1999: 41; see also Kwinter 2002: 10).

Encounters constitute much of the founding morpho-genesis of an extended case as it is moving into its own future(s).[13] Encounters enable thinking on how persons interacting are delivering to themselves and to others the futures they are in the process of creating—doing this in units that though of micro scale are often supra-individual—and having a social life, however ephemeral, of their own. One thing is certain: there is absolutely no point in arguing that encounters simply mirror and reproduce the social order that is giving them birth. Change is generated no less in the micro domain than in the macro—it is the scale and multi-dimensionality of macro change that make it so weighty, imposing, and consequential as it drives into and hammers micro domains, so often those of everyday mundane existence. If we argue that encounters mirror or incapsulate the social order from which they derive, we deny the emergence of internally generated change. The generating of change in micro domains is indeed consequential for the living of mundane lives.

The growth and emergent form of the encounter are one. The encounter may be called a "morphogenetic moment-event" (Kwinter 2002: 8–10), and so uncertainty and indeterminacy are its edges as it shapes—thus, it is virtual in its combinatorial capacities (see Kapferer 1997 on virtuality). Built into the encounter is the fact that it will end, and so, to whatever degree, built in no less is the rupture of its participants from one another's presence. These also are the edges at which encounters slide into the emerging extended case, as the analyst puts this together. The end of an encounter, the rupturing of presence among co-participants, is when the loss of one kind of relatedness, that of co-presence, may be turned into another—expectations of relatedness in the future. For Max Weber, this probabilistic expectation of relatedness in the future is the basis of the social relationship. Thus, he argued: "Let it be repeated and continuously kept in mind, that it is only the existence of the probability that, corresponding to a given subjective meaning complex, a certain type of action will take place, which constitutes the existence of the social relationship" (Weber 1964: 119).

For the extended-case analyst, the movement from the encounter that *was* to the encounter that *may be* is the interstitial zone of time/space from which the case takes shape. Once a subsequent encounter comes into existence, perhaps with some of the same participants as before, another micro component of a case may be added, depending on its significance for the analysis. This probably requires joining the continuousness of Bergsonian time to time understood as consisting of ruptures and breaks in movement (see Game 1997: 121), or, perhaps in a more Proustian way, to the notion that different sorts of encounters are creating their own senses of time that are integral to the ways in which they emerge.[14] William James's comment (cited in Game 1997: 121) that time comes in drops may also help one perceive how encounters form in drops, flowing into one another to shape the extended case, which in turn blots them into a broader, more comprehensive understanding of social order.[15]

In writing my doctoral thesis in Manchester during 1969–1970, I used the perspective outlined above to analyze interactions I had observed in a number of sheltered workshops for the aging (Handelman 1973, 1977, 1987). I discovered that different kinds of workshop encounters, themselves phenomena emerging through interaction, structured these settings through time. These workshop settings were themselves emerging and changing in ongoing ways through tiny encounters. It was not merely that interaction was ruled, structured, incapsulating more macro orders, in Gluckman's terms; rather, a sequence of interaction took form, though this form often was uncertain even as it was practiced into form. Whatever the emergent organization of the form, it made its own little contribution to the structuring of the workshop in which it took place.

At the time, I did not understand that in tracking these encounters through time I was doing an extended case. I foreground this once more because Manchester anthropology simply did not address in detail the micro domains of interaction in which much of extended cases was grounded and through which they continued to emerge. On the other hand, Goffman, whose thoughts inspired me to think in these directions, had made a number of starts in analyzing emergent interaction through discussions of encounter, 'focused gathering', and the like, but he had never followed through on these. True, the structures I studied were tiny, but their implications were not.

I argued that much of mundane life in these little structures was local, that is, the emergent product of interaction there. These little structures had to be analyzed in terms of greater ones, but if this were the only direction of the analysis, the fuller significance of life on the ground would be utterly skewed. So though the representatives of large institutions could smash these little structures to smithereens, as long as they continued, they were full of the living of life. I argued that much of what was significant about life on the ground for those who lived there emerged from the practice of interaction there, and was not accountable directly to great institutions. In this regard, much of the interaction had what art historian Henri Focillon called emergent "events," which shape their environment rather than being produced by it (cited in Kracauer 1969: 143–144). The further implications of my position for the extended case were clear, though I did not see them then. Had the practitioners of the extended case begun their analysis in micro domains of interaction (instead of summarizing these, sometimes summarily indeed), this could well have effected their conclusions.

When I was writing a book on one of these workshops (Handelman 1977), this thinking put me on a collision course with Max Gluckman. In the foreword (never published) to the book, he took strong exception to the theoretical position outlined above.[16] He did not accept my argument for the emergence of social order through encounters; more vigorously, yet unsurprisingly, he utterly rejected my standpoint that emergence within micro domains could have any effects on macro domains (or levels, as he referred to them). He wrote in the foreword (Gluckman 1974: xv): "I am interested in major political structures, not small areas of negotiation, and in major developments in social organization, not in the small shifts of power within the miniscule type of social setting with which Handelman is here concerned." He continued (ibid.: xvi): "Clearly, the processes of 'emergent re-orderings of social and structural reality' [with which the study was concerned] in this sheltered workshop can have little effect on the wider social domain." In this particular instance, Gluckman was right. But was he correct in theoretical terms or, more to the point, epistemologically, ontologically?

Epistemologically, he invoked his argument, present throughout *Closed Systems and Open Minds* (Gluckman 1964), that "the analyst has at some point to close off the system of interdependencies he is analyzing and treat other events at the margin of that system as if they are simple, even when he knows them to be complex; but he has to keep his mind open to the possibility that his closure has been effected at the wrong points, and that he has to take into account those complexities" (Gluckman 1974: xvii). More ontologically, in his view my argument for the significance of emergent social order was demolished once 'higher' normative levels of institution were brought to bear. In my view, he had pinched off his analyses "at the wrong points" so as to obviate the ongoing ways in which social practice could generate change in social order, even when more powerful forces demolished, co-opted, or subverted these emergent properties. In today's language, 'resistance' (despite its wasteful, debilitating overuse) is an emergent property of social practice.

For that matter, we might have been able to reach some agreement on the above point. However, at issue, though unstated, was whether the extended-case study would lead into and broach directly the indeterminacy and uncertainty of social life. In Gluckman's view, indeterminacy and uncertainty were fed back into higher-order systems and utilized in their service. In my view, he tended to pile meta-level upon meta-level in an effort to maintain higher-level systemic integration (see Gluckman 1968). Yet indeterminacy and uncertainty are crucial to our inability, ultimately, to know social orders that cannot be other than processual. I have no doubt that the extended case relates directly to this problematic, one already embedded in the dynamics of the forming of encounters. The extended case, emerging into existence through time, intrinsically processual, becomes recognizable as micro historical, as history-in-its-becoming, which we know largely as meaning-in-its-making through time. The extended case encompasses the processuality of temporality from the minute encounter through social institutions, foregrounding the potentiality of more macro organization emerging from micro organization.

## The Processuality of the Extended Case as Prospective Micro History

Earlier I noted that Jayawardena understood Gluckman's concept of social situation as a historical precipitate. Yet anyone who does situational analysis should recognize that history continues to precipitate, so that field research is in no small way the ongoing awaiting of whatever social situations are becoming, since they are in processes of becoming. Situational analysis is not so much time-bound as it is time-dynamic. This was recognized with utmost clarity, even if underplayed, once situational analysis turned into the extended-case method. The immediate scale of these dynamics is often that of the micro, and this places no small part of the analytical onus once more on interaction and social practice. Of equal significance, the perspective of the researcher becomes *prospective*, and a prospective perspective is inevitably one of emergence and change. The extended case is developed through the time-dynamic of present becoming future, and so the case becomes micro history.[17]

There is no principled epistemological distinction between an anthropology grounded in the study of social practice and an anthropology that does micro history. The practice of encounters in real or near-real time necessarily glides, slips, or trips into micro history, while micro history emerges prospectively from the temporal practices of social life. Doing extended-case analysis is doing micro history, though not in the direction usually posited by anthropologists or historians, since the emphasis is squarely on the emergent properties of social ordering (see Jayawardena 1987: 41).

The extended-case study opened time/space (descriptively and analytically) to the practice of process and denoted the foregrounding of practice as intrinsically dynamic. The extended-case study tells us that so long as the anthropologist does not perceive social life as the reductionist instantiation of norms and values, nor as the reductionism of methodological individualism, nor as the dialectical outcome of interplay between the ideal and the real, then social life needs to be understood as processual in its prospective accomplishments of making something of the random and the predictable, and of everything in between. The prospective perspective of the extended case pays close attention to how social life is practiced into existence. The problematic of emergence is that of the creating and re-creating of social life through practice, and of how this is done in the domains in which we live most of our lives, intensely, significantly. The practices of everyday living are complex, delicately nuanced, deeply textured, just as, so often, the powers of the macro—of great force, domination, and control by institutions—brutally and directly flatten micro existences. In itself, this is an excellent reason to pay close attention to the ongoing, emergent creation of social life.

In Manchester anthropology, the extended-case study followed particular human beings through their uncertain daily lives, as these lives came into being, prospectively. I surmise that the anthropologists who followed such pathways were often surprised by the emergent character of micro-social living, even when they organized emerging phenomena into vehicles for discussing cyclical processes, for example, as did Turner (1957) with the idea of "social drama." I emphasize once more that emergence is intrinsic to interaction through time, as is how the emergent effects its own emergence and so, too, the conditions that enabled it to come into existence (Mihata 1997: 32, following G. H. Mead; see also Chang 2004). Only a prospective perspective that joins anthropological thinking (like that of the extended case) to micro history can hope to detail how this is occurring. No other analytical perspective developed through anthropology has been as sensitive in tracing the processual, indeterminate character of living as has that of the social situation and extended case. This has significant implications for a micro-historical anthropology.

As noted, to study process through a series of observable events emerging into phenomenal existence is to do a form of micro history, though one usually not recognized as such. Instead of going back in time (regardless of the length of the duration), one goes forward, following the emergence and development—unfolding, reproductive, haphazard, chaotic—of social practices in the present as these become futures. But prospective history is no less history than is retrospective history, since time present unceasingly is becoming time past. And prospective history is undoubtedly micro historical, since even acts that may turn out to have momentous consequences in yet unknown futures are coming into existence in some micro domain or in a network of domains.

The most likely, quite prosaic reason that prospective history is not recognized as such is that history is defined by historians. Collingwood, following Dilthey, argued that the historian could not represent historical events as if they had presentness, given their remoteness in time, which resulted in both the historian's inability to observe and his or her need to infer. Thus, Collingwood (1957: 54) declared: "The historian's business is to know the past, not to know the future." Is it not likely that today most historians would concur with this statement? Yet as Jayawardena (1987: 43) points out, the study of social situations "can also reveal potentialities that, though now submerged, could become dominant." Indeed, many anthropologists do prospective history, especially prospective micro history, without recognizing it as such. The field anthropologist who interacts with the same people through time necessarily does a prospective micro history of social practice, as present becomes past, moving into future (see, for example, Handelman and Leyton 1978). There is no contradiction between studying the emergence of social life during interaction (occurring necessarily through time), the emergence of social life in more complex situations (requiring studying a variety of different, related, overlapping encounters), and the emergence of social order through an extended case (occurring only through time). In comparison with the historian, the 'time of experience' of the ethnographer, the period during which the ethnographer experiences events, is highly resonant with the 'time of knowledge', the period during which he or she analyzes these field materials (see Motzkin 1992 on the historian).[18] But when the ethnographer does traditional, retrospective micro history, social practice recedes from view, experience becoming more minimal, while knowledge increases proportionately (see Kracauer 1969: 104–138).

Throughout this discussion I have avoided referring to encounter, social situation, and extended case, as *levels* in relation to one other, or in relation to more macro structures. Instead, I have referred to them as *domains* of social organization. If one refers to levels, the logic of organization between levels is necessarily hierarchic, with the higher-order macro levels encompassing, or at least subsuming, lower levels.[19] Lower levels, then, derive from higher ones; in Gluckman's terms, the lower level incapsulates the higher. Higher, normative order generally rules throughout levels, and if there is emergence, it may well be thought of as resistance to more encompassing, dominant levels. This is more or less where Gluckman began his thinking on the analysis of the social situation. I am not claiming that such ordering does not exist. But so does that which Goffman (1983) referred to as the interaction order with its "loose coupling"—or "partial connections" (Strathern 1992)—to other orders and the encounter with its emergent organizing properties. The differences between domains are those of scale, ranges of power, and organizational capacity to structure other domains, among other qualities. In any event, no macro domain can account fully for emergent phenomena in interaction, in interpersonal behavior, or in patterns of connectivity among persons in concert.

Emergence is a much more extensive and intensive matter than is resistance to domination (cf. Scott 1990). Emergent phenomena index the creation of variation and variability in practices of living, a dynamic never ceasing, though the great bulk of emergent variation does not enter social life (Handelman 1977). Therefore, understanding emergence from within a domain (contra Schwimmer 1990) is crucial to comprehending numerous micro-social changes. This especially is why the relatedness of the extended case to encounters and to micro history should be theorized. Perhaps this is where Gluckman did not initially grasp the potentialities of explanation in the extended-case approach. The extended case, in its capacities to move through permutations of the living of human life among and between human beings, is no more limited than is social life itself.

## Prospective Time and Duration

From the prospective perspective, time is less seamless and more episodic, opening up the study of encounters and social situations to different senses of causality while reinforcing the necessity of discovering how to move among modalities of time continuous and time abrupt.[20] Recently, political scientist William Reno (1998: 45) has likened change that occurs with rupturing speed, spreading like chain reactions or brush fires within Africa's weakest states, to the concept of "punctuated equilibrium" of the natural scientist, Steven Jay Gould (Gould 2002: 765–784; Gould and Eldridge 1993). In macro-evolutionary theory, punctuated equilibrium indexes periods of relatively abrupt, sudden, sweeping changes in the fossil record that 'punctuate' periods of lengthy stasis, periods of equilibration during which species successfully maintain themselves without major evolutionary shifts (thereby putting to the question Darwin's theory of gradual, continuous, evolutionary change). Gould's idea is enticing as an analogy for thinking about social change. When mutually reinforcing systems lose their equilibria, change, often highly destructive of social order, spirals with speedier tempos—intensively, ferociously. Not only is the continuousness of time shattered, but also time speeds up, rushing headlong toward its denouements.

Though I have argued that the prospective perspective of encounters and of the extended case is oriented toward the ongoing, continuous emergence of social life through its practice, there is no denying the speedy appearance of temporal ruptures and radical changes in the micro and the macro. Nonetheless, an idea such as punctuated equilibrium invokes lengthy periods of relative reproduction rather than change. Is it necessary to reconcile my emphasis on the ongoing emergence of ordering through social practice with its speedy rupture after long periods (in micro terms, in macro terms) of relative stasis? My feeling is that these dimensions exist side by side, each constituted by different configurings of existence. To integrate these dimensions within a single scheme of temporality would be to damage the power of each to organize and reorganize social life.

Despite my theoretical disagreements with Gluckman, I perforce return to a concept of his that enables living more gently with the conundrum of continuous and punctuated temporalities—his idea of the 'structural duration'.

Gluckman (1968: 221) argued that different institutions or organizations have different structural durations: "The 'structural duration' of an institution is that period of time required to work out the implications of its rules and customs within the biological, ecological, and social environment. This period of time, the duration, is contained within the structure of an institution, and it is only in terms of expositing the institution through that duration that we can work out the interdependence, the systematic structure, between the elements that comprise the institution." Gluckman was not referring to historical time but to time that enables an institution to go through many of its regular alterations or changes that make it as it is, that can only be witnessed through time, and that constitute the cultural and social fullness of that institution.[21] Structural duration indexes the institution through the temporal organization of its own interior processes. This enables us to comprehend how institutions are constituted through their own temporalities—their own tempos, rhythms, disturbances, equilibrations. This thinking is somewhat analogous to Gould and Eldridge's conception of periods of stasis in macro evolution, periods that of course are highly dynamic with life, but non-evolving. This is no less so for Gluckman's dynamic conception of equilibrium through the structural durations that comprise much social organization.

In my terms, structural duration is not limited to macro scales, but is entirely evident as well on micro scales. The emergence of encounters demonstrates that certain of their formations are strongly durational in more structural terms—for example, encounters that are ritual, ritual-like, ritualistic—while other formations are much more open-ended, though if they become integral to social relationships, then they too acquire more ritual-like properties. The idea of structural duration enables distinguishing how, during periods of relative stasis in micro domains, the forms of encounter, even as they emerge, are tending to reproduce micro orders (though little changes continue to accrete). During periods of punctuation, structural durations are destroyed and great changes ensue, as they do in the macro domains of institutions. The power of the extended case is focused in its capacity to relate to, yet to distinguish among, different temporalities of the organizing propensities and dissolutions of social life. The extended case has the capacities to distinguish among emergence, structural duration, stasis, punctuation, showing how these dynamics are especially in play, in process, during particular, prospectively historical time spans.

As noted, I have avoided identifying scale and complexity of social phenomena with hierarchy, with levels, with the elementary (indeed, commonsensical) idea in so much social-science thinking that macro encompasses micro and thus that micro derives from macro. The positing of levels as encompassing and encompassed makes the possibility of micro influencing macro virtually impossible. As Kracauer (1969: 126) commented, micro events arrive at macro altitudes in a "damaged state." Yet the extended-case study remains one of the few ways of studying how domains of social order, each with its own integrity, its own periodicities of structural duration, its own periods of stasis and the eruption of punctuation, join and part as the intersection of radical differences in social organization. Gluckman understood but did not accept this. Very much to this point, Kracauer (1969: 130) noted: "The belief that the widening of the range of *intelligibility* involves an increase of *significance* is one of the basic tenets of Western thought. Throughout the history of philosophy it has been held that the highest principle, the highest abstractions, not only define all the principles they formally encompass but also contain the essences of all that exists in the lower depths. They are imagined as the 'highest things' in terms of both generality and substance" (italics in original). The history of field-research anthropology in the twentieth and now the twenty-first century may be understood as an unresolved struggle with this premise. Yet the extended case has the capacity to highlight this struggle in its manifold complexity, challenging anthropologists to recognize just how emergence and reproduction, radical difference and radical sameness, are generated continuously in social orders—how social orders forming *out* of themselves collapse *into* themselves, so often with quite certain yet quite unpredictable outcomes.

## Acknowledgments

I wrote this essay while a Research Fellow at the Max Planck Institute for the History of Science, in Berlin, during the autumn of 2004. Telephone conversations with Bruce Kapferer helped me see past some of my own conceptual blockage. Bruce told me of William Reno's work. My thanks to Terry Evens for his comments. Another version of this essay focuses on varieties of micro history that I have called retrospective, atemporal, and prospective (Handelman 2005b).

Don Handelman is Sarah Allen Shaine Professor Emeritus of Anthropology and Sociology at the Hebrew University of Jerusalem and a member of the Israel Academy of Sciences and Humanities. He has been a Fellow of the Netherlands Institute for Advanced Study, the Swedish Collegium for Advanced Study in the Social Sciences, Collegium Budapest, the Institute for Advanced Studies at The Hebrew University, the Max Planck Institute for the History of Science, and the Olof Palme Visiting Professor of the Swedish Social Science Research Council. He is the author of *Models and Mirrors: Towards an Anthropology of Public Events* (1998) and *Nationalism and the Israeli State: Bureaucratic Logic in Public Events* (2004); the co-author, with David Shulman, of *God Inside Out: Siva's Game of Dice* (1997) and *Siva in the Forest of Pines: An Essay on Sorcery and Self-Knowledge* (2004); and the co-editor, with Galina Lindquist, of *Ritual in its Own Right: Exploring the Dynamics of Transformation* (2005).

## Notes

1. Gluckman and his colleagues took what we call 'practice' as integral to the generating of social living, rather than theorizing its existence in the manner of Bourdieu (1977) or, to a lesser extent, de Certeau (1984). The Manchester School did not use the language of practice. Nonetheless, as Kapferer (1987) points out, there are strong affinities between Gluckman's approach through situational analysis and that of Bourdieu.

2. The idea of abduction (dated to the 1860s; see Brent 1998: 3) was one of Charles Sanders Peirce's great contributions to a comprehension of how knowledge is created. Peirce understood abduction as a third form of inference, distinct from induction and deduction. Abduction can be equated to guessing (in the instance of anthropology, perhaps 'educated guessing' is appropriate). By contrast, as Brent (ibid.: 349) comments: "Deduction reiterates what we know, and induction tests or generalizes knowledge that we already have." Guesses, tentative conclusions, "are the only form of inference that originates knowledge" (ibid.). As Eco and Sebeok (1983: vii) maintain: "Abduction makes its start from the facts, without, at the outset, having any particular theory in view, though it is motivated by the feeling that a theory is needed to explain the surprising facts … Abduction seeks a theory. Induction [by contrast] seeks for facts." Muir (1991: xix) points out: "Peirce argued that a method should not be chosen for its security or its guarantee of certain answers but for its potential for fruitfulness … there is an inverse relationship between fruitfulness and security … Abduction … is the most fruitful and least certain method."

3. On Gluckman's critique of segregation through the analysis of the social situation, see especially Cocks (2001).

4. The sociologist Michael Burawoy has taken the extended case in a direction distinct from that of the Manchester group. The Manchester approach often began with what may be called 'found' events or materials—a ritual, a situation, a particular informant—and went on from there, usually as an abductive voyage of discovery. Burawoy begins as a theoretician bent on making certain connections between domains of inquiry. He does not follow his nose, knowing full well where he is going and why. He asserts: "Fieldwork is a sequence of experiments that continue until one's theory is in sync with the world one studies" (Burawoy 1998: 17–18; see also Burawoy et al. 1991).

5. I would think that the extended-case analysis also encouraged the development in Central African anthropology, at Manchester and elsewhere, of open-ended social network approaches to the study of social fields, though to my knowledge this relationship has yet to be documented (see Mitchell 1974: 281). The development of network studies was the Manchester way of theorizing social interaction. Network studies gave close attention to the character of network links among persons, in other words, to emerging and extant social relationships. In studying these aspects of the practice of social life, the Manchester anthropologists thereby skipped straight to the analysis of social relationships, without spending much time thinking on the doing of interaction as such or on its emergent properties.

6. The classic formulation in anthropology of the emergence of form is that of Gregory Bateson's (1972) conception of schismogenesis (first published in 1935), one of the few attempts in the social sciences to think through a logic of emergence that creates difference. Schismogenesis can be understood as the generating of difference from within interaction. Both sorts of schismogenesis discussed by Bateson (symmetrical, complementary) generate different kinds of meta-communication that in turn shapes interactions-to-come. The same can be argued more generally for the emergence of encounters, of series of encounters, and for the ways in which the analyst shapes the extended case.

7. Goffman's view of ritual was primarily Durkheimian and accorded well with that of Gluckman (see Gluckman 1962; see also Collins 1988 on Goffman's interaction ritual).

8. The idea of emergence is present more implicitly in the kinds of conversational analyses that developed out of early ethnomethods in the work of Harvey Sacks, Emanuel

Shegloff, Gail Jefferson, and others, as well as Peter McHugh's (1968) study of defining the situation. Yet their close analyses of utterances in verbal interaction is not only a sociology of native accounts and accounting practices but one that is strictly account-able to analytical—indeed, scientific—precision, utterance by utterance, and therefore often additive in its understanding of how people put together their situational rules of making sense, making order. Sadly, recent theoretical discussions of case analysis (with the exception of Burawoy; see note 4) make virtually no mention of the Manchester extended case (see Ragin and Becker 1992).

9. There are, of course, institutional venues—bureaucratic, administrative, legal, edu-cational—specializing precisely in procedures of rupture and reductionism (see Handelman 2004).

10. See Evens (1977) for a pertinent critique of methodological individualism, especially in the work of Fredrik Barth. Interestingly, Barth's variety of methodological individualism is being adopted now by some of the Italian micro historians, such as Giovanni Levi. In these works, Barth's (1966) idea of generative models of social interaction is applied to historical situations of competition and conflict (see Gregory 1999: 103). Generally, there is a powerful resurgence of the economistic theorizing of interaction. For a per-spective from psychology, see Colman (2003). Goffman himself was highly ambivalent to methodological individualism. His thinking was trapped between perceiving the indi-vidual as shaped by normative order and by the agency of the individual's interactional strategies and tactics that nonetheless reproduced this order. I believe this left little space for theorizing the structuring capacities of social units such as the encounter or the focused gathering.

11. Here I am thinking of 'fold' in somewhat of the way that Deleuze (1992) uses the idea in his discussion of Leibniz and the baroque.

12. For thoughts on how the idea of fold may be applied to the study of ritual, see Handel-man (2005a).

13. Extended-case analysis may also be done retrospectively (see Handelman 1976).

14. To my knowledge, Goffman had little to say on how encounters create time.

15. This argument is equally applicable to encounters in cyberspace.

16. As long as Max was alive (he died on 13 April 1975), I felt duty bound to include his foreword in the book. After his death, I decided not to include it. He had used the fore-word to critique another senior (not British) anthropologist, and though I thought he was wrong to do so, I would not edit his text to omit this small portion. A carbon copy of Max's typescript is in my possession. For a rosier view of Max's forewords to books by those who had participated in the Bernstein Israeli research scheme (as both Terry Evens and I had), see Moshe Shokeid (2004). Shokeid's perception of the entire project is quite different from mine.

17. See, too, Staley (2002) on the history of the future, treating scenarios of the future as the analysis of history. Nonetheless, this is distant from analyzing social practice as micro history in the making.

18. This distinction between the time of experience and the time of knowledge is Motzkin's.

19. This use of encompassment does not address directly Louis Dumont's (1970) argument for the hierarchical nature of the idea, which depends on a Hegelian-like dialectical syn-thesis of micro and macro orders. Were I to address this issue here, I would emphasize that my argument is more systemic than dialectical. David Shulman and I (Handelman and Shulman 2004) have argued for a Hindu cosmos that is held together interiorly, from within itself, rather than by Dumontian encompassment, which requires order to be held together from outside itself, from its exterior, in keeping with a Hegelian-like synthesis that holds together by being exterior to thesis and antithesis. My thanks to Terry Evens for raising this issue.

20. Somewhat analogous thinking has also entered the analysis of formal organizations (see Weick and Quinn 1999).

21. On this problematic, understood through the history of the human-made, see Kubler (1962).

# References

Assad, Maria L. 1999. *Reading with Michel Serres: An Encounter with Time*. Allbany: SUNY University Press.

Barth, Fredrik. 1966. *Models of Social Organization*. London: Royal Anthropological Institute of Great Britain and Ireland, Occasional Paper No. 23.

Bateson, Gregory. 1972. "Culture Contact and Schismogenesis." Pp. 61–72 in *Steps to an Ecology of Mind*. New York: Ballantine.

Borges, Jorge Luis. 1998. "The Garden of Forking Paths." Pp. 119–128 in *Collected Fictions*. London: Allen Lane.

Bourdieu, Pierre. 1977. *Outline of a Theory of Practice*. Cambridge: Cambridge University Press.

Brent, Joseph. 1998. *Charles Sanders Peirce: A Life*. Bloomington: Indiana University Press.

Burawoy, Michael. 1998. "The Extended Case Method." *Sociological Theory* 16, no. 1: 4–33.

Burawoy, Michael, et al. 1991. *Ethnography Unbound: Power and Resistance in the Modern Metropolis*. Berkeley: University of California Press.

Chang, Johannes Han-Yin. 2004. "Mead's Theory of Emergence as a Framework for Multi-level Sociological Inquiry." *Symbolic Interaction* 27, no. 3: 405–427.

Cocks, Paul. 2001. "Max Gluckman and the Critique of Segregation in South African Anthropology, 1921–1940." *Journal of Southern African Studies* 27, no. 4: 739–756.

Collingwood, R. G. 1957. *The Idea of History*. New York: Oxford University Press.

Collins, Randall. 1987. "Interaction Property Chains, Power, and Property: The Micro-Macro Connection as an Empirically Based Theoretical Problem." Pp. 193–206 in *The Micro-Macro Link*, ed. J. C. Alexander et al. Berkeley: University of California Press.

_____. 1988. "Theoretical Continuities in Goffman's Work." Pp. 41–63 in Drew and Wooten 1988.

_____. 2000. *The Sociology of Philosophies: A Global Theory of Intellectual Change*. Cambridge, MA: Harvard University Press.

_____. 2004. *Interaction Ritual Chains*. Princeton, NJ: Princeton University Press.

Colman, Andrew M. 2003. "Cooperation, Psychological Game Theory, and the Limitations of Rationality in Social Interaction." *Behavioral and Brain Sciences* 26, no. 2: 139–153.

De Certeau, Michel. 1984. *The Practice of Everyday Life*. Berkeley: University of California Press.

Deleuze, Gilles. 1992. *The Fold: Leibniz and the Baroque*. London: Athlone Press.

_____. 1994. *Difference and Repetition*. London: Athlone Press.

Devons, Ely, and Max Gluckman. 1964. "Conclusion: Modes and Consequences of Limiting a Field of Study." Pp. 158–261 in Gluckman 1964.

Drew, Paul, and Anthony Wooten, eds. 1988. *Erving Goffman: Exploring the Interaction Order*. Boston: Northeastern University Press.

Dumont, Louis. 1970. *Homo Hierarchicus*. London: Paladin.

Eco, Umberto, and Thomas Sebeok, eds. 1983. *The Sign of Three: Dupin, Holmes, Peirce*. Bloomington: Indiana University Press.

Epstein, A. L., ed. 1967. *The Craft of Social Anthropology*. London: Social Science Paperbacks in association with Tavistock Publications.

Evens, T. M. S. 1977. "The Predication of the Individual in Anthropological Interactionism." *American Anthropologist* 79, no. 3: 579–597.

Game, Ann. 1997. "Time Unhinged." *Time and Society* 6, no. 2/3: 115–129.

Garbett, G. Kingsley. 1970. "The Analysis of Social Situations." *Man* (n.s.) 5, no. 2: 214–227.

Giddens, Anthony. 1988. "Goffman as a Systematic Theorist.' Pp. 250–279 in Drew and Wooten 1988.

Gluckman, Max. 1958. *Analysis of a Social Situation in Modern Zululand*. Manchester: Manchester University Press.

_____. 1961. "Ethnographic Data in British Social Anthropology." *Sociological Review* 9, no. 1: 5–17.

_____, ed. 1962. *The Ritual of Social Relations*. Manchester: Manchester University Press.

_____. 1963. *Order and Rebellion in Tribal Africa.* New York: Free Press of Glencoe. (The chapter titled "Rituals of Rebellion in South-East Africa" was originally the Frazer Lecture of 1952.)

_____, ed. 1964. *Closed Systems and Open Minds: The Limits of Naïvety in Social Anthropology.* Chicago: Aldine.

_____. 1967. "Introduction." Pp. xi–xx in Epstein 1967.

_____. 1968. "The Utility of the Equilibrium Model in the Study of Social Change." *American Anthropologist* 70, no. 2: 219–237.

_____. 1974. "Foreword." Unpublished typescript to Handelman 1977.

Goffman, Erving. 1961. *Encounters.* Indianapolis: Bobbs-Merrill.

_____. 1974. *Frame Analysis.* New York: Harper and Row.

_____. 1983. "The Interaction Order." *American Sociological Review* 48: 1–17.

Gould, Stephen Jay. 2002. *The Structure of Evolutionary Theory.* Cambridge, MA: Harvard University Press.

Gould, Stephen Jay, and Niles Eldridge. 1993. "Punctuated Equilibrium comes of age." *Nature* 366 (18 November): 223–227.

Gregory, Brad S. 1999. "Is Small Beautiful? Microhistory and the History of Everyday Life." *History and Theory* 38, no. 1: 100–110.

Handelman, Don. 1973. "Gossip in Encounters: The Transmission of Information in a Bounded Social Setting." *Man* (n.s.) 8: 210–227.

_____. 1976. "Bureaucratic Transactions: The Development of Official-Client Relationships in Israel." Pp. 223–275 in *Transaction and Meaning: Directions in the Anthropology of Exchange and Symbolic Behavior,* ASA Essays in Social Anthropology, vol. 1, ed. Bruce Kapferer. Philadelphia: ISHI.

_____. 1977. *Work and Play Among the Aged: Interaction, Replication and Emergence in a Jerusalem Setting.* Assen: Van Gorcum.

_____. 1987. "Micro-structure and Micro-process: Interaction and the Development of Infrastructure in Two Israeli Work Settings." Pp. 75–101 in *Power, Process and Transformation: Essays in Memory of Max Gluckman,* ed. Bruce Kapferer. Special issue of *Social Analysis,* no. 22.

_____. 2004. *Nationalism and the Israeli State: Bureaucratic Logic in Public Events.* Oxford: Berg.

_____. 2005a. "Introduction: Why Ritual in Its Own Right? How So?" Pp. 1–32 in *Ritual in Its Own Right: Exploring the Dynamics of Transformation,* ed. Don Handelman and Galina Lindquist. Special issue of *Social Analysis* 48, no. 2.

_____. 2005b. "Microhistorical Anthropology: Toward a Prospective Perspective." Pp. 29–52 in *Critical Junctions: Anthropology and History beyond the Cultural Turn,* ed. Don Kalb and Herman Tak. New York: Berghahn Books.

Handelman, Don, and Elliott Leyton. 1978. *Bureaucracy and World View: Studies in the Logic of Official Interpretation.* Newfoundland Social and Economic Studies No. 22. St. John's: Memorial University of Newfoundland.

Handelman, Don, and David Shulman. 2004. *Siva in the Forest of Pines: An Essay on Sorcery and Self-Knowledge.* Delhi: Oxford University Press.

Jayawardena, Chandra. 1987. "Analysis of a Social Situation in Acheh Besar: An Exploration in Micro-history." *Social Analysis* 22: 30–46.

Kapferer, Bruce. 1972. *Strategy and Transaction in an African Factory.* Manchester: Manchester University Press.

_____. 1987. "The Anthropology of Max Gluckman." *Social Analysis* 22: 3–21.

_____. 1997. *The Feast of the Sorcerer.* Chicago: University of Chicago Press.

Kracauer, Siegfried. 1969. *History: The Last Things Before the Last.* New York: Oxford University Press.

Kubler, George. 1962. *The Shape of Time: Remarks on the History of Things.* New Haven, CT: Yale University Press.

Kwinter, Sanford. 2002. *Architectures of Time: Toward a Theory of the Event in Modernist Culture.* Cambridge, MA: MIT Press.

McHugh, Peter. 1968. *Defining the Situation: The Organization of Meaning in Social Interaction.* Indianapolis, IN: Bobbs-Merrill.

Mihata, Kevin. 1997. "The Persistence of 'Emergence.'" Pp. 30–38 in *Chaos, Complexity, and Sociology: Myths, Models, and Theories,* ed. Raymond A. Eve, S. Horsfall, and M. E. Lee. Thousand Oaks, CA: Sage.

Mitchell, J. Clyde. 1959. *The Kalela Dance.* Manchester: Manchester University Press.

_____. 1974. "Social Networks." *Annual Review of Anthropology* 3: 279–299.

_____. 1983. "Case and Situational Analysis." *Sociological Review* 31, no. 2: 187–211.

Motzkin, Gabriel. 1992. *Time and Transcendence: Secular History, the Catholic Reaction, and the Rediscovery of the Future.* Dordrecht: Kluwer Academic Publishers.

Muir, Edward. 1991. "Introduction: Observing Trifles." Pp. vii–xxiii in *Microhistory and the Lost People of Europe,* ed. Edward Muir and Guido Ruggiero. Baltimore: Johns Hopkins University Press.

Ragin, Charles, and Howard S. Becker, eds. 1992. *What is a Case? Exploring the Foundations of Social Inquiry.* Cambridge: Cambridge University Press.

Reno, William. 1998. *Warlord Politics and African States.* Boulder, CO: Lynne Rienner Publishers.

Schwimmer, Eric. 1990. "The Anthropology of the Interaction Order." Pp. 41–63 in *Beyond Goffman: Studies on Communication, Institution, and Social Interaction,* ed. Stephen Harold Riggins. Berlin: Mouton de Gruyter.

Scott, James C. 1990. *Weapons of the Weak.* New Haven, CT: Yale University Press.

Sharrock, Wes. 1999. "The Omnipotence of the Actor: Erving Goffman on 'the Definition of the Situation.'" Pp. 119–137 in *Goffman and Social Organization: Studies in a Sociological Legacy,* ed. Greg Smith. London: Routledge.

Shokeid, Moshe. 2004. "Max Gluckman and the Making of Israeli Anthropology." *Ethnos* 69, no. 3: 387–410.

Staley, David J. 2002. "A History of the Future." *History and Theory* 41: 72–89.

Strathern, Marilyn. 1992. *Partial Connections.* London: Rowman and Littlefield.

Strong, P. M. 1988. "Minor Courtesies and Macro Structures." Pp. 228–249 in Drew and Wooten 1988.

Turner, Victor W. 1957. *Schism and Continuity in an African Society.* Manchester: University of Manchester Press.

Van Velsen, Jaap. 1967. "The Extended-Case Method and Situational Analysis." Pp. 129–149 in Epstein 1967.

Weber, Max. 1964. *The Theory of Social and Economic Organization.* New York: Free Press.

Weick Karl E., and Robert E. Quinn. 1999. "Organizational Change and Development." *Annual Review of Psychology* 50: 361–386.

*Chapter 4*

# SITUATIONS, CRISIS, AND THE ANTHROPOLOGY OF THE CONCRETE*
## The Contribution of Max Gluckman

*Bruce Kapferer*

The contemporary ethnographically focused, fieldworking, university discipline of anthropology was established during a time of crisis, at a major turning point in world history. Anthropology's founders—those who identified many of its initial defining methodologies, its vital questions, its conceptual and theoretical foci—made their innovations at intense periods of change in the years between and following the world wars of the twentieth century. The diverse and often hot and turbulent forces that were present in those times were especially powerful in anthropology. Many anthropologists refused to acknowledge

*This is a revised version of the first Max Gluckman Memorial Lecture, presented at the University of Manchester on 17 May 1997.

Notes for this chapter begin on page 147.

these forces openly but rather presented themselves as voyagers into the cold periphery, far from a dynamic and uncertain world. This kind of conceit has been increasingly and rudely challenged over recent years by anthropologists and other scholars. They do so at a time of new crisis and change.

At the start of the new millennium, global realities have shifted much of their direction compared with Gluckman's time. Then, European imperial and colonial expansion had passed its peak and was in rapid decline. The sovereign nation-state was in almost universal ascendance. Both colonialist and what can be called statist ideologies were ingrained in the anthropology that took root in Britain and elsewhere. However, the circumstances that saw the rise of such an anthropology have now significantly altered. The post-colonial nation-state has seen a decline in its power, with its sovereignty, borders, and territory not only being redrawn or transgressed but also giving way to social and political formations and processes that cannot be easily conceived in the neatly bounded ways often associated with state orders. Currently, the dominant catchword is globalization, and accordingly much anthropology has developed appropriate concepts and concerns as new crises develop involving the expansion of capital into new domains, the development of innovative forms of labor extraction, the formation of new patterns of ethnic strife and political violence, among others. The questions that Gluckman raised before recent trends became clearly established have achieved even sharper relevance. Many of the opinions he held—among them the importance of abandoning such totalizing and homogenizing concepts as society and culture—have become commonplace.

The anthropology of Gluckman and of those he grouped around him (at the Rhodes-Livingstone Institute in Zambia, at Manchester, and later in Israel) concentrated on the themes of crisis and change.[1] These themes occupied center stage in their work at a time in the history of anthropology when such topics were more an afterthought than the major focus of interest. Gluckman's Manchester group of anthropologists explored issues that were considered by other prominent anthropologists to be marginal to anthropology, if indeed they were regarded as being anthropology at all.[2] Thus, the group worked on urban and industrial processes, ethnicity, labor migration, village societies in the circumstances of monetization and global capital expansion, the invention of and contradictions in power and authority under the conditions of colonial rule, the dilemmas of modernization, local politics as the fulcrum of changes and transformations in the societies of dominant centers as well as those at the colonial or post-colonial periphery, immigrant and settler communities and their inventions and reconstructions of tradition, and many others. Indeed, it was Gluckman and his associates who largely pioneered issues and themes that in many quarters these days are conceived to be vital to a reconstruction of anthropology as, through and through, the study of modernity. In this effort they attacked some of the central conceptual and theoretical schemes of British anthropology, overhauling them or at least attempting to adapt them to their new concerns, all the while searching for new constructs that would enable anthropology to engage authoritatively with a contemporary world.

Of prime concern for Gluckman and his colleagues was the question that if human social existence is one of constant change (Gluckman's guiding claim), of continual flux, how can it be explored so that social reality can reveal the forces and processes of its formation? This is the problematic that set the signature methodology of situational and extended-case analysis of Gluckman and his Manchester group. The situational idea, the hallmark of the approach of Gluckman's so-called Manchester School, embodies the central orientation of his, at the time, relatively distinct direction in anthropology. It at once marks out the domains of the complexity and flux of social life and becomes the means for entering within them so that they reveal the forces that are engaged in the generation and production of such complexity and flux. My discussion will address this contribution of Gluckman and some of its possibilities.

Gluckman's ideas clearly were shaped by the social and political circumstances of his native South Africa and the community of intellectuals, many of them Jewish, who were radically critical of the colonial realities of Southern Africa and its deep-seated racist policies. His writings on Southern Africa and the research schemes that he established as director of the Rhodes-Livingstone Institute (RLI) in Zambia (then Northern Rhodesia) were influenced by the strongly socialist views of many of his peers. He was, of course, already highly conscious of the role of Manchester in the development of socialist ideas and working-class history when he moved from a temporary lectureship at Oxford in 1949 to take the chair of the Social Anthropology Department at Manchester University. The location of the department in the premises of an old girls' school that had once been the site of a factory owned by Friedrich Engels's father was a source of considerable pride. Many of those who gathered around Gluckman at Manchester in the early years, some of whom also pursued their research in Central Africa (where the RLI operated as a vital field station), were left-oriented, a few of them being members of the Communist Party, which Gluckman himself never joined. However, Gluckman's anti-colonial opinions and radical sentiments resulted in his being denied entry to Northern Rhodesia for some 17 years until Zambian Independence in 1964, when I first met him.[3] I recall the considerable excitement with which he was greeted by many Lozi who then occupied senior posts in the newly won government. His African reputation was to precede him to Australia, where in 1960 the government barred his entry into its colonial territory of Papua New Guinea.

While Gluckman's background and socialist leanings were highly important for his methodological commitments, the distinction of his situational approach had many antecedents. It was a bricolage born of a wide reading and a generous interest in, and acknowledgment of, the work of others. Clearly, the focus of historians on significant events and their elaborations of the periods whose process the events illuminate were a major influence. He acknowledged the enormous importance of Malinowski's fieldwork method and the latter's great eye for detail and his concern to follow through the ramifications of particular practices, avoiding the neat compartmentalization into preordained categories that had been the pattern of earlier anthropologists (see Gluckman's [1961b: 6] contrast of Junod's ethnography with that of Malinowski). He was alive to the importance of Evans-Pritchard's notion of situational selection, which he viewed as critical to an anthropology that should be aware that norms and values vary in diverse situated circumstances and are far from homogeneous. Evans-Pritchard's classic study, *Witchcraft, Oracles and Magic among the Azande* (1937), was of huge methodological influence. Gluckman saw the importance of Evans-Pritchard's contextualization of a key problematic recognized by the people under study and the examination of it in different circumstances of practice. Evans-Pritchard both dissolved the general category of witchcraft (Zande notions could not be reduced to European commonsense opinion) and asserted the importance of ethnographic specificity. However, while Gluckman stressed the importance of ethnographic (and historical) particularity, he did not see this as opposed to the establishment of sociological generalization, as was the tendency of Evans-Pritchard. On the contrary, Gluckman saw generalization or theoretical knowledge as being premised on the particular, discerning in the events of practice the ground of logics of human action that were not limited to specific times and places. Undoubtedly, here Freud's invention of psychoanalysis and his in-depth interrogation of human experience and systematic building up of case/life material were crucial to the development of Gluckman's perspective. Freud demonstrated how the thorough investigation of unique cases of crisis revealed deep underlying themes of motivation. He showed the hidden forces behind events and how their interrelation in the course of a life exposed definite patterns. Through an exploration of the unique and the unusual, Freud maintained that theoretical understanding of potentially universal worth could be produced. These were ideas that were to realize their impact both in situational analysis and later in the development of the extended-case method by Gluckman's colleagues. Marx is overtly important for reasons similar to those of Freud. Marx's concept of contradiction and how its forces engender historical process is major for Gluckman's thought. Durkheim is also key. This is so because Durkheim's stress on the social as a legitimate focus of inquiry in itself reinforced Gluckman's view (following Radcliffe-Brown) that anthropology's distinct scientific contribution lay in the exploration of the logics and structures of social action in which the consciousness of human subjects was constructed. Gluckman never denied the worth of other perspectives, but his emphasis on Durkheim gave him cause to effect a transference of perspectives on the situation and the event of crisis in other areas of knowledge—such as those of Freud for psychology and Marx for political economy—into the then still young and emerging discipline of anthropology.

When Gluckman started at Manchester, British social anthropology was developing in several directions, pushing the dominant paradigm of structural functionalism to its limits. Toward the end of Gluckman's career, some anthropologists in Britain and elsewhere were becoming increasingly critical not only of anthropology's colonial complicity but of the concepts and theories that appeared to be strongly associated with it. Gluckman (1968) expressed a reaction to some of these developments in his Plenary Address at the American Anthropological Association in 1966. I recall the time when he presented a preliminary version of this essay at the Manchester seminar. The closing statements (present in the published version) given at the seminar were directed at his young staff, who were trying to establish different routes both against and within his tradition. As usual, in that seminar great humor was mixed with intellectual serious-ness, and Gluckman delighted with his own outrageous bombast (the Zulu king bailed up in his own kraal?).[4] He failed to conjure the same general mood when he attempted a repeat performance in the very different academic context of the American Anthropological Association meetings. Here he cut a conservative figure for several reasons, some of them political. It was an error of judgment that was nonetheless a mark of his intellectual commitment, one of his most appealing qualities. The time was the beginning of the Vietnam War, and some intellectuals in the US were becoming critical of their nation's imperialist strategy. Gluckman defended structural functionalism, but it was an attempt to demonstrate a complexity and subtlety in his own more materialist position (vis-à-vis Leach).[5] He appeared politically conservative in a context wherein the colonialism of the past appeared to be reasserting itself in Amer-ica's imperialist present. This was a time of dalliance with Marxism in the US and in Britain and France, but in structuralist and occasionally culturist guise.[6] It was also the start of the American-dominated post-modernist movement in anthropology, which was aspiring to assume the radical mantle and was to be effective in reorienting the character of much anthropology.

Gluckman had misread the crisis of the socio-political situation in which he was in. This was in its own way tragically ironic for a scholar who had been at the forefront of an anthropology that was critical of colonialism (in sharp contrast to Leach and Firth, for example, who were far more conservative, both socially and politically). The irony was even stronger given Gluckman's overall methodological orientation, which, as I will describe, is not to be reduced to the study of events, despite their significance in the approach. Gluckman's recommendation of situational analysis is an insistence that anthropology and anthropologists should be aware that the subjects of their inquiry, as well as the anthropologists themselves, are always engaged within the changing forces of history. This is so whether practices appear to express a traditional conti-nuity (a repetitive process) or a time of radical transformation (revolutionary in dynamic, whereby the ongoing processes of social life are overturned and dramatically redefined).

For Gluckman, the term 'situation' refers to a total context of crisis, not just contradictory and conflicting processes but a particular tension or turning, a point of potentiality and of multiple possibility. This conception of the situation as crisis demands an understanding that micro dynamics are always integral within macro forces, and that these larger processes must be attended to if anthropological explanation and understanding are to achieve any kind of ade-quacy. A major point that Gluckman stresses is that it is in crisis—in the situa-tion as crisis and specifically in events that constitute concentrated and intense dimensions of the overall crisis of the situation—that the vital forces and prin-ciples already engaged in social action (or taking form in the event itself) are both revealed and rendered available to anthropological analysis. Perhaps it is paradoxical that some scholars (e.g., Burawoy 2000) are rediscovering a value in Gluckman's perspective at what appears to be a new period of crisis in world history, one of globalization or neo-imperialism. Situational analysis provides one kind of methodological strategy that enables the often small-scale focus of the anthropologist or sociologist to open out to an understanding of larger historical processes that otherwise is at risk of being obscured.

## Gluckman's Situational Analysis

Gluckman's idea of the situation and of situational analysis is complex. This is especially so in his early statements, which I will concentrate upon here: the essays written in the 1940s and collected in *Analysis of a Social Situation in Modern Zululand* ([1940] 1958; hereafter, *A Social Situation*), and the short essay, *An Analysis of the Sociological Theories of Bronislaw Malinowski* (1949; hereafter *Malinowski's Sociological Theories*), which was published around the time he came to Manchester. In *A Social Situation*, what Gluckman means by 'social situation' must be taken at several levels. The idea, not yet formalized, is all the more exciting and pregnant with possibility because of this.

There are three interconnected essays that are brought together in the 1958 Rhodes-Livingstone version of *A Social Situation*. Clyde Mitchell, the then director of the RLI, was keen that they should be published together as he felt that they represented Gluckman's orientation and the spirit of his inspiration as a whole. The three essays follow an analytical progression: the first establishes situational analysis as grounded in the recording and analysis of events of practice (the famous example is of those events surrounding the bridge opening in what is now KwaZulu Natal in South Africa); the second concentrates on the overall dynamics of the larger historical situation in which the events recorded by Gluckman are occasioned and achieve further significance; the third consists of a theoretical abstraction that is intended to allow for generalization beyond the observed and historical particularities of the situation. The key idea is that it should be possible to argue backwards from the abstract theoretical statements to the practices upon which the theories are grounded.

This last concern relates to Gluckman's demand from his colleagues and students to record the events of practice in great detail, even an excess of detail—more than was seemingly required for the analysis presented. Gluckman was aware that ethnographic recording is a highly selective activity, guided by the ethnographer's predispositions and location in the developing course of events. In his essay on the bridge opening, he is careful to declare his own positioning and makes a conscious effort to show how his own status as a member of the dominant white order was a factor in his ethnographic construction (Gluckman [1940] 1958: 10–11). His interest in an excess of detail is intended to compensate for processes of selection and to expose the material to the test of alternative interpretations. In line with this position, Gluckman would encourage, as part of his anthropological training method at Manchester preliminary to fieldwork, the detailed reanalysis of the work of other anthropologists, an insistence that produced some uneasiness among his colleagues elsewhere in the profession.[7]

There is a larger point here. Gluckman considered that the initial test of an interpretation or theory lay with the original material (or restudy) itself. The expansion of the theory, and also its further verification and elaboration, was to be through the examination of comparative ethnographic materials. In his view, comparison should not involve the consideration of examples taken at random or out of context and engaged merely to illustrate preformulated ideas (as in the work of Sir James Frazer, whose approach he would critically address in teaching) that were not thoroughly questioned through the ethnography itself. Rather, comparison should initially develop systematically, attending to variations in practice across a region in which there are broad similarities in historical circumstance, institutions, language, and customs between peoples. Only after this has been done (and a relatively secure basis for ideas established) should the method be extended farther afield, and here the comparative method should be thoroughly alive to contextual and value divergences, testing the extent to which such differences permit the confirmation (or not) of larger generalizations that are built through comparison. This was a major logic behind the Rhodes-Livingstone/Manchester research program in Central Africa that Gluckman attempted to repeat in Israel.[8]

The seminar tradition established at the RLI and continued at Manchester was in many ways a practice of Gluckman's ideas.[9] The spirit of this seminar was one that intentionally challenged the authority of the ethnographer, of the anthropologist. Outsiders who encountered it on the occasion of being invited to present their own materials were often taken aback, some feeling insulted (e.g., Schneider 1995: 127–129). This was especially so if the visitor clung to the precious trappings of academic status, for this was against the egalitarian ethos that Gluckman encouraged.[10] All were equal before the evidence, the validity of interpretations resting in the capacity of the material to withstand counter-interpretations. The reputation of the anthropologist as defined in university hierarchies was not a guarantee of either the worth of the material or the ethnographer's analysis. Gluckman himself experienced his own treasured interpretations of his own ethnography being overturned in the seminar and would acknowledge the worth of the analyses of his peers and juniors. The excitement at the thought of discovery in this seminar and the enthusiasm it generated, especially in the early days, should not be underestimated. However, this exuberance did decline in the later years, the seminar sometimes degenerating into the meaningless point scoring that afflicts many a seminar. At its best, the intellectual rough and tumble of the Manchester seminar could be likened to the kind of situational analysis that Gluckman championed, a crisis of interpretations wherein new insights and understandings were always a possibility.[11]

I will return to some of the above considerations shortly but at this point wish to underline Gluckman's approach to the situation as both a vortex of change or process and a way of conceiving, organizing, and theorizing about it. In many ways, 'process' became the preferred term among the Manchester group because as Gluckman stressed in *A Social Situation*, everything is change—the forms of social and political life are continually in flux. Change is the very condition of human existence. Furthermore, there is no unchanging primordial condition or static beginning or prior point of fixity in relation to which change can be measured. The very idea of culture change was problematic for Gluckman, especially if it represented culture as some kind of bounded and relatively motionless totality. What anthropologists described as cultures, he contended, were simply moments in a differentiating and open process. He argued for the distinction between the often idealized self-perception of a people of their culture and the more messy realities of historically shifting processes of cultural formation and practice that he would refer to as a "hodge-podge" (Gluckman 1961b: 11). He was to prefer the concept of custom to culture. His notion of custom was not unlike Bourdieu's (1977) much later concept of habitus, whose dispositional import is continually shifting.[12] The idea underpins Gluckman's (1955a) perspective on the legal process among the Barotse wherein, through the jurisprudential concept of "the reasonable man," he understands judgments in relation to personal crisis as continually adjusting rule and value. In effect, cultural abstractions come into being through a practice of interpretation in which value is always in process and never static or stable.

In *A Social Situation*, what are described as events (or occasions, such as the bridge opening) and situations, or situations as events, or events as situations are effectively moments of social life in the very process of formation. There is some lack of clarity in the use of terms, with 'situation', for example, referring both to a larger social and political complexity in which different kinds of events occur as well as to the events themselves and the particular structural process manifest in them.

But the most important feature of Gluckman's approach is that the event or situation is in an active rather than passive relation to the production of ethnographic understanding and the construction of theory. It is not intended as an illustration of larger processes and therefore passively representing what is already known; rather, it is a particular point of entry that opens toward a knowing that is not already apparent. Thus, the event or situation, as the raw material in Gluckman's sense, calls forth or demands its understanding. It constitutes the problematic to be investigated. It might be said to generate material for its own comprehension. It becomes the site from which to enter into wider realities and draws their complexity into particular focus, thus yielding interpretational possibility. The event or situation begins the process of analytical revelation.

The events of the bridge opening pose the questions, and in pursuing their answer, Gluckman opens out to the complexity of Zululand and beyond into the broader social and political arena of South Africa. The answers require a discussion of the structure of black-white relations in the wider social world, the cross-cutting allegiances and involvements between the Zulu and the white-controlled administrative order, the hybridization and invention of Zulu 'tradition' in the interests of the administrative ceremonial of control. These and other themes (the unities produced through conflict, the social and political complications of Zulu labor migration to the Rand mines) were to be expanded by Gluckman and his Manchester colleagues in later articles and books.

Gluckman is careful to point out that the picture he presents of South Africa is a view from the bridge opening in Zululand. The implication is that it is but one perspective of the larger scheme of things. Other processes would necessarily come into focus within the reality of South Africa, and a different slant on the scene would emerge if viewed from another angle. Although he discusses a series of underlying principles, in the orientation that he presents, he refuses the kind of totalizing ethnography—the claim to comprehensive description or understanding—that some ethnographers of his time, and some even today, assert. He insisted that such ethnographic completeness is impossible because of the different points from which ethnographers must enter the worlds of their interest and the continually differentiating complexity of such realities. I stress this, for it underlines another important aspect of his situational approach.

The idea of the situation can be conceived of as a kind of net that the analyst casts over complexity, thereby bringing together a diversity of dynamics and different processes without asserting that in reality they constitute an integrated unity. The situation is a way of addressing issues of the social while avoiding some of the pitfalls in the employment of concepts such as society (and culture) that might suggest a degree of coherence that is not in fact the reality. However, Gluckman constantly argued for a distinction to be made between the complexity captured in the situation, on the one hand, and the concepts used to make analytical understanding of that complexity, on the other. Notions of system, social field, structure, and equilibrium that he engaged are not to be confused with reality but rather should be understood as abstract constructs for the illumination of the dynamics or processes that are gathered into the situation (Gluckman [1940] 1958: 56).

Gluckman situates the micro dynamics of the bridge opening within the macro-historical processes that are in various ways integral to the events of the bridge opening. These are also conceived from a situational-analytic perspective. They underline the orientation he was developing toward a concentration on change and process and the idea of the situation itself as a moment of process that discloses particular dynamics. He focuses on the historical situation of the Zulu emergence within the Nguni population and the rapid transformation (over approximately five years) of the Zulu into an expansionist state—and the period of terror (*mfecane*) that accompanied this. The two historical moments he discusses are also slices of time, as it were. Their process and the changes that are effected in their dynamic are, in his analysis, effectively distinct.

The former (the context of the initial Zulu emergence) is an example of change effected through what on the surface appear to be unchanging socio-political principles and institutions. The conflicts arising on the basis of what he discerned to be fundamental socio-political cleavages or contradictions were capable of being managed within the conventional scheme or pattern of established practices. Gluckman ([1940] 1958, 1955b, 1963) was to refer to this as repetitive change, that is, social practices and institutions that endured despite conflicts (indeed, they were engaged as a means for resolving conflicts) but were also, and by this fact, a dynamic in the generation of change. Sahlins (1980) makes a very similar point much later regarding the transformations of ancient Hawaii into modernity, which he expressed in the phrase "plus ça change, plus c'est la même chose." The forms of life among the Nguni peoples stayed the same while things were changing, for example, with the establishment of a relatively independent Zulu polity. The moment of rapid Zulu state expansion (under Shaka) is a situation when social and political institutions and practice are in numerous ways reconfigured, a period of revolutionary change that took the Zulu and other peoples in the region in radically new directions. The periods of repetitive and revolutionary change were different reactions to a growing crisis—the penetration into what is now known as the KwaZulu Natal region of South Africa by white settlers and the growing incorporation of the region into the global economy. The dynamics of repetitive change were at first capable of managing the crisis indexed by the increased conflicts founded in new socio-economic contradictions. However, the crisis reached such a point—manifested in territorial restrictions for the Zulu and others—that conditions for a spectacular transformation were set. This was mediated through the extremely innovative agency of Shaka Zulu.

I note here that a strength of Gluckman's situational approach is his recognition of individual agency. Nonetheless, he conceived this largely as being conditioned within structural dynamics, individual creativity, as in Shaka Zulu's case, realizing the potentiality of social forces or being motivated in the spaces created by gathering socio-political contradictions. He saw the emergence of such individual creative innovation as having the effect of switching the course of history in particular ways, as with the Zulu expansion. The stress that Gluckman places on the importance of individual agency through his situational approach, and without losing the advantages of a concern with structural processes, takes him beyond Durkheimian perspectives and especially Radcliffe-Brown, a major influence on his thought (van Velsen 1967).

Through the three moments of time or situations of Zulu history (including the moment of the bridge opening), points of change were identified both in relation to particular crises and with respect to their specific dynamics whereby the crises were overcome. In other words, the processes described and marked out by each situation were a kind of freeze-framing of different processes arranged in historical sequence. This represented a continuity of processes from the past into the present and effectively isolated out the often overlapping dynamics that underpinned the changes and transformations affecting the populations in the periods covered. More abstractly, Gluckman (see [1940] 1958: 46–52; 1968) conceived of the sequenced situations of change and process to be successive equilibria. This was, for him, a theoretical construction (a further freezing of the dynamic) in the interest of grasping more analytically the particular kind of dynamic structure engaged in the change. In this sense, the notion of equilibrium was not a static concept, of which he has been routinely criticized, but, as Gluckman was to insist, a theoretical way into the grasping of complex processes. His idea of equilibrium is appropriate to his situational approach and does not contradict his general project to develop an anthropology thoroughly concerned with change.

Much of Gluckman's later work and the developments of his Manchester colleagues are implicit in *A Social Situation*. Methodologically, the roots of what was to become known as the extended-case method—pioneered by Mitchell and brought to brilliant fruition by Victor Turner—are evident in this work (see, too, Kapferer 1972; Long 1968; van Velsen 1964). Gluckman's insistence that there are different forms (or dynamics) of modernity operating contemporaneously is evident in *A Social Situation*. They became the strong point of his "townsmen are townsmen and tribesmen are tribesmen" (Gluck-man 1960, 1961a), which refused traditional-modern contrasts that were then current and still continue in some anthropological quarters. In his situational analysis is the early statement of his 'cross-cutting ties' thesis through which he was to understand the persistence of such oppressive and evil systems as apartheid (see also Gluckman 1955b). He stressed the importance of the forces of global capital (which set the conditions for a systemic unity of cooperation and conflict[13]) and the whites' technological command of greater instruments of violence, but these were not alone in effecting the continuity of a gross order of social inequality. He also underlined the fact that systems based in contradiction and opposition could be modified by cross-cutting ties, the resulting ambiguities of power and allegiance overcoming (or delaying) the tendency of the system to blow itself apart or form another order of integration (a point of Marx's *Eighteenth Brumaire of Louis Napoleon*, of which he was aware).

Gluckman's situational perspective, oriented to detecting the multiplicity of structural processes, was effectively continued by Mitchell (1956a) and Epstein (1958) in their Copperbelt studies. And they pursued the implication of cross-cutting allegiances, which indicated that the thoroughgoing structural or racial-class divide through all areas of social relations (what Gluckman referred to as the 'dominant cleavage') on the mines allowed for less modification of the opposition than in the commercial areas where African social relations were more fragmented and subject to the complexities of cross-cutting loyalties. The more divisive and shifting pattern of relations among commercial workers inhibited the degree to which they could effectively contest white power, their political party organization being less potent, at least for a while, than African miners' trade unionism. The broader point of Gluckman's anthropological intervention in *A Social Situation* was that the endurance of orders through time was not by any means necessarily a function of cultural and social homogeneity but a potentiality of different patterns of internal differentiation (a reason why he was interested in Durkheim's *The Division of Labour*). His cross-cutting ties idea is a development of Durkheim and also of the significance he saw in Evans-Prichard's Nuer studies, whose notion of balanced opposition he was to pursue but in the circumstances of modernity. Thus, Gluckman indicated in *A Social Situation*, and expanded in later work, that the lack of balance in fundamental opposition—the overweening power of whites over blacks, in the South African instance—spawned social fragmentation and conflict on the weaker side of what he identified as the dominant cleavage augmenting the naked power of the South African apartheid regime.[14]

## Situational Analysis and a Polemic for an Anthropology beyond Malinowski

Gluckman's *Malinowski's Sociological Theories* spells out without complication some of the key analytical implications of *A Social Situation* for a new anthropology in which both change and process are critical issues and also for an anthropology that engages positively with the contributions of other disciplines. *Malinowski's Sociological Theories* communicates the forceful energy of the young Gluckman, a scholar certain of his vision and willing to tackle a lion of the discipline. It has all that sense of critical enthusiasm that was to draw scholars to him and around which the excitement of his Manchester School was to build. While he recognizes the major importance of ethnographic fieldwork, Gluckman stresses the significance of other ways of knowing. The value of fieldwork is in relation to other forms of knowledge, whose insights have to be taken seriously and not simply rejected out of hand. This, in his view, was an important failure of Malinowski, whose particular, overdetermined dependence on fieldwork to the exclusion of other modes of understanding threatened the isolation of anthropology and its marginalization in the pursuit of human knowledge.

Gluckman's critique of Malinowski has all the force of outrage as well as the excitement of the formation of a different orientation. For Gluckman, Malinowski, in the posthumously published *The Dynamics of Culture Change* (1945), had betrayed the possibilities of his own innovation of long-term fieldwork in the Trobriands—the defining method of anthropology. Having disregarded his own anthropological edict to attend to knowledge gained from the field, Malinowski's misunderstandings in the South African case, characterized by conceptual faults and triviality, are thoroughly exposed. Gluckman is scornful of Malinowski's rejection of historical knowledge and his treatment of the Africans of Southern Africa prior to European invasions as if they are "people without history," to use Eric Wolf's (1992) well-known phrase.[15] Gluckman shows how Malinowski ignores historical processes among African populations before the colonial conquest and how the different courses of both African and European history coincided in a specific way to create numerous effects that were integral to the crisscrossing coordinates of the South African situation and the social and political formations emergent within it, including the development of apartheid. Overlooking one history, Malinowski also ignores his own, and Gluckman demonstrates that if Malinowski had attended to the historical processes engaged in the formation of Northern European and American industrial capitalism, he would have been far more astute in grasping the complexities of the racial situation in Southern Africa and the severe plight of the African populations. In Gluckman's analysis, Malinowski fails to see the structures in the dynamics of change—all he sees is disruption and dislocation, both personal and psychological. What Malinowski describes in South Africa as breakdown and disorganization in the situation of industrialization and urbanization are, in Gluckman's view, themselves new structural forms. It is an argument that Gluckman and his colleagues, especially Mitchell, were to use in a more sympathetic critique of Godfrey Wilson's *The Economics of Detribalization* (1941–1942), a study of the Zambian town of Kabwe (Broken Hill). While Wilson saw the importance of attending to global capitalist forces, he did not realize sufficiently that the forms of life he described were innovative forms relative to the urban context itself and not necessarily broken-down or modified traditional practices somehow out of place in the town.[16]

Malinowski considered the complex ethnic composition of South Africa to be one of cultures in contact. But for Gluckman, cultures do not come into contact as if they are bounded, independent entities. Such a reified and totalized view, anathema to Gluckman and his followers, came close to the segregationist vision of those in power in South Africa.[17] Gluckman considered it preposterous that an anthropologist of Malinowski's standing and with an awareness of the importance of long-term fieldwork should offer advice to the authorities on the basis of so little fieldwork knowledge. Here is the first clear statement by an anthropologist concerning anthropological complicity in the structures of colonial domination. Gluckman's critique has relevance for many contemporary anthropologists engaged in consultancy. While Gluckman did not underrate the importance of culture (custom, value), he insisted (contra the Malinowski of *Dynamics*) that cultural practices should be subordinated to sociological rather than culturological analysis. In his critique of Malinowski, Gluckman reasserts the argument of *A Social Situation* whereby cultural processes are to be understood through the complex forces of a social world in which cultural ideas and values are at play and in continuous construction. The cultural community is not the universe of analysis for Gluckman, as it is for Malinowski, but rather a socio-cultural field whose boundaries are constantly changing and being breached and which is planed by various economic, social, and political forces.

Gluckman was opposed to a relativizing and totalizing anthropology of the kind threatened by Malinowski's argument, which treated cultures or societies as sealed-off entities, an approach that had become entrenched in certain parts of Britain and across the Atlantic. Gluckman's early statements are still fresh and maintain much of their point for a contemporary anthropology acutely conscious of globalizing realities. However, many current anthropologists, anxious to shrug off what they see to be the embarrassments of the past, have eschewed structure, often opting instead for a revitalized individualism (in which agency opposes determinism). This has also presaged a return of psychologism, though perhaps of a different order from that which Gluckman reacted to in Malinowski.[18]

Malinowski saw cultural integration as being equated with individual psychological health: cultural breakdown was the cause of individual breakdown. The implication is that culture is reducible to being a property of the mental state of persons, an attitude of mind. This position is risked in those postmodern perspectives that, while refusing cultural normative or integrationist arguments of the kind of Malinowski (or of some North American cultural anthropology), nonetheless stress culture as an individual property and as being diverse in its interpretive possibility because of this.[19] Be this as it may,

Gluckman underscores the force of culture and value in and through social and political processes. In this sense, culture and value are not viewed as breaking down or becoming disorganized; rather, they assume new significance in a different order or process of socio-political relations. Here Gluckman is undeniably Durkheimian in spirit. The individual life is also inseparably a social life, and the objective of anthropology is to explore those social processes and orders that are integral to certain forms of individual expression and orientation, including even an impetus to the destruction of both the self and society.

If Gluckman was antagonistic toward psychologism (i.e., toward misconceiving what may in fact be a socio-political process in a reduction to individualist psychological terms, most often of a commonsense variety), he did not eschew the importance of other kinds of explanation outside of anthropological or sociological ones. Thus, he was interested in the potentiality of psychoanalytic understanding, attempting to use it to explain why Shaka Zulu in particular should be the major person to initiate both the Zulu expansion and the character of the Zulu terror.[20] Gluckman contends that it is Malinowski's ethnographic or fieldwork chauvinism, together with his cultural relativism, that results in a premature dismissal of Freud's assertion of the universality of the Oedipus complex (despite the fact of Malinowski's interest in Freud). Gluckman suggests that a closer examination of the Trobriand ethnography (along the lines, perhaps, of what Gluckman recommends in situational analysis) might have supported Freud (see Devons and Gluckman 1964: 236–240). Malinowski was doubly at fault, for Gluckman claims that he neither addressed his own material rigorously enough nor considered sufficiently the insights of non-ethnographically based investigation.

The ideas that marked Gluckman's initial prescriptions for anthropology, which invoked much excitement and were to shape much of the research at the RLI and at Manchester, became, expectedly enough, more formalized in later statements. Thus, the Gluckman of *Closed Systems and Open Minds* (1964) appears as the authoritative figure of an established view rather than the slayer of dragons of his earlier statements. For some, the later statements are an intellectual folly, typical of a tendency to excess and exaggeration. In the Manchester corridors, the title of the later work was inverted (the joke was "closed minds and open systems"), and many considered that Gluckman was unwarrantedly excluding far too much from what he appeared to regard as legitimate anthropological practice (see, e.g., Shokeid 2001: 859). But Gluckman was attempting to define the particular contribution of anthropology as a specific disciplinary practice so that it might enter into productive discourse with other forms of knowledge—which was the clear point of *Closed Systems and Open Minds*. Undoubtedly, he was convinced of the Durkheimian position that the socio-cultural, *sui generis*, constitutes the distinctive subject matter of an anthropology. This is where anthropological fieldwork knowledge must lie.

While anthropologists must be aware of the theories and findings of other fields of inquiry into the conditions and nature of human beings, they cannot be jacks-of-all-trades and masters of none. Gluckman had a keen literary sense, but I think that Geertz's attempt to be a Renaissance man would not have met with his approval. The complexity of the human situation demands that anthropologists must delimit their research analytically. In other words, they should not attempt to present total explanations or expect to collect all that may be relevant and often beyond their competence. His point is neither one of necessary expediency (the impossibility of knowing all there is) nor one that demands the wearing of blinkers. The argument is against empiricism (virtually foundational in the idea of fieldwork from Malinowski to the present), insisting on the constructive and selective nature of anthropological work. He argues for a thoroughgoing awareness of what this involves, even when anthropologists make use of the knowledge and research of other fields. He does so by demonstrating positively, through a critical assessment of cases of anthropological fieldwork of his colleagues, the kind of pragmatic selections anthropologists make in their ethnography and the reasoning behind them. Gluckman's argument for analytical and theoretical closure, I think, carries forward some of the ideas he presented in *A Social Situation* relating to the impossibility of producing a total theory of human social complexity. What anthropologists can only hope for is partial understanding—a fact that Gluckman presents with characteristic optimism. Anthropological theoretical understanding must be only partial because this is intrinsic to theoretical work per se. The act of theorizing is in all known instances, whether in the sciences or social sciences, a practice of closure—a relatively conscious process of selective exclusion. And it is in this very aspect of closure that can be found its potency for discovery and understanding.

Gluckman's situational analysis, and the idea of the extended case that developed from it, was integral to his concern to pursue the development of anthropology as a rigorous science that would extend the horizons of knowledge concerning the social life of human beings. He was thoroughly sociological in orientation, and this was vital in his rejection of any kind of relativism that refused the production of general understanding that could not go beyond the particular case. The anthropology that he strove for was to be grounded in a close attention to practice and to the values engaged whose specificity would both test general propositions and lead to new ones. Comparison was central in this regard. Through comparison, the theoretical abstractions won from the investigations of a particular case should be tested against the variations within similar practices obtainable from the same general region (where the variations were constituted under the same broad historical/cultural conditions). The idea was for the field of comparison to expand progressively and systematically, resulting in the formation of a general hypothesis and theory. This notion of the comparative method was concerned with deriving the key terms and categories for comparison from observed practices, and with achieving a close identity between abstract categories (formed independently of the material) and activities on the ground. Gluckman's major demonstration of the method was in his divorce hypothesis, in which he sought to establish the connection between different rates of marital separation and forms of kinship, marriage rules, and control over property (an extension of aspects of Friedrich Engels's 1884 treatise, *The Origin of the Family, Private Property and the State*). The approach, of course, is an elaboration on that of Durkheim and of Radcliffe-Brown and is thoroughly consistent with the view of situational analysis as an ethnographic method corresponding to experimental proce-dure in the scientific laboratory, as Gluckman and many of his colleagues saw it. Mitchell was to make an aspect of this more explicit in his discussion of the typicality of events as one cornerstone of the situational analysis and extended-case perspectives. The issue of typicality is a matter of importance in the testing of propositions that might flow from the investigation of particular events or situations. One such approach is through statistical or mathemati-cal procedures (something that Gluckman encouraged and that was pursued, for example, by Mitchell). However, as Mitchell (1983) explains, whether an event or situation is typical or not is beside the point—and even misses it. No event or situation can be typical, especially given Gluckman's view that all is in process. Everything is in some way or another different and potentially unique. What the anthropologist seeks is patterns or principles integral to processes that can form the basis for generalizations. Situational analysis and the extended-case method were ways of achieving this.

Most of Gluckman's methodological directives were attacked. Leach, Gluckman's most forceful intellectual foe, signaled a paradigm shift toward Lévi-Strauss's structuralism. In the first Malinowski Lecture in 1961 at the London School of Economics and Political Science (LSE), Leach dismissed as empiricism the 'butterfly collecting' attention to detail for detail's sake. He condemned the hither-and-thither collection of ethnographic facts to support an anthropological assertion or hypothesis without due attention to conceptu-alization, meaning, and context: all factors that could completely subvert any pretense to the claim of having discovered a general truth. Leach and Gluck-man shared a common project, but relative to Gluckman, Leach reduced, in a cultural, topological approach, the importance of contextualization and ethno-graphic detail that Gluckman championed and which he saw as the great con-tribution of Malinowski. Leach advocated a mathematical abstractionism and intellectualism that transcended context and excluded situated practices. In the papers collected into *Rethinking Anthropology* ([1961] 2004), Leach attacked Gluckman's comparative method and especially the divorce hypothesis. The cultural variations in the meaning of concepts relating to marriage, kinship, and property, for example, could not be subsumed in a general nomothetic sys-tem of classification. Leach was also critical of Gluckman's equilibrium model, considering him to be obsessed with stability. Of course, there was merit to the criticism, but in hindsight both scholars were committed to similar paths.[21]

As I have suggested, Gluckman's comparative method was intended to over-come some of the difficulties of abstract classifications that were insensitive to cultural and social context. I think that Gluckman (1968) accurately defended himself against Leach's critique of his approach to equilibrium, demonstrating that Leach's own work among the Kachin accorded with his approach. Leach's famous charge against ethnographic 'butterfly collecting' expressed the central raison d'être of Gluckman's much earlier situational analysis and the develop-ment of the extended-case perspective from it.

## Situational Analysis: A Prolegomena for Reassessment and Extension

Situational analysis and the extended-case method had their roots in a positivist social science, but their intention was to reach beyond the limitations of such social science and, indeed, to match the methods of science. The poverty of much social-science positivism is that it superficially mimics science rather than attempting to apply its investigative procedures—in part, Gluckman's aim. Situational analysis and the extended-case method were not envisaged as aids to mere description or as illustrations of arguments, ideas, or theories developed independently of the methods. Gluckman and his colleagues inveighed against the description of situations and of events thrown up within them being presented as 'apt illustrations' of already formulated theories or opinions. Rather, as I have indicated, situations and events were to be the base ground, the material whose investigation in and of itself would generate new theories and understandings of a potentially general kind. The situation and the event were to be routes into discovery.

Whether situational analysis and the extended-case method were true to their aims is an open question. Clyde Mitchell, in personal comments, would routinely raise the point, arguing that situational analysis and the extended-case method did not completely overcome the problem of the case as apt illustration. Mitchell was self-critical in this regard, finding difficulties with his own study, *The Kalela Dance* (1956a), one of the best examples of the situational approach. This study does make a discovery regarding ethnicity and the distinctive order of urban-industrial life that goes beyond the suggestions in Gluckman's *A Social Situation*, although it is Gluckman's initial perspective that makes Mitchell's insights all the more possible. Mitchell, through his presentation of the composition of urban dance groups, a content analysis of the songs, and descriptions of daily events, shows the distinct and variant nature of urban ethnic identity and, furthermore, how it is engaged in the formation of social relations rather than being solely an expression of them.[22]

Undoubtedly, Mitchell could have pursued such insights through conventional ethnographic means. *The Kalela Dance* is in many ways such an ethnography, and Mitchell, forever the modest scholar that he was, would argue that his account of *kalela* was really a method for focusing and organizing his argument. However, I suggest that the concept of situation is significant for Mitchell's study, nonetheless. This is so because the very idea of situation challenged notions of system homogeneity or overall coherence. The concept opened Mitchell to the potentialities of the contexts he explored and the practices he encountered, indeed, encouraging him to conceive of them as, in different ways, dynamic and structural processes of the complex realities that threw them up.

However, Mitchell has an important point, i.e. situational analysis remains trapped in the idea of the case or event as illustration despite the effort to the contrary. But without in any way relinquishing the importance of Gluckman's situational idea and general methodological approach, I wish to pursue them further, to see in what other ways they can realize a potentiality to open out to discovery.

## Situational Analysis and the Post-structuralist Intervention of Deleuze and Guattari

There is in my view a degree of correspondence between Gluckman's situational idea, as I have presented it, and the contemporary post-structuralism of Deleuze and Guattari (1994). The latter are concerned with articulating different procedures for extracting knowledge from the ongoing processes and phenomena of existence or what they call 'actuality' (to distinguish this from the virtual or the constructions of the real within actuality). Their objective is to place different forms of knowledge creation into parallel relation, indicating points of conjunction and cross-fertilization. They reject a knowledge hierarchy that puts science in a dominant relation to other disciplines (social sciences, humanities), assigning them a lesser value. It was just such a hierarchy that influenced Gluckman's concern to develop a method for anthropology that would match that of science (and informed his *Closed Systems and Open Minds*, which otherwise as a project, if not in execution, has some resonance with Deleuze and Guattari's exercise). This, I believe, places constraints on Gluckman's idea, rooted as it is in the positivism of the time, inhibiting it from better realizing some of its potential of discovery.

Deleuze and Guattari enable, I think, a slight redrawing of the situational and extended-case idea, highlighting certain aspects of what I regard to be its enduring value. My aim, too, is to break with certain features of Gluckman's sometimes premature drive to develop universal explanations at too great a distance from the phenomena concerned. The extension of the situational analysis and extended-case method that I offer here is to turn it more intensely to a consideration of the socio-cultural practices that are drawn into its net. Gluckman takes events and situations to be the raw material of his analyses, but his interpretation sometimes overcomes and reduces the authority of those who are the producers of his raw material. My point is that he ultimately excludes possibilities of the discursive processes he encounters, subsuming them to his own predetermined assumptions, while refusing aspects of the raw material that might facilitate other theoretical constructions. Overall, however, I remain committed to the spirit of Gluckman's concern, which is to arrive at conceptual and theoretical understanding on the basis of recorded events or practice that transcend their particularity and enabling the development of broader theoretical generalizations, yet without losing touch with the specifics upon which the generalizations are grounded.

Deleuze and Guattari write of existence (actuality[23]) as a chaos of myriad changing, shifting, and competing processes, whether in the material, physical worlds of scientific interest or the realities of the actions of human beings, the focus of concern of philosophers and social scientists. Existence is a potentiality in a plethora of continual becomings. The scientist, they suggest, engages technical apparatuses to interrupt the infinite speed of chaotic actuality (the rapidity of its constant formation and re-formation). In Deleuze and Guattari's view, scientists descend into the phenomenon by slowing or interrupting its infinite speed (as in catalysis or the use of particle accelerators). Thus, scientists establish a state of affairs within the chaotic process (what Deleuze and Guattari identify as a 'virtual' within the 'virtuality of chaos') whose coordinates they have determined.[24] Philosophers of the flux of human actualities, Deleuze and Guattari claim, operate in a similar way. Rather than establishing a scientific state of affairs, philosophers engage with the chaos of life as a plane of immanence. They operate with slices of time, as it were, freeze-frame them, and engage with the potentiality captured through a diversity of concepts that are directly appropriate to the practices with which they engage.

Indeed, Gluckman in *A Social Situation*, as I have outlined earlier, addresses the situation and the event as effectively freeze-framed sections of the historical temporality of continually emerging life processes. The event thrown up in crisis, which might be grasped as the situation (or also a state of affairs), appears as a fleeting moment on the plane of immanence. But more than a particular actualization of the situation, the event is also a potentiality that reaches beyond the situation from which it emerges. This is all the more so at moments of crisis, the main condition of the event, in the perspective of Gluckman and his colleagues. The event regarded in this way cannot be reduced to the situation, cannot be a mere illustration of the situation, but is instead a generative moment, a site of emergence on the plane of immanence, which is the situation.

It is Turner (1957, 1968) in his Ndembu studies who realizes most fully this implication of Gluckman's methodological innovation when it is re-expressed in the post-structuralist terms of Deleuze and Guattari. More than an explication of the Hegelian/Marxist logic, which is inherent in Gluckman's concepts of structural cleavage, systemic contradiction, etc., Turner's studies present events as social dramas (that internally reflect a dynamic of discord, rupture, and resolution), as successive moments of emergence. The situation of the Ndembu, their plane of immanence (see especially Deleuze 1986; Deleuze and Guattari 1994), is conditioned at a point in time of converging lines of complexity (e.g., the development of cash farming, labor migration) that excites contradictions in Ndembu social life (that of the virilocal principle in relation to matrilineality) made manifest in political struggle. Not only are such principles integral to socio-cultural life revealed in the events of crisis, but socio-cultural forms begin to take on new significance and start to express original possibilities—in Turner's analysis, the development of the *chihamba* cult. The events do more than illustrate principles at work—they indicate new dynamics in formation. Turner's (1974) later work was to carry forward the idea of the event, the drama, as a moment of excess, origination, and restructuring, especially in his work on ritual through the concept of liminality.

The descent into the event via the situational and extended-case method involves the interrogation of the dynamics of the event as such and as itself a phenomenon of emergence (see also Kapferer 1972). Thus, the event cannot be reduced to being merely an expression or reflection of the larger social and political plane in which it has irrupted. The treatment of events as mere representations of larger processes is almost a trivialization of much of the intention behind the direction of the situational perspective as Gluckman and his colleagues, Turner especially, were developing it. The event is a site of creativity or of generation whose analysis may disclose an understanding of the potentialities of social forces or structural processes that are not yet apparent in the lived environment or larger contexts of the event's occurrence.

Turner, as he extends from situational analysis, maintains a close integration of practice with value or the symbolic. The value is vital in the practice—not somehow independent of it. There is not, as in Gluckman, a separation of the two and a privileging of practice (in a universalist sociological rationalism) over value, or a submission of practice to value as in much anthropological idealism. Gluckman effectively refused aspects of the authority of the sociocultural practices with which he engaged, overlooking their capacity to reveal insights and understanding beyond the categories of explanation he imposed upon them. They were regarded as reflections of general sociological principles that his engagement of the method of comparison across cultural and social space affirmed. Thus, he reduces the complexity of the Swazi royal *incwala* ritual to being a demonstration of the social ordering or maintaining function of conflict. This significance of the rite for Gluckman is the general principle that it discloses and which he considers to be repeatedly confirmed in a variety of disparate practices elsewhere, ranging from Nuer feuding and Azande sorcery and witchcraft, to gossiping among anthropologists. Gluckman ignores Swazi cosmology and the arguments of the Swazi embedded in it. As some have indicated (e.g., Beidelman 1966), his typing of the Swazi songs of hatred to their king in the *incwala* ceremony of royal renewal as 'rituals of rebellion' obscures a Swazi understanding that the songs have constitutive force in the sacrificial transformation of the king and his capacity to embody and instigate the regeneration of socio-political realities. Gluckman's idea of conflict, insightful as it is, precedes the evidence and conditions its interpretation.

What I am saying is that Gluckman tends to oversimplify and overlook critical aspects of the practices themselves and the values and particularly the interpretations that the subjects make of their own action and that are embedded in the discourse of practice. What is emergent from this discourse, perhaps intensely so in the crisis of events, can give rise to theoretical understanding of wider application. However, Gluckman largely suppresses this possibility of the anthropological imagination and its potential for the discovery of theory through the exploration of grounded practices that his notion of situational analysis and the extended-case method might facilitate.

## Situational Analysis, the Discourse of Practice, and the Ethnographic Imagination

Gluckman's overall orientation is set within the Cartesian method of radical doubt. This causes him, and many others in anthropology, to reduce the importance of the discursive practices and other forms of reflection (interpretation, critique) that members of human populations have developed based on their own experience and circumstance. The Cartesian principle inhibits the degree to which the practices and interpretations of the ethnography challenge or disrupt the commonsense or theoretical thought of the anthropologist. Radical doubt is rarely turned against the anthropologist's conventional or abstract wisdom (Kapferer 2001a). The anthropologist may attempt to control for these by at first postulating radical cultural difference and otherness, which frequently risks inverting the kind of universalizing rationalism that Gluckman insisted on and replacing it with a cultural relativism that, in my opinion, Gluckman rightly resisted. Much discussion in anthropology still appears to be enmeshed in what strikes me as an irresolute dialectic between cultural relativism, on the one hand, and an anti-essentialist universalism, on the other. One attempt to correct this, the suspension of disbelief, may effect an entry into the constituting terms of other realities, yet nevertheless it effectively maintains the authority of the established views of many an anthropologist by the very fact of suspension itself. The view of the anthropologist is only *suspended* and not exposed to being overthrown as a possibility of a thoroughgoing investigation of the implications of the discursive practices encountered.[25] I am indicating one direction for development through the situational perspective that may open the way for the anthropological imagination to produce genuinely original and counter-intuitive thought of a scientific kind. This is so in the sense that it escapes the Scylla of relativism and the Charybdis of affirming established thought usually integral to the metropolitan world of the anthropologist.

Let me introduce a brief example to indicate the direction I am taking, which is to engage the situational method to explore cultural assertions in the circumstances of their practical production and recognition. I draw on Steven Friedson's (1996, 2005) excellent explorations of African music-trance healing and trance dancing. In *Dancing Prophets* (1996), Friedson discusses the music-dance events in which Tumbuka healers, or *nchimi* in Malawi, bring forth *vimbuza* spirits in their patients and in themselves to attack the witchcraft and other forces of illness that are destroying the bodies of their clients. The *vimbuza* are the energies or spirits of the peoples (but also animals, most especially the lion) who have invaded or otherwise powerfully affected Tumbuka realities. *Vimbuza* are engaged by healers to do battle with the agents of witchcraft. They (a multiplicity of *vimbuza* may be involved in a particular music-trance event) must be brought into the bodies of both healer and client but also must be withdrawn from their bodies—for *vimbuza*, like so many agents of healing the world over, are ambiguous agents, powerful for curing but also themselves dangerous and capable of causing illness and death in the bodies of those whom they enter. The healers consider that their drumming is a key technique—in Friedson's terms, a clinical necessity—for calling up the *vimbuza* and indeed manifesting them within their own bodies and those of their patients.

Healers and patients are emphatic that they actually encounter the spirits, that the *vimbuza* are really objectively there, that they are beings immediately given to direct experience. The *vimbuza* are present in the flesh, as it were. Now as anthropologists, we have no problem with this regardless of whether we are universalists or relativists. In terms of psychoanalytic theory, an anthropologist might understand the experience as an objectification and projection of deep psychosexual conflicts that manifest themselves as a real feeling of spirit inhabitation. For the relativist, the Tumbuka's definition of their experience is real in its consequence and for this reason just as valid as any other explanation. But either way, Tumbuka cultural ideas are viewed as surface expressions, and the anthropologists remain in their own cocoon. The opinions of the Tumbuka are not examined in their authenticity or in the fullness of the Tumbuka's own encounter with their reality. The Tumbuka are insistent that the *vimbuza* are in the music.

Friedson turns to the Tumbuka events of music-trance, the musical techniques and the different rhythms out of which the *vimbuza* are produced, developing a thought inspired by Gestalt psychology and the experimental work on visual illusions. The example is the well-known Necker cube, which demonstrates a classic figure-ground illusion. Our perception of the cube is what Gestaltists call multi-stable; that is, what we perceive as the front or back of the cube shifts as we stare at it, the one orientation of the cube disappearing as the other becomes dominant. And this is not all there is to it. If you look at the Necker cube intensely, other images may appear in it, such as the body of an insect with six legs or a diamond-shaped gem. These are not formed to our conscious awareness until we are told. They do not exist for us independently of our meaningful construction of them, but this does not mean that they do not exist outside our constructions. They are available to us, immediately given in our perceptual field, as potentials of actuality that are awaiting our specific construction of them.

Friedson demonstrates through an investigation of the variations in Tumbuka drumming that sound illusions (of the kind that the Necker cube illustrates for visual perception) are created in the alternating rhythms of Tumbuka music-trance. Given up to the music in dance, healers and their patients can encounter illusions of coming into contact with solid energies, experienced by the dancers as the possessing motion of the spirits as they pass into and out of the body. The Tumbuka have come to recognize these actual illusions of the music as *vimbuza* and, being culturally attuned to so recognize them, will rapidly come into and out of spirit possession, manifesting a number of different *vimbuza* as the rhythms shift. The illusions are not merely inventions of cognition but are available within the immediate illusory structure of the music. The Tumbuka are right about the *vimbuza*. They are produced in the music.

Furthermore, Friedson opens up possibility by worrying away at Tumbuka statements in the context of a close exploration of the situated practical production of experience. He suggests that there may be a correspondence between different forms of trance experience in this region of Africa and specific kinds of musical patterns. This is not merely cultural difference but differences formed around the variations in the structuring of sound (also cultural productions) that might have larger import, not just for understanding trance processes but in the wider study of auditory perception. The cultural intuitions and inventions of the Tumbuka taken seriously by the ethnographer generated an original insight. Furthermore, Tumbuka understanding mediated through the method of the anthropologist is enabled to participate with other scientific and non-scientific orientations in the expansion and generation of a rigorous understanding.

Although Friedson does not explicitly engage the Gluckman or Manchester situational or extended-case approach, it is within the spirit of the work's perspective. Moreover, Friedson shows how the interrogation of situated practice, the methods of production, and the discourse of interpretation that relates to practice can lead to a theoretical discovery that transcends the particular.

I am neither engaging culture to explanation nor attempting to explain culture. Rather, I am recommending a close investigation of ethnographic phenomena that not only accepts the authenticity of the participants' statements about their experiences but also comes to an understanding at a more abstract level that maintains an identity between the phenomena as immediately grasped by participants and a more general theorizing. In this sense, the theoretical understanding arises in and through the phenomena and does not deny its possibility. Friedson, in my view, has done just this. Through a close investigation of the musical events of possession dance, he has revealed a new understanding of the potentialities of human experience. He has articulated a discovery that the Tumbuka themselves have made regarding the possibilities of a particular kind of musical illusion.[26]

My next example comes from my own fieldwork in Sri Lanka on healing rituals and anti-sorcery rites (Kapferer 1983, 1995b, 1997, 2000). Here I followed the lead of Victor Turner, who, as I commented earlier, realized the potential of the extended-case or situational approach in his ritual analyses. Turner's work on Ndembu rituals began by applying Gluckman's structural-functionalist 'rituals of rebellion' perspective to the Ndembu material. Turner definitely pushed Gluckman's idea much further, but the ritual events were still strongly representational, even if they were certainly not 'apt illustrations'. But Turner's later work involved a reorientation whereby the extended-case or situational-analytical approach was far more powerfully engaged so that the Ndembu rites were to give up their own discursive logic. Turner then used what he saw as a key dimension of their discursive process (what he addressed as the 'liminal', a key point of transition and transformation) to develop a conceptual and theoretical orientation toward larger social and political issues outside the realm of ritual. Although his approach to liminality was suggested in the earlier ritual analyses of Van Gennep, Turner's exploration of the dynamics of Ndembu ritual, via the extended-case approach, threw up possibilities of the liminal whose implications went beyond either Van Gennep's argument or the immediate pragmatic purposes that the Ndembu had for their own cultural inventions. In a major sense, Turner's application of the extended-case method to ritual paralleled Freud's approach to dreams and to myth (I think consciously so). Turner thus went some way toward realizing Gluckman's vision for situational analysis to achieve its objective of discovery.

The events defined in the practice of some ritual can perhaps be regarded as 'folk' versions of situational or extended-case analysis. This is so in many respects with the elaborate anti-sorcery healing rites practiced by Sinhala Buddhists in Sri Lanka, which are typically performed at major times of personal and social crisis. While they represent in numerous symbolic ways the dimensionality of such crises, they are also techniques for entering within what is conceived to be the existential heart of the crisis. Within the context of the rites, the ritual specialists who perform them see themselves, among many other aspects, as making critical adjustments to the coordinates of space and time that intersect in a particular victim's life trajectory and that cause the victim's suffering and may visit affliction on his or her household.

The major sorcery rites I recorded can be conceived as technologies or machines for entering within what Deleuze and Guattari might call the chaotic dynamics of human realities and for making necessary corrections within them. The idea is to reconstitute victims as persons who have regained their agency in ongoing realities and the construction of their life course, a capacity that the Sorcerer destroys. The rites are not representations of lived social and political realities (a major direction of much anthropological analysis of ritual; see Kapferer 2005b) but rather dynamic structures for engaging with the processes of reality formation. In a major sense, they are a praxis of specific theoretical (cultural) constructs of reality and world formation within the Sinhala Buddhist environment of their performance. They are a 'virtual' (in the sense of Deleuze and Guattari) and thus do not model reality (as Geertz, for example, classically approaches rite), but rather suspend the ongoing motion of the real, holding vital aspects of its speed in abeyance, as it were, so as to descend within the flux that is reality to engage with some of its key forces of formation (Kapferer 1997, 2005b).

Let me briefly concentrate on the mythopraxis and dynamic logics of the most elaborate of Sinhala Buddhist anti-sorcery rites, a ritual known as the *Suniyama*. As I have developed extensively elsewhere (Kapferer 1988, 1997), the critical dynamics of the rite have relevance for an understanding of state/anti-state political violence, particularly the intensity of human destruction, not just for Sri Lanka but more generally. The major argument of the rite is contained in its governing myth, the well-known Buddhist story of King Mahasammata, his creative act of the socio-political ordering of the state and society, and the events surrounding the healing of the first sorcery victim, his queen (Kapferer 1997, 2000; see also Tambiah 1976). The idea of the rite is to put victims through a series of practices that cured Mahasammata's queen. The ritual replication of these socially and personally regenerative acts (which, among other things, restores victims to speech silenced by sorcery) returns victims and their households to their full capacity to participate in the taken-for-granted activities and projects of everyday life.

A central discursive logic articulated through the practice of the rite is the contest between two mutually incompatible sets of principles: those of the Sorcerer (a leveling, horizontally radiating, ego-centered, deterritorializing force) and those of the State (a hierarchializing, bounding, and delimiting force). Their relation, which is played out in a variety of ways in the course of the rite, is not one of order to disorder, nor is it one of a Hegelian dialectical kind in which contradictory principles are resolved in a higher synthesis of ultimate unity. The destructive potency of the Sorcerer and also that possibility of the State are emergent properties of their relation and not of essentialized characteristics existing independently. Each manifests its particular determining and violent potential through the other, which in the performance of the rite synergically intensifies violent forces that are expressed toward the end of the rite in the destruction (by the Sorcerer) of Mahasammata's Cosmic Palace, the central ritual edifice. What can be described as the disordering violence of the Sorcerer is a product of the ritually expressed Sorcerer-State conjunction that also manifests the disordering violence of the State. The poetics of the ritual discourse conceive of the structurally incompatible forces of the Sorcerer (the Sorcerer as incompatible with the structures of the ordering hierarchy of the State) as already present and intimate within the State (the fault in its order) *prior* to the Sorcerer's ritual revelation.

The idea of the Necker cube and the Gestaltist notion of multi-stability is suggested through the structure of the ritual discourse. The dynamics of State and Sorcerer are incontrovertible. While they emerge in the context of the other, they also operate to cancel each other out—as figure to ground. Thus, the Cosmic Palace of Mahasammata suppresses the presence of the Sorcerer, who, when he makes his appearance in a dramatic event of the rite, destroys and levels the Palace.

The dynamic logic of rite can be applied to aspects of recent violence in Sri Lanka. I refer specifically to the events of insurgent and state terrorism among the Sinhala population that came to a peak in 1989–1990 (see Kapferer 1996, 1997, 2001b). The occasion was the uprising of the Janatha Vimukthi Peramuna (People's Liberation Movement), an organization of largely disaffected Sinhala urban and rural youth, against the Sri Lanka government. This could be understood as a movement representing some of the social and political fragmentation within the Sinhala population that occurred as a result of what Gluckman would have recognized as the dominant ethnic cleavage between Tamils and Sinhalese that had developed from the ashes of the anti-Tamil riots of 1983 (see Kapferer 1988, 2001b; Tambiah 1986). In accordance with Gluckman's analysis in *A Social Situation*, this crystallization and stabilization of the ethnic division resulted in a gathering fragmentation on either side of the cleavage manifested in a proliferation of often mutually hostile political groups. This was one factor in the creation of a complexity of cross-allegiances and other ambiguities that contributed, in my opinion, to the endurance of the war—a routinization of continuing violence as the state of affairs.

The youth uprising expressed a particular structural process that operated, like many terrorist movements worldwide, in a cell-like pattern interconnected laterally across space by ties of kinship and friendship. It was a hidden structure that became visible during the night, whereas the forces of the state, which it opposed, commanded the day. The dynamic of the state, concerned with controlling territory and barricading itself against the threat of its opponents, was hierarchializing, whereas that of the insurgents was deterritorializing.

Both state and insurgent violence was considerable, perhaps the greatest toll coming as a result of destruction by state forces. (Some counts had the number of state victims as being in the range of 100,000 youths killed in a few months, but the true figures are unlikely to be known.) The state violence had a hierarchical structure, suspected insurgents being identified in terms of abstract classificatory categories of village, caste, age, etc., and took a bounding, territorializing form. The victims of government violence were often burned in tires, the bodies defaced and personal identities erased. Placed at the boundaries of villages and towns, the dead were effectively declared to be outside the order of the state and without an identity. Insurgent violence showed another structure and dynamic, that systematic with the Sorcerer. Thus, insurgent violence was of a highly personal nature, the bodies being mutilated in a way that was an expression of the identity of the victim, a blowing up of identity rather than its erasure (see Kapferer 1996, 1997, 2001b).

For a time, there was an extraordinary intensity of killing, and I suggest, following the line of argument in anti-sorcery ritual, that some of the intensity (and the extreme senselessness of the killing) was driven in the contradiction of two mutually exclusive dynamics. In the major anti-sorcery rite, this is expressed at the peak moment of absolute incompatibility that ends the rite— when the figure of the Sorcerer becomes dramatically manifest in the midst of the Cosmic Palace. As I have noted, the Sorcerer revealed in Mahasammata's ordering realm becomes possessed in a frenzy of violence during which the Cosmic Palace is destroyed. Similarly, what might be regarded as the excess of violence that took place between state forces and insurgents was an emergent phenomenon of the engagement of two very different forms of social and political realization. The degree of violence, the annihilatory dimensions of it, which at the time almost brought ordinary civil life to a standstill, was a force driven by the relation of incompatibility and was not reducible to the dynamics of either one.

The process I have outlined is compatible with Deleuze and Guattari's (1988) discussion of state and war machine dynamics, which they develop to a considerable extent from the examination of ethnographic materials. But the concept is explicit in the sorcery ritual materials, which do not require reference to these scholars.

My argument asserts that the relation between sorcery and the kind of political violence referred to is thus at the abstract level of dynamics. There is no statement whatsoever of a causative relation between sorcery beliefs and practice, on the one hand, and contemporary violent politics, on the other.[27] My point is that they share a shape in their dynamics, this dynamic in no way indicating a direct cultural or historical link between the two. Obviously, the dynamics I have isolated by searching through the ethnography for the bare dimensions of the processes involved can be extracted from the observation of state and insurgent terror worldwide, quite apart from sorcery practices. But I do indicate that ritual formations may indeed pick up on the dynamics of human processes that have a high degree of universal potential and, moreover, impart to them a sharper delineation or definition in their mythopraxis. In this sense, sorcery practices, especially given their ontological direction in the historical context of Sri Lanka (the rites I have discussed were born in state systems that were subject to manifold kinds of resistance), may be acutely sensitive to the dynamics of social and political processes. They distill a dynamic that has distinct empirical workings out under different historical conditions, these different conditions, nonetheless, sustaining the relevance of the ritual and its dynamics in very different historical realities. History, in effect, reinvents the relevance of the dynamic. Moreover, ritual has its own method of abstraction—a dimension of myth and of its practice in performance—that not only can draw into focus critical aspects of dynamics in its own realities but can point up the possibilities of dynamics elsewhere that may be otherwise relatively obscured.

Ritual, I have stated above, may be addressed as a folk version of situational analysis or extended-case method. I am given to this observation as a consequence of Gluckman's idea. However, treating rite consciously in situational-analytic terms—as Turner effectively did in his own analyses of rite—demands that it be examined as a process that may include a number of different dynamics (as is the case with Sinhala healing rites). Furthermore, I have attempted to expand Gluckman's idea not only by following the particular logics of the dynamics but also by extracting from them the potentialities of their argument for the investigation of other phenomena that are outside the strict domain of rite. Without denying the importance of Gluckman's own interpretations of situations and theorization of them, it is possible that the value of the situational perspective may be expanded by giving more sociological authority to the arguments of the discursive practices (both their interpretations or conceptualizations and those that are embedded in the structures of practice) that are integral to the constitution of events and situations.

## In Retrospect

From the standpoint of contemporary anthropology, Gluckman and his Manchester School's methodological intervention does not appear as innovative today as it seemed when many of us just starting our careers joined his department. The relatively close group of scholars among whom Gluckman's ideas developed spread out in many instances to form departments of their own. The situation of the Manchester Department in Gluckman's day was itself in dynamic tension, contributing to the excitement, with colleagues and students either following his methodological prescriptions or reacting against them. Occasionally, this was productive, but undoubtedly a few directions were dead ends. Paradoxically, the potentiality of Gluckman's ideas were as much open to decline as they were to innovation, even negating such imaginative possibilities. The notion of fission and fusion, which was anthropologically popular in his time, and the idea that all systems contain the seeds of their own demise, which Gluckman particularly favored, were applicable to some degree both to his Manchester School and to his preferred methodology. However, I must add another observation. As I noted at the outset, situational analysis was already a bricolage of many influences. Gluckman was open, as were his Manchester colleagues, to investigate the potential of other perspectives that could be introduced into the Manchester situational perspective. American symbolic interactionist and ethnomethodological approaches attracted interest, especially among the younger generation, as did the transactionalist perspectives then taking root (see Barth 1966; Kapferer 1976). I think this capacity of the idea to continually reinvent itself by absorbing new perspectives that were ultimately antagonistic to some of Gluckman's more important premises had the entropic effect of exhausting any specific originality for anthropology that the Manchester perspective may have had (see also Werbner 1984).

One major route from Gluckman's situational approach was Clyde Mitchell's (1969) development of social networks. This was explicitly related to the situational insistence on structural diversity and its key concern to attend to individual agency without losing the significance of larger structural forces, including the structure of social relations developing around individual actors yet not entirely reducible to them. For Mitchell, the concept of social network was to be a tool for the analysis of complexity and especially of large-scale processes that did not lose connection with the persons on the ground. Mitchell was particularly interested in the biographic dimensions of network analysis— the way it enabled the exploration of the construction of ego-centered relations and their changing import by focusing on the movement of particular individuals through a variety of contexts (here, one elaboration of the extended-case idea)—and the promise it held out for more analytical rigor (see Epstein 1969). Mitchell was interested in the application of various mathematical forms of analysis (see Garbett 1970, 1980; Mitchell 1974), and Gluckman, enthusiastically in support, began to include network ideas in the reinterpretation of old arguments (e.g., the divorce hypothesis).

A major import of the social-network concept is its aim to overcome what Gluckman and Mitchell conceived to be a disadvantage of the community-centeredness and localism of conventional anthropological fieldwork, which sometimes missed the fact that significant social relations were not bounded by the idea of community, anthropologists often inventing the idea of community when there was none. Situational analysis and the extended case already offered a way out, but Mitchell saw the potential of carrying the point further. The explicit connection between situational analysis and the extended case, on the one hand, and the concept of social network, on the other, is evident in a study by Epstein (1969) on the Copperbelt and in my own work (Kapferer 1972) in industrial/factory contexts in Kabwe (Broken Hill). Mitchell (1969) developed the idea initially used by John Barnes (his Central African colleague and a student of Gluckman) in his Norwegian study (Barnes 1954) and also by Elizabeth Bott (1957) for her study of family and class in London. In Norway and in London, the kind of anthropology that focused on small, localized communities was not appropriate (in Norway, people in rural areas are sometimes widely scattered in small clusters or homesteads across a difficult terrain) and far more problematic in urban concentrations characterized by movement, often migratory. With Barnes, Bott, and especially Mitchell, the idea of network became more than a metaphor.

In many respects, the concept of network, as that of situational and extended-case analysis, ran afoul of more individualist theories that were on the rise in the latter part of Gluckman's life. Some of these, such as transactionalism (see Bailey 1969; Barth 1966; Kapferer 1976), opened up contradictions that were implicit within the situational idea, overcoming the importance of structural dynamics and process as forces on human action (generated by individuals but not reducible to them) that Gluckman constantly insisted on bridging.[28]

Scholars during Gluckman's heyday and since have concentrated their analyses around events and situations. Both Geertz and Sahlins have focused in a significant way on the structure and processes of events, but they have been strongly relativist. This is certainly so with Geertz (1973). Sahlins's (1980) brilliant work on Hawaii effectively stops when Hawaii becomes part of larger realities and the events that he discusses have a high degree of inner consistency (as the wider structural/cultural context) that I think Gluckman and his colleagues would have contested. Sahlins's most recent work (2004), while thoroughly independent of any influence of Gluckman's Manchester tradition, in my view, carries the thrust of Gluckman's approach, which is to address larger problems of a global nature through the event. Sahlins, I think, probably realizes more successfully than Gluckman did the event as a source for the discovery of larger theoretical understanding, but he is nonetheless constrained within the linguistic and symbolic frame of American cultural anthropology, which, as I have said, does not fully escape the kind of relativism to which Gluckman was opposed. For Gluckman, it was in the event and the situation that the suggestions for analysis were to be found. The idea should never be merely illustrative or a gimmick by which to engage with larger developments, for it was always pregnant with possibilities (potentially breaking free of cultural constraints) that were yet to be realized and which the action emergent within it was likely to be integral in producing.

If Gluckman's perspective is no longer distinctive, itself being overtaken by events, it anticipated many later developments, and its relevance still continues. This is especially so in an era of globalization, as I noted at the beginning of this discussion, and in a context of anthropological revision, when there is a cry in some quarters for a multi-sited field strategy (Marcus 1998), the point of which lay behind situational analysis and the kinds of problems upon which Gluckman and his colleagues focused. In my view, Gluckman's methodological innovation remains important, for while it is doubtless open to many improvements, it amounts to one of the few attempts (see also Handelman 1998; Sahlins 2005) to theorize the status of the situation and the event and to lay out a procedure and a demonstration of their significance for the development of a specifically anthropological understanding.

Gluckman is still an inspiration to the many of us who were influenced by his energy and thought. His generosity, humor, and warmth were not only the defining character of the man but a critical dimension of his intelligence, whereby he easily acknowledged the contributions of others and tried to develop his own thought around them. Perhaps of greatest and most enduring importance was his commitment to the discipline of anthropology and his drive to make it thoroughly critical and alive to the problematics of the contemporary world.

### Acknowledgments

I wish to thank Richard Werbner for inviting me to present this lecture and for the many influential conversations and reminiscences about Gluckman and the Manchester tradition that we have engaged in since we first met in Zambia in 1964.

The late Kingsley Garbett, Andrew Roberts, Olaf Smedal, and the editors of this volume have discussed aspects of the overall argument of the essay with me, and I am grateful to them. Much of my discussion is, of course, based in my membership of the Manchester group in the latter days of Gluckman's presence before he took a post in Oxford, and on personal discussions with both Gluckman and Clyde Mitchell concerning the situational approach.

Bruce Kapferer is a Fellow of the Australian Academy of Social Sciences and is currently Professor of Social Anthropology at the University of Bergen, Norway. He was affiliated with the Rhodes-Livingstone Institute (1963–1966) and was later appointed to the Department of Social Anthropology at the University of Manchester (1966–1973). He was subsequently Foundation Professor of Anthropology at the University of Adelaide and at James Cook University, as well as Professor and Chair at University College London. In 2005 he was Davis Senior Fellow at the National Humanities Center, North Carolina, and has held other research fellowships at other institutions, among them the Center for Behavioral Sciences, Palo Alto, the Netherlands Institute for Advanced Studies, and the University of Manchester. His published books include *A Celebration of Demons* (1983), *Legends of People, Myths of State* (1988), and *The Feast of the Sorcerer* (1997). He has recently edited *Beyond Rationalism* (2002), and has co-edited, with Angela Hobart, *Aesthetics in Performance* (2005). Currently, he leads a Norwegian Research Foundation project located at Bergen on contemporary state formations and their effects. He is continuing major fieldwork in South Asia, Southern Africa, and Australia.

## Notes

1. The essay is largely confined to the South-Central African period of the Manchester anthropological development. There are several important studies and reflections on Gluckman and the Manchester approach that add much to what I discuss here. I recommend the overall appraisal of the Manchester tradition written by Richard Werbner (1984). Richard Brown (1979) presents a useful account of Gluckman's accession to the directorship of the RLI in Zambia. The research program that Gluckman developed there and the crucial link between the RLI and Manchester were of central importance to the development of the Manchester School. Van Donge (1985) gives a consideration of the RLI and Manchester rural studies in South-Central Africa, while Schumaker (2001) engages in critical historical reconstruction of the fieldwork practice, as well as the nature of the socio-political realities in which the fieldwork was conducted.
2. Epstein (Yelvington 1997) tells of an event in the corridors of the LSE regarding a remark made by Leach to Firth concerning Epstein's interest in urban processes as not being anthropology.
3. Brown (1979) and Schumaker (2001) point out that Gluckman and his colleagues were in compromised positions as members of the dominant colonialist white community in Central Africa. Brown (1979: 537) discusses the fact that in his days as director of the RLI, Gluckman was keen to be involved in colonial administrative projects and that he was disaffected by not being taken seriously. But Brown (ibid.: 538, 540) also underlines Gluckman's critical attitude toward the colonial administration and his general support for the program of decolonization.

4. The conclusion to the seminar and his Plenary Address is as follows: "One may learn something from examination; dismissal teaches one nothing. If we call others 'asshead,' we may be in *A Midsummer Night's Dream* (Act III, sc. 1), looking through bully Bottom's mask." Gluckman enjoyed every second of the barb, which brought hoots of derision from those at the seminar. The moment was thoroughly enjoyed by all.

5. Major criticisms of structural functionalism, involving systemic closure of determinism and homeostasis, were starting to develop. As I consider more fully later in this discussion, Gluckman, stressing both dynamics and individual agency, radically departed from later much-criticized aspects of structural functionalism. He saw closed systems purely as constructions for the establishment of theoretical conceptualizations that should be testable through comparative analysis.

6. Firth (1975) and Bloch (1983) downplay the influence of Marx on Gluckman and the Manchester School. Firth complains that Gluckman tended to overplay the socially integrative functions of conflict. But he misses the point that Gluckman makes a distinction between conflict and contradiction: the former is a surface feature of social processes, while the latter is vital as the underlying force of history and transformations in it. This is certainly systematic with my reading of Marx, and I think that Gluckman makes something of a refinement, trying to understand why the effect of the working out of dominant cleavages, as he would state, often does not result in the revolutionary changes that might be expected. As I will explain, this is thoroughly evident in his work on Zululand. Bloch, writing in the heyday of structural Marxism, implicitly suggests that Gluckman is not Marxist enough, despite the obvious influence not only in Gluckman's *Analysis of a Social Situation in Modern Zululand* ([1940] 1958) but also in his *Economy of the Central Barotse Plain* ([1941] 1968). Gluckman and his colleagues (e.g., Worsley 1956) may have been more materialist than Bloch might have wished, but the influence of Marxist thinking is clear. Certainly, it is more evident than in Firth or others at the time. Bloch's own affair with Marxism occurred much later—when it was radical chic. In the race to hold the radical high ground, Bloch gives the pole position to the far more politically conservative Edmund Leach. Bloch also downplays Gluckman's and his colleagues' critique of the colonialism of British social anthropologists, citing one or two exceptions. But Gluckman's point is generally valid. It is possible that the politics of British social anthropology at the time that these assessments were made accounts for a certain freedom with the facts.

7. The reanalyses of Malinowski's Trobriand material by Singh Uberoi (1962) and of Meyer Fortes's Tallensi ethnography by Worsley (1956) provide some of the outstanding published examples of the kind of reinterpretation encouraged by Gluckman. In Gluckman's view, these constituted a kind of test as well as an extension of the original understandings.

8. Van Teeffelen (1977) surveys the Israel program and gives it a high success rating compared to the Central Africa group. I think he is mistaken. The Israel program was an attempt to repeat the Central Africa program, in which all of the methodological innovations of Gluckman and his colleagues were achieved. In Central Africa there was a unity of purpose and, above all, a deep sense of issue and problem to which most were committed. In my opinion, the Israel scheme did not achieve anything approaching the import of the Central Africa work as far as the significance for social anthropology is concerned.

9. The style of the seminar owed much to the intellectual style of Gluckman (viewed as eccentric by some) and his concern to open up 'facts' to interpretation. Gluckman often saw this as a cooperative intellectual exercise. Folklore has it that the first RLI seminar took place in the Zambezi River (the RLI was initially situated at Livingstone before it moved to Lusaka). One seminar is purported to have taken place while Gluckman was having his hair cut (Clyde Mitchell, personal communication). The field-training exercise that Gluckman, after he had assumed the directorship of the RLI, took his researchers on in the Lamba resettlement area had many of the trappings of Gluckman's conception of the seminar as a practical work session in anthropology (see Mitchell and Barnes 1950; Schumaker 2001: 86). In other words, the RLI seminars, and later the seminars at the department in Manchester, were never conceived as formal sessions for the presentation of ideas and ethnography but rather working events. In effect, the seminar presenter

gave material that would then be seriously worked on in the spirit of a workshop. It was expected that all would attend as part of their commitment to research.

10. I have discussed elsewhere (Kapferer 2003) Gluckman's egalitarian ethos. Gluckman's image of the African chief or king was very much at the forefront of his imagination. This perception was of a person who is a *primus inter pares*, that is, a person who embodies to the highest degree the qualities (generosity, selflessness) that are the core organizational properties of the group and who is otherwise no different from those whom he commands. Put another way, material difference, the trappings of status, and other forms of social distinction should not be an impediment to social interactions with peers. Gluckman's famous insistence that his colleagues should accompany him to Manchester United football games (an idea initiated by Peter Worsley and at the time expressive of an egalitarian and ideological unity with the working class) was, for Gluckman, a ritual expression of unity over difference. Given the intellectual and personal conflicts that were often a feature of life in the Manchester department, attendance at the games sometimes had the ambience of what Gluckman might himself have called "the peace in the feud" (see Gluckman 1955b).

11. Epstein (Yelvington 1997: 292) presents a picture of Firth's LSE seminar in the 1950s and comments on Firth's ability to control the discussion and keep it to the point. While he admires this, he also remarks that he found the LSE seminar occasions "quite freezing." He did not like the way students were picked on. I think the account Epstein gives indicates a very hierarchical and controlled event quite in contrast to the 'heat' of the Manchester seminar.

12. In my interpretation of Bourdieu's use of the concept of habitus, developed in relation to Durkheim, Mauss, Levi-Strauss, and Merleau-Ponty, there is a major move away from a deterministic structuralism of more or less fixed oppositions to one in which these oppositions come into selective and changing relation (with consequently shifting import) relative to the movement of persons. This is exemplified in Bourdieu's (1977) discussion of the Kabyle house, where the import of the structures of habituated lived space—in which consciousness is continually formed and re-formed—changes and shifts relative to the movement of persons through it (body hexis). The person in movement or engaged in practices within this habitus is in a creative and generative relation to the meaningful potential of the habitus. This meaning is contingent on practice and is further contingent when the person embodying such meaningful potential or through such practice enters external realities; that is, the contingencies of external realities have further influence or changing influence on the meaning generated in the habitus, the orientation or disposition toward the world being established through the habitus. The external reality is, in Bourdieu's conception, an open horizon, contingent in this sense. This is the idea that Gluckman favored, albeit in different terms earlier on, refusing the notion of society and of culture as closed systems except as clear heuristic constructions for the purpose of analysis.

13. Of course, the point here was/is that Africans and white settlers cooperated in the political economy of an industrial/industrializing society that opened up conflicts between them founded in the very structural dynamics of the capitalist forces at work and to which they were all committed.

14. Crehan (1997) attacks Gluckman and by extension the RLI group of anthropologists for adopting an ahistorical approach to their research, concentrating particularly on the notion of tribe. Although she asserts that she is focusing on Gluckman's student text, *Politics, Law and Ritual in Tribal Society* (1965) and does not wish to address his work as a whole, this does seem to be a little disingenuous, given that the article appears to be a critical statement on the overall RLI position. She reiterates common criticisms, for example, the static structural functionalism of the equilibrium model, the idea that the RLI use of tribe tended to overlook history and change and stressed homogeneity. It is a pity that Crehan did not try to comprehend Gluckman in the context of his work as a whole and especially in terms of his overall paradigm that is established in *A Social Situation* and in *Malinowski's Sociological Theories*. This paradigm is integral to the fieldwork assumptions of Gluckman's RLI colleagues. Crehan in her particularizing in fact takes the approach of Gluckman and his RLI colleagues out of context. I might add that Terence Ranger's stress on the role of tribal categories as colonially invented traditions

for the purpose of colonial control, to which Crehan refers approvingly, was developed in the context of a full consciousness of the RLI research.

15. Gluckman's analysis indicates how Western political and economic processes were part of African history well before this was reflected in African consciousness, even though their impact could already be shown to be a factor in the transformation of African social and political institutions. He also depicts how forces integral within African political dynamics had repercussions for transformational processes in Europe, for example. Here he certainly prefigures Eric Wolf's (1992) important development. I add that in certain ways it is in advance of Sahlins's much later analysis. In a critical sense, Sahlins's (1980) analysis of the cultural and political transformation of ancient Hawaii is an extension of Malinowski's culture contact theory of social transformation (see Kapferer 1988). Gluckman might have argued that the changes that Sahlins describes for Hawaii were already motivated in a European presence in the Pacific well before they came into active contact with Hawaiians.

16. Ferguson (1999) criticizes the RLI and Manchester School anthropologists on a number of counts, among them their liberalism rather than radical Marxism and their compromised political situation in the context of white colonial control. Certainly, they were not hard-line radicals and, indeed, were compromised—a condition of most anthropologists including Ferguson. But given this, the Manchester members were sharply critical of prevailing white colonialist and politically ideological arguments. Ferguson echoes especially the critique of Magubane (1971) against Mitchell whom Magubane charged continued dominant ideology through the concept of 'tribalism'. Magubane, as others have pointed out, egregiously misinterpreted Mitchell's point. This was that what Mitchell identified as tribalism was a thoroughly modern ethnic construct constituted as a kind of social stereotype in the circumstances of urban/industrial life (see Kapferer 1995a, 1995c). Magubane, in effect, interpreted Mitchell's concept as an anthropological primitivist, traditionalist stance. Quite the opposite to Mitchell's position which, following Gluckman, is antagonistic to those colonialist interpretations, certainly racist, that conceived of Africans as tribal people in town, i.e., unaccustomed to urban life and to be civilized into its structures. Mitchell's argument is entirely the reverse to Magubane's presentation of it and which Ferguson approvingly reissues. Ferguson, keen to present the radical or politically correct view, actually ends up supporting a conservative position that he might otherwise oppose. Strangely, Ferguson (also Burawoy [2000], who follows the same line of attack) regards Mitchell as a protagonist both of a modernization project and of a gradualism that was part of the legitimation of colonial orders, integral to a civilizing process. The whole tenor of Mitchell's approach is, in fact, in accord with that of Ferguson and indicates the critical role of rural ties in urban life even before the collapse of the mining industry, which is the context of Ferguson's ethnography. Furthermore, in Mitchell's analysis, this is neither entirely a function of colonial restrictions nor one of an enduring traditionalism. Rather, Mitchell was concerned with examining migration and urban processes as taking place in a complexly interrelated field of social and economic relations that included an understanding of the importance of rural ties. He was interested in forms of analysis that to some extent overcame rural-urban contrasts and oppositions that influenced many urban studies.

Ferguson's argument is additionally strange because he claims that Godfrey Wilson's orientation as set out in the *Economics of Detribalization* is the more appropriate stance rather than that of Mitchell. This is based on a confusion. Wilson is the modernization theorist who sees Africans as both tribal traditionalists in town and people who are gradually adapting to its environment (in the process of becoming modern). (For Wilson, Africans are traditionalist in rural areas, but as Mitchell and Gluckman pointed out these areas are also modern, but in a different way, because they are subject to the forces of capital of which colonial structures were a part.) Mitchell, Gluckman and others in the Manchester School were sharply opposed to what they regarded as adaptationist arguments which they also saw as thoroughly congruent with an American cultural relativism and culturalism that they attacked routinely. The whole argument of Fergusons's work is based on an extreme misunderstanding of fairly straightforward arguments. Ironically he in fact supports a position to which he is actually opposed, brought about by an acute misreading and his eagerness to draw out his own distinction. As few of his readers are likely to read Wilson he gets away with what is tantamount to premeditated academic homicide.

Ferguson's general position is premised on the collapse of the mining industry in Zambia which implies Mitchell, Epstein and the other urban anthropologists of the time might have predicted. Certainly their divinatory expertise was undeveloped!. He then goes on to say that urbanization is all about style, a way of life—echoing Louis Wirth—that is as much a dimension of rural life as urban life. The peoples in Zambia are in a globalized world dominated by capital—precisely the position of the Manchester School. Adding salt into the wound Ferguson then goes on to explain the expansion of the importance of rural ties in the circumstance of urban/industrial decline and the generation of great uncertainty. The argument in fact follows the line of Mitchell (the point of his arguments on migration, stabilization and especially his development of the concept of social network) but Ferguson effectively appropriates it as his own post-modern originality.

17. Adam Kuper (1999) reiterates the same overall point. Interestingly, he does not cite Gluckman, whose argument had the political courage that Kuper's lacks. Instead, Kuper references the work of Schapera and Radcliffe-Brown, whose influence Gluckman himself acknowledged but whose larger political implications Gluckman took considerably further.

18. See the essays in Kapferer (2005a) for criticisms of this trend.

19. In seminars and in private discussion, Gluckman and others in the Manchester tradition (especially Mitchell) would inveigh against what they called the "culture in the head" psychologistic position of much anthropology. This was not to say that human beings did not have value orientations in their life-worlds. What the Manchester group resisted was the implication of culture as some kind of totality that was embedded in individual skulls. Not only is culture not to be totalized in such a way, but also, they insisted, whatever culture is (and it is always situationally engaged), it is produced and has its effect through interactive and other structural processes that cannot be reduced purely to the mind.

20. Macmillan (1995: 42) records that Zulu authorities complained to the white administration that Gluckman was asking too many intimate questions about sex. This has resonance with Gluckman's often-expressed view that Shaka was ridiculed in his sexuality (he was said to have a small penis) and that this accounted for aspects of his ambition and violence. I think Macmillan's finding indicates Gluckman's interest in Freud and his concern to relate psychosexual conflicts and orientations to socio-political action. Gluckman would be routinely opposed on this point in seminars, which might have inhibited the full publication of his Zulu material. I offer this suggestion very hesitantly indeed.

21. Gluckman and his Manchester colleagues were interested in Leach's materialist turn in his Sri Lanka study *Pul Eliya* (Leach 1961). They saw this as very similar to the direction they had taken well before, though caustic comments were passed to the effect that it read like "underanalyzed field notes," implying that it would have benefited from the closer analysis recommended in the situational analysis and extended-case perspectives.

22. Ferguson (1999: 207–233) presents a post-modern, cosmopolitan version of the situational arguments of Mitchell and others for the Copperbelt. He entitles one section "Analysis of a Social Situation in (Post) Modern Zambia" (ibid.: 218–230). In this (re)presentation, culture becomes reduced to style, the kinds of performances he discusses echoing very much the material collected by Mitchell and the broad points about the culture concept presented by Mitchell and by Gluckman. But the analysis is a total trivialization of the situational analysis approach. There is no attempt to explore the structural dynamics of the situated particular or the larger, more global structural processes affecting action at the local level. With no effort at all to engage with specifics, Ferguson reduces what might be suspected as very different contexts and their dynamics (a point of situational analysis) into a congealed similarity further compounded by the use of generalized, spongy terms, such as 'cosmopolitanism' and 'globalization', that, in too many analyses of a post-modernist nature, threaten to say a great deal about nothing. In the end, there is a kind of uniform and universalizing process at work, the very contradiction of the orientation of situational analysis.

23. What they denote as 'actuality' might also be referred to as the 'really real' in the positivist sense, that is, reality as it may exist independent of any human constructive or interpretational exercise to describe what reality is or may be defined as being.

24. Deleuze and Guattari understand science to address a chaos of existence (a complexity of myriad structuring processes rather than a disorder), which is defined "by its infinite speed with which every form taking shape in it vanishes. It is a void that is not a nothingness but a *virtual*, containing all possible particles and drawing out all possible forms, which spring up only to disappear immediately, without consistency or reference, without consequence" (1994: 225). They build on the work of Ilya Prigogine and Isabelle Stengers, *Entre le temps et l'éternité* (Between Time and Eternity) (1988), particularly their discussion of the crystallization of a superfused liquid below its crystallization temperature.

25. W. I. Thomas's famous dictum that "if men define situations as real, they are real in their consequences" enables non-anthropological interpretations to be sustained but in an ultimately non-threatening relation to established anthropological theorizing or predispositions.

26. Another brilliant example of the direction I am taking is Mimica's (1992) account of a New Guinea people's counting system. Through an interrogation of the practice (which involves a tacking back and forth into the cosmology and social world of the people), Mimica demolishes anthropological argument that peoples in New Guinea have a primitive, even childlike (after Piaget) notion of counting. He then demonstrates that the dynamics of the counting disclose the potentialities of higher mathematics, further arguing that the imagination of mathematics is to some degree an extension of the processes of embodiment of human beings.

27. Some critics of my earlier work on nationalist violence in Sri Lanka (Kapferer 1988) state that I have said that Sinhala nationalism is an outgrowth of sorcery exorcisms. I do not say this. What I do argue is that they metonymically share a common dynamic. Other commentators have picked up my comparison of nationalist violence with the violence that is apparent in exorcism. Here I was arguing for a metaphoric connection. Indeed, I would suggest that in a sense nationalism and exorcism share at least one feature in common (but again, there is no suggestion of a causative connection)—they both can be conceived as rites of cleansing. My general point was that any connections in the symbolism of sorcery and modern nationalism were connections that were established through nationalist discourse.

28. While Gluckman was interested in the development of individualist approaches, he did insist on the priority of social-structural formations and dynamics. Two scholars whose work interested him were George Homans and later Fredrik Barth, but he preferred the more structural work of these scholars over their development of individualist social exchange or transactionalist perspectives. Gluckman was particularly impressed by Homans's historical study of thirteenth-century English villagers and Barth's study of the Swat Pathans (which Gluckman taught in his introductory first-year classes). He saw his own approach as the best, and its worth as being reflected in the early work of Homans and Barth. One anecdote in the latter days of Gluckman's presence at Manchester illustrates the point as well as the humor of the man. The occasion was when he invited Homans to present a seminar. Gluckman, in deference to Homans, who had suffered a heart attack and was a non-smoker, wrote "NO SMOKING" in large chalk letters on the blackboard behind where Homans was seated. Homans began his talk to the assembled staff, opening by saying that he was going to talk about a great British social anthropologist, even though the scholar concerned was not exactly English. All of us gathered were shifting nervously because we thought it was going to be another self-affirmation for Gluckman. Max appeared to be holding his head in mock self-effacement. Homans repeated that the social anthropologist was not English. Homans paused and the tension built. Suddenly, Homans in raised tone declared, "And that anthropologist ... is ... BARTH, Fredrik Barth!!!!" Gluckman looked up, surprised (we all sighed in relief). He immediately got up and, with a large grin on his face, went to the blackboard, rubbing out his notice and replacing it with "SMOKING ALLOWED!"

# References

Bailey, Frederick G. 1969. *Stratagems and Spoils.* Oxford: Blackwell.

Barnes, J. A. 1954. "Class and Committees in a Norwegian Island Parish." *Human Relations* 7: 39–58.

Barth, Fredrik. 1966. *Models of Social Organization.* London: Royal Anthropological Institute of Great Britain and Ireland, Occasional Paper No. 23.

Beidelman, T. O. 1966. "Swazi Royal Ritual." *Africa* 36: 373–405.

Bloch, Maurice. 1983. *Marxism and Anthropology.* Oxford: Clarendon Press.

Bott, Elizabeth. 1957. *Family and Social Network.* London: Tavistock.

Bourdieu, Pierre. 1977. *Outline of a Theory of Practice.* Cambridge: Cambridge University Press.

Brown, Richard. 1979. "Passages in the Life of a White Anthropologist: Max Gluckman in Northern Rhodesia." *Journal of African History* 20: 525–541.

Burawoy, Michael. 2000. "Introduction: Reaching for the Global." Pp. 1–40 in *Global Ethnography,* ed. Michael Burawoy et al. Berkeley: University of California Press.

Crehan, Kate. 1997. "'Tribes' and the People Who Read Books: Managing History in Colonial Zambia." *Journal of Southern African Studies* 23, no. 2: 203–218.

Deleuze, Gilles. 1986. *Cinema 1: The Movement-Image.* Trans. H. Tomlinson and B. Habberjam. London: Athlone Press.

Deleuze, Gilles, and Felix Guattari. 1988. *A Thousand Plateaus.* Trans. Brian Massumi. London: Athlone Press.

_____. 1994. *What Is Philosophy?* New York: Columbia University Press.

Devons, Ely, and Max Gluckman. 1964. "Conclusion: Modes and Consequences of Limiting a Field of Study." Pp. 158–261 in Gluckman 1964.

Epstein, A. L. 1958. *Politics in an Urban African Community.* Manchester: Manchester University Press.

_____. 1969. "Gossip, Norms and Social Network." Pp. 117–127 in *Social Networks in Urban Situations,* ed. J. Clyde Mitchell. Manchester: Manchester University Press.

Evans-Pritchard, Edward E. 1937. *Witchcraft, Oracles and Magic among the Azande.* Oxford: Clarendon.

Ferguson, James. 1999. *Expectations of Modernity: Myths and Meanings of Urban Life on the Zambian Copperbelt.* Berkeley: University of California Press.

Firth, Raymond. 1975. "Max Gluckman, 1911–1975." *Proceedings of the British Academy* 61: 479–496.

Friedson, Steven M. 1996. *Dancing Prophets: Musical Experience in Tumbuka Healing.* Chicago: University of Chicago Press.

_____. 2005. "Where Divine Horsemen Ride: Trance Dancing in West Africa." Pp. 109–128 in *Aesthetics in Performance: Formations of Symbolic Construction and Experience,* ed. Angela Hobart and Bruce Kapferer. Oxford and New York: Berghahn Books.

Garbett, G. Kingsley. 1970. "The Analysis of Social Situations." *Man* (n.s.) 5, no. 2: 214–227.

_____. 1980. "Graph Theory and the Analysis of Multiplex and Manifold Relationships." Pp. 191–232 in *Numerical Techniques in Social Anthropology,* ed. J. C. Mitchell. Philadelphia: Institute for the Study of Human Issues.

Geertz, Clifford. 1973. "Deep Play: Notes on the Balinese Cockfight." Pp. 412–453 in *The Interpretation of Cultures.* New York: Basic Books.

Gluckman, Max. [1940] 1958. *Analysis of a Social Situation in Modern Zululand.* Manchester: Manchester University Press for Rhodes-Livingstone Institute.

_____. [1941] 1968. *Economy of the Central Barotse Plain.* Rhodes-Livingstone Papers, no. 7. Manchester: Manchester University Press.

_____. 1949. *An Analysis of the Sociological Theories of Bronislaw Malinowski.* Oxford: Oxford University Press.

_____. 1955a. *The Judicial Process among the Barotse of Northern Rhodesia (Zambia).* Manchester: Manchester University Press.

_____. 1955b. *Custom and Conflict in Africa.* Oxford: Blackwell.

_____. 1960. "Tribalism in Modern British Central Africa." *Cahiers Etudes Africains* 1: 55–70.

_____. 1961a. "Anthropological Problems Arising from the African Industrial Revolution." Pp. 67–82 in *Social Change in Modern Africa,* ed. A. Southall. Oxford: Oxford University Press.

_____. 1961b. "Ethnographic Data in British Social Anthropology." *Sociological Review* 9: 5–17.

_____. 1963. *Order and Rebellion in Tribal Africa*. London: Cohen and West.

_____, ed. 1964. *Closed Systems and Open Minds: The Limits of Naïvety in Social Anthropology*. Chicago: Aldine.

_____. 1965. *Politics, Law and Ritual in Tribal Society*. Oxford: Blackwell.

_____. 1968. "The Utility of the Equilibrium Model in the Study of Social Change." *American Anthropologist* (n.s.) 70, no. 2: 219–237.

Handelman, Don. 1998. *Models and Mirrors: Towards an Anthropology of Public Events*. New York and Oxford: Berghahn Books.

Kapferer, Bruce. 1972. *Strategy and Transaction in an African Factory*. Manchester: Manchester University Press.

_____, ed. 1976. *Transaction and Meaning: Directions in the Anthropology of Exchange and Social Behavior*. Association of Social Anthropologists Monograph Series. Philadelphia: Institute for the Study of Human Issues.

_____. 1983. *A Celebration of Demons: Exorcism and the Aesthetics of Healing in Sri Lanka*. Bloomington: Indiana University Press. (2nd ed. published jointly in 1992 by the Smithsonian Institution Press and Berg Press.)

_____. 1988. *Legends of People, Myths of State: Violence, Intolerance and Political Culture in Sri Lanka and Australia*. Washington, DC: Smithsonian Institution Press. (2nd ed. published in 1998 by Smithsonian Institution Press.)

_____. 1995a. "Bureaucratic Erasure: Identity, Resistance and Violence: Aborigines and a Discourse of Autonomy in a North Queensland Town." Pp. 69–90 in *Worlds Apart: Modernity through the Prism of the Local*, ed. Daniel Miller. London: Routledge.

_____. 1995b. "From the Edge of Death: Sorcery and the Motion of Consciousness." Pp. 134–152 in *Questions of Consciousness*, ed. A. Cohen and N. Rapport. London: Routledge.

_____. 1995c. "The Performance of Categories: Plays of Identity in Africa and Australia." Pp. 55–80 in *The Urban Context*, ed. A. Rogers and S. Vertovec. Oxford: Berg Press.

_____. 1996. "Remythologizing Discourses: State and Insurrectionary Violence in Sri Lanka." Pp. 159–188 in *Legitimation of Violence*, ed. D. Apter. London: Macmillan.

_____. 1997. *The Feast of the Sorcerer: Practices of Consciousness and Power*. Chicago: Chicago University Press.

_____. 2000. "The Sorcery of Consciousness: A Sinhala Buddhist Discourse on the Dynamics of Consciousness." *Journal of Cognition and Communication* 33, no. 1/2: 97–120.

_____. 2001a. "Anthropology: The Paradox of the Secular." *Social Anthropology* 9, no. 3: 341–344.

_____. 2001b. "Globalization, the State and Civil Violence in Sri Lanka." *Bulletin of the Royal Institute for Inter-Faith Studies* 3, no. 2: 59–111.

_____. 2003. "Erindring om forgangne tider: Gluckman og Manchester-skolen i social-antropologiens historie." *Jordens folk* 38, no. 3: 11–14.

_____. 2005a. *The Retreat of the Social: The Rise and Rise of Reductionism*. New York and Oxford: Berghahn Books.

_____. 2005b. "Ritual Dynamics and Virtual Practice: Beyond Representation and Meaning." Pp. 35–54 in *Ritual in Its Own Right: Exploring the Dynamics of Transformation*, ed. Don Handelman and Galina Lindquist. Special issue of *Social Analysis* 48, no. 2.

Kuper, Adam. 1999. *Culture: The Anthropologists' Account*. Cambridge, MA: Harvard University Press.

Leach, Edmund. 1961. *Pul Eliya: A Village in Ceylon: A Study of Land Tenure and Kinship*. Cambridge: Cambridge University Press.

_____. [1961] 2004. *Rethinking Anthropology*. Oxford: Berg.

Long, Norman. 1968. *Social Change and the Individual: A Study of the Social and Religious Responses to Innovation in a Zambian Rural Community*. Manchester: Manchester University Press.

Macmillan, Hugh. 1995. "Return to the Malungwana Drift: Max Gluckman, the Zulu Nation and the Common Society." *African Affairs* 94: 39–65.

Magubane, Bernard. 1971. "A Critical Look at Indices Used in the Study of Social Change in Colonial Africa." *Current Anthropology* 12, nos. 4–5: 419–445.

Malinowski, Bronislaw. 1945. *The Dynamics of Culture Change*. New Haven, CT: Yale University Press.

Marcus, George E. 1998. *Ethnography through Thick and Thin*. Princeton, NJ: Princeton University Press.

Mimica, Jadran. 1992. *Intimations of Infinity*. Oxford: Berg.

Mitchell, J. Clyde. 1956a. *The Kalela Dance*. Rhodes-Livingstone Paper No. 27. Manchester: Manchester University Press.

_____. 1956b. *The Yao Village: A Study in the Social Structure of a Nyasaland Tribe*. Manchester: Manchester University Press.

_____, ed. 1969. *Social Networks in Urban Situations*. Manchester: Manchester University Press.

_____. 1974. "Social Networks." *Annual Review of Anthropology* 3, no. 4: 279–299.

_____. 1983. "Case and Situation Analysis." *Sociological Review* 31: 187–211.

Mitchell, J. C., and J. A. Barnes. 1950. *The Lamba Village: Report of a Social Survey*. Cape Town: University of Cape Town Press.

Prigogine, Ilya, and Isabelle Stengers. 1988. *Entre le temps et l'éternité*. Paris: Fayard.

Sahlins, Marshall. 1980. *Historical Metaphors and Mythical History*. Ann Arbor: Michigan University Press.

_____. 2004. *Apologies to Thucydides*. Chicago: Chicago University Press.

_____. 2005. "Structural Work: How Microhistories Become Macrohistories and Vice Versa." *Anthropological Theory* 5, no. 1: 5–30.

Schneider, David M. 1995. *Schneider on Schneider: The Conversion of the Jews and Other Anthropological Stories*. Ed. Richard Handler. Durham, NC: Duke University Press.

Schumaker, Lyn. 2001. *Africanizing Anthropology: Fieldwork, Networks, and the Making of Cultural Knowledge in Central Africa*. Durham, NC: Duke University Press.

Shokeid, Moshe. 2001. "Obituary for A. L. Epstein." *American Anthropologist* 102, no. 4: 858–859.

Tambiah, S. J. 1976. *World Conqueror and World Renouncer*. Cambridge: Cambridge University Press.

_____. 1986. *Sri Lanka: Ethnic Fratricide and the Dismantling of Democracy*. London: I.B. Tauris.

Turner, Victor W. 1957. *Schism and Continuity in an African Society: A Study of Ndembu Social Life*. Manchester: Manchester University Press.

_____. 1968. *The Drums of Affliction: A Study of Religious Processes among the Ndembu of Zambia*. Oxford: Clarendon Press.

_____. 1974. *Dramas, Fields and Metaphors: Symbolic Action in Human Society*. Ithaca, NY: Cornell University Press.

Uberoi, Singh J. P. 1962. *Politics of the Kula Ring*. Manchester: Manchester University Press.

Van Donge, Jan Kees. 1985. "Understanding Rural Zambia Today: The Relevance of the Rhodes-Livingstone Institute." *Africa* 55, no. 1: 60–76.

Van Teeffelen, T. 1977. *Anthropologists on Israel: A Case Study in the Sociology of Knowledge*. Amsterdam: Antropologisch-Sociologisch Centrum, University of Amsterdam, Papers on European and Mediterranean Societies.

Van Velsen, Jaap. 1964. *The Politics of Kinship: A Study in Social Manipulation among the Lakeside Tonga of Nyasaland*. Manchester: Manchester University Press.

_____. 1967. "The Extended-Case Method and Situational Analysis." Pp. 29–53 in *The Craft of Anthropology*, ed. A. L. Epstein. London: Tavistock.

Werbner, Richard P. 1984. "The Manchester School in South-Central Africa." *Annual Review of Anthropology* 13: 157–185.

Wilson, Godfrey. 1941–1942. *An Essay on the Economics of Detribalization in Northern Rhodesia*. Rhodes-Livingstone Papers, nos. 5-6. Livingstone, Northern Rhodesia: Rhodes-Livingstone Institute.

Wolf, Eric. 1992. *Europe and the People without History*. Berkeley: University of California Press.

Worsley, Peter M. 1956. "The Kinship System of the Tallensi: A Re-evaluation." *Journal of the Royal Anthropological Institute* 86, no. 1: 37–75.

Yelvington, Kevin A. 1997. "An Interview with A. L. Epstein." *Current Anthropology* 38, no. 2: 289–299.

# SECTION II

# HISTORICIZING EXTENDED CASES

# PREFACE
Historicizing the Extended-Case Method

*T. M. S. Evens and Don Handelman*

In 1949, Gluckman was appointed to the new Chair of Social Anthropology at the University of Manchester, with the intention of founding a new department. At the time, he was teaching at Oxford, in Evans-Pritchard's department. During the visit there of a Dutch colleague, Gluckman was introduced to him as leaving shortly for Manchester. He responded: "Ah, in the same way as X has left the department at _____ to go to _____." Evans-Pritchard remarked: "No, not in the same way. X is a refugee; Gluckman is a colonist" (Gluckman 1972: x). Gluckman, the colonial and colonist, remained devoted to Evans-Pritchard, his mentor, and hankered from time to time to find his way back to the Oxbridge ecumene.

Yet something else took intellectual shape in Manchester, something that had begun long before and much farther away than Oxford. Gluckman had begun his voyage at the anthropological periphery of South Africa, colonized twice over, as the offspring of Jewish immigrants from Russia in a colonial outpost of Northern Europe. Deeply affected by his experiences there, he had attended Oxford as a Rhodes Scholar (he was an excellent athlete) and had returned to forge and temper his path-breaking thinking in the British colonies of Central Africa. Before taking up a lectureship at Oxford in 1947, he had headed the Rhodes-Livingstone Institute for Social Research in Northern Rhodesia, recruiting students and colleagues who later became the research core of the Manchester School. Evans-Pritchard sent him down to build Oxford in Lancashire, yet Gluckman had another agenda, one quite unlike that of the anthropologies of Oxbridge, one that steered away draft by draft from the symmetrical abstractions of social structure that dominated Oxford, away from the pretty clockwork aestheticism that always pervaded the Cambridge anthropology of Edmund Leach, his great enemy, who was upper-crust British to the core.

When Leach (1984: 20) wrote of Gluckman, "If anyone had asked me then [1938–1939] or later what I thought of Gluckman, I would probably have said that I considered him to be an uncivilized and fundamentally uneducated egocentric whose attempts at theoretical generalization were of quite puerile incompetence," this was not merely a statement of personal antipathy toward yet another foreign *parvenu* but one that opened to quite distinct aesthetics of practicing the discipline of anthropology. Despite Leach's (ibid.: 12) inane claim that, *inter alia*, Gluckman remained wedded to "homeostatic social equilibrium," it was indeed Edmund Leach who, despite his disclaimers, remained mired in, as it were, High Church structural principles and structuralist transformations until the end of his days. Gluckman, as we argue in the introduction, moved toward studying what we are calling the practice of practice, the study of the hurly burly of social life in its myriad complexities, contradictions, and always emerging dynamics. Little by little, though never fully so, this steering became self-steering, at least for a while, and this is why, if only for a little while, one can refer to the Manchester School of Anthropology.

The contributions to this second section show how deeply Mancunian dynamics were embedded in broader intellectual climates and how integral such dynamics were to the doing of this kind of anthropology, and not solely in field research. David Mills takes a social-constructionist perspective on how Gluckman fashioned (and perhaps self-fashioned) claims to a distinct and distinctive approach that came to be viewed as a uniquely Manchester anthropology. He argues that it was only in the 1950s, long after the bridge-opening articles had appeared, that Gluckman started to write about the case-study approach as an innovation lodged in the Rhodes-Livingstone Institute, and that he did so perhaps in response to the interest that others, especially Clyde Mitchell, but likely Victor Turner as well, expressed in these articles—and likely no less in response to the criticism of his peers, who preferred the delineation of abstracted bony principles of social skeleton, with bits of apt illustrative flesh adhering here and there. Mills perceives Gluckman's 1961 article, "Ethnographic Data in British Social Anthropology," as an attempt to fashion a distinctively anthropological genealogy for thinking about the extended-case study. He mentions that Fred Eggan took issue with Gluckman's pointed focus on case materials. This is an interesting twist, since Eggan, influenced by Radcliffe-Brown during the latter's stay in Chicago during the 1930s, was perhaps the major figure in post-war American anthropology who called for the integration of British structural functionalism and the American study of 'process' and history (Eggan 1954: 745). In this instance, the Manchester approach lined up against both the British and most of the American, finding more affinity with Chicago sociology.

Thus, Mills shows that Clyde Mitchell, early on, was fully aware of W. I. Thomas's idea of the definition of the situation, which Mitchell referred to as the 'situational approach', and probably with Thomas and Znaniecki's path-breaking sociological monograph, *The Polish Peasant in Europe and America* (1918), in which they discuss the significance of studying "concrete situations." In other words, the Chicago School of Sociology—which studied social situations through case studies (but not in any sense of an extended case)—had a significant, if embryonic, influence on the fashioning of a distinctive Manchester anthropology. A related question not addressed is whether the post–World War II Chicago contemporaries of the Manchester group, with their continuing appreciation for "the nature and obdurate character of the empirical world" (Colomy and Brown 1995: 29), had any impact on the emerging Manchester School.

Mills mentions that the case-study method "was as much about an approach to writing as an approach to research itself." The point is worth emphasizing. All of us know that the most difficult act of anthropological writing is the evocative yet substantive detailing of ethnography itself. The social situations of obdurate life are simply the most complex of social phenomena. Writing social situations positioned Manchester anthropology early on at the crux of turning the dynamics of social life into those of its inscription, even as Gluckman argued the value of literature for anthropology (see Frankenberg, this volume) without entombing culture within text-as-text, as Geertz and his apolitical American lit-crit hit mob had succeeded in doing by the 1980s in their quest for poetic (yet more often poetistic) shortcuts to doing ethnography. (Gluckman and his wife, Mary, devotees of Shakespeare, would declaim the Bard together in the privacy of their home.) This did not mean that all Manchester anthropologists were equally up to the task, though Victor Turner certainly was, as he developed the extended case into the social drama (see especially Turner 1974). Nonetheless, the problematic was recognized, salient.

Marian Kempny asks what it was that made Manchester anthropology fully a 'school', given that "theory as such was not a subject of inquiry," and given that Manchester anthropology had not generated a distinctive body of theory adopted by its members. Kempny makes useful points in this regard, outlining factors that held Manchester anthropologists together despite their numerous differences. Here we highlight two of these that were quite distinctive to and productive for Manchester anthropology, helping to shape the Manchester perspective yet never receiving the attention they deserved: the seminar and the reanalysis.

Post-war American academia turned more and more to corporate managerial models for its self-fashioning. Going into the university was going to the office; specialized committees and sub-committees proliferated; deans became professional bureaucrats; and the departmental seminar became a polished set-piece, an artful presentation of the individual self in the scholarly boardroom, responded to with degrees of polite comment, question, critique, and wit, depending on the status of speaker and respondent. American anthropologists, like American academics generally, were (and are) thin-skinned in discussion and debate, and little of intellectual substance came or comes from their seminar occasions. The individual positions the self before the intellect; the self is wounded; the intellect offers no buffer (David Schneider at Manchester was one case in point; see Frankenberg, this section).

Manchester was quite the contrary, always intensive and highly social (see Kapferer and Frankenberg, this volume), and Manchester seminars often were learning experiences, more endeavor than set-piece. Gluckman instituted the Seminar Week—a week of seminars, morning and afternoon, for five consecutive days during the last week of each term. The presenters were faculty, PhD students returned from the field, and guest speakers. The department practiced and lived seminar during that week, in the rough-and-tumble of discussions in which the position of speaker might be co-opted by others midway through a presentation that turned into a discussion—on topics varying from the nit-picking to the far-ranging. Often the presentation and discussion were on field materials, on how they did and did not fit together, the significance of either, or both. By and large, with Gluckman's tutelage, department members learned to think together with one another, while buffering their sensitive and precious souls from the substance of perspective and critique, though always retaining the right to accept criticism—or not. Both of us came to a parting of the ways with Gluckman over our PhD theses, but his bottom line was, as he expressed this to one of us: "Finally, it's your work, not mine." In other words, the decision is yours, as is, no less, the responsibility.

Not to put too fine a point on this, seminar discussion was no less the practicing into existence of anthropology through praxis, not the formulation of theory as meta-design, but the relentless, theorizing search for dynamics and patternings of complexity through what Peirce would have recognized as the logic of abduction, crucial to any anthropology of discovery and sadly lacking from today's anthropologies of ideological premise, presumption, and pronouncement. Not for nothing did Gluckman call anthropology a craft.

At his intellectual peak, Gluckman had the wonderful capability to listen to an argument in seminar and then, taking those selfsame materials, produce a counter-argument that re-explained those very materials that he then handed back to the lecturer. He did this not by going outside the parameters of the materials presented, nor by invoking another theory as more powerful to the task at hand, but by paying infinite attention to the minutiae of ethnographic detail, to the practicing of ethnography as it grew and took shape in the seminar room, and to the patternings implicit in this that could be highlighted to understand the field materials in a radically other way. Occasionally, a seminar would emerge as an embryonic extended case, as it was practiced into existence inside and outside the seminar room. Doing the ethnography of ethnography as it was collected in the seminar room was no less in its own way the praxis of theory and method—and it was fundamental to the idea of reanalysis.

Manchester taught the reanalysis of the classics, as Kempny writes, yet it went way beyond this. In the first instance, in Gluckman's view one learned from the ethnographies of others. He made a point of stressing just how easy it is to critique destructively, often by invoking countervailing theories, yet, appositely, just how difficult it is to critique constructively. He would say that there was always something valuable in the work of another, and that our task was to discover this. The crux to doing so was to learn to respect ethnography for its own sake, as a site of the obdurate social, cultural world in its myriads of complexity. Ethnography was to be learned from, yet in and by that very learning we were to make it our own, so that we could then rethink the details of ethnography in terms of what there is, not in terms of what there should be, could be, would be, used to be, must be.

Thus, first and foremost, as we stated above, analysts must stay within these parameters in the reanalysis, in intensive rather than extensive labor, exhausting the capacities of the data as much as possible from within themselves, afterwards adding to this while continuing the reanalysis. A powerful tool for learning and practicing the analysis of ethnography, and for continuously honing one's skills, reanalysis in the Manchester mode complemented the praxis of the extended case and the Manchester seminar. Both of us, much more than most anthropologists, have invested time and effort over the years into doing a wide range of reanalyses, from which our own anthropologies have only benefited (Evens 1984, 1989, 1994; Handelman 1998).

Ronnie Frankenberg is a lateral, transverse thinker, and his highly personal memoir juxtaposes much insight and information on positioning Gluckman in South Africa, Rhodesia, and Manchester—on Gluckman tensing between Marx and Freud, the most powerful thinkers on conflict in the conflicted nineteenth century—on Gluckman moving to rhythms of conflict and asymmetry yet trapped to degrees within those of functionalism. Above all, Gluckman was a highly politicized and political man, raised in South Africa, alienated from the system he was part of, and, no less, an anthropologist studying that very system, yet one that was both the problem and the problematic. Frankenberg argues that in writing the bridge articles, Gluckman was making a deliberate intervention in the language of anthropology as it was constituted in South Africa and in the anglophone world: he sought to undermine the absolute cultural difference that characterized and therefore legitimated the colonial practice that became apartheid and, too, its support from the prevalent anthropology there. Conflict came to the fore in Gluckman's work *because* he insisted on the singularity of multiplicities, on open systems that could not ignore the asymmetries and clashes between multiplicities, so that one could not refuse to analyze practices before one's very eyes. So, too, the anthropologist was one of these multiplicities, albeit a tiny mote of a multiplicity, but nonetheless a subject among subjects, shaped, moved, acting, acted on. In our understanding of Frankenberg's reading, Gluckman advocated studying the practice of practice long before many of the Americans discovered what they think is practice theory.

# References

Colomy, Paul, and J. David Brown. 1995. "Elaboration, Revision, Polemic, and Progress in the Second Chicago School." Pp. 17–81 in *A Second Chicago School? The Development of a Postwar American Sociology*, ed. Gary Alan Fine. Chicago: University of Chicago Press.

Eggan, Fred. 1954. "Social Anthropology and the Method of Controlled Comparison." *American Anthropologist* 56: 743–763.

Evens, T. M. S. 1984. "Nuer Hierarchy." Pp. 317–334 in *Différences, valeurs, hiérarchie: Textes offerts à Louis Dumont*, ed. J. C. Galey. Paris: Éditions de l'École des Hautes Études en Sciences Sociales.

_____. 1989. "The Nuer Incest Prohibition and the Nature of Kinship: Alterlogical Reckoning." *Cultural Anthropology* 4, no. 4: 323–346.

_____. 1994. "Mythic Rationality, Contradiction and Choice among the Dinka." *Social Anthropology* 2, no. 2: 99–114.

Gluckman, Max. 1972. "Introduction." Pp. ix–xxix in *The Allocation of Responsibility*, ed. Max Gluckman. Manchester: Manchester University Press.

Handelman, Don. 1998. *Models and Mirrors: Towards an Anthropology of Public Events.* 2nd ed. New York: Berghahn Books.

Leach, Edmund. 1984. "Glimpses of the Unmentionable in the History of British Social Anthropology." *Annual Review of Anthropology* 13: 1–23.

Thomas, William I., and Florian Znaniecki. 1918. *The Polish Peasant in Europe and America: Monograph of an Immigrant Group.* Boston: Gorham Press.

Turner, Victor. 1974. *Dramas, Fields, and Metaphors: Symbolic Action in Human Society.* Ithaca: Cornell University Press.

*Chapter 5*

# MADE IN MANCHESTER?
## Methods and Myths in Disciplinary History

*David Mills*

Unlike several contributors to this volume, I never knew or was taught by Max Gluckman. My fascination with his charismatic influence on post-war social anthropology in Britain has been piqued by my research on the discipline's political history. Of the Oxford-based troika behind the foundation of the Association of Social Anthropologists (ASA) in 1946, an initiative led by Evans-Pritchard and abetted by Meyer Fortes, Gluckman was the most expansive and innovative in his vision of anthropology's contribution to the social sciences. This energy is reflected in the reputation he created for the Manchester Department of Anthropology and Sociology. The later narrowing of his broad methodological vision and theoretical inquisitiveness mirrored the discipline's own institutionalization within British universities.

In this essay, I explore three main themes. I trace in Gluckman's writings and teachings, and those of his associates and students, the gradual invocation of the case-study method as a unique Manchester School innovation. Schumaker (2001: 252) describes one funding application that Gluckman wrote in 1962 in which

---

Notes for this chapter are located on page 178.

he presented the Manchester Department's particular approach as the product of Central African fieldwork, as Manchester's "mythic charter." Yet as Schumaker acknowledges, myths are not enacted by charters alone. They require dedicated cultural work. Manchester's reputation, almost unique within anthropology, as having been a theoretical 'school' with a particular history and mythology was not achieved by Gluckman's charisma alone, vital though this was. Gluckman deliberately and strategically built the department's collective reputation around a constellation of research and writing practices that he gave a distinct imprimatur. These included a team-based approach to field research and an emphasis on the reanalysis of earlier anthropological work. The practice of repeatedly citing and discussing each other's research was particularly key to the creation and transmission of a departmental mythos and to the shaping of a collective memory about the work carried out in Northern Rhodesia. Gluckman's shrewd understanding of academic politics combined with his dominant personality—engaged, committed, forceful, impatient, sometimes overweening and bullying—to cultivate a sense of intellectual common purpose within the department. The boyish bonhomie of enforced trips to watch Manchester United play football was all part of Gluckman's identity-building project. Viewing themselves as a group of eclectic and left-leaning marginals in an upper-middle-class academic discipline, both students and colleagues looked on Gluckman as their intellectual figurehead.

Secondly, I explore the development of the case-study method by early American sociologists. I suggest that British anthropologists were relatively unfamiliar with this history and that the Chicago School debates of the 1920s and 1930s were rarely discussed. Consciously or not, Gluckman crafted a specifically anthropological genealogy of the rise of a method with which he became so closely associated. While the influence of Gluckman's legal training (he did one year of an LLB at Witwaterstrand) and his interest in psychology are often acknowledged as having potentially inspired the case-study method (both legal and psychoanalytic practice revolve around the analysis of a particular 'case'), the sociological connection deserves more prominence.

Lastly, I suggest that the methodological advances of this period are a neglected part of the Manchester Department's history. One is Gluckman's pioneering insistence on team-based fieldwork as a way of carrying out systematic social survey and anthropological research. The other is his advocacy of a judicious combination of qualitative and quantitative approaches to data collection. His championing of a balanced use of ethnographic and statistical analysis is a neglected part of the collective memory of the Manchester School, partly because it chimes a discordant note with the discipline's contemporary qualitative identity.

This chapter draws on a variety of archives, including the voluminous and energetic correspondence Gluckman kept up with his students. This, too, is a form of history making. Like individuals, disciplines tell histories in particular ways, and these narratives involve conscious forgetting as well as careful remembering. As Platt (1996: 260) notes in her history of American sociological methods: "[A]mong the factors affecting the transmission of reputations and the collective memory are the disciplinary boundaries drawn in constructing the history of sociology. The history of sociology is assumed to be about 'sociologists', which implies the exclusion from it of other people." Handelman (1976: 7), in an apt metaphor, once described Gluckman as the "bridge spanning the growth and fluorescence of anthropology," but I am as interested in the bridges not built and the opening ceremonies not held as much as those that were. The history of anthropological method, I would argue, has to be depicted on a broad intellectual canvas.

## Making Methods, Making History

I begin with the discussion and writing that surrounded the method itself. In the annals of social anthropology, the extended-case study method has come to be synonymous with the approach to research and writing advocated by Max Gluckman and his students—in short, the Manchester School. How, over time, does one isolate and claim ownership of a method as an intellectual object or product, separable from the broader skein of social science research practices? This is not just a chance occurrence or the objective reckoning of history; Gluckman was instrumental in this process. Manchester's association with this method was the result of his repeated attention to it, in the socialization of his students and in seminar discussions, the circulation of research papers, and the dissemination of methodological manifestos. This was particularly possible in a discipline such as anthropology, where an appropriate research habitus in the field was (and still can be) primarily passed on through anecdote and mystique. In her history of US sociological research methods, Platt (1996: 2) argues that one cannot assume that methodological thought "follows directly from general theory, or in its turn directly determines methodological practice." Gluckman retold the history of the Manchester School through its methodological insights. For this investigation, I too have attended to the ways people spoke, wrote, and taught about the method.

The story begins in 1940 with the publication of *Analysis of a Social Situation in Northern Zululand* (Gluckman [1940] 1958). It was one of Gluckman's earliest—and, for many of his students, arguably the most influential—publications, though at this point he did not refer to it as a case study. Its evocative description of a bridge-opening ceremony in Zululand, and his use of the event to discuss the conflictual politics and history of South African race relations, made it a germinal text for others. Writing more than 40 years later, Frankenberg (1982: 32) was still of the view that this would be the one text he would take if "banished to a desert island ... in the hope that it was inhabited and that fieldwork was possible." Gluckman's students, particularly Clyde Mitchell, impressed upon Gluckman the importance of his paper. Originally published in an early edition of the *Journal of Bantu Studies,* which many found difficult to access, it was republished 18 years later in two parts in the Rhodes-Livingstone Papers. In a foreword to the 1958 version, Mitchell explains that these essays had "not become as widely known as they should" and that Gluckman had been reluctant to republish the articles given that he would rather now "rephrase" the problems in a different way (Mitchell 1958).

Gluckman ([1940] 1958: 8) begins simply, noting how "a series of events as I recorded them on a single day" are "the starting point for my analysis." He goes on to point out how one should use the evidence comparatively, and therefore inductively, suggesting that "social situations are a large part of the raw material of the anthropologist" (ibid.). More pertinently, from the events the anthropologist observes "and their inter-relationships in a particular society he abstracts the social structure, relationships, institutions etc. of that society" (ibid.). Gluckman justifies his use of the term "social situations" on the grounds that he is analyzing them "in their relationship with other social situations in the social system of Zululand" (ibid.: 9). There is a discrepancy here between his view that he could have taken any such "events or situations in modern day-to-day Zululand" and his subsequent comment that he deliberately chose "these particular events from my note books because they illustrate admirably the points I am at present trying to make" (ibid.: 10).

At this early point in his career, Gluckman does not attempt to contrast this approach with those of earlier anthropologists or to proclaim it to be a methodological advance. Indeed, writing in 1944 about the "difficulties, achievements and limitations of anthropology," he is somewhat disparaging about an untheorized focus on "events," noting that "sociology has formulated relations between specific types of events which are scientific relations, and not pure descriptions of particular events" (Gluckman 1944: 39). He had met Radcliffe-Brown in Oxford in 1938 and had clearly been influenced by the latter's insistence on understanding the logic of social relations and not simply the import of individual cases. Gluckman uses this to back up the broader thrust of his article that "sociology is becoming a science" (ibid.), a view to which he remained committed throughout his career.

In 1944, Gluckman was able to put his methodological and theoretical principles into practice as the first set of research fellows arrived at the Rhodes-Livingstone Institute (RLI), of which he was by now director. Appointed with funds from the Colonial Social Science Research Council, the fellows included Elizabeth Colson, John Barnes, and Clyde Mitchell. Gluckman's plan for the RLI included an ambitious seven-year research program of survey work and studies across Northern Rhodesia (Gluckman 1945).

In his 1948 report as RLI director, Gluckman details his unusually hands-on approach to research training, noting that "I was planning to take our new officers into some field for a short time, to introduce them to African life, and to show them certain field-research techniques," which for Gluckman included "an analysis of demographic data, budgets, and of labour migration figures" (Gluckman 1948: 70). The field site chosen was the Lamba reserve on Ndola, and while Gluckman was quickly called away to meetings in Lusaka, his report notes that "it has proved a most useful exercise in training us to collect quantitative data in a single scheme, and in developing a method of analyzing such facts as matrilocality, divorce rates, type of kinship organisation within a village, on a quantitative basis" (ibid.). Mitchell later acknowledged the importance of that field trip and of the training/data analysis that followed at Cape Town under Isaac Schapera, writing (Mitchell and Barnes 1950: ix): "Not only did the Institute provide the finances for academic and disinterested research, but it also created the framework in which a group of sociologists, of divergent interests and backgrounds, could work on common problems." Schumaker (2001: 109) describes how during this field school Gluckman impressed upon the group the "necessity of collecting sufficiently detailed data that would enable one to analyse it later from angles not anticipated while in the field." For Gluckman, the exercise posed "problems of what data we can measure and how to measure them, and above all, of whether we are measuring the correct things" (Gluckman 1948: 78). He also felt it helped set lines along which "the institute officers, as a team, can collect comparable data in their different areas" (ibid.). This focus on comparable and controlled statistical data collection—which is equally characteristic of the work of Mitchell, Barnes, and Colson, and even of the first half of Turner's (1957) *Schism and Continuity in an African Society*—is rather a less well-remembered methodological contribution of the Manchester School.

Gluckman wrote a rather didactic introduction to the published Lamba study in which he criticized the survey team's dependence on quantitative methods. "I may say at once," he notes, "that I consider the team collected too much demographic data, at the expense of sociological material" (Gluckman 1950: 10). He goes on to set out his qualms about the use of statistical data: "Quantitative analysis, such as that made by Mitchell and Barnes, appears to me to afford an excellent approach to the problem of comparing the kinship and village structure of these peoples. But we must first make sure that we are measuring the right things … quantitative analyses may thus assist, particularly in comparative work, studies in this field of social anthropology. They can never be sufficient for a proper interpretation, which must be rooted in a close personal knowledge of the people" (ibid.: 11). He also queries a more general striving "after representative samples which can be used for quantitative judgements, if this distracts our attention from our main purpose, an understanding of the social structure of the people" (ibid.: 18). With similar intellectual modesty, he suggests that what Barnes and Mitchell call a random sample is better described as a "casual" sample: "A candle compares unfavourably with a powerful electric light, but in the absence of electricity is much better than unrelieved darkness. Therefore I consider that we should continue to collect data of this type, even where our samples are casual" (ibid.: 19).

Yet Gluckman defends their approach nonetheless, and in his later work he continued to advocate a careful and judicious (perhaps read anthropological!) use of quantitative data. Recognizing his own lack of familiarity with quantitative methods, Gluckman had planned to go back to the UK in 1946 to take a course in social statistics at the London School of Economics and Political Science, but he was unable to get a sea passage just after the war. Instead, Mitchell coached him in the potentials of statistical analysis, as he was better able to see its limits.

In writing about the training he had organized for his Lamba research team, Gluckman made no mention of the techniques of participant observation or of the case-study approach. Instead, one of the first explicit references to a "situational approach" was in a letter from Mitchell to Gluckman in Oxford in November 1948:

> Incidentally did you know that W. I. Thomas died last year? He is the person that I get the situational approach from and it is an approach which I think holds quite a lot of answers to our difficulties. I got the idea first of all from 'Gestalt' psychology which with psychoanalysis formed the basis of the NUC [Natal University College] BA course. As applied to social psychology for example they explained away instincts by pointing out that in a certain situation a certain response was evoked, the response being conditioned by the factors in the situational field. Thomas then put in the idea about 'defining the situation' which I take it you know it quite well—you see I use it a lot [e.g.] chief versus commoners and chiefs vs. DC situations.[1]

Gluckman responded to Mitchell the following month:

> I agree with you that the approach through 'situations' is crucial. That is what we try to teach here! You know that EP [Evans-Pritchard], who also owes it to Thomas and Znaicki [*sic*], used it as his basis; so does Meyer, so do I try. EP also uses gestalt methods often without knowing it. At least he claims never to have read gestalt psychology.[2]

When I first came across this correspondence, I was intrigued. The work of the American sociologist W. I. Thomas had never been openly referenced in Gluckman's methodological writings. The influence of gestalt psychology on this generation of anthropologists is similarly left implicit, though Malinowski's use of Freudian ideas was well-known (Stocking 1986). Gluckman makes only one passing reference to psychoanalysis in *Politics, Law and Ritual in Tribal Society* (1965); otherwise, any mention is usually made by analogy, such as his suggestion that the "case-method would bring to the monographic analysis some of the penetration which Freud brought to the study of human personality" (Gluckman 1967: xvi).

This reference to Thomas leads me to the crux of this essay—the relationship between Chicago sociologists and the work of the Manchester School.

## The Chicago School and the Case-Study Method

Who were William Thomas and Florian Znaniecki? Thomas, described by Ross (1991: 348) as "the Chicago Sociologist who did the most to create a new model for Sociology," was a close compatriot of Robert Park at the University of Chicago, where he taught for 20 years, and his popular anthropology course on social origins was highly influential. Combining romantic sensibilities with cosmopolitan sympathies, Thomas, who came from a rural Virginia background, drew on his training and reading in anthropology—in which he hoped to find "the laws of social physics"—and *Volkspsychologie* in his study of race and ethnic relations in Chicago. He also became a consultant to the city's Vice Commission. Indeed, his commitment to what Malinowski later dubbed "participant observation" got him into trouble after he publicly admitted that his research had involved "association with prostitutes, thieves and bums" and that he had "met many women in many places which would be called compromising" (Thomas, quoted in Ross 1991: 309). He was later fired from the university after being arrested in a hotel with a married woman, and the scandal led the university to cancel the planned publication of his research. However, the scandal did no harm to the work's success when it was subsequently published by a private Boston press.

Thomas's research into Polish immigration and the creation of a new Polish-American society had begun after he was awarded a $50,000 grant to study the problem of immigration. Adopting a liberal standpoint that was sympathetic to immigrant cultures and committed to racial equality, Thomas sent his students into the city to do anthropological research. He defined his own work as a study of social psychology, of attitudes among immigrations toward modernization and assimilation. The research was carried out with Florian Znaniecki, a young Polish philosopher involved in the Polish nationalist movement. Together they drafted their momentous five-volume, 2,250-page monograph *The Polish Peasant in Europe and America*, a paradigmatic work for this new empirical social science and perhaps, in the language of contemporary anthropology, the first attempt at a multi-sited ethnography. Its authors stated their aim as creating a "nomothetic science … to interpret as many facts as possible by as few laws as possible" (Thomas and Znaniecki 1918: 62) and to "use in this work the inductive method in a form which gives the least possible place for any arbitrary statements" (ibid.: 76).

For 1918, this was a revolutionary text. Taking seriously the importance of starting from subjective experience, it drew extensively on personal documents and oral histories. Its theoretical statements were brief in comparison. One of the volumes consisted simply of a 300-page autobiography of a Polish immigrant of peasant origin, while another included a lengthy correspondence carried on between family members in Poland and America. Its theoretical introduction set out the principle of attending to "concrete situations" in a way that would later be echoed by Gluckman and his protégés: "Now while the task of science is to analyse by a comparative study the whole process of activity into elementary facts, and it must therefore ignore the variety of concrete situations in order to be able find laws of causal dependence of abstractly isolated attitudes or values on other attitude or values, the task of [our] technique is to provide the means of a rational control of concrete situations" (ibid.: 70). Thomas and Znaniecki saw this as a solution to the difficulties of studying whole societies "with the total complexity of problems and situations which constitute their social life" (ibid.: 19). Instead, they averred: "[W]e can work on special social problems, following the problem in a certain limited number of concrete social groups and studying it in every group with regard to the particular form which it assumes" (ibid.). While the text was critically acclaimed for its subject matter, for the authors, the "Polish peasant was selected rather as a convenient object for the exemplification of a stand-point and method" (ibid.: xii).

The sociologist Herbert Blumer, in an influential critique of Thomas and Znaniecki's work, acknowledged the groundbreaking nature of the text's attempt to outline a "methodology essential to the study of social life" (Blumer 1949: 5). He queried, however, if its use of personal documents met scientific require-ments of "representativeness, adequacy, reliability and validity of interpreta-tion" (ibid.: 44), and pointed out the dilemma such work presented for social research. While he accepted that it "conclusively shows the need of recognizing and considering the subjective factor in human experience" (ibid.: 78), his main concern was that the "documents do not seem to be an effective test of the theo-retical ideas one may develop regarding human or group behavior" (ibid.).

Blumer was not an advocate of a statistical approach himself, but many in his generation were, and Platt (1996: 13) demonstrates how in this pre-war period US sociology was divided by a "marked quantitative/qualitative, humanistic/scientific controversy." Before the war, the main cleavage was between those advocating the case-study method and practitioners of the statistical method. She notes one Chicago departmental picnic in the 1930s, where the case-study prac-titioners faced off the statisticians at baseball! Platt traces the rise and fall of the explicit use of the term 'case study', tracing its probable origins to social work. After World War II, only the older generation was familiar with the term, and the disciplinary cleavage became one between approaches based on surveys and those based on participant observation (Platt 1997). This was partly because of the critiques of Blumer and others, and partly because increasingly sophisticated questionnaires and statistical sampling techniques made the separation less necessary or obvious. Abbott (1999: 25) suggests that Blumer's celebrated attack "helped bury life-history analysis as a sociological method until the 1950s."

It was precisely in the 1950s that Gluckman began to write about the case-study approach as an RLI innovation, perhaps sparked by the interest of Mitch-ell and others in republishing his 1940 paper (now known as "The Bridge"), but also by critical praise for his account of Barotse jurisprudence, made up of a number of legal case studies (Gluckman 1955). He was not the only one writing about the method, which was much discussed among his students. Cunnison, who arrived at the RLI in 1948, recalled in an interview with Schu-maker (2001: 78) that it was "The Bridge, the Bridge, all the time the first few years." John Barnes (1958: 47), in his inaugural lecture, compared the evolu-tion in ethnographic writing style that it typified as the distinction between an account of "a church service with elaborate symbolism and ceremonial but few distinctive roles" and "a Russian novel, with a host of characters whose changing positions relative to each other and to the external world constitute the plot." The analogy serves to remind us that the much-trumpeted case-study method was as much about an approach to writing as an approach to research itself. Gluckman, who came from a literary family, admired Malinowski both for his methodological inventiveness and the freshness of his writing. Perhaps this explains his lack of interest in tracing a methodological genealogy. If he was aware of the Chicago School and its debates, he didn't let on.

## Critiques and Elaborations

As the profile of this new methodological approach grew, so too did criticism from others, and Gluckman found himself increasingly defending his students' work. Raymond Firth once commented that Gluckman "was very sensitive to criticism ... in seminars he stood up good-humouredly to assaults by colleagues and pupils upon his ideas, but he was indefatigable in hunting down critics in print" (Firth 1975: 494). Writing to Mitchell at great length and with some exasperation in 1958, Gluckman rebuffed I. M. Lewis's view that the RLI material was "dull": "The truth is that the detailed case-study method which we are developing, largely out of the big case in your book, does strike people brought up on Evans-Pritchard's kind of analysis as dull. And even Meyer is not impervious to this feeling. He was one of the people who with EP [Evans-Pritchard] and Radcliffe-Brown urged me to cut down my cases in my book—and I just had to tell him that I could not do my analysis except out of cases. He (Meyer) felt Vic's [Victor Turner's] cases were too long, and he was very critical of Van Velsen's long use of case material."[3] Aware of van Velsen's sensitivity to such criticism, Gluckman insisted that if van Velsen "feels that it is the right way to analyse he must have the courage to stick to it." He declared himself resigned to the fact that "we just have to recognise that people brought up on the very abstract analysis that EP does will not appreciate case material. And we have only learnt to appreciate it largely by working over again the work of Firth, Fortes and EP himself."[4]

In a 1961 article on the use of ethnographic data, Gluckman begins constructing a new and specifically anthropological lineage of thinking about the case study, arguing that its roots as a method went back to Malinowski's (1922) use of cases in *Argonauts in the Western Pacific*, an approach he called the method of "apt illustration" (Gluckman 1961: 7). Gluckman felt that "Malinowski and the next generation of anthropologists" (in which he included himself) had used observational data to analyze a "general outline of the culture, or the social system, according to our main theoretical bent ... we then used the apt and appropriate case to illustrate specific customs, principles of organization and social relationships" (ibid.: 8). This in no way demeaned what Gluckman saw as Malinowski's "outstanding contribution," his data, the "raw material of the novelist, the playwright, the biographer or autobiographer, all drawing directly on social life, rather than on the facts which the theoretical anthropologists of the nineteenth and early twentieth century had available to them" (ibid.).

Gluckman noted a second use of cases, whereby from a description could be extracted the general rule of custom or social relationship. Here he mentioned his own "Bridge" article, Malinowki's analysis of language in Trobriand fishing, and Fortes's discussion of Gold Coast fishing ceremonies: "We called these complex events social situations, and we used the actions of individuals and groups within these situations to exhibit the morphology of the social structure. But it was still the social morphology that we were aiming to present" (Gluckman 1961: 8). He went on to describe a third stage in this theoretical development: "But younger anthropologists ... have found weaknesses in our method. They still ask for more case material ... this new kind of analysis treats each case as a stage in an on-going process of social relations between specific persons and groups in a social system or culture ... and showing how these incidents, these cases, are related to the development and change of social relations among these persons and groups, acting within the framework of their social system and culture. Where this method has been applied to monographs using the method of apt illustration, quite a different picture of a social system emerges—a more complex, less rigid, less highly interconnected picture" (ibid.: 9).

As an exemplar of this use of the case-study method that "treats each case as a stage in an on-going process of social relations between specific persons and groups," Gluckman cited Clyde Mitchell's work and his eight-page account of witchcraft accusations over six years in a single Yao village (Mitchell 1956). Gluckman maintained (1961: 12): "Mitchell's employment of this data is the first example I know in British anthropology of the new use of the extended-case method." Interestingly, Mitchell does not draw attention to this approach in his own text, and most of his examples are short accounts of structural disputes, rather unlike Gluckman's rich ethnographic evocation of the bridge opening. The ethnographic style is very different, but for Gluckman the continuities lie in the intellectual questions being addressed.

Gluckman does not shy away from the problems associated with the method, noting that "since the method is clearly fruitful, these problems must be faced and overcome, and not cited to obstruct the development of the method." He goes on to suggest that "the increasing use of statistics, in a more refined form, by anthropologists, provides an important safeguard to issues of typicality" (Gluckman 1961: 13). Finally, he pleads for a change in the manner of comparison, asking anthropologists to again "accustom themselves to welcoming great ethnographic detail, including descriptions and analyses of extended cases, as in the 1920s and 1930s we welcomed the rich detail of Malinowski's books ... I believe it is fatal to become, like Leach, bored with ethnographic fact" (ibid.: 16).

Eggan, responding to this article, was far from convinced. Among what he called possible "complications" to Gluckman's call to "concentrate all our attention on case materials seen over time" was the issue of sampling, since the "essence of the method is in the co-operation required for intensive study, and this can seldom be achieved with cases selected at random" (Eggan 1961: 22). Reiterating the difficulties of defining and setting limits to a case, he stated that Gluckman's predilection for ethnographic detail made him sound "very much like American ethnologists of the 1920s" (ibid.). He saw little distinction between Gluckman and Evans-Pritchard's work, as both for him still viewed social anthropology's heuristic role as being "descriptive integration" rather than attempting to "generalise by comparison" (ibid.). Eggan ends by explicitly drawing the reader's attention to the Chicago School debates.

Why was it left to Eggan to situate the case-study method within the Chicago tradition? One answer is that Gluckman may not have actually read Thomas and Znaniecki's work or have been aware of its importance for American sociology. In the introduction to *Closed Systems and Open Minds*, a discussion about the limits of disciplinary understanding and knowledge, Devons and Gluckman make a case for "specialisation and keeping to one's own last in the social sciences in order to develop theoretical understanding." They argue that "it is highly dangerous to trespass beyond the limits of one's competence, and that to exercise this competence one must abstain from becoming involved in the problems of others" (1964: 19). This does not justify a studied ignorance of methodological debates. A more likely and pragmatic reason is that Gluckman relied on his students to do his reading for him. Famously, he preferred to learn about people's ideas by inviting them to stay. Frankenberg recalls how he once sent Gluckman a copy of Erving Goffman's *The Presentation of Self in Everyday Life*, which Gluckman never read, and that it was five years before Goffman came to give a seminar at Manchester.[5] A final reason may simply be that Gluckman did not feel it was incumbent on him to historicize the methods that he felt he had pioneered at the RLI.

Instead, it was left to Gluckman's students to reconcile some of the contradictions. One of the fullest responses to Eggan's critique was by Clyde Mitchell in a foreword to van Velsen's *The Politics of Kinship* (1964). For Mitchell, "the case method or 'situational analysis' is not a substitute but a supplement to conventional structural analysis," a point he feels Eggan "apparently missed … when he raises the question of the typicality of the cases used in the analysis" (Mitchell 1964: xiii). Mitchell goes on to argue that "the extended-case method is in no way a substitution for quantitative methods of study" and that where possible the anthropologist "presents data in quantitative form" (ibid.: xii). Drawing on his sociological background, Mitchell historicizes this methodological debate for the first time. "This use of 'case material,'" he argues, "is different from that proposed by sociologists some 25 years ago when a controversy arose between antagonists, some of whom advocated case-study methods and some 'statistical' methods as if they were mutually exclusive alternatives" (ibid.). Mitchell ends by noting that "an excellent modern example of the combined use of quantitative observational and extended-case methods is in Turner's study of the social processes in Ndembu villages." He also suggests that the issue of typicality "is irrelevant since the regularities are set out in the description of the overall social structure … in a sense the more atypical the actions and events described in the case history, the more instructive they are, since the anthropologist uses case material to show variations can be contained within the social structure" (ibid.: xiii).

Jaap van Velsen, who was one of the most forceful advocates of the case-study method, begins his monograph with a chapter on method entitled "A Note on the Situational Analysis." He claims the term 'situational analysis' as his own, arguing that it is more appropriate because the word "case [has] been used with so many different meanings" (1964: xxv). He insists on its methodological importance because "by this method the ethnographer presents the reader with abstractions and inferences from his field material but he also provides some of the material itself. This should put the reader in a better position to evaluate the ethnographer's analysis not only on the basis of the internal consistency of the argument, but also by comparing the ethnographic data and the inferences draw from them. Particularly when several or most of the actors appear again and again in different situations, the inclusion of such data should reduce the chances that cases become merely apt illustrations" (ibid.: xv–xvi). Van Velsen suggests that this allows the reader to develop his own alternative interpretations of the materials, and that the "author using situational analysis is more exposed—he has put more cards on the table. The reader's position is more like that of a reader of an historical work who can go back to the documents and check up on the author's interpretations and conclusions" (ibid.: xxvi).

The overlapping theoretical and methodological interests of Gluckman and his students, and their extensive cross-referencing and cross-citation, all served to emphasize a distinctly Manchester approach to anthropology. Throughout the 1960s, Gluckman and his students reiterated the importance of this approach in a number of forewords written for each other's books. Gluckman went over the same ground in his own introductory textbook, *Politics, Law and Ritual in Tribal Society* (1965). Each time, Gluckman argued for the importance of restating and reworking a case, often generously acknowledging his students' advances, but also positioning himself as a forerunner of the development of the extended-case study. As Frankenberg (1982: 32) notes: "[H]e was not and did not claim to be entirely original, but he made creative use of ideas, whatever their source." Gluckman's leadership style may not have endeared him to some, but it was central to developing the department's wider academic reputation.

As the method became increasingly popular, Gluckman felt that some of its advocates had taken the approach too far. Two years before he died, Gluckman wrote an article critiquing the use of case studies—particularly in legal anthropology—in isolation from other methods, pointing out that "if the study of disputes is erected it can be as stultifying as the reporting of rules on their own. Disputes illuminate social process, but disputes cannot be understood without knowledge of social process" (1973: 636). He used this intervention to question what in his view were misinterpretations of Turner's *Schism and Continuity* that dwelt on Turner's analysis of "social dramas." For Gluckman, "Almost all anthropologists who have used his book seem to have overlooked the first 90 pages ... which contain a detailed, and often quantified analysis of the external environment and the structure of Ndembu society" (ibid.). He went on: "Turner necessarily gives an account of what I sum up as 'praxis' and he has to include statements of rules, and of how most 'reasonable' and even 'upright' persons behave. Only in this background is he able to analyse how social dramas—which often take the form of disputes—arise in the history of a set of people and influence the future course of their relationships" (ibid.).

Turner's later work dispensed with this "background" and focused increasingly on the performative and symbolic aspects of Ndembu ritual. To the end, however, Gluckman defended the simultaneous use of quantitative and qualitative analysis. In his 1965 *Politics, Law and Ritual in Tribal Society*, Gluckman again advocates a balanced use of both methods, while noting: "Quantitative and statistical analysis are important tools of analysis, but they are tools only." Invoking the views of the sociologist Homans, he concludes: "Let us make the important quantitative, and not the quantitative important" (1965: 175). He later described the increasing use of statistics by anthropologists as an "important safeguard" (1967, cited in Mitchell 1983). His insistence on this balanced application of methods is a less appreciated aspect of the Manchester School's legacy.

After Gluckman's death, Clyde Mitchell continued to work on the epistemological questions raised by the use of case studies, and to seek to answer the critiques made of it by quantitative sociologists. In a 1983 article, he points out the "confusion between the procedures appropriate to making inferences from statistical data and those appropriate to the study of an idiosyncratic combination of elements or events which constitute a 'case'" (Mitchell 1983: 187). While acknowledging the innovations wrought at Manchester, he questions Gluckman's call for the use of "statistical analysis as a counter-measure to the untypicality of case material," as it did not precisely elaborate on how this counter-analysis should proceed. Questioning an easy assumption of complementarity of the two approaches, Mitchell returns to the 1930s work of Znaniecki, this time with an explicit discussion of Znaniecki's contribution and his distinction between statistical and logical inference (Znaniecki 1934). Mitchell (1983: 198) argues that the two approaches are quite independent: "[W]e infer that the features present in the case study will be related in a wider population not because the case is representative but because our analysis is unassailable." How and when one can claim that one's "analysis is unassailable" is unfortunately left unexplored by Mitchell! Nonetheless, he goes on to argue that "the extent to which generalisation may be made from case studies depends upon the adequacy of the underlying theory and the whole corpus of related knowledge of which the case is analysed rather than on the particular instance itself," and that "the single case becomes significant only when set against the accumulated experience and knowledge that the analyst brings to it." For Mitchell, logical inference is "based on the validity of the analysis rather than on the representative-ness of the events" (ibid.: 190).

It is a subtle and brave defense of the case-study method as it developed at Manchester, even if Mitchell recognizes that the term itself refers to "several very different epistemological entities" (1983: 210). For him, the method insists on the inseparability of sociological data from the role and position occupied by the observer. In making the case for the continuing importance of case studies within a broader ethnographic and sociological project, Mitchell offers a fitting historical legacy to the ambitious methodological charters espoused by Gluckman and his Manchester School.

---

David Mills is a lecturer at the University of Birmingham and works for C-SAP (Sociology, Anthropology and Politics), part of the Higher Education Academy, which promotes debates about, and research into, the learning and teaching of anthropology. He has written about the political history of social anthropology and is currently carrying out research into concepts of training in the social sciences. His publications include *Teaching Rites and Wrongs: Universities and the Making of Anthropologists* (2004), co-edited with Mark Harris.

# Notes

1. MSS Mitchell papers, Rhodes House, Oxford Box 5/1 ff 30 Clyde Mitchell (JCM) to Max Gluckman (MG) 2/11/48.
2. Ibid., 5/1ff 34 MG to JCM 15/12/48.
3. Ibid., 5/1 ff 216 MG to JCM 05/02/58.
4. Ibid.
5. Interview with Ronnie Frankenberg, 11 December 2001, Stoke on Trent.

# References

Abbott, Andrew. 1999. *Department and Discipline: Chicago Sociology at One Hundred*. Chicago: Chicago University Press.

Barnes, J. 1958. "Social Anthropology in Theory and Practice: An Inaugural Lecture." Pp. 47–67 in *Arts: The Proceedings of the Sydney University Arts Association*.

Blumer, H. 1949. *Critiques of Research in the Social Sciences: I. An Appraisal of Thomas and Znaniecki's "The Polish Peasant in Europe and America."* New York: Social Science Research Council.

Devons, Ely, and Max Gluckman. 1964. "Introduction." Pp. 13–20 in *Closed Systems and Open Minds: The Limits of Naïvety in Social Anthropology*, ed. Max Gluckman. Edinburgh: Oliver & Boyd.

Eggan, Fred. 1961. "Ethnographic Data in Social Anthropology in the US." *Sociological Review* 9: 19–26.

Firth, Raymond. 1975 "Max Gluckman." *Proceedings of the British Academy* 51: 479–496.

Frankenberg, Ronald. 1982. *Custom and Conflict in British Society*. Manchester: Manchester University Press.

Gluckman, Max. [1940] 1958. *Analysis of a Social Situation in Modern Zululand*. Rhodes-Livingstone Papers, no. 28. Manchester: Manchester University Press for Rhodes-Livingstone Institute. (Originally published in *Journal of Bantu Studies*.)

_____. 1944. "The Difficulties, Achievements and Limitations of Social Anthropology." *Rhodes-Livingstone Institute Journal* 1: 22–43.

_____. 1945. "The Seven-Year Research Plan of the Rhodes-Livingstone Institute." *Rhodes-Livingstone Institute Journal* 4: 1–32.

_____. 1948. "Director's Report to the Trustees of the Work of the Years 1944–46." *Rhodes-Livingstone Institute Journal* 6: 64–80.

_____. 1950. "Introduction." Pp. 3–20 in Mitchell and Barnes 1950.

_____. 1955. *The Judicial Process Among the Barotse of Northern Rhodesia*. Manchester: Manchester University Press.

_____. 1961. "Ethnographic Data in British Social Anthropology." *Sociological Review* 9: 5–17.

_____. 1965. *Politics, Law and Ritual in Tribal Society*. Manchester: Manchester University Press.

_____. 1967. "Introduction." Pp. xi–xx in *The Craft of Social Anthropology*, ed. A. L. Epstein. London: Tavistock.

_____. 1973. "Limitations of the Case-Method in the Study of Tribal Law." *Law and Society Review* 7, no. 4: 611–642.

Handelman, Don. 1976. "Some Contributions of Max Gluckman to Anthropological Thought." Pp. 7–14 in *Freedom and Constraint: A Memorial Tribute to Max Gluckman*, ed. Myron J. Aronoff. Assen: Van Gorcum.

Malinowski, Bronislaw. 1922. *Argonauts of the Western Pacific: An Account of Native Enterprise and Adventure in the Archipelagoes of Melanesian New Guinea*. London: George Routledge and Sons.

Mitchell, J. Clyde. 1956. *The Yao Village: A Study in the Social Structure of a Nyasaland Tribe.* Manchester: Manchester University Press.

_____. 1958. "Foreword." Pp. ix–x in Gluckman 1958.

_____. 1964. "Foreword." Pp. v–xiv in van Velsen 1964.

_____. 1983. "Case and Situation Analysis" *Sociological Review* 31, no. 2: 187–211.

Mitchell, J. C., and J. A. Barnes. 1950. *The Lamba Village: Report of a Social Survey.* Cape Town: University of Cape Town Press.

Platt, Jennifer. 1996. *A History of Sociological Research Methods in America.* London: Routledge.

_____. 1997. "The Development of the 'Participant Observation' Method." Pp. 32–51 in *Methodology and Experience.* Vol. 4 of *The Chicago School: Critical Assessments*, ed. K. Plummer. London: Routledge.

Ross, Dorothy. 1991. *The Origins of American Social Science.* Cambridge: Cambridge University Press.

Schumaker, Lyn. 2001. *Africanizing Anthropology: Fieldwork, Networks, and the Making of Cultural Knowledge in Central Africa.* Durham, NC: Duke University Press.

Stocking, George. 1986. "Anthropology and the Science of the Irrational: Malinowski's Encounter with Freudian Psychoanalysis." Pp. 13–49 in *Malinowski, Rivers, Benedict and Others: Essays in Culture and Personality.* Vol. 4 of *History of Anthropology*, ed. George Stocking. Madison: University of Wisconsin Press.

Thomas, William I., and Florian Znaniecki. 1918. *The Polish Peasant in Europe and America: Monograph of an Immigrant Group.* 5 vols. Boston: Gorham Press.

Turner, Victor. 1957. *Schism and Continuity in an African Society.* Manchester: Manchester University Press.

Van Velsen, Jaap. 1964. *The Politics of Kinship: A Study in Social Manipulation among the Lakeside Tonga of Nyasaland.* Manchester: Manchester University Press for the Rhodes-Livingstone Institute.

Znaniecki, Florian. 1934. *The Method of Sociology.* New York: Farrar and Rinehart.

*Chapter 6*

# HISTORY OF THE MANCHESTER 'SCHOOL' AND THE EXTENDED-CASE METHOD

*Marian Kempny*

## Manchester Anthropology and Different Meanings of the 'Research School'

Despite the fact that the Manchester School in many respects belongs now to the history of anthropology, its legacy still attracts a lot of attention. However, in order to get a fresh insight into the nature and foundations of this approach that once evolved around the Department of Social Anthropology and Sociology of the Victoria University of Manchester, some further historical and theoretical inquiries are necessary. There have been several vast areas of dispute about this tradition, out of which I take up one that I believe to be both important and often misinterpreted. To my mind, there is a question as to what extent the term 'school' is an adequate description of the phenomenon being discussed. Numerous and recurrent references made by the historians of anthropology to 'Manchester School' seem to rule out any skepticism about its existence.[1] At the same time, Clyde Mitchell, a person counted among the most prominent members of the school, in a personal communication surprisingly enough declared:

---

Notes for this chapter begin on page 197.

"Seen from the outside, the Manchester School *was* a school. But seen from the inside, it was a seething contradiction. And perhaps the only thing we had in common was that Max [Gluckman] was our teacher, and that meant we wrote ethnography rich in actual cases" (quoted in Werbner [1984] 1990: 152–153).

Moreover, in the title of a recently rediscovered manuscript authored by Gluckman and written as a part of his application for research funds—"The History of the Manchester 'School' of Social Anthropology and Sociology"— Gluckman himself, the unquestionable founder of this tradition, put the word 'school' in quotation marks.[2] This raises the question as to whether the term 'Manchester School' was chosen by people, based in that department, who constituted this tradition or was rather a label imposed from outside. It has also to do with suggestions that perhaps in the case of the history of social anthropology, a less theoretically laden description—such as the term 'Manchester anthropology'—might be more suitable. Nonetheless, in Gluckman's above-mentioned document, one can also find, quoted with approval, the earliest recognition that a new school in anthropology had emerged, which appeared in a review by Mary Douglas of William Watson's (1958) book, *Tribal Cohesion in a Money Economy*.

Douglas (1959: 168) states in her review: "From the many and illuminating references to the researches of other Manchester and Rhodes-Livingstone anthropologists, whether they have worked in Central Africa or other fields, it is evidently time to salute a 'school' of anthropology, whose publications are developed through close discussion, and where each worker's work is enhanced by his focus on a common stock of problems." In the same document, Gluckman put special emphasis on the collective nature of the Central African research and the distinctive and significant character of the school. Additionally, in order to underline the fact that the school had already become known internationally, thanks to "the quality of its work," Gluckman refers to the appreciation given to him in the French academia by stating: "[W]hen lecturing at the Sorbonne I was introduced as leader of *l'Ecole de Manchester* by Professor Georges Balandier, who also wrote in an article on 'Structures sociales traditionelles et changements economiques' in *Cahiers D'Etudes Africaines* (1960: 2), when discussing the importance of a dynamic approach to the problems of changing Africa: 'C'est un point du vue qu'ont également choisi les anthropologues anglais de l'Ecole de Manchester'" (Gluckman n.d.).

Clearly, it was not only for administrative purposes that Gluckman pointed out in his communication several basic features of the school. Among them, the most crucial one seems to be that about teamwork in accordance with a firmly coordinated plan. Yet it is also a similar methodology worked out while attacking common problems of the study of change in the tribal situations that Gluckman (n.d.) put forward when describing the school's uniqueness: "I think the main characteristics of our school developed out of a combination of working out comparable techniques for detailed studies of tribes, presenting series of incidents affecting the same groups of persons within a social morphological framework, validated by sophisticated numerical and statistical analyses (inspired by Barnes, Colson and Mitchell)."

It is easy to recognize in this statement a sketchy description of the extended-case method, which was to become a trademark of Mancunian anthropology. This methodology has produced many excellent and original studies, as well as having had an impact on the way of doing ethnography in non-Manchester-trained circles. As a result, one can argue that even today leading contemporary anthropologists in America, who were trained in Britain, demonstrate notice-ably Mancunian characteristics in their approach.[3] Still, the adoption of this particular methodology did not necessarily produce substantive ideas, nor was there always satisfaction with its approach. In fact, the key problem is that except for the concern with social process, conflict, and change, no unified body of theory can be attributed exclusively to the Manchester tradition.[4]

In brief, whereas the Manchester anthropology is recognized as a school even far beyond its provenance, it is far from clear which theoretical innova-tions, if any, seem to be typically Mancunian.[5] In addition, the purpose of the school is not well defined. As acknowledged by Richard P. Werbner, himself an Africanist, its scope from the very outset was broad and encompassed a wide range of studies of British and Indian villages, as well as tribal politics and peasant economies, including research in urban settings in Britain. However, the roots of the Manchester tradition can be traced to Max Gluckman's direc-torship of the Rhodes-Livingstone Institute of Social Studies (RLI) in British Central Africa, where he was second director of the institute and attracted to it a spate of field researchers.[6] The field research in Africa seems still to be a vital factor that accounts for the strength of individual ties with and one's feelings of belonging to the Manchester School. In what follows, I will try to substanti-ate this claim and pinpoint other features on which specificity of this 'school' might rest. Of course, all this initially requires some thoughts about the mean-ing of the very concept of 'school' in the social sciences.

In order to avoid the danger of using this term in a trite and purely persua-sive way, I will attempt to clarify its basic meanings. Following Jerzy Szacki (1975), one can distinguish between scientific or intellectual 'schools' in an institutional sense, in a psychological sense, and in a typological sense. These different understandings also indicate separate ways of articulating the issue in question. First, let us consider the Manchester School from an institutional point of view, which means that the interests, concepts, and concerns unique for a certain group of scholars are perceived as produced and sustained within the same institutional framework.

Seen from such a perspective, the Manchester School was in fact nested in two different, though very closely entangled, institutions: the RLI (later renamed the Institute for Social Research of the University of Zambia) and the Department of Social Anthropology and Sociology of the Victoria Uni-versity of Manchester. These institutions and their personnel constituted a material base for an intellectual tradition still proudly referred to by many as the 'Manchester School'. In this context, one can look at the Manchester School as a far-flung network of scholars and researchers that encompasses several generations and undoubtedly is a unique phenomenon in the history of British anthropology.

At the same time, I would fully agree with Lyn Schumaker (2001: 4), the author of a recent monograph of the school entitled *Africanizing Anthropology. Fieldwork, Network, and the Making of Cultural Knowledge in Central Africa,* that when writing the history of anthropology, a focus on the social and cultural factors in the particular historical situation of the Manchester School is as important as its intellectual genealogies and connections. However, while endorsing her claim about the importance of social and cultural contexts, which calls attention to the role played by the colonial culture and by missionary and administrative practices in shaping the work of anthropologists in Africa, I take another tack and deal with the foundational myths of the Manchester School as an anthropological research school.

To my mind, the significance of Manchester as a "first-class research school" (Gluckman n.d.) is beyond any doubt, but it goes beyond the Central African research. Advanced training and studying in Manchester meant for students something more than pure apprenticeship that made them specialists in African anthropology. It had to do with shaping the feelings of solidarity focused around Gluckman as well as with developing craftsmanship in anthropological research (or social research).[7]

By juxtaposing the focus on the Manchester School as a broader intellectual category and the history of RLI as a more local, African-centered phenomenon, one can see the constitutive factors for this school being regarded as a frame of individual identifications and thereby gain psychological insight into the Manchester School. The intellectual school in such an understanding might be based on a different principle than belonging to a more-or-less centered network of colleagues involved in direct and intense interpersonal relations and focused around a certain point source, i.e., an intellectual leader. Such a principle, which might constitute a school in science corresponding to the idea of solidarity without propinquity, can be most adequately expressed in terms of the reference group model (cf. Szacki 1975: 175). In this case, belonging to a particular 'school' is determined not by immersion in a particular institutional and personal setting but by adherence to a defined set of ideas about research procedures or to a conceptual or theoretical framework treated as reference points in any research activities.

To grasp the features that can help unravel the specificity of Manchester anthropology, tracing the commonalities by means of which researchers who have never worked together, or never even met, attack and theorize research problems is as important as investigating the Manchester School's legends and anecdotes by means of which its members have been able to construct their own identities. Such a view on the nature of the school in science also draws our attention to the third sense of the meaning indicated above. The so-called typological approach indicates that the term 'school' might be applicable to a group of scientists singled out because of the common traits discovered in their methodology or theory, even when they have never identified themselves with this particular group. It is worthwhile to consider whether the term 'Manchester School' might function also as an entirely analytical description of a separate type of anthropological practice.

Within the confines of this essay, I can examine only some basic aspects of the Manchester School in the quest to determine its identity. These include its African origin, its Oxford connection, the charismatic leadership of Max Gluckman, and the Manchester seminar, which generated innovations in anthropological methods. By scrutinizing these factors, I hope to clarify what made this tradition, regarded as a major force in British social anthropology in the 1950s and 1960s (cf., e.g., Kuper 1983: 128), a 'school'.

## The African Roots of the Manchester School

The history of the school begins with Max Gluckman's post-graduate training, when he took over as director of the Rhodes-Livingstone Institute in British Central Africa in Livingstone (then Northern Rhodesia). Founded in 1937, the RLI was the first social science research institute in Africa, and from 1941, under Gluckman's directorship, it operated as an anthropological field research center. Its appointed team of research workers were involved in the study of neighboring areas of Central Africa in accordance with a coordinated plan drafted by Gluckman himself.[8]

From the very outset, Gluckman worked closely at the RLI with Barnes, Colson, and Clyde Mitchell in order to give them basic field training. In addition, Barnes and Mitchell got instruction from Isaac Schapera at Cape Town. Together with Gluckman, they also did two field surveys as their main postgraduate training, which resulted in the writing up by Mitchell and Barnes (1950) of a report of one of these surveys. During this period, the reciprocal visits to the field sites and the RLI-based conferences at its first headquarters stimulated within the circle of trainees, teachers, and colleagues an intellectual exchange that facilitated standardization of research practices. The first of these conferences, which took place in 1947, served to coordinate the researchers' projects and the ways of reporting on their respective fieldwork. Each researcher gave a presentation to the seminar that needed a systematization of data at an early stage and faced a critique from Gluckman and the other participants. As Mitchell recalled it: "Field methods were the most important focus of the seminars—crucial—and this built us into a team, with all having a similar approach. Max Gluckman emphasized concrete documentation and kept quoting Malinowski to us" (quoted in Schumaker 2001: 107). In addition, the gathering of comparable data made the RLI a storehouse of field notes, which could be consulted and commented on by other researchers. One can also claim that an important additional factor, which influenced the coherence of the team and drew its members together, was the publication of some of the early work of Gluckman's students, including contributions to the *Rhodes-Livingstone Institute Journal* and a notable edited collection, *Seven Tribes of British Central Africa* (Colson and Gluckman 1951).

The function of such integrative activities in the development of the Manchester School became even more visible as Gluckman made growing use of the seminars and publications to further develop the approach while at Oxford and, finally, during his period at Manchester. Gluckman moved to Oxford in 1947, but it was in 1949, when he became the chair of social anthropology at the University of Manchester and when the Department of Social Anthropology and Sociology was set up, that he started to develop the institutional foundations of the school. Its core principle consisted of a close collaboration between the Manchester Department and the RLI. The mechanism that linked these institutions together is plainly described in Gluckman's (n.d.) document:

> [W]hen I moved to found a Department of Social Anthropology at Manchester, she [Colson—the subsequent director] had all her Research Officers come to me for advanced training and to do their Ph.D. degrees. After preliminary training at Manchester, they went to Central Africa, returned to Manchester, went again to Central Africa, and then back to Manchester. This policy was continued by Mitchell, who succeeded Colson, when owing to temporary ill-health she had to leave the tropics and became first a Simon Fellow, and then Senior Lecturer, at Manchester. In this way Turner, A. L. Epstein, van Velsen, Watson and Gann (an historian), all did their main preparation and writing-up at Manchester, though of course they were supervised in the field by Colson and Mitchell who organized conferences at which they were also taught.

As a matter of fact, due to the strong ties of the RLI with the metropolitan university and with founding organizations supporting it (especially the Simon Research Fund), Gluckman was able to bring the RLI directors (Colson and Mitchell) for longer periods to Manchester, to send Barnes to do fieldwork in Norway, to appoint as fellows and visiting professors many outstanding workers (Ian Cunnison, A.L. (Bill) Epstein, Max Marwick, Victor Turner, and William Watson), and to have their books published. The whole group produced out of their research a well-coordinated stream of publications.[9] In this context, it is worth expanding on the role of the Central African research, which remained for a long time the core of the Manchester departmental research program and which has been recognized as one of the most significant programs of research in the history of social anthropology. While building up the department, Gluckman considered that in order to develop a research school, a common focus would be needed and, in a natural way, opted for Central Africa. He not only opened the career path for the RLI anthropologists who later obtained posts in Manchester but also encouraged his Manchester students who were interested in Africa to take jobs in the RLI.[10]

To sum up, Gluckman provided at Manchester the solid foundations for the training of and the writing up of results for successive groups of RLI fieldworkers, as well as the established interconnections necessary to construct a unified body of theory and method, all of which fully deserves the name of Manchester School. It allows returning to my initial question: What made the Manchester anthropology a 'school'? If the emphasis is put on field research methods based on some basic procedures as its *differentia specifica*,[11] one nonetheless must note that from the moment he set up the department at Manchester, Gluckman can be said to have paid greater attention to theory.

I discuss this claim in more detail later on, but it is doubtful whether even during its early period the Manchester group was a school in a strongly typological sense, which implies adherence to a body of theory. Whereas Mitchell denies the theoretical focus of the RLI seminars (cf. Schumaker 2001: 108–109), Fred Bailey, a member of the first generation of Mancunians, recalls that theory did not form the major topics of discussion during the departmental seminars at Manchester in the early 1950s (Wenner-Gren 2003 interview). There is no doubt, though, that at Manchester Gluckman used the reanalysis of renowned ethnographies—and also those produced under the RLI approach—as a teaching technique wherein the same data were analyzed from a number of different perspectives to check the usefulness of specific theories. In other words, the Manchester seminars became the testing ground for innovations born in the field.

In trying to identify the relationship between Manchester and the RLI, it seems that although Gluckman's move to Manchester finally fostered theoretical inclinations among members of the group, Lyn Schumaker (2001: 151) is right in holding that "this research school's emergence and group character had already evolved in the field." Many of Gluckman's initiatives during this period confirm that, as he told Mitchell in 1949, he intended to "build a new RLI" at Manchester. This is the main reason why he sought to retain the association of the RLI people with the department.

## The Oxford Lineage of Manchester

It is the RLI activities that provide the background against which an adequate description of the Manchester School's development becomes possible. The best illustration of the thesis that the RLI experience actually begot the Manchester anthropology is the Oxford lineage of the school. Gluckman himself was a Rhodes Scholar at Oxford, where he obtained his PhD in 1936, and Barnes, Mitchell, and Ian Cunnison likewise earned doctorates from Oxford between 1950 and 1952. At the same time, Manchester was established clearly as an alternative to the structural approach typical of Oxford anthropology.[12] Paradoxically, the alternative became apparent when Gluckman took a lectureship at Oxford in October 1947, bringing with him Barnes, Colson, and Mitchell. The group had developed close cooperation during research in Africa, though settled many miles apart in the field, and this process of evolving a tight-knit working group continued when they moved to Oxford. They ran biweekly Rhodes-Livingstone seminars on their own, working over theoretical problems and research techniques, with Gluckman teaching Cunnison (then newly appointed to the RLI) and other post-graduate students. Two of them— Mary Douglas and John Middleton—were later regarded as crucial members of the Oxford structural school.

Although Gluckman officially acknowledged the merits of teachings that his students received at that time from E. E. Evans-Pritchard and Meyer Fortes at Oxford, it seems that he rather believed that they had been properly trained at the RLI and as a group were able to compete with already established anthropological schools.[13] In addition, this period in Oxford resulted in the construction of the above-mentioned collection, *Seven Tribes in British Central Africa,* with articles written by Gluckman, Colson, Barnes, and Mitchell based on their recent fieldwork and on seminar presentations given at the Institute of Social Anthropology at Oxford. All this raises the question as to what this period meant for the RLI team, who were establishing their identities as part of the Oxford structuralist tradition dominated by Evans-Pritchard's scholarship (cf. also Werbner [1984] 1990).

Gluckman himself was doubtless greatly influenced by Evans-Pritchard and showed an attitude of respect toward Oxford, but in the first generation of his trainees, the feelings of dissatisfaction with the structural functionalism of Cambridge and Oxford and with Radcliffe-Brown were easily noticeable and widespread.[14] For this reason, it is much more convincing to interpret the Oxford period as a formative experience for the development of a separate RLI identity quickly transformed into a Mancunian one than to look at the Manchester School as an outgrowth of Oxford structural functionalism. In effect, the Manchester School came to the fore as a team deeply rooted in Central African research—a tight-knit group that maintained its separate identity in the face of the prestige of the Oxford and Cambridge traditions.

## The Department of Social Anthropology and Sociology at Manchester

Although this problem is well studied, the answers given to the need of describing the Manchester School's inception and of periodizing the developments in the department are not entirely unanimous. In a clear way, when Manchester's Department of Social Anthropology was set up in 1949, two meanings of the scientific school identified above—the institutional and the psychological—evidently resonated as almost conterminous. The Oxford seminars strengthened the ties among the scholars who shared common experiences of field research and constituted a nucleus of the prospective school. A very strong case supporting such a view is made by Schumaker (2001: 37ff.), who argues convincingly that in terms of the genealogy of the school, it was exactly the shared involvement in fieldwork of the first group of RLI people who transferred to Oxford and finally to Manchester that created a foundational group experience, which was subsequently enhanced when the team presented themselves as a whole to academia and to the wider public.[15] However, very soon the new Manchester Department started to recruit a new group of novices who came not only from African field research sites.

As I see it, then, the institutional growth of the department shows that explanations given by Vincent (1990), who describes the beginnings of the Manchester School by tracing out its Oxford theoretical ancestry, and by Schumaker (2001: 37–38), who introduces a category of "field generation" in order to describe the formative stages of the school, are not fully compelling. In fact, at the beginning the situation was different—both more complex and more banal.

There is no doubt about the RLI roots of the school. Even in the early 1960s, Gluckman intended to continue with Central African anthropology as a core of the departmental research and expand it further. From his document on the history of the department (Gluckman n.d.), one can learn that he planned to develop "socio-anthropological studies" in Tanganyika and Kenya. In this connection, he tried to appoint to a post in the department Martin Southwold, an East Africanist working in Sudan, and wanted to send "at least occasional students" to West Africa.[16]

Nevertheless, from the very outset he also accepted into the department students and researchers who had no interest in Africa or had been educated in different disciplines, especially those trained in sociology. After World War II, there were also social circumstances that pushed some categories of people to seek a university education. In fact, it is not easy in retrospect to determine the decisive factor that attracted research students to the department. As Bailey (Wenner-Gren 2003 interview) recalls: "Max provided us with jobs. Max had a new department; Max had money, at least in small quantities. Of course most of us, except Frankenberg, were ex-soldiers and eligible for further-education grants … I don't think that there was a system of recruitment [to the department]."

In fact, the expansion of the tight-knit group into the bidisciplinary department over time altered the situation of full cohesion within the school. The dividing lines seem to go along three main criteria. The most obvious was the generational difference, but, as suggested above, no less important was the fact of different regional interests. Last but not least was the closeness of Gluckman's disciples to his theoretical concerns and methodological views. The concurrence among these criteria would suggest that as far as the Manchester School is concerned, the three senses of the intellectual school previously distinguished have coincided. Actually, their full concurrence came about only at the very early stages, and it is the very process of the gradual dispersion of the school that Werbner ([1984] 1990) expressed in the hypothesis about its evolution from a close-knit group to a loose-knit network linking widely dispersed scholars.

As Vincent (1990) observed, whereas the members of the first generation of student-collaborators of Gluckman (born in 1911) were born between 1918 (Barnes and Mitchell) and 1929 (Ronald Frankenberg), the members of the second generation were born between 1934 and 1940. The first age cohort included, in addition to the Central Africanists already mentioned, F. G. Bailey and T. S. Epstein (both doing their research in India), Abner Cohen, Emrys Peters, and Frankenberg. A full roll call of the second generation of Mancunians is more problematic. Vincent's (1990: 461) list includes the following names: M. J. Aronoff, G. K. Garbett, N. E. Long, E. E. Marx, S. Deshen, J. M. Pettigrew, B. Sansom, M. Shokeid, J. Singh Uberoi, R. P. Werbner. But this list does not seem complete without such names as D. M. Boswell, T. M. S. Evens, D. Handelman, B. Kapferer, and P. Harries-Jones. Werbner ([1984] 1990: 154) mentions, in turn, a third generation consisting of Manchester students of the school's early members, most of whom did not do their fieldwork in Africa. Notable exceptions are the students of Clyde Mitchell who, being based at the

University College of Rhodesia and Nyasaland in Salisbury (Southern Rhodesia) until the mid-1960s, was able to adhere to the research tradition of the RLI by sending his pupils to the field in south-central Africa.

In general, the perspective suggested by an analysis of the Manchester School in terms of personal relationships between its members belonging to different generations discloses the significance of variation in regional interests that might weaken or strengthen the feelings of belonging to the network, with Gluckman as its point source.[17] At the same time, the focus on regional interests enables conceptualization of the idea of the school as a heterogeneous setting with core locations and more marginal ones. It allows distinguishing at Manchester, during the time of Gluckman's chairmanship, three categories of persons: the first was composed of the RLI old-timers and Central African students; the second was associated with the study of Israeli society and consisted of researchers from Israel, Canada, the United States, and Britain, who came to Manchester mainly in the 1960s; the third was made up of "the odd men, people on the fringe, or if you wish to put it in this way people on the margins" (Bailey, personal communication).[18] Obviously, these three sets of people have not always been internally homogeneous. For example, Abner Cohen, a Jewish member of the school in its early days, who did not belong to the 'Israeli contingent' involved in the Bernstein project, came to work with Emrys Peters, who was himself studying Arabs in the Middle East.

It is worthwhile to emphasize that the conditions of marginality in the department were not so unproblematic as it might appear. One should also take into account the combination of the two disciplines within the department, which was reflected by the existence of a group of sociologists developing research on rural and urban life in Britain but also in general sociology.[19] Again, however, it turns out that Gluckman did not care about the labels—sociology or anthropology—as long as the research was done in accordance with the tradition that dominated the department. That is why R. J. Frankenberg, T. Lupton, Sheila Cunnison, V. Pons, D. Allcorn, and W. Watson, although appointed to sociological positions, were regarded as social anthropologists and their research as social anthropological in nature. As a result, an individual's marginality or more central location within the network could not depend solely on an incessant preference for African studies.[20]

Therefore, in order to take up the issue of marginality properly, it is necessary to deepen our understanding of Manchester anthropology as a school by introducing a typological sense of the term. It means that one should try to find out whether, in taking into account all of these various groups and marginal people, there are some features they share that mark them as typical of Manchester and distinct from those involved in other kinds of methodological or theoretical approaches. For instance, according to Bailey (Wenner-Gren 2003 interview), the minimal set of such features connected with the theoretical issues carried over from the RLI days boils down to several categories—conflict, process, and change—and to a slightly hostile attitude toward the study of culture as arrays of ideas divorced from actions in the world. Although the central motifs were those of conflict, opposition, social change, and social order, the works of Mancunians abounded in a conceptually brand-new vocabulary, which includes the following categories (to list just a few among many more): the social field, inter-calary roles, situational selection, cross-cutting ties, dominant cleavage, redressive ritual, processual change, and processional form (see Werbner [1984] 1990: 152).

In more general theoretical terms, it implies the focus on the dynamics of social systems and the search for models that could account for continuity in and the collapse of social order. The concept of 'rituals of rebellion' is perhaps the most widely known example of Gluckman's explanation of dialectic between continuity and discontinuity and how the latter could contribute to social cohesion. Yet again, as Adam Kuper (1983: 148ff.) argues, the immediate inspiration for Gluckman's approach should be looked for in the work of the Oxford structural functionalists—Radcliffe-Brown and Evans-Pritchard. Nevertheless, even from this point of view, Mancunian theories illustrate a potential development of Oxford orthodoxy. Within the confines of this essay, I am unable to discuss the issue of how strongly Gluckman stuck to central tenets of structural functionalism;[21] however, undoubtedly in one respect this issue went far beyond the classical functional issues of system equilibrium in which Gluckman's and his followers' views on colonial societies were rooted. It was the relations of power and domination present in the white-ruled Central African societies that emerged in their studies, which for the first time provided an additional appropriate context of RLI activities and the Mancunian approach.

The early RLI scholars were fairly left-wing and sympathetic to the working-class,[22] but later the broad statement "We are all Maxists here" became a jibe that reflected a Marxist aroma hanging around Max Gluckman's department. In reality, the fact that they perceived their commitment to anthropology partly in political terms reflected mainly their anti-racist and anti-colonial attitudes. Consequently, many of the RLI workers had great difficulty getting into the field because of their political sympathies, and RLI scholars were treated with great suspicion by colonial authorities. Gluckman himself became a prohibited immigrant and was not to be allowed back to Barotseland until independence.[23] As a result, this group practiced anthropology with an awareness of the political ramifications of social situations in colonial societies and the ethical responsibility of anthropologists. It partly explains the anti-cultural, strongly sociological bias of Manchester-style research.

In light of the above, it is helpful once again to quote Bailey's (Wenner-Gren 2003 interview) reply to the question of the specific properties and foundations of the Manchester School: "Well, this identity, one can say, of Manchester [School] was basically connected with Gluckman and where Gluckman came from, which is Oxford and structural functionalism. And identity is also connected with politics, but it was a left-wing politics. And each of these movements had a little rebellion against it, and in its core were also people who weren't aware of Marxism and didn't know much about it."[24]

Therefore, while looking for common features, it is probably easier to identify a stock of common problems, a core of shared values, or even a specific lifestyle[25] than to depict a theoretical framework that might account for the strongly manifested solidarity of Mancunians. At the same time, the solidarity itself seems to diversify the membership. The Africanists with RLI experiences have shown a stronger allegiance to the group than people who have worked elsewhere. Finally, then, while thinking about the Manchester School in a typological sense, labels such as 'Marxist' or 'non-Marxist' definitely are less important than the extent to which, and the way in which, those researchers tackled in their studies similar problems and applied the same research tool-kit to come up with sometimes similar answers. In the domain of methodology, it is especially the extended-case method, which evolved out of Gluckman's situational analysis, that reached the status of a yardstick.[26]

## Max Gluckman, Manchester Seminars, and the Extended-Case Method

In view of what has been said so far, it is absolutely impossible to find a pattern or to chart the gradual development of the school without taking into account Max Gluckman and his personal leadership. It is also hard to sketch the portrait of the Manchester School without a mention of Gluckman's personal charisma. He attracted a strong personal loyalty but sometimes brought about the banishment of some 'people on the margins' to the outer perimeter of his circle of students and colleagues. As remembered by Bruce Kapferer (1987), a lecturer in the department in the 1960s, a gradually deepening status distance and differences of power between Gluckman and his followers might have led to the estrangement of younger colleagues.[27] Numerous forewords to the books of his students and colleagues expressed Gluckman's awareness of his influence in inspiring their research and writings while recognizing that their insights animated his own imagination. The consequences of such developments were described by Kapferer (1987: 3): "[T]hose who were not caught up in his enthusiasm, those whose ideas were not pushed as part of Gluckman's own intellectual development, often felt left out and expressed bitterness." Likewise, according to Shokeid (1992), Gluckman's energy, generosity, and parental power unsurprisingly led to competition for his attention and the resources under his control.

However, as I see it, his contribution to the emergence of the school in the institutional sense was much more important and exceeded his role in shaping the identities and feelings of belonging to the Gluckman-centered network. Schumaker's (2001) study gives a rich documentation of the expansion and achievements of the Central African research orchestrated by Gluckman. The famous "seven-year plan" (Gluckman 1945) launched at the RLI led to a unique, systematic regional research that in many ways changed how anthropology has been practiced since then. At the same time, although the success of Gluckman's African scheme was unprecedented, as Kapferer (1987: 5) put it: "African anthropology WAS anthropology." However, after the first decade of the RLI under Gluckman, only Colson and Mitchell continued to do Central African fieldwork. Despite Gluckman's vision of resuming the Central African research on its former scale, the earlier policy of concerted research failed to be a viable option in the 1960s. Instead, Gluckman attempted to repeat within the Manchester Department the African team-research success story by initiating rural and industrial studies in Britain and by sparking a research scheme conducted in Israel. The scale of Gluckman's endeavors and his predilection for the coordinated character of research are revealed especially by his involvement in the Israeli Bernstein project, which occupied the major part of his time and efforts during the last 12 years of his life.

All of this suggests the relevance of a team-focused way of working in shaping the identity of Manchester anthropology. At the same time, Gluckman's conscious efforts to create a most favorable environment for organized research materialized in particular in the development of the famous seminars at Manchester, which derived from seminars and conferences held at the RLI headquarters. The enormous role played by these seminars in the consolidation and expansion of the school in a psychological sense is well documented. Both the Central African and Israeli research projects resulted in long lists of publications, the authors of which have in their works acknowledged Gluckman and fellow Mancunians, but often the departmental seminar itself, reflecting its unusually creative and integrative potential.[28] Gluckman (n.d.) has himself drawn a picture of the seminar in a suggestive way that evokes a notion of the "mythic charter" he needed to narrate the birth of the school (cf. Schumaker 2001: 253). Yet the persuasive nature of his description notwithstanding, this indicates as well that the seminar provided a forum where the Manchester School as a typologically separate intellectual formation was forged and renewed over time.

It is worthwhile to identify the scholars invited to take part in this intellectual endeavor in its initial phase to make clear that the seminar attracted not only anthropologists. Participants in the seminars in the 1950s were Oxbridge dons—M. Fortes and E.E. Evans-Pritchard, but also S. N. Eisenstadt, E. Goffman, G. C. Homans, T. Parsons, and E. Shils (some of whom were Simon Visiting Professors at Manchester). At the same time, the interdisciplinary character of the seminar was connected with the regular attendance of Manchester scholars from other fields, particularly philosopher Dorothy Emmet, economist Ely Devons, and political scientist W. J. M. Mackenzie. Gluckman's (1964) edited collection, *Closed Systems and Open Minds*, shows that such an association with representatives of other disciplines bore fruit, as far as a reflection on the conditions and determinants of anthropological knowledge is concerned. Gluckman and Devons discuss there the seminar papers of Turner, Bailey, Bill Epstein, Lupton, Sheila Cunnison, and Watson to come up with conclusions about the basic procedures by which fields of study in anthropology are demarcated.

In fact, the topics discussed in the volume—the reduction of internal complexity of reality under study, the circumscription of a field of research and analysis, the legitimate use of the findings of other disciplines in anthropological studies—reflected the dominant and enduring motifs of the research seminars at Manchester, though articulated in a more abstract way. No doubt, in many respects the Manchester seminars resembled the RLI ones. They were mainly devoted to presentations of field material or reanalyses of classic ethnographies, thus confirming that, in general, theory as such was not a subject of inquiry. As Bailey (Wenner-Gren 2003 interview) recalls such occasions: "They always began with a case or with a piece of fieldwork, and an argument developed from that. And the theoretical things [then] came out of that. This wasn't a straight discussion about what theory is, [though you could say that] we had theoretical discussions. They arose in the context of particular events that were recorded in Central Africa or India, or whatever else it was. So we were to some extent theoretical."[29]

There is little doubt that the researchers trained by Gluckman and his followers tended to approach social reality with a viewpoint different from the position of pre-war structural-functional anthropology. In principle, however, in Bailey's opinion,[30] it was due not to a body of theory but rather to a common, unified methodology that one can regard the Manchester anthropology as a 'school' in the most taxing, typological sense. This is not to say that it is impossible to identify the basic theoretical themes running through the writings of Mancunians,[31] yet the focus was principally on discussing research findings and teaching and modifying field methods through the collective efforts of the seminars' participants. Nevertheless, at the same time one can claim that the advancements in methods were channeled through a distinctive theoretical stance typical of Mancunian anthropology. This is why in what follows I try to cast some light on the theoretical underpinnings of the most important innovation in anthropological inquiry attributed to the Manchester School, namely, the extended-case method.

The best way to explore these supposed links between theory and method is to look at an important article, first published in 1940 in the *Journal of Bantu Studies*, resulting from Gluckman's early fieldwork in Zululand. Titled "Analysis of a Social Situation in Modern Zululand," and popularly known as "The Bridge," the article deals with the events surrounding the ceremonial opening of the first bridge in Zululand built under the new schemes of local development. It contains a thorough description of "several events which were linked by [Gluckman's] presence as an observer, but which occurred in different parts of Northern Zululand and involved different groups of people" (Gluckman [1940] 1958: 8–9). It is disputable whether or not the method portrayed in "The Bridge" was already that of an extended case. For example, individual actions were regarded as important in the context of macro processes with some neglect for the problem of individuals choosing between one set of structural norms and another (cf. Frankenberg 1982; Werbner [1984] 1990). Nevertheless, Gluckman's detailed analysis meant a sea change in the mode of presenting ethnographic material.

As to its theoretical ramifications, Gluckman's approach implies that the complex events he refers to as "social situations," within which the actions of individuals and groups involved take place, are seen as the reflection of the complexity of social structure. In contrast to Bronisław Malinowski's theory of culture contact, Gluckman describes Africans and Europeans in their various social roles, directed by different motives and interests, as symbolically and structurally divided but intimately interrelated in a single social system. But his analysis of the situation in Zululand raised further theoretical issues—the problem of the achievement of equilibrium in the system, which due to instability of the situation requires accommodation of conflicts; the issue of the relationship between structural constraints and individual choice within the unstable systems; the issue of how macro processes are reflected in individual actions and produce in turn "standardized but unplanned relationships and associations." For Gluckman's followers, this was the extended-case method, which promised to cope with all of the weak points of structural-functional approaches.

As Gluckman ([1940] 1958: 2) himself put it: "[S]ocial situations are a large part of the raw material of the anthropologist. They are events he observes, and from them and their interrelationships in a particular society he abstracts the social structure, relationships, institutions, etc., of that society. By them, and by new situations, he must check the validity of his generalizations." This approach also related to the question as to what form the field material should be in when presented to the reader. Instead of presenting tidy abstractions and inferences from the field material, the anthropologist would provide the reader with some of the material itself. Needless to say, the researcher who presented extended cases had less leeway to shape or even disfigure the data.

Later, such a way of presenting and dealing with ethnographic data was called "situational analysis" (van Velsen 1967) and meant the analysis of the case "as a stage in an on-going process of social relations between specific persons and groups in a social system and culture" (Gluckman 1967: xv). In addition, an adopted situational frame of reference differed from Oxford-style structural-functionalist description in supplementing the analysis of the static of the structure with an account of the actions showing how individuals in particular structural positions cope with the complicated choices they face. Consequently, one can claim that by means of the integration of case material, situational analysis seeks to integrate variations, exceptions from structural regularities, and accidents into descriptions of regularities. All this indicates that dissatisfaction with conventional modes of presenting ethnographic material in which extended-case analysis was grounded spurred Gluckman to envision theoretical reformulations and methodological innovations.

Finally, when looking for the tenets of the Manchester School, it seems to be the gradual development of the extended-case method that represents an enduring thread linking together the modes of methodological training and theoretical inquiries imposed at the different stages of the institutional growth of the school. The constitution of the school seen in this way indicates the significance of the method itself imparted by Gluckman to his followers and students during frequent and intense exchanges at the seminars run at the RLI and later in Manchester. This is proven by the observations of historians of anthropology that the RLI research officers on their arrival in 1946 were familiarized with "The Bridge," which was thoroughly discussed at the institute. For example, Schumaker (2001: 78) quotes in this respect Ian Cunnison's remark: "The Bridge, the Bridge, all the time the first few years." The results of this kind of training are especially vividly noticeable in the manner of presenting material and its analysis employed by Mitchell (1956) in his early monograph

*The Kalela Dance.* While trying to emulate the same method as Gluckman, Mitchell starts with a description of the dance itself and then relates its basic features to the system of relationships within the social setting under study. However, in order to do this, he had to take into consideration the whole system of black-white relationships in Northern Rhodesia. As he put it: "[B]y working outwards from a specific social situation ... the whole social fabric of the Territory is therefore taken in" (Mitchell 1956: 1). In other words, only by tracing particular elements of social events back into the society at large is the researcher able to demonstrate their significance to the social life.

Several accounts of different scenes at the Manchester seminars that reveal the theoretical significance of the extended-case method and the nature of its formative quality are available in the anthropological literature. One remarkable scene, pictured by Edith Turner (1985: 5), describes a seminar in which her husband Victor Turner presented for the first time his application of the extended-case method to his Ndembu ethnography: "With controlled excitement he read the story of Sandombu; and he analyzed its stages—breach, crisis, redress, reintegration—the social drama as the window into Ndembu social organization and values. Now you see the living heart. Max sat, his hands folded on top of his bowed bald head. When it was over, he raised his head, his eyes burning. 'You've got it! That's it.'"

The type of analysis of social situations worked out by Turner is documented later in his *Schism and Continuity in an African Society* (1957) and confirms that the Manchester anthropology had its own distinctive way of exploring social action and change. In addition, situational analysis gave rise to the transformation of the very category of 'social situation' into concepts of 'social drama', 'social field', and 'arena', which, for instance, became key categories of the processual paradigm in political anthropology (cf. Vincent 1990: 337ff.). In this context, the issue of theoretical advancement returns. I think it is not an exaggeration to claim that it was due to the methodologies of situational analysis, extended cases, and 'social dramas' that the Manchester approach to social structure and social change was innovative. As Don Handelman (1987: 73) makes it clear, these methodologies have enabled Mancunians to produce new sorts of data, which can described as interactional, and demonstrate the complex interplay between social relationships and the choices of individuals, between institutions and customs. Handelman regards such a view on the relationships between macro and micro order as the essence of the anti-reductionist position of the Manchester School. Accordingly, although Mancunian studies remain structural analyses, they have always tried to interpret the observed reality by introducing another important dimension, that is, an analysis of social interaction and the complexities of social process. At the same time, the Manchester anthropology has also implied the recognition of the complexity of the real social world as being constituted in the day-to-day mundane living of ordinary people.

As a result, many of the theoretical issues discussed during the Manchester seminars of the 1950s and 1960s anticipated much of what Anthony Giddens and Pierre Bourdieu would later write about structure and agency. Instead of monostructural models of social reality, the seminar participants wanted to understand structures in action. Bailey (Wenner-Gren 2003 interview) assesses the situation that was typical by the early 1950s: "The general idea was there, certainly. It came to us not as 'agency' but as 'action theory,' which is the notion that people take initiatives, do things that have effects on the structure. We believed it was necessary to recognize the complexity of the real world. When you look at *The Nuer*, it is so easy to read, so beautiful, because vast amounts of material have been put on one side. So many questions are not asked or [are] simply left unanswered in the interest of simplifying everything down to a single pattern that explains everything. That was not the Manchester way."

From Gluckman's point of view, the school's development was a basic product of the improvement of extended-case study methods, which led to greater interest in the complexity of "each unique period and parcel of history; in the life-histories and lives of individuals; in the choices that individuals have available to manipulate to their advantage" (Gluckman 1968: 234). He was also quite frank in pointing out an inexorable dilemma that the anthropologist has to cope with—when one reduces the complexities of data in the structural analysis of interaction patterns, one loses much of the process of actual social life. Finally, then, it turns out that in contrast to a 'structural-functional study', the critical point for the Manchester school was a concern for the immediacy of everyday social life and real-world agency. In effect, the search for the logic of stability that was typical of structural functionalism was supplanted within this school by an attempt to describe the alternative courses of action that are available and to understand the logic of praxis. No doubt, this approach came about for methodological reasons in order to avoid the loss of the uniqueness and richness of the ethnographic data.

## Conclusions

To sum up, the RLI and the Department of Social Anthropology and Sociology in Manchester under Max Gluckman for many years included a core group of Mancunians and many people more loosely connected with the center who influenced each other by sharp, at times harsh, criticism in and out seminars, by working together, and by spending time together away from work. The ethnographies produced from the seminars organized by Gluckman arguably are among the most outstanding written by anthropologists at that time. Their authors (Barnes, Bailey, Colson, the Cunnisons, the Epsteins, Frankenberg, Marwick, Mitchell, Turner, van Velsen, Watson, and Gluckman himself) established new standards and patterns of anthropological field research and analysis. These developments have in turn made possible a sort of empirical rediscovery and conceptual replication of Gluckman's findings, thanks to the shared sophisticated methods of gathering data during fieldwork. Thus, while considering the Manchester School in a strict sense of the term—that is, the typological sense—the emphasis must be placed on the extended-case method.

Its development gradually constitutes a theoretically laden framework, set also in general terms, that in particular aims at analyzing the interrelation of the structural regularities and the actual behavior of individuals that petrifies social life as much as generating its constant change. In other words, it is the tight integration of methods and theorizing that determines the exceptionality of the Manchester School.[32] One can argue that the Mancunians were united by a near homology of methods and theory, and for this reason, despite the apparent lack of high-flying theorizing among most of them, the Mancunian anthropology remains a distinctive school of thought of a weight hardly to be surpassed by other currents in social or cultural anthropology.

## Acknowledgments

As this essay is partially based on oral history and archival work, as well as formal and informal interviews with the members and associates of the former Department of Social Anthropology and Sociology of the Victoria University at Manchester, my thanks are due to many people and institutions. I owe a great debt to all Mancunians for their time and their encouragement. Several foundations provided financial support for my research: the Fulbright Commission of the US Government, the Israel Academy of Sciences and Humanities, the British Academy, and the Wenner-Gren Foundation for Anthropological Research.

---

Marian Kempny (1954–2006) was Professor of Sociology at Warsaw University and also served as Head of the Culture Theory Unit at the Institute of Philosophy and Sociology, the Polish Academy of Sciences. He had done field research in Cieszyn Silesia and was a member of a group of scholars who reintroduced the works of Malinowski to Polish social science. Kempny had a number of books to his credit. Two of these, for which he served as co-editor, appeared in English: *Cultural Dilemmas of Post-Communist Societies* (1994) and *Identity in Transformation: Postmodernity, Postcommunism, and Globalization* (2002). Much of his work was devoted to the study of anthropological knowledge, social theory, and cultural analysis.

## Notes

1. See, for instance, Kuper (1983: 128ff.) and Vincent (1990: 276ff.), or Barnard (2000: 84ff.) for a more recent work. The most extensive account of the Manchester School in terms of its theoretical content has been provided by Werbner ([1984] 1990).
2. This document (Gluckman n.d.) was written around 1962.
3. This point is made, for instance, by Moshe Shokeid (1988–1989). However, one can try to give an explanation for this by examining the intellectual lineages of leading anthropologists in America, as in the case of the Comaroffs and Victor Turner, an intermediary of the Mancunian tradition.
4. One can even reasonably argue whether there was any theory developed there at all. Such an opinion was expressed by Fred Bailey in February 2003 in an interview

recorded by myself for the Wenner-Gren Anthropological Archives program. At the same time, Werbner ([1984] 1990) who discusses various strands of the Manchester tradition, concludes that although the Manchester School now has no overriding theoretical focus, the distinctive approaches that the school developed have not ceased to be of theoretical interest.

5. Gluckman (n.d.) himself discloses that many theoretical innovations of the school have had their roots elsewhere: "I stress again that though we did work closely together, we never failed to consult the work of others on the same problems, as a reference to any of our books will show. I myself used American sociological jurisprudence in my book on *The Judicial Process Among the Barotse* (1955), as did A.L. Epstein [1953] in his studies [of urban courts]; Mitchell brought reference-group theory from American sociology into British anthropology (*The Kalela Dance*, 1956); Watson himself used for his book on labour migration not only our own research, but also work by South African anthropologists, and by economic historians on the same situation in Britain. And so forth."

6. The Manchester School also included later anthropological studies in Israel under the umbrella of the 'Bernstein project', starting in 1963 (see Marx 1980).

7. What is noteworthy, it is quite likely that Gluckman himself used the term 'sociology' more often than 'anthropology' in order to describe the kind of research he had in mind while focused on the issue of how systems with important racial conflicts and cleavages could manage to function (cf. Schumaker 2001: 34).

8. Gluckman (n.d.) writes about this group as the "first-class people: Elizabeth Colson (now Professor of Anthropology at Brandeis University), J. A. Barnes (now Professor of Anthropology at the Australian National University), J. H. Holleman (now Director of the Social Studies Research Unit at the University of Natal), and J. C. Mitchell (now Professor of African Studies at the University College of the Rhodesias and Nyasaland)."

9. In Gluckman's unpublished document, the outcome of 30 books and "booklets" and numerous articles is mentioned.

10. The gradual weakening of the institutional ties with the RLI might be perceived as a major blow to the Manchester School. Bruce Kapferer has implied that the virtual dying away of the creative fieldwork connection between the Mancunian and Central African research brought about Gluckman's efforts to repeat the African model with a program of concerted research in Israel (the so-called Bernstein project). See Olaf Smedal's interview with Kapferer (http://www.anthrobase.com/Txt/S/Smedal_Kapferer_01.htm).

11. Mitchell is especially outspoken in this respect: "The Manchester School was not a school but a set of research studies based on basic procedures" (quoted in Schumaker 2001: 107).

12. Such a claim is overtly made by van Velsen (1967: 139), who links the methodological developments of Mancunians with "the reaction to structuralism [i.e., to structural functionalism] as formulated by Radcliffe-Brown and developed by some of his students."

13. Cf. Schumaker (2001: 151), who refers to Gluckman's 1949 letter to Clyde Mitchell.

14. As Bailey commented upon it (Wenner-Gren 2003 interview): "This left Max—I think—very, very, not exactly troubled, but uncertain because he had a huge respect and affection for Radcliffe-Brown and Evans-Pritchard and—I think—a part of it was a rebellion against this on our part. Because their theory was too remote from the empirical facts that we were talking about, we were describing. It didn't explain things, except obvious things that everybody knows, very clear, it didn't explain change directly. I mean, we need to know what the structural things do, we need the framework to talk about change, about the process of change, but it wasn't enough, of course."

15. Schumaker (2001) mentions, for example, radio talks given by the team that were organized by Gluckman to popularize their research.

16. As Gluckman (n.d.) described it: "[I]n the early 1960s a Central African program restarted with Garbett holding a Fellowship of the International African Institute at Salisbury and with two Manchester students (Werbner and Lang) gone to Salisbury to do their fieldwork for the PhD with Mitchell." Mitchell resigned from the RLI directorship

in 1966 to take up Gluckman's offer of a professorship at Manchester, a move that in the end undermined the Central African program.

17. The inscription in Mitchell (1969) reads: "To Max Gluckman, point-source of our network."

18. As Bailey explains (Wenner-Gren 2003 interview): "I put myself in that one—I went to India, and Scarlett Epstein was one, she went to India too. There were others whom you might not know. There was a guy called Allcorn, who worked in London on teenage youth, Emrys [Peters] of course, it's another part of Africa ... And there is a generation that ... still, kind of, adheres to one another of this group. You know these Israelis, the other one I can think about was [Bruce] Kapferer who came late via RLI and Mitchell. I wonder even whether he did his PhD in Manchester. I know that his book is very heavily influenced by Mitchell and Manchester."

19. As Gluckman (n.d.) explains: "I had myself to take on the teaching of sociological theory, and instead of getting a Senior Lecturer in Sociology, we appointed as Lecturer, W. Watson, who before studying two tribes in Northern Rhodesia for the Rhodes-Livingstone Institute, had carried out research in Scotland. Out of this work, Watson developed a view of patterns of social mobility, for the study of which in the Lancashire town of Leigh, we got a grant from the Nuffield Foundation."

20. Frankenberg's case is telling example here. Instead of African fieldwork, he started research on rural problems at Manchester and in 1957 published a book, *Village on the Border*, praised by Gluckman as an excellent anthropological study. But it emerged out of necessity when Frankenberg was caught by surprise by deportation from a West Indian island where he had intended to do his fieldwork (Frankenberg [1957] 1989: 171ff.).

21. Gluckman himself modified his initial position on the nature of social systems and social change to accentuate that such mechanisms as 'the peace in the feud' or 'rituals of rebellion' express the dialectic between cohesion and conflict, which stimulate the political activity of main actors within the system (Gluckman 1963).

22. Their South African background is often given as an explanation (Kuper 1983: 144; Schumaker 2001: 109–110).

23. Paradoxically, Mancunian anthropology is also accused of being a 'colonial science'. See van Teeffelen (1977, 1978) and Shokeid's (1988–1989) rejoinder.

24. His view is shared by Bruce Kapferer (2000), who holds: "Many were members of the Communist Party (though Gluckman was not, rather his wife, Mary; Gluckman was merely sympathetic) such as Bill Epstein, Bill Watson. Vic Turner, before he turned Catholic, was one of the intellectual spokesmen for the British Communist Party. But many, such as Clyde Mitchell, were more liberal in their politics."

25. It is reflected in their labeling as 'the cloth-cap boys', which underlines the contrast between their social position and that of upper-middle-class Oxbridge. Additionally, their passion for football, which went hand in hand with an allegiance to Manchester United, Gluckman's favorite football team, was an indicator of the strong working-class affiliations of Mancunians (Fred Bailey and Mike Aronoff, personal communications with author).

26. The exclusively Mancunian methodological handbook, *The Craft of Social Anthropology*, edited by Bill Epstein (1967), is an example of the product of the core group with Central African experience.

27. In comparison with the first generation of Mancunians, Gluckman's students later became considerably younger and more career dependent. In addition, Gluckman was less directly involved in their projects, with senior colleagues serving as academic intermediaries (see Shokeid 1992).

28. Furthermore, sometimes words of appreciation appeared in books written by scholars from outside Manchester whose works were discussed within the seminar. Compare such acknowledgments in Elisabeth Bott's (1957) *Family and Social Network,* and in Eric Hobsbawm's ([1959] 1965) *Primitive Rebels.*

29. Shokeid (1992: 235) mentions in this context the "shock treatment" he experienced when he transferred from the grand theory of Eisenstadt's Sociology Department at

Hebrew University, Jerusalem, to the Manchester Department, with its seminars focused on reporting simple facts and minute observations.

30. As Bailey recalls it (Wenner-Gren 2003 interview), there was no "body of theory akin to what, for instance, makes 'Durkheim and his young men' a distinctive school. At the time I was there I don't think that had begun to develop. We didn't have a clear position on the map of grand theory in sociology."

31. See especially the insightful essays by Handelman (1976) and Werbner ([1984] 1990).

32. I would like to credit Don Handelman with making this point clear to me in his editorial remarks on a draft version of this essay.

# References

Balandier, G. 1960. "Structures sociales traditionelles et changements economiques." *Cahiers d'Etudes Africaines* 1, no. 1: 1–14.

Barnard, A. 2000. *History and Theory in Anthropology*. Cambridge: Cambridge University Press.

Bott, E. 1957. *Family and Social Network: Roles, Norms and External Relationships in Ordinary Urban Families*. London: Tavistock.

Colson, E., and M. Gluckman, eds. 1951. *Seven Tribes of British Central Africa*. London: Oxford University Press for the Rhodes-Livingstone Institute.

Douglas, M. 1959. "Review: W. Watson, *Tribal Cohesion in a Money Economy*." *Man* 59, no. 270: 168.

Epstein, A. L. 1953. "The Role of African Courts in Urban Communities of the Northern Rhodesian Copperbelt." *Rhodes-Livingstone Journal* 13: 1–26.

_____, ed. 1967. *The Craft of Social Anthropology*. London: Social Science Paperbacks in association with Tavistock Publications.

Frankenberg, R. [1957] 1989. *Village on the Border*. Manchester: Manchester University Press. (Reprinted: Prospect Heights, IL: Waveland Press.)

_____. 1982. "Introduction: A Social Anthropology for Britain?" Pp. 1–35 in *Custom and Conflict in British Society*, ed. R. Frankenberg. Manchester: Manchester University Press.

Gluckman, M. [1940] 1958. "Analysis of a Social Situation in Modern Zululand." *Journal of Bantu Studies* 14: 1–30, 147–174. (Reprinted as Rhodes-Livingstone Papers, no. 28, by Manchester University Press for the Rhodes-Livingstone Institute.)

_____. 1945. "The Seven-Year Research Plan of the Rhodes-Livingstone Institute." *Journal of the Rhodes-Livingstone Institute* 4: 1–32.

_____. 1955. *The Judicial Process Among the Barotse of Northern Rhodesia*. Manchester: Manchester University Press.

_____. 1963. *Order and Rebellion in Tribal Africa*. New York: Free Press of Glencoe.

_____. 1967. "Introduction." Pp. xi–xx in Epstein 1967.

_____, ed. 1964. *Closed Systems and Open Minds*. Edinburgh and London: Oliver & Boyd.

_____. 1968. "The Utility of the Equilibrium Model in the Study of Social Change. *American Anthropologist* 70, no. 2: 219–237.

_____. n.d. "The History of the Manchester 'School' of Social Anthropology and Sociology." Unpublished manuscript.

Handelman, D. 1976. "Some Contributions of Max Gluckman to Anthropological Thought." Pp. 7–14 in *Freedom and Constraint: A Memorial Tribute to Max Gluckman*, ed. Myron J. Aronoff. Assen: Van Gorcum.

_____. 1987. "Micro-Structure and Micro-Process." *Social Analysis* 22: 73–102.

Hobsbawm, E. J. [1959] 1965. *Primitive Rebels: Studies in Archaic Forms of Social Movement in the 19th Century*. New York: W.W. Norton.

Kapferer, B. 1987. "The Anthropology of Max Gluckman." *Social Analysis* 22: 3–21.

_____. 2000. "An Interview." *Antropolog Nytt* 3. http://www.anthrobase.com/txt/S/ Smedal_Kapferer_01.htm.

Kuper, A. 1983. *Anthropology and Anthropologists: The Modern British School.* London: Routledge and Kegan Paul.

Marx, E. 1980. "Introduction." Pp. 1–14 in *A Composite Portrait of Israel,* ed. E. Marx. London and New York: Academic Press.

Mitchell, J. C. 1956. *The Kalela Dance.* Rhodes-Livingstone Papers, no. 27. Manchester: Manchester University Press for the Rhodes-Livingstone Institute.

_____, ed. 1969. *Social Networks in Urban Situations.* Manchester: Manchester University Press.

Mitchell, J. C., and J. A. Barnes. 1950. *The Lamba Village: Report of a Social Survey.* Cape Town: University of Cape Town Press.

Schumaker, L. 2001. *Africanizing Anthropology: Fieldwork, Networks, and the Making of Cultural Knowledge in Central Africa.* Durham, NC: Duke University Press.

Shokeid, M. 1988–1989. "'The Manchester School in Africa and Israel' Revisited: Reflections on the Sources and Method of an Anthropological Discourse." *Israel Social Science Research* 6, no. 1: 9–23.

_____. 1992. "An Anthropologist's Work between Moving Genres." *Ethnos* 57, no. 3–4: 234–244.

Szacki, J. 1975. "'Schools' in Sociology." *Social Science Information* 14, no. 2: 173–182.

Turner, E. 1985. "Prologue: From the Ndembu to Broadway." Pp. 1–15 in *On the Edge of the Bush: Anthropology as Experience,* ed. E. Turner. Tucson: University of Arizona Press.

Turner, V. W. 1957. *Schism and Continuity in an African Society.* Manchester: Manchester University Press for the Rhodes-Livingstone Institute.

Van Teeffelen, T. 1977. *Anthropologists on Israel: A Case Study in the Sociology of Knowledge.* Amsterdam: Antropologisch-Sociologisch Centrum, University of Amsterdam, Papers on European and Mediterranean Societies.

_____. 1978. "The Manchester School in Africa and Israel: A Critique." *Dialectical Anthropology* 3: 67–83.

Van Velsen, J. 1967. "The Extended-Case Method and Situational Analysis." Pp. 129–149 in Epstein 1967.

Vincent, J. 1990. *Anthropology and Politics.* Tucson: University of Arizona Press.

Watson, W. 1958. *Tribal Cohesion in a Money Economy.* Manchester: Manchester University Press.

Werbner, R. P. [1984] 1990. "The Manchester School in South-Central Africa." *Annual Review of Anthropology* 13: 157–185. (Revised version in *Localizing Strategies: Regional Traditions of Ethnographic Writing,* ed. R. Fardon. Edinburgh and Washington: Scottish Academic Press and Smithsonian Institution Press.)

*Chapter 7*

# A BRIDGE OVER TROUBLED WATERS, OR WHAT A DIFFERENCE A DAY MAKES[1]
From the Drama of Production to the Production of Drama

*Ronald Frankenberg*

## Double Metonym, Multiple Experience

Like many before me, I call Gluckman's paper, "Analysis of a Social Situation in Modern Zululand," by its accepted nickname, "The Bridge." "Analysis" is too bland, as perhaps its more cautiously self-conscious users intended it to be. I could have called it by a new name: "The Journey." It is, after all, also about metaphorical and real journeys, one in particular, to and from a real bridge built in 1937–1938 by engineers for the Natal Provincial Government in South Africa. Anne Salmond (1982) has pointed out how, in contrast to the Maori, European and especially anglophone poets and anthropologists, from T. S. Eliot to E. E. Evans-Pritchard, lived and wrote and sought to transform the lives of others, always-already in terms of stories about real and metaphorical (super-real or surreal) journeys, secular pilgrimages, and modernist knightly quests. The philosophical bases, derived from both Athens and Jerusalem (Arnold [1869] 1993; Lambropolous 1993), share a concern with journeys, questings, and questions about them. A day's journeying is a central trope of modernist and realist literature, as well as of ethnographic analysis (see Joyce [(1922) 1997] and Woolf [(1925) 1992]; very recently, see Cunningham [1999] and MacEwan [2005]; see also Doty [2002] and, for a post-modern 'Raymond Chandlerized' version of Eliot's 1922 *The Waste Land*, converted into a graphic novel, see Rowson [1990]; and even in music, the original version of Vaughan Williams's *London Symphony* [(1913) 2000] records in music a day's walk across the city).

Migrant laborers would be able to cross the bridge in Natal in one direction. Both the beneficent and the coercive activities of an increasingly powerful, but ultimately self-destructing, South African state would cross it in the other. For Gluckman, it was to be *the* bridge to a new kind of politics and anthropology, a new kind of intellectual commitment and protest. His work has since been interpreted and developed in many different ways, but it has come to be recognized by many, and not just by Gluckman's students, as a major crossing-point for anthropology (see, for example, Burawoy 1991; Hannerz 1980; Parkin, Caplan, and Fisher 1996; Vincent 1990, 2002; most surprisingly, see also Hennen 2004). I here propose that although it had its roots in earlier anthropology in South Africa and elsewhere (with anti-imperialist undertones not appreciated by Magubane [1969, 1971]), Gluckman's work was, more loosely than often claimed but nevertheless certainly, influenced by ideas from Marx and Freud.

It was part of a general 'modernist' culture of literature and the other arts that came about during World War I and continued between the wars and up through World War II. This many of us have only just begun to understand as we become more conscious of the links between the anthropology of the real and the general literature of the period. E. M. Forster coined the slogan "only connect," and James Joyce ([1922] 1997) compressed the long years of Homer's *Odyssey* into an eternity-encompassing single day (16 June 1904) in the life of Dublin and *its* long-established 'bridges' (see also Hannerz 1980: chap. 4 and esp. 158–159 for discussion and 356 for references). Many post-colonialist theorists have nonetheless neglected this aspect of Gluckman's work,

David Pocock, who later became a professor of social anthropology at Sussex and who, Korah-like, had preceded me from Highgate School to Cambridge, returned to lecture to the school's Masaryk Society. Having switched from Eng. Lit. to Arch. Anth., he expounded on the relationship between English literature and anthropology, and told us of Evans-Pritchard's views on T. S. Eliot's *Notes Towards the Definition of Culture*, which he said might appear in the literary journal *Scrutiny*.[2]

Later, on one memorable evening, I found myself electioneering with Bill Watson and the physicist P. M. S (Paddy) Blackett (later president of the Royal Society), who attended anthropology seminars when he could. We were parked in a car in St. Peter's Square, Manchester, awaiting instructions for our next assignment. An informal mini-seminar developed, and led by Max, my seniors told me I must learn to write 'science' to be read as if it were literature. Later, in his preface to *Village on the Border* ([1957] 1990), Max praised me—rightly or wrongly—for doing just that. It was almost as good as a novel, he wrote.

I happen to be one of a diminishing number of survivors who encountered "The Bridge" before they met Max Gluckman and who crossed over it into a new career. I first met Max himself in the fall of 1949, when I was just 20 years old and beginning anthropology. A miserably precocious schoolboy and undergraduate, I had studied natural sciences for seven years at school and university, culminating with elementary biochemistry. The 15-year gap between my oldest sibling and myself, as well as my father's late-nineteenth-century Polish revolutionary past, meant that I already had a more-than-average knowledge of Marx and Freud. I approached Max at the speaker's table after he had spoken on Zande skepticism at a meeting of the respectably unrespectable Cambridge Heretics Society. I had chosen this event, because of his presence, as the alternative attraction to a meeting of the official Anthropology Club. I asked Max where I could get a complete copy of "Analysis of a Social Situation in Modern Zululand" ([1940] 1958). It had not yet become *my* 'bridge', but I had somehow found and read the first two parts through a reference generated by John Peristiany, visiting successor from Oxford to Evans-Pritchard, who had recently moved there from Cambridge. Peristiany was tutor for the East (i.e., non-Gwilym Jones, non-Nigerian) African Studies course. No Cambridge library seemed to take *Bantu Studies*, however, and I could not find the sequel. Max's response was to ask me to join him and Phyllis Deane for dinner at the Blue Boar Hotel.

After some desultory correspondence, including his providing a complete copy of the text, Max and I met again (significantly [?], nine months later) at Cheadle Hulme Station, where at the insistence of Radcliffe-Brown—who, unlike Max, thought Anthropology Departments should have students—I had been invited for two days of interview. As I got off the train, Gluckman asked first, "What part of South Africa are you from?" Hearing that I was not South African at all, he asked, "Why do you want to be a bloody anthropologist then?" My reply, inappropriate but more insightful than I knew,[3] was that his were the only anthropological writings I had discovered that seemed to take account of both Freud and Marx.

Before I left for home in London two days later, I was accepted for a master's course, which was about to be created,[4] on Radcliffe-Brown's suggestion that, like his one-time mentor, the Oxford anarchist theorist, Prince Kropotkin, I had been studying chemistry and, after training, would be just what the department needed to solve the problems surrounding the unusual constitutional role of queen mothers in the East African lacustrine states. These women balanced the power of male kingships by living even more extremely by the principles of reigning without ruling. In the end, I limited myself to one such state, Rwanda, and what seemed to me to be the most crucial, if more directly socio-political, problems of inequality—those between Tutsi nobles and cattle-owners, the agricultural Hutu, and the forest Twa.

"The Bridge," and its implied "shared journey," metonyms and metaphors for South African unity, became one of the principal metaphorical sites of the beginnings of post-positivism and a doorway to so-called post-modernism in British social anthropology.[5] It was also, serendipitously, my personal birth rite and birthright.[6]

## Post-positivism or Literary Modernism

The totally anecdotal myth—and no doubt partially mythical anecdote—of a small part of my protracted initiation ceremonies into the discipline is also a field report on other aspects of both Gluckman's practice and his always inspiring, but often (beneficially?) confused and conflated, theoretical positions. As others have pointed out, he remained, at least overtly, committed to Radcliffe-Brown's positivist palaeo-Durkheimian stance, and was gratified when Evans-Pritchard (1948) confirmed his shared acceptance of this in his inaugural lecture at Oxford. He clearly felt betrayed when Evans-Pritchard (1951) publicly acknowledged his abandonment of this position in the Marett Lecture two years later. Gluckman expressed his views in letters to Evans-Pritchard and to others, which, as was his wont, he dictated publicly in his large office/seminar room in the presence of whoever happened to be around. Neither fieldwork and its analysis, nor professional debate, nor even administrative duties and professorial correspondence were solitary pleasures (nor were they allowed to be part-time ones) in the Manchester Department of the 1950s.

Despite following these principles in his fieldwork in Barotseland, where perhaps he pushed participation to its ultimate extreme (Brown 1979), it was still to be some time before Gluckman was able to pursue openly the implications of the 'bridge' approach in his analysis of Barotse law and to treat Lozi cases as a set of linked situations—of which he had shared experience, as well as exemplars of processes—rather than merely as sources of attributes for quantitative analysis. In this he was encouraged by A. L (Bill) Epstein as well as by his reading of A. P. Herbert's ([1927] 1935) wisely comical *Punch* articles on the "Uncommon Law," prefaced in the book version by the Lord Chief Justice of England.[7] As I shall suggest later, the difference between other approaches and the post-positivism of Gluckman and his immediate followers lies in the fact that when the latter *do* quantify, they do so to confirm the typicality of situated process rather than to predict the probability of generalized outcomes. When it occurs, the use of quantitative rather than of qualitative description is (or was intended to be) related to the problems in which scholars are currently interested. Barnes and Mitchell, as trained mathematicians, like other (sometimes, even natural) scientists, knew exactly when (and especially when *not*) and how to count in order "to add an air of verisimilitude [or at least 'scientific legitimation'] to an otherwise bald and unconvincing narrative."[8] They also knew how and when to incorporate the experience of the observer in so deciding. The training program for new research officers at the RLI under Gluckman, Colson, and Mitchell sought to ensure that they also always did so.

Later, Rhodes-Livingstone Institute (RLI) research officers such as Epstein (1967) and van Velsen (1967), in Epstein's edited book, presented situational analysis as a purely technical, fieldwork analysis device, first, because this book was seen by its authors and its editor precisely as a manual of technical practice; second, because they both sought to be robustly atheoretical in the grand schema sense; and, finally, because they felt no need to theorize fieldwork. Audrey Richards told me that she and Malinowski saw themselves primarily as anthropological naturalists in the tradition of biological empiricists rather than of theoretical evolutionists. They lived in the field but did not see themselves, in their scientific role, as part of it.

Van Velsen and Epstein, unlike most of their predecessors, were both also 'natural fieldworkers', but they also saw themselves as an organic part of the field. This prompted political and societal alarm in both official colonial government and copper mine management circles. They both aroused suspicion, as had Gluckman in Zululand, for their comportment in the field: Gluckman had been accused of inappropriately adopting Zulu dress; van Velsen was reproached for his barefaced, sometimes bare-nearly-all (lack of) dress code in the village; Epstein incurred fear and hostility for his continual presence at miners' union meetings with a cigarette in the corner of his mouth and a beer bottle in hand (Powdermaker 1962, 1966).

Marilyn Strathern (1987: 281ff.) was characteristically more attentive than most to the actual argument of Thomas Kuhn (1970). She followed him in pointing out that new scientific paradigms, like other forms of cultural change, are not invented or inserted: first, they become necessary, then present, and, only in the last instance, visible to their practitioners. Indeed, she suggests and argues cogently that in the social, as opposed to natural, sciences "they are less applicable than appears at first sight" (Strathern 1987: 282). She also, interestingly, refers in a footnote (ibid.: 279) to the fact that Edwin Ardener's (1972) seminal paper, "Belief and the Problem of Women," ironically became a feminist text. Ardener's article was, of course, based on the use of 'paradigm' as a term of linguistic analysis rather than its applied metonymic use in science. It described the way that women in the grasslands of Cameroon, like pre-Kuhnian scientists, without theorizing or naming their actions, shifted paradigms from femineity to femininity and back, through a kind of lived auto-anthropology in actions that spoke more loudly than words.

## Auto-anthropology or What?

We also owe to Strathern the most useful suggestion that auto-anthropology is the study of a society using its own analytical language, shared by the ethnographer. I am still not entirely convinced of the necessity for making this useful distinction as part of the required general evaluation and analysis of all ethnographic work in one's 'own' society. It is, however, as crucial to "The Bridge" as Emanuel Marx has argued it is to his and other Israeli work, since it has now become clear that Gluckman was making a consciously deliberate intervention to define and to redefine the analytical language of anthropology, especially in his native land of South Africa. Historians writing about "The Bridge," both in South Africa and elsewhere, have joined Gluckman in arguing that he was writing not only *as* a South African but also, at least initially, *to* and *for* South Africans. He is specifically seeking to restate and to widen (sometimes paradoxically by narrowing, that is, by making more specific) the boundaries of their analytical language. He does this in relation to black and colored South Africans as well as to the then current German and Dutch colonial practice and *volkskundlich* ethnology. The problem is, of course, that the groups involved, as observers and as observed, themselves had several situational and general languages at their command. Furthermore, their choice of which to choose shifted quite rapidly, even within a short period of time. (This is one of the reasons why the analysis of a single day or a single ritual event may be particularly useful, especially if it is presented in relation to its historical and spatial context. In literature, Virginia Woolf, James Joyce, and recently Michael Cunningham, Mark Doty, and Ian MacEwan have all recognized and represented this well.)

Gluckman's central argument draws attention to the overt enactment of latently shared understandings of the meaningful diversity of shared analytic, research, and day-to-day languages. He seeks to demonstrate, and to build on, a unity that emerges from the intellectual conflict in which he is involved with other white anthropologists as a political animal as well as an anthropologist-observer. He shares the conflicts within the unity of celebration at the bridge, perceiving himself as an embodied representative of some of the several apparently conflicted categories that participate. Lyn Schumaker (2001: 41–50), in a chapter of her history of the RLI titled "Archetypal Experiences," and in a section within it intriguingly called "The Dancing Anthropologist," is able to build on Gluckman's demonstration (many years ahead of his time) that this extended to the language of the body itself (see Shilling 2005: esp. chap. 6, "Musical Bodies"). In the language of the twenty-first century, the RLI researchers opened themselves to the policy of sharing embodied experience with their subjects. She points to the sharp difference in the dress and demeanor of Gluckman compared with P. J. Schoeman of the Afrikaans University of Stellenbosch and the latter's pupil, J. F. Holleman, whom she interviewed personally. Even so, Schumaker seems to treat the distinction too lightly, since she does not emphasize the difference this made to the anthropologists' ability to evoke the 'whatness' of their several accounts (see Joyce [1922] 1997). Perhaps influenced by later post-modernist arguments, she sees it, despite herself, in general merely in terms of Gluckman building "reflexivity into his text."[9] She does not fully realize what was recognized by some, especially his opponents, at the time—that he had introduced a qualitative change into the nature of social anthropological fieldwork in general. He did this, first, by substituting for mere direct observation what later came to be called (borrowing from Chicago sociology) 'participant observation'.[10] Second, he saw that fieldwork findings had now to be analyzed theoretically in a new way.[11] Gluckman had in fact introduced, as a principled and theoretical method, participant observation in the full sense of the biblical 'stranger within the gates'—someone who lives within the bounds of a social entity but is, in some sense or other, not entirely of it. I suggested naively in my very brief magazine article on the subject (Frankenberg 1963) that the full participant-observer technique results, like a course of psychoanalytic treatment, in a process of counter-transference and positive and negative transference (see also Drucker-Brown 1985). The end of analysis for the therapeutic couple lies in the total or partial dissolving of the transference. For the social analyst, that is, unsurprisingly, the place where it *begins*.

A less mealy-mouthed scholar, the poet and classicist Anne Carson ([1986] 2000), in *Eros: The Bittersweet*, has elucidated the classical Greek metaphor, which expounds the unity of all love, *eros*, as process in action, in life, literature, and philosophy—all of which, in the words of Sappho, are bittersweet. I have only space here to refer to Carson's preface in which she repeats and comments on a Kafka story, "The Top," about a philosopher who frequents the company of children in order to grab their tops as they spin: "To catch a top still spinning makes him happy for a moment in his belief 'that the understanding of any detail, that of a spinning top for instance, was sufficient for the understanding of all things.') Disgust follows delight almost at once and he throws down the top and walks away." He repeats his actions again and again.

"The story," Carson explains, "is about the delight we take in metaphor. A meaning spins, remaining upright on an axis of normalcy aligned with the conventions of connotation and denotation; and yet, to spin is not normal, and to dissemble normal uprightness by means of this fantastic motion is impertinent. What is the relation of impertinence to the hope of understanding? To delight?" She concludes that she finds it hard to believe that the philosopher chases after tops to achieve his or her professional goal of understanding. In Carson's view, s/he (perhaps like an anthropologist) uses the search for understanding in order to justify chasing tops.

## Emanuel Marx: Post-positivist Fieldworker and Neo-positivist Analyst

This characteristic of simultaneous presence and absence in participant observation is picked up in practice, in an equally imaginative but characteristically more lucid and scientifically rigorous way, by Emanuel Marx, who was also consciously engaged in virtual auto-anthropology. At least in his pioneering earliest definition of the characteristics of the extended-case method (E. Marx 1972, 1976), he says that a principal factor in the possibility of his employing it was his prior acquaintance and continued association with those involved (1976: 2). Despite this disclaimer, and his initially implied and later highly original development of a distinctive Israeli anthropology for the twenty-first century, I think that Marx is, even in his early work, fulfilling Strathern's criterion of auto-anthropology as a project whose theoretical basis emerges from the encultured thought processes of the ethnographer rather than those of the studied. Just as in the case of Gluckman and other Africans—and, indeed, of Strathern and other inhabitants of New Guinea—the end product of success is a dynamic, even oscillating hybrid.

As Gluckman argued in "The Bridge," the cultural presuppositions of the participants are different and may seem segregated at the outset. When they disperse, their limited partial interaction having ended, they have taken steps toward dynamic dualities or eventual multiplicities of thought and practice. This does not mean that conflict, contradiction, or irony have ceased or will inevitably cease to exist; it means merely that the field in which their activity is enacted and can be analyzed is at once physically more extensive and beneficially made more concise and potentially precise.

Emanuel Marx's work is post-positive in his inclusion of himself within the field of study (1976: 2–3): "My material derives chiefly from my own observations and from detailed reports of the participants in each incidence of violence. I had known all the persons involved before they acted violently and continued to associate with them after the incidents." In other ways, it harkens back to a more formal view of the relationship between the observer in command of theory and the observed, whose actions are consciously chosen but not fully consciously thought out. He continues (ibid.: 3):

> The case method makes systematic use of interconnected series of field data for sociological analysis. In this method the facts are arranged around an analytical topic; in addition, they should provide information on a wider range of subjects. The analytical topic is the thread that links the facts in a consecutive narrative. The case is thus not a slice of real life lifted straight out of the anthropologist's notebooks, but a sociological construct bringing together facts in a systematic order. This fundamental point, in particular, has sometimes been ignored by social scientists, who assumed that facts whose interconnection derives from a concern with a certain person or group, or a certain locality, or because they occurred within a certain time span, do therefore constitute a case, and that such a case is a significant unit for sociological analysis. A case of this kind may qualify for literary treatment, as it possesses the elements of dramatic unity. But its utility for sociological purposes is strictly limited.

Indeed, but if it were always true, its utility for literature, as we now understand it, would be not merely limited but totally absent. Marx goes on to explain how before he put pen to paper with case studies, he spent many hours in the study, classifying, analyzing, and developing a specifically sociological framework. In other words, the expertise of sociologists and anthropologists (like that of novelists and playwrights, and often even poets) lies in the questions they learn to ask at the beginning. These rarely lead to new answers but rather to new questions that they are now newly qualified to ask, at the apparent end of, or perhaps pause in, their work.

Participant observation, along with other ways of being partially estranged in the field situation, was for Emanuel Marx, as for others, a role fraught with both danger and power. Its overenthusiastic adoption by Gluckman led to his temporary and then permanent expulsion from Zululand. In different power circumstances, it also gave rise to the Celtic saints and the place name prefix 'Llan' in Wales (Bowen 1956), as well as to a new royal dynasty in Cyrenaica (Evans-Pritchard 1949). It made my own use of situational analysis in Glynceiriog possible but led to the embarrassment of being denounced on the radio as a German spy and to being interviewed by the police. At the same time, participant observation suggested to me how conflicts were handled in committees and other village groups. When they employed me as a teacher, the National Union of Mineworkers had the wisdom to bar me from union membership, ensuring that I did not emulate the Sanusiya in Cyrenaica and try to take over the union itself or use it as a steppingstone to political power. One of my successors, Kim Howell, who subsequently earned a PhD, had been allowed to remain a member as a miner himself. He became a 'real' union official, was elected to Parliament, and now is the minister for higher education in the government formed by New Labour. Learning the role of the stranger by direct experience enabled me to analyze at a distance war-time decisions, the role of psychiatrists in the courts, the practice of management consultancy. I was even able to analyze aspects of Greek tragedy, with the approval and help of Moses Finley, G. S. Kirk, J.-P. Vernant, and P. Vidal-Naquet, at an enlarged seminar in 1966, which grew into a Gluckman-edited volume, *The Allocation of Responsibility* (1972).[12]

In "The Bridge," Gluckman questions the unambiguous boundedness of groups. By identifying and discussing phases of the ceremony that unite and divide different subsections, he even moves toward (or at least opens the way for) the network vision of situated social process that Barnes and Mitchell and their students were going to develop and use so effectively in Zambia and carry home to the anglophone world.

Beyond this, as Hugh Macmillan (1995) has argued and as Paul Cocks (2001) has elaborated more recently, Gluckman's work, like that of Radcliffe-Brown, Schapera, Malinowski, and the historian W. M. Macmillan before him, was a political intervention that sought to undermine the nationalists' claim that anthropological science was on their side. As Cocks points out, both Radcliffe-Brown and Schapera accepted cultural difference but saw it as in the process of being modified. Schapera, less hindered by positivist theory and indeed more at home in South Africa and possessing detailed knowledge based on fieldwork, was more conscious both of outside forces for change and of internal social change and diversification. Both scholars opposed segregation, but neither had the theoretical vision to see the already ongoing "formation of a single social system being the basis for any positive alternative—in their own terms, a 'functional' rather than a 'dysfunctional' society—thus undermining their own critiques" (Cocks 2001: 745). Cocks goes on to argue at length that, unsurprisingly, at the time when Gluckman accompanied Schapera on a field trip in 1930 and at least until submitting his BA (Hons.) thesis in 1933, Gluckman did not have the theoretical basis to improve upon his mentors.[13] Later however, as Cocks puts it, following in both senses Gluckman's argument, albeit with the benefit of hindsight and much subsequent literature (ibid.: 753): "The fundamental point that Gluckman was making was not simply that blacks and whites were part of a single social system, but that it was precisely what differentiated them from each other that formed the basis for their integration. Although 'on the whole' they had 'different modes of life, customs and belief', the need to cooperate resulted in their having 'to adapt to each other in socially determined ways when they associate with one another.'" Gluckman, however, had no illusions about on which side of what he later came to call a 'dominant cleavage' lay white and black ultimate power and economic control. His use of terms such as 'equilibrium' and 'community' led Phyllis Kaberry (1957) and others astray,[14] despite his clear statement in several parts of the text (see Gluckman [1940] 1958: 2, 13, 26) and in a footnote rejoinder added to the Rhodes-Livingstone Paper version (ibid.: 35; see also Vincent 2002: 60). Gluckman wrote: "I did not intend to convey that Zulu and White formed an harmonious, well integrated lot of people, but a lot of people co-operating and disputing within the limits of an established system of relations and cultures." It was left to historically minded anthropologists and anthropologically well-informed historians to extract the full value from the insights and findings yielded by these studies (see K. Marx [1869] 1973).

Gluckman, even (or perhaps especially) at home in South Africa, had many left-wing 'liberal' friends, some active, including union leaders, like Sachs, and Jack Simons, a professor of law, and his wife, Rae Alexander, the activist historian of the South African Communist Party. It was the informal task of the two last mentioned to meet new RLI research officers off the boat in Cape Town and act as guides to, and interpreters of, the realities of African life. At least one research officer, van Velsen, who later worked closely with Simons in Lusaka, expressed shock that his first night in Africa was in the household of a 'Bolshevik'. Some of these were known Communists, and some were not; some had studied Freud (Wulf Sachs and the Joffe brothers were professional psychoanalysts), and some Marx. Since it was fashionable in South Africa, as it was for some of us in North London and later Cambridge, some researchers may have studied both together in the attempted synthesis of Wilhelm Reich. As a 1930s intellectual, Gluckman had an intelligent and reasonably informed interest in both; I do not believe, however, that he had ever systematically studied Marxism, certainly not to the extent that Raymond Firth had, let alone Worsley, Turner, or even myself. Later Gluckman knew psychoanalysis to a greater extent as an analysand, but not to the greater academic and professional standard that Fortes did. His propensity to support his own students and other scholars who shared his radical approach and innovative style, even if they were Marxist, earned him, by a sort of guilt-by-association process, a reputation for himself being Marxist, which, among other things, led to his being excluded from New Guinea. Schumaker implies that Gluckman's interest in material culture arises not from his materialism *tout court* but from his 'Marxist materialism'. It is clear from the published literature that his interest in the economy was fueled in Zambia by common sense and Phyllis Deane and in African agronomy by W. M. (Bill) Allan, and that his discussion of the theoretical relationships between anthropology and economics were influenced by the very conservative but independent-minded Manchester economist, Ely Devons. None of these scholars had any time for Marx as an economist or, indeed, for any sort of involvement as general political activists, let alone as part of the so-called extreme left.

Nevertheless, Mitchell (1987: 3–6), like many Marxists, was, ironically, totally mistaken in supposing that what distinguished his own work from certain other urban sociologists such as Castells and Harvey was that the others were 'constrained' by their Marxism from arguing from local situational process to global structural process. They chose their method to match their problem, just as he did. The fact that they focused one-sidedly on structural determinants, if it is a flaw at all, arises from the way that they chose to use the method of so-called historical materialism. It does not arise from any necessary feature of that method itself. They leave out—as was, in my view, also a central cause of the downfall of the Soviet Union—the dialectic of theoretically argued and physically imposed reality coming face to face with how it is lived and experienced. They do not see it as central to their argument and perhaps expect us to add it for ourselves. They may have been too optimistic! Nor, of course, was Engels in *Condition of the Working Class* alone of the famous duet, as Mitchell suggested, in describing in detail what actually happens on the ground, although he did have more first-hand experience of it. Textbook expositions of *Capital* (K. Marx [1867] 1976) are usually purely theoretical. The book itself describes, frequently in meticulous detail drawn from medical reports and the observations of the founders of public health and the geography of disease, how people lived, endured, embodied, and altered their life situations.

What Marx did know and could analyze at first hand, as could Engels, were the 'small-p' political situations on which changes in ultimate systemic power might depend. "The Bridge" once more links us metonymously with this. Worsley suggested in seminar discussion that it and Gluckman's 1952 Frazer Lecture were to the micro sociology of internal African politics of the colonial twentieth century what Marx's ([1869] 1973) "The 18th Brumaire of Louis Bonaparte" was to the politics of nineteenth-century Europe. Gluckman wrote ([1940] 1958: 32–33):

> Through all these periods of Zulu History, in the equilibrium of the ruler-subject relationship, the force of organisation behind the ruler was balanced against division in the ranks of the ruled. Intriguers for power sought popular support and the people, in order to escape from intolerable oppression, turned to those men who were near in their power to their rulers. When a ruler transgressed these rules, his subject knew of no other political system, nor could they establish another under the social conditions prevailing. They could be rebels not revolutionaries. The king's danger came from rivals who could be installed in his place, with similar powers in a similar organisation: he was deposed, but his office remained unaffected, as is shown in the ability of his successor immediately to undertake religious functions, to symbolise the values of the society, and to express them in ceremonial.

Gluckman goes on to describe what we would now sometimes describe as a hegemonic ideology. Interestingly, however, and perhaps also somewhat romantically, he inverts it by saying that the rulers in general accepted the same values as their people. After expanding his analysis of political equilibrium in more detail in the following paragraph, he continues: "Economic interests also checked fissiparous tendencies. As in the past, the chief controlled allocation of tribal land and all his subjects were entitled to some. His subjects had to render him labour service. In addition, many of his subjects lived on cattle he had loaned them for use and so they dared not break with him." He describes the wealth and armed power that subsequent kings had inherited from the successful tyrant, Shaka, and continues: "The king could not himself consume this wealth nor change it into capital under the rudimentary mode of production which persisted unchanged" (Gluckman [1940] 1958: 34).

Gluckman sees that there is a kind of class division here. He denies it in Barotseland (see Gluckman passim and cf. Frankenberg 1978) but recognizes that the Zulu's own mode of production mainly falls short of commodity production and of capitalism, although the social formation of which it had become part is capitalist dominated. Gluckman (1954) returned to the repetitive aspect of the Zulu polity in his Frazer Lecture, in which he considers the ritual aspects of the contrast between the possibility of revolution and the actuality of rebellion and argues, using Hilda Kuper's Swazi field material as a starting point, that such rituals are possible only and precisely because revolutionary change is not even an imaginable option. In such circumstances, ritual and even forceful rebellion merely serve to strengthen the existing power. Zulu and Swazi may despise and attack the king, but in doing so they express support for monarchy, which they are in fact thereby defending (see the discussion of coercive and symbolic violence in E. Marx 1976). Gluckman (1954: 24) thus writes: "Every Rebellion therefore is a fight in defence of royalty and kingship; and in this process the hostility of commoners against aristocrats is directed to maintain the rule of the aristocrats, some of whom lead the commoners in revolt."

Within a different cultural context and in a different stage of industrial development of capitalist social relations, Karl Marx's analysis of political maneuverings in Paris in the late 1840s and the early 1850s used similar kinds of observation and ways of analysis and reached, in part, similar conclusions but was written more in the style of the romantic literature of his day than in the austere modernism of Gluckman and Mitchell. He too shows, albeit on a longer time line and in a more complicated class situation, how in different phases, different groups underwent fission and fusion, according to situational changes in the National Assembly and in Paris, which arose directly from their own interaction. At the time, it only partially appeared to them to reflect the gross structural divisions in the country at large, which they often barely recognized or even misrecognized. The outcome was in fact, in this case also, the strengthening of the central state, which the protagonists had intended to weaken. Marx saw this as in the long term desirable, since the process was ripening the economy and the central role of the state, readying it for its hopefully eventual and inevitable takeover by the forces of the proletariat. As he himself put it, "Well grubbed, Old Mole."

## Abner Cohen: The Ritual Drama of Symbolic Politics; Victor Turner: Symbols and the Politics of Ritual Drama

When Abner Cohen arrived in Manchester in 1956, it was another cataclysmic and politicized year, both for the world (Suez and Hungary) and for Gluckman's department. Cohen joined a group of scholars and teachers who, like himself, but unlike me, had done battlefield work (sometimes on planes and ships) before they had done anthropological fieldwork. I remember Abner explaining how, while still in Iraq, he had worked translating Marxist classics into Arabic and that he had avoided a similar fate to those alleged to be Communists, but who were certainly Jews by cultural affiliation and had been hanged eight years before, only by escaping through the back of the house, while members of his family stalled the police at the front. I like to think of this as an exemplary myth. Cohen perhaps began at that moment to understand through his own practice the empowerment that comes from symbolic and practical action, cultural performances inseparably combining the expressive and the instrumental. He made his way to Israel, where, like so many, he became a soldier and in his case an excellent educationist, earning an external first-class degree from London University and reading widely in English literature.

After corresponding with Gluckman, he decided to study anthropology in the Manchester Department. His move to Manchester (appropriately, given the department's supposedly Marxist, and latently Freudian, *Platzgeist*) was overdetermined. Gluckman's already-established family connections with and interests in Israel and his cooperation with established Israeli scholars, such as the tragically short-lived Yonina Talmon-Garber and Shmuel Eisenstadt, were factors, as were his planned recruitment of accomplished young scholars to foster, his openness to non-dogmatic radical theory and practices of many kinds, and his interest in creative literature in general and Shakespeare in particular. I am not sure how often, if at all, Cohen subjected himself to football half-time seminars on pragmatic and ceremonial tactics, or readily empathized with, or even recognized, Manchester United as the department's dominant symbol.

But above all, what drew Cohen and others to Manchester was, as David Parkin (1996) explains in his introduction to a festschrift volume for Cohen, "The Bridge"—the study of a remote place that illuminates at once centuries of history compressed into a single day of events. This, as I have already argued above, began the transformation of the scope of social anthropology beyond the internal or external colonial other and toward more sophisticated theoretical possibilities in the same way as did similar developments in literature (Joyce's *Ulysses*, Woolf's *Mrs Dalloway*, and Solzhenytsin's *Day in the Life*, for example). "The Bridge" has elements drawn from Durkheim and Marx but owes its radical attraction to the realization not only that the ethnographer is there as a person but also that (long before the methodological individualist confusion sown around the topic by some, but not all, post-modernist approaches) s/he has to be recognized as part of a system of social relations in which s/he is, like it or not, fully included. Gluckman presented himself, as I have suggested, correctly, not only as part of the problem, but also as part of the problematic. He saw the apparent unity despite diversity, which led to the classification of Manchester as a 'school' in terms of collective representations arising from its shared methods of fieldwork. This meshed with the exercise of a collective craft. In seminars, theoretical situational analyses passed through the refining process of lived pragmatic situational analysis. Visitors did not always perceive what was going on: David Schneider and David Aberle were respectively angered and saddened. Others, such as Shils and Homans, happily and astutely joined the play, while Goffman, on a visit, unsurprisingly took charge.

Despite theoretical differences and subsequent careers focused on different continents and in different traditions, Victor Turner and Cohen, in complementary ways, carried Gluckman's focusing-down a stage further. Gluckman explored the drama of politics on a national scale to illuminate the local, while Abner did so on the local scale to help understand the national (Cohen 1981, 1993)—different sides of the same coin, contradictory conjoined theses of the same dialectic. Both Abner and Turner also advanced from the plurally lived but differentiated experiences of a whole single day to the unstable embodied moment, a fulcrum and/or turning point at once empty of mundane social content yet saturated with the possibility of perduring meaning. Vic Turner (with his wife Edie), first in his sharing of the Ndembu experience, built his analysis of their ritual around the central liminal social silences that he discerned as being at the heart of their political, religious, and symbolic practices. He then realized, together with Edie, its wider relevance in their own shared similar experience in the Eucharist and in pilgrimages of his newfound and her rediscovered Catholic faith.

Abner strengthened his own and his reader's theoretical conviction with a wider but just as deeply analyzed ethnographic range, of which one example (Cohen 1979) is built, as at the Notting Hill and other carnival masquerades, on the deafening noise of simultaneously competing and complementary Trinidadian and Jamaican musics, steelband and calypso (with dancing and dress to match). This last is consistent with the Jewish Talmudic tradition of speaking at once, supposedly simultaneously with many voices, while recognizing the productive inevitability of dissent and argument about it. This is an outlook shared within Jewish culture by the religious, the observant, and the semi-observant, and by those, such as Freud and Abner Cohen, who assert a generalized but totally skeptical respect for all religion accompanied by a secular agnosticism and a sense of wonder at the diversity of ways in which people create and reinforce power (micro for Freud, micro and macro for Cohen) through the deployment of ritual and ceremonial symbolism (see Slezkine 2004). These issues are tellingly discussed in Abner's (1979) remarkable summarizing paper, "Political Symbolism," written during a Stanford sabbatical and printed in the *Annual Review of Anthropology*. (This is one of a trilogy with Turner's [1975] "Symbolic Studies" and Vincent's [1978] "Political Anthropology: Manipulative Strategies"—three grandchildren of "The Bridge.") In it, Cohen developed ideas he had first put forward 10 years before (Cohen 1969) and counters the arguments of both Turner and Firth against him—that his view of ritual as political was reductionist. He demonstrates by a creative use of Marx's thinking that the apparent contradiction between rituals of the self (births, marriages, and deaths, for example) and the rituals of political power (including the enhanced Creole cult of the dead in Sierra Leone and mortuary rituals surrounding Lenin and Mao) can be resolved by empirical and theoretical analysis of their obligatory nature, whether experienced as external coercion or embodied compulsion. Marx and even, perhaps unsurprisingly Althusser, Marx's *Normalien* successor, come together with Durkheim to refute reductionism and to leave Foucault at the starting blocks.

As we have seen, while they thought in terms of continuing social processes, Manchester scholars did so in different ways. Some described successively linked processes (Epstein and van Velsen). Some perceived fragmenting and reuniting cycles (Colson, Bailey, Barnes, and Mitchell). They all wrote about the partially unpredictable but always ongoing production of difference and similarity, units and collectivities, boundaries and unboundedness. Each society, even every situation and ephemeral moment within each society, was different. Each, however, was involved in multiple, overlapping, and intertwined processes. As a politically conscious South African, Gluckman chose to see and to recognize the overlap and, unlike most of his compatriots, to use it. Abner Cohen, a scholar-soldier in Israel, like Emanuel Marx understanding Arabic and Hebrew and the similarities and differences of their (temporarily) conflicting cultures, chose for his first professional foray into anthropology a study of Arab border villages in Israel (Cohen [1965] 1972). The understanding that he forged and purified there he applied especially in his 1979 study of carnival divisions between Afro-Caribbeans and others, as well as within the cultural realities that at once united and divided them.

In 1970, after my then rarely possible month's tour of China, at the tail end of the Cultural Revolution, Abner invited me to talk at a School of Oriental and African Studies seminar on ritual and religion, titled "Political Symbolism in the Cultural Revolution." Afterwards, he sent me a paper of his (Cohen 1969: 219) in which he had marked a paragraph that illustrates the breadth of his vision and deserves to be the last word: "[T]here can be no social order without the 'mystification' of symbolism. This is true, not only of capitalist societies, as Marx maintained, but also of socialist societies, where emblems, slogans, banners, mass parades, titles, patriotic music and songs, and inevitably, the 'world view' of dialectical materialism—these and a host of other symbols play their part in the maintenance of political order. 'Secularisation' writes Martin (1965: 169) 'is less a scientific concept than a tool of counter-religious ideologies.'"

---

Ronald Frankenberg was the youngest to graduate from Gluckman's department in 1954. He earlier read natural sciences and some anthropology at Cambridge. He did research on British communities and on medical anthropology in Zambia and in Britain. He retired in 2002, having divided his time equally between Brunel and Keele in the UK for about 12 years. He works freelance as an honorary fellow of Keele and of the Centre for Jewish Studies in Manchester. He spent much formative time in the US, helping to found *Medical Anthropology Quarterly* and the critical medical anthropology caucus of the Society for Medical Anthropology of the American Anthropological Association. He received the first Virchow Prize (1986), the Malinowski Medal (1993), and the AARG best conference paper (1995). He taught briefly at Berkeley and Case Western Reserve, as well as in Zambia, Tanzania, Norway, India, and Finland, and he worked as education and research officer for the Welsh Miners Trade Union. His books include *Village on the Border* (1957) and *Communities in Britain* (1964). He edited a tribute volume to Gluckman, *Custom and Conflict in British Society* (1982), and *Time, Health and Medicine* (1992). Recent papers are on Asian women in the British National Health Service and Gramscian medical anthropology.

## Notes

1. A famous anti-appeasement statesman, Alfred Duff Cooper (aka Lord Norwich), called his 1953 memoirs *Old Men Forget*, presumably because it sounded better and snappier than *Old Men Remember (Not Only Too Much but Also Often Inaccurately)*. Be warned. I might well have called mine *Old Men Mythologize*.

2. In addition to Pocock and myself, other sixth-form contemporaries on the anthropological and Africanist journey were Anthony Forge, Tim Goodland, and Terence Ranger. W. W. Skeat was a nineteenth-century predecessor.

3. The South African-exiled Communist psychoanalyst, Max Joffe, was a great friend of and influence on Gluckman, and when I messed up in my first interview for an RLI job, I was sent to him to see if I was neurotic or stupid. He decided the latter, but Gluckman wrote to Audrey Richards at Makerere saying that I was brilliant but neurotic. She replied by telegram that Makerere was a research institute, not a mental hospital.

4. The other potential students, Bailey and Worsley, older and wiser ex-officers, were not required, as I was, to do coursework and written examinations.

5. I use the term 'post-positivism' to avoid confusion arising from the fact that the term 'post-modernism', when related to science, means inter alia the recognition that effective 'scientific' observers can be neither outside nor mutually independent of what they observe. In relation to literature and the arts in general, the term 'modernism' is used for similar perceptions of narrators, graphic artists, film directors, and tellers of tales. Richard Hamilton is to Joyce as Joyce is to Dublin. The synecdochical approach of the best gluckmanist post-bridge anthropology establishes bridges by helping to demonstrate the non-existence of the cultural gap between created science and creative literature.

6. This is one answer to the agonized question—"Surely, not again?"—of my former head of discipline, Adam Kuper, when told of this essay. Another is that each time I have written it, I have been writing in a different intellectual and political situation. One of the lessons of the original paper and its readers who write it anew is that each of us continually becomes a different same person (see Frankenberg 2002).

7. Sir Alan Patrick Herbert (1890–1971) was a regular contributor to the comic magazine *Punch* from 1910 until his death. Herbert served in Parliament from 1935 until 1950 as a representative for Oxford University and was largely responsible for the 1937 bill liberalizing English divorce law. He was knighted in 1945. His autobiography, *A.P.H.: His Life and Times*, appeared in 1970.

8. See Kapferer's (1987: ix) comment in the foreword to Mitchell's *Cities, Society, and Social Perception*: "The reader will see how Mitchell always *argues* through the mathematical and statistical techniques he develops. Thus he shows how certain aspects of mathematical and statistical method fail to penetrate some aspect of the problematic areas of cultural perception or social action as ethnographically encountered. He accordingly elaborates a particular technique, and so the principles which systematically underlie perceptions of urban life, migration ..., etc., are revealed more clearly before the analytical gaze." Alas, the fellows of Nuffield College, who wisely elected him to their number, nevertheless seemed unable to follow his example. See also Mitchell (1956) and most cogently (1983; passim and especially the conclusion, 93):

   > In case studies statistical inference is not invoked at all. Instead the inferential process turns exclusively on the theoretically necessary linkages among the features in the case study. The validity of the extrapolation depends not on the typicality or representativeness of the case but open the cogency of the theoretical reasoning.
   >
   > In terms of this argument case studies may be used analytically—as against ethnographically—only if they are embedded in an appropriate theoretical framework. The rich detail which emerges from the intimate knowledge the analyst must acquire in a case study if it is well conducted provides the optimum conditions for the acquisition of those illuminating insights which make formerly opaque connections suddenly pellucid.

9. Schumaker's (2001: 43) full text reads: "Gluckman built reflexivity into his text by using his own movements and behavior during the course of the day to explore the racial politics of the larger context. This is significantly different from Malinowski's use of a photograph of his tent to authenticate his presence as a participant-observer in Trobriand society. Although Gluckman's description of his own movements also textually authenticates his presence, while in the field itself he used this device as a self-conscious method to achieve an understanding of the political and racial situation. Moreover, in the resulting text he directly addressed the question of how far the anthropologist or any other European could enter into Zulu society, a question that, rather than simply supporting the efficacy of participant-observation, highlighted its limitations in a racially charged situation."

10. Susan Drucker-Brown (1985) suggests that I inadvertently formalized this in print for the first time in *New Society* when the editor asked me to write an article on it, and I naively assumed that it was accepted usage in anthropology as well as sociology.

11. The link with the method, if not its name, is made by Mitchell (1987: 296–301).

12. Other contributors were Sally F. Moore, Emrys Peters, P. T. W. Baxter, Basil Sansom, and Richard Werbner. The conference was also attended by Professor Charles L. Black Jr. from Yale Law School, Dorothy Emmett, Meyer Fortes, Simon Pembroke, and Gordon Rose. The book begins with a revised version of Gluckman's Marett Lectures and is dedicated to Evans-Pritchard. The conference was initiated by Moses Finley, who invited the other classicists to help Gluckman (and, very incidentally, me) to make his references to classic texts more rigorous. Gluckman (1972: xxvii) wrote: "But Mr Dacre Balsdon of Exeter College and Professor Moses Finley of Cambridge made clear to me that I must do much work on the problem." Significantly, although all the articles relied heavily on the research philosophy of "The Bridge," only Gluckman himself refers directly to it. The others, by this time, took it for granted.

13. Cocks and Hugh Macmillan are in dispute about the latter's father's influence on Gluckman's development of the arguments in "The Bridge." I have, however, neither the knowledge nor the interest to judge between them. Gluckman, in my presence, showed regard and respect for Schapera as his teacher and as his senior colleague (he once severely rebuked Watson for addressing Schapera disrespectfully by an intimate nickname without being invited to do so). W. M. Macmillan's demeanor and age inspired respect without any prompting; Gluckman introduced him with awe and admiration.

14. As the use of the term 'community studies' later did in British and American sociology.

## References

Ardener, Edwin. 1972. "Belief and the Problem of Women." Pp. 135–158 in *The Interpretation of Ritual,* ed. Jean La Fontaine. London: Tavistock.

Arnold, Matthew. [1869] 1993. "Culture and Anarchy." Pp. 55–211 in *"Culture and Anarchy" and Other Writings,* ed. Stefan Collini. Cambridge: Cambridge University Press.

Bowen, Emrys G. 1956. *The Settlements of the Celtic Saints in Wales.* Cardiff: University of Wales Press.

Brown, Richard. 1979. "Passages in the Life of a White Anthropologist: Max Gluckman in Northern Rhodesia." *Journal of African History* 20: 525–541.

Burawoy, Michael. 1991. "The Extended-Case Method." Pp. 271–287 in *Ethnography Unbound: Power and Resistance in the Modern Metropolis.* Berkeley: University of California Press.

Carson, Anne. [1986] 2000. *Eros: The Bittersweet.* Normal, IL: Dalkey Archive Press. (Published originally by Princeton University Press.)

Cocks, Paul. 2001. "Max Gluckman and the Critique of Segregation in South African Anthropology, 1921–1940." *Journal of Southern African Studies* 27, no. 4: 739–756.

Cohen, Abner. [1965] 1972. *Arab Border Villages in Israel: A Study of Continuity and Change in Social Organisation.* Manchester: Manchester University Press.

_____. 1969. "Political Anthropology: The Analysis of the Symbolism of Power Relations." *Man* 4, no. 2: 215–235.

_____. 1979. "Political Symbolism." *Annual Review of Anthropology* 8: 87–113.

_____. 1981. *The Politics of Elite Culture: Explorations in the Dramaturgy of Power in a Modern African Society.* Berkeley: University of California Press.

_____. 1993. *Masquerade Politics: Explorations in the Structure of Urban Cultural Movements.* Oxford: Berg.

Cunningham, Michael. 1999. *The Hours.* London: Fourth Estate.

Doty, Mark. 2002. "Poem: The Hours." *London Review of Books.* 14 November.

Drucker-Brown, Susan. 1985. "Participant Observation: A Social Anthropologist's Use of the Label." *Cambridge Anthropology* 10, no. 3: 41–73.

Epstein, Arnold L., ed. 1967. *The Craft of Social Anthropology.* London: Tavistock Publications.

Evans-Pritchard, E. E. 1948. "Social Anthropology: An Inaugural Lecture." Delivered before the University of Oxford, 4 February. Oxford: Clarendon Press.

_____. 1949. *The Sanusi of Cyrenaica.* Oxford: Clarendon Press.

_____. 1951. *Social Anthropology: Past and Present.* The Marett Lecture. *Man* 50: 118–124.

Frankenberg, Ronald. [1957] 1990. *Village on the Border.* 2nd ed. Illinois: Waveland Press. (Originally published by Cohen and West in London, 1957.)

_____. 1963. "Participant Observers." *New Society*, 7 March. (Reprinted in Frankenberg [1957] 1990.)

_____. 1978. "Economic Anthropology or Political Economy: The Barotse Social Formation." Pp. 31–68 in *The New Economic Anthropology*, ed. John Clammer. London: Macmillan.

_____, ed. 1982. *Custom and Conflict in British Society.* Manchester: Manchester University Press.

_____. 2002. "The Bridge Revisited." Pp. 59–64 in Vincent 2002. (Extracted from "Introduction" to Frankenberg 1982.)

Gluckman, Max. [1940] 1958. *Analysis of a Social Situation in Modern Zululand.* Rhodes-Livingstone Paper, no. 28. Manchester: Manchester University Press for the Rhodes-Livingstone Institute.

_____. 1954. *Rituals of Rebellion in South-East Africa.* The Frazer Lecture, 1952. Manchester: Manchester University Press.

_____, ed. 1972. *The Allocation of Responsibility.* Manchester: Manchester University Press.

Hannerz, Ulf. 1980. *Exploring the City: Inquiries Toward an Urban Anthropology.* New York: Columbia University Press.

Hennen, Peter. 2004. "Fae Spirits and Gender Trouble: Resistance and Compliance Among the Radical Faeries." *Journal of Contemporary Ethnography* 33, no. 5: 499–533.

Herbert, A. P. [1927] 1935. *Misleading Cases in the Common Law.* London: Methuen.

Joyce, James. [1922] 1997. *Ulysses: A Reader's Edition.* Ed. Danis Rose. Basingstoke: Macmillan-Picador.

Kaberry, Phyllis. 1957. "Malinowski's Contribution to Fieldwork Methods and the Writing of Ethnography." Pp. 71–92 in Firth 1957.

Kapferer, Bruce. 1987. "Foreword" Pp. v–xv in Mitchell 1987.

Kuhn, T. S. 1970. *Structure of Scientific Revolutions.* 2nd ed. Chicago: Chicago University Press.

Lambropolous, Vassilis. 1993. *The Rise of Eurocentrism: Anatomy of Interpretation.* Princeton, NJ: Princeton University Press.

MacEwan, Ian. 2005. *Saturday.* London: Jonathan Cape.

Macmillan, Hugh. 1995. "Return to the Malungwana Drift: Max Gluckman, the Zulu Nation and the Common Society." *African Affairs* 94, no. 374: 39–45.

Magubane, Bernard. 1969. "Pluralism and Conflict Situations in Africa: A New Look." *African Social Research* 7: 529–554.

_____. 1971. "A Critical Look at the Indices Used in the Study of Social in Colonial Africa." *Current Anthropology* 12, no. 4–5: 419–445.

Martin, David. 1965. "Towards Eliminating the Concept of Secularisation." Pp. 169–182 in *The Penguin Survey of the Social Sciences*, ed. Julius Gould. Harmondsworth: Penguin Books.

Marx, Emanuel. 1972. "Some Social Contexts of Personal Violence." Pp. 281–321 in Gluckman 1972.

_____. 1976 *The Social Context of Violent Behavior: A Social Anthropological Study in an Israeli Immigrant Town*. London: Routledge and Kegan Paul.

Marx, Karl. [1869] 1973. "The 18th Brumaire of Louis Bonaparte." Pp. 143–249 in *Surveys from Exile*. Harmondsworth: Penguin Books.

_____. [1867] 1976. *Capital*. Vol. 1. Harmondsworth: Penguin Books.

Mitchell, J. Clyde. 1956. *The Kalela Dance: Aspects of Social Relationships among Urban Africans in Northern Rhodesia*. Rhodes-Livingstone Papers, no. 27. Manchester: Manchester University Press.

_____. 1983. "Case and Situation Analysis." *Sociological Review* 31: 187–211.

_____. 1987. *Cities, Society, and Social Perception: A Central African Perspective*. Oxford: Oxford University Press.

Parkin, David. 1996. "Introduction: The Power of the Bizarre." Pp. xv–xl in Parkin, Caplan, and Fisher 1996.

Parkin, David, Lionel Caplan, and Humphrey Fisher, eds. 1996. *The Politics of Cultural Performance*. Providence and Oxford: Berghahn Books.

Powdermaker, Hortense. 1962. *Copper Town: Changing Africa, the Human Situation on the Rhodesian Copperbelt*. New York: Harper and Row.

_____. 1966. *Stranger and Friend: The Way of an Anthropologist*. New York: W.W. Norton & Company.

Rowson, Andrew. 1990. *The Waste Land*. London: Borgo Press. (Graphic novel treatment of Eliot 1922.)

Salmond, Anne. 1982. "Theoretical Landscapes: On Cross-Cultural Conceptions of Knowledge." Pp. 65–86 in *Semantic Anthropology*, ASA Monograph, no. 22, ed. David Parkin. London: Academic Press.

Schumaker, Lyn. 2001. *Africanizing Anthropology: Fieldwork, Networks, and the Making of Cultural Knowledge in Central Africa*. Durham, NC: Duke University Press.

Shilling, Chris. 2005. *The Body in Culture, Technology and Society*. London: Sage.

Slezkine, Yuri. 2004. *The Jewish Century*. Princeton, NJ: Princeton University Press.

Strathern, Marilyn. 1987. "An Awkward Relationship: The Case of Feminism and Anthropology." *Signs: Journal of Women in Culture and Society* 12, no. 2: 276–292.

Turner, Victor. 1975. "Symbolic Studies." *Annual Review of Anthropology* 4: 145–161.

Van Velsen, Jaap. 1967. "The Extended-Case Method and Situational Analysis." Pp. 129–149 in Epstein 1967.

Vincent, Joan. 1978. "Political Anthropology: Manipulative Strategies." *Annual Review of Anthropology* 7: 175–194.

_____. 1990. Anthropology and Politics: Visions, Traditions, and Trends. Tucson: University of Arizona Press.

_____, ed. 2002. *The Anthropology of Politics: A Reader in Ethnography, Theory and Critique*. Oxford: Basil Blackwell.

Williams, Vaughan. [1913] 2001. *London Symphony*. World premiere recording; the original version of Symphony No. 2. London Symphony Orchestra. Richard Hickox, conductor. Colchester, Essex, UK. CHAN9902.

Woolf, Virginia. [1925] 1992. *Mrs Dalloway*. Annotated ed. Intro. and notes by Elaine Showalter; text edited by Stella McNichol. London: Penguin Books.

# SECTION III

# CASE STUDIES

# PREFACE
Extended-Case Studies—Place, Time, Reflection

*T. M. S. Evens and Don Handelman*

Extended-case studies originated and flourished in multiple sites in Central Africa as British colonialism waned. The extended-case study method was created and shaped in response to complex social situations that emerged from and through ongoing and at times profound changes in the ways in which social and moral orders were put together. The extended case and situational analysis have from their very beginnings been cognate with complexity in social ordering, with the non-linearity of open-ended social fields, and with recursivity among levels of social ordering. Manchester methods originated as a result of profound shifts in the practice of anthropology and contributed to turning these changes into the practicing of ethnographic praxis. Yet over time, the explicit valuing and evaluating of Manchester perspectives disappeared from view. Witness the inane, reductionist comment by George Marcus (1995: 110) (a member of the American lit-crit hit mob of the 1980s), limiting "the extended-case method" (with no mention of Manchester) to "small-scale societies," where it has been "an established technique ... in the anthropology of law" (with no mention of Gluckman).

The scholars who have contributed to this section do not adopt the extended case uncritically or with the utmost of confidence that the method is equal to the task of practicing the ethnography of complex social situations. Three of the essays are themselves meta-commentaries on the use of the extended case, bringing forth doubt—at times radical—and reflection on whether and how the method can be used fruitfully. It is worth noting that this shift in perceiving the extended case reflexively began with Victor Turner's rhetorically pregnant formulation of the social drama (Turner 1957), which he later took in two directions—that of the social drama made historical (Turner 1974) and literary (Turner 1971), and that of performance embedded within and activating the very matrices of the practice of social drama (Turner 1984). Through the social drama as a medium of performing dynamics of process, Turner implicitly emphasized the reflexive turn that the extended case could take.

Karin Norman (who studies European social orders; see Norman 1991) discusses two cases of Kosovar refugees in Sweden. The first takes shape within shifting spatial and temporal fields, as a family of refugees make its way through myriad uncertainties in the day-to-day lives of its members, no less in the face of governmental policies of classification that, as Norman writes, "create and maintain refugees and refugeeness as a separate social category and experience." So, too, Norman's own experiences with family members are pervaded by uncertainty, much of which gains clarity, at times partial at best, only in retrospect. The second case is positioned within a social psychiatric facility for refugees, where personnel diagnose and treat the mental dispositions of refugees in order to prevent their suffering from post-traumatic stress disorder further along in their immigrant experience. Given the linear determinism built into this bureaucratized set-up and its mission to uncover illness, the facility and its operation are pervaded by certainty. Refugees referred there for diagnosis unsurprisingly are found to be in need of treatment, so that, one may say, the existence of the facility is justified and the work of preventing the fuller emergence of mental disorders continues.

The contrasts between the cases lead Norman to question, reflexively and epistemologically, what it is that constitutes a case. She asks this through the ways in which she herself is constituting her field research and her positioning within it. She reflects on the first case as more of an extended case, one that in her terms demonstrates dynamics through its practices. The second case approximates more an apt illustration, instantiating the predictability that issues from the practice of commonsensical medical premises in a bureaucratic organization. Nonetheless, we note that the apt illustration also shows the strategic value of place as a research venue, generating certain kinds of (bureaucratic, medical) cases that an extended case in broader social venues might well not pick up with such pithy clarity.

The three studies that follow return to African locales in or near the heartlands of the Manchester approach. C. Bawa Yamba continues an extended case of witchfinding in Zambia that he has documented elsewhere (Yamba 1997). In terms somewhat analogous to those of Norman's cases, his demonstrates the unintended consequences of a Swedish project for HIV/AIDS prevention that intended to promote 'capacity building'—the persuading of local people to take responsibility for the AIDS epidemic. Contrarily, the project brought about the invitation to a witchfinder to help battle AIDS, leading to the deaths in poison ordeals of 16 people. The witchfinder was sent to prison; local life conditions worsened in manifold ways; the fears of witchcraft returned and grew; and calls for the return of the witchfinder were renewed. Yamba demonstrates what an extended-case approach can do so well by following the ongoing emergence of local practice in its changing contexts, pervaded by uncertainty and unpredictability, together with the abductive responses of the anthropologist.

Yamba expresses radical doubt in the extended-case method, suggesting that anthropologists do such work as a matter of course in their field research (see

Yamba 1995). In other words, extended case-ness simply goes together with intensive fieldwork through time. One difference, nonetheless, lies in knowing anthropologically, in the epistemological sense, and hence demonstrating knowledge, thereby practicing this knowledge into anthropological existence without its slipping into an aptness of illustration. Intriguingly, Yamba recalls the advice of Clyde Mitchell to analyze data until its potentials for extrapolation and interpretation are exhausted. This would mean returning to the same materials (with additions and emendations) and playing with these materials as ideas occur (on play and playfulness, see Lindquist and Handelman 2001). This indeed is how the reanalysis of ethnography should be done. Moreover, this could well mean publishing more or less the same materials in different analytical versions without any definitive finality. Yet the highlighting of such ongoing uncertainty is hardly acceptable in academia, unless camouflaged as startling discovery. In the academic culture of counting publications, each piece is ideally an independent creation that must be accountable as distinct and separate in order to (again) count toward accruing the material rewards of academia.

The late Björn Lindgren uses the crisis engendered by the appointment of a female chief to succeed her father in southern Zimbabwe to discuss how an extended case can inform us about the politics of ethnicity and its conflicts. He uses his formation of the case to demonstrate a cross-section of social and cultural dynamics through which the protagonists negotiated and practiced their values and interests. Thus, the protagonists in the crisis invoked histories and nationalisms, manipulated ethnic affiliations, and questioned gender hierarchies to ground and substantiate their different claims. Through these optics, Lindgren critiques Fredrik Barth's constructivist understanding of ethnicity. Ethnicity, argues Lindgren, is not a basic identity; instead, its form and substance must be related to other social phenomena and to historical changes that contextualize ethnic identification. He argues further that this approach, no less social than that of Barth, does not obviate culture, which he refers to as the ideas, experiences, and feelings that infuse persons through their existential practices.

Sally Falk Moore first went to Tanzania in the 1960s to study the impact of imposed, intentional, planned change—African socialism—in a broad social field. In her discussion here, she sets out to analyze, through a small-scale event, an aspect of that impact and also to address the nature of the extended-case study. Her efforts seem to us to pivot on the analytical problems presented by the persistent (and pestiferous) dichotomies of structure and process, and subjectivity and objectivity. Acknowledging throughout the radically innovative character of Gluckman's contribution, she nonetheless argues, in line with the current anthropological turn to reflexivity, for greater emphasis on the need to attend to the constructional role of the ethnographer in case studies and also on, given the increasing shrinkage of global political and economic distance, the importance of extending cases in space as well as time. In doing so, she draws a distinction between 'case' and 'event', regarding events as "moving sub-segments of process", and uses 'process' to refer to a variety of social arrangements that do and do not change through time.

Because she sees her case study as focusing on seemingly unconnected rather than connected events (a picture and distinction that fall in logically with her emphasis on the ethnographer's share in the constituting of a case), she does not regard it as an extended case in the proper sense. Focused intricately on an instance of conflict between an aged German inn-keeper and some local African (Chagga) officials, Moore's case study highlights a particular place, the Kibo Hotel on the slopes of Mount Kilimanjaro. In this respect, she makes place into the locus of the occurrence of events, thus providing an ethnographic strategy for constructing case from place considered through time as well as space. In effect, a social history of place is formed through the events that occur in and around this locus, itself a changing, layered, and shifting field, such that, in her terms, events become the 'diagnostics' of process.

## References

Lindquist, Galina, and Don Handelman, eds. 2001. *Playful Power and Ludic Spaces: Studies in Games of Life*. Special issue of *Focaal: European Journal of Anthropology*, no. 37.

Marcus, George. 1995. "Ethnography in/of the World System: The Emergence of Multi-sited Ethnography." *Annual Review of Anthropology* 24: 95–117.

Norman, Karin. 1991. *A Sound Family Makes a Sound State: Ideology and Upbringing in a German Village*. Stockholm: Stockholm Studies in Social Anthropology, no. 24.

Turner, Victor W. 1957. *Schism and Continuity in an African Society: A Study of Ndembu Village Life*. Manchester: Manchester University Press.

_____. 1971. "An Anthropological Approach to the Icelandic Saga." Pp. 349–374 in *The Translation of Culture*, ed. T. O. Beidelman. London: Tavistock.

_____. 1974. *Dramas, Fields, and Metaphors: Symbolic Action in Human Society*. Ithaca: Cornell University Press.

_____. 1984. "Liminality and the Performative Genres." Pp. 19–41 in *Rite, Drama, Festival, Spectacle: Rehearsals Toward a Theory of Cultural Performance*, ed. John J. MacAloon. Philadelphia: Institute for the Study of Human Issues.

Yamba, C. Bawa. 1995. *Permanent Pilgrims: The Role of Pilgrimage in the Lives of West African Muslims in Sudan*. Edinburgh: Edinburgh University Press.

_____. 1997. "Cosmologies in Turmoil: Witchfinding and AIDS in Chiawa, Zambia." *Africa* 67: 200–223.

*Chapter 8*

# THE WORKINGS OF UNCERTAINTY
## Interrogating Cases on Refugees in Sweden

*Karin Norman*

> "Looking at something changes it. It's called the Uncertainty Principle," says the shrewd lawyer as he 'looks' at a murder.
>
> — Coen brothers' film, *The Man Who Wasn't There*

How do specific social realities move the analysis in different directions, shaping the construction of a case? And how do experiences during fieldwork emerge in forming subsequent cases?

The ethnographic description of this essay concerns two different social realities of Kosovo Albanian refugees in Sweden and the social dynamics and bureaucratization of their refugeeness. While attempting to construct cases from this material, the endeavor has simultaneously raised the question of what constitutes a case and what may instead turn out to be 'apt illustrations'.

---

Notes for this chapter begin on page 249.

The general ethnographic problem presented refers to processes of becoming and being a refugee and the implications in everyday life and in more restricted encounters of policies of classification that create and maintain refugees and refugeeness as a separate social category and experience, whereas everyday life in exile is both "fluid" and "indeterminate" (Moore in Turner 1977: 64; cf. Moore 1986).

The aim is to explore the analytical implications of circumscribing a 'field' in time and space and the shifting relationships that developed with informants. In large measure, the issue is one of reflexivity. As Phyllis Gorfain puts it: "[L]ike epistemology, reflexivity does not address *what* we know but *how* we think we know" (1986: 209; emphasis in original). For my purposes, this connects with how fieldwork was conducted and with the subsequent attempt at constructing cases from the ethnographic material. The experiences of fieldwork open up to an awareness of the uncertainties inherent in social life and in the contradictions inherent in being a social person. This process of coming to know through experience requires time. When fieldwork is very brief or untimely focused, the complexity of uncertainty may well slip from analytical view. However, the kind of case one is able to construct cannot be reduced to time or fieldwork methods. Within specific institutional realities, persons may create and uphold the image of certainty, denying uncertainty experiential and practical relevance for the actors involved. In particular, this is the logic of bureaucratic organizations, their taxonomies and mechanisms of control (Handelman 1990; Herzfeld 1992), which, I argue, has significant consequences for the differences between how my cases are constructed. In other words, the two cases have their theoretical limitations and potentials in relation to both the social realities they problematize and the challenges of the case-study method.

The first case, based on my first and longest fieldwork among refugees in Sweden during most of the 1990s, is composed of a small set of persons related through ties of kinship. Their lives are in many ways circumscribed by government refugee policy and bureaucratic practice, but their family relationships and activities complicate and reach beyond such bureaucratized boundaries and certainties. It is a fieldwork whose delimitations in time and space expand and contract, and it is characterized by my own close and complex association with a small number of households over many years. My understandings and interpretations shift and change, depending a great deal on the indeterminate and varying quality of our relationship and the informants' changing everyday lives.

The second case, from a short-term fieldwork conducted several years later in a different part of Sweden, is a field constituted by a greater number of actors connected to one another in terms of work within a social-psychiatric organization for refugees. It has more distinct boundaries in time and space, and my own more detached and less complex relationship with informants gives observation precedence over participation. The social reality presented in this case appears more coherent than the other but is rather more rudimentary. It is about a hierarchically organized institution where the main actors tend to tuck loose ends away, promoting the certainty of seemingly observable results.

The analysis then develops from a disconcerting sense of predictability, which is, I argue, also a problem of the constitution of this particular field, of modern bureaucratic taxonomy as it is put into action. Whereas the first case opens up more directly to the uncertainties of social reality and experience and to what has been referred to as "the surprise of anthropology" (Shweder 1997) or "the serendipity of fieldwork" (Pieke 2000), the restrictive form of the social interactions and relationships in the second case sets a limit to such 'surprises', unless one moves beyond this field. In quite different ways, both cases raise issues of reflexivity—its meanings, possibilities, and flaws.

Another difference between the two cases and the circumstances of their development is that the first emanates from a fieldwork that was initially an unplanned development of an ongoing study. It is theoretically tuned to the fluidity of social relationships and everyday social interaction, but specific in the sense of relating to experienced meanings of refugeeness. The second study, in contrast, was more instrumentally circumscribed in time and space, growing out of an initial request from the informants themselves to study (an evaluation, in their terms) their specific goal-oriented activity. The study was thus a critical examination of the relationship between the staff's local practice and the ideologies they were relating to. Such differences between the two studies have also had repercussions in the way the cases have been constituted, the extent of ethnographic detail, and the theoretical and methodological problems around which they revolve.

## Case 1: Concealing and Revealing—the Case of the 'Missing' Father

In modern state bureaucracies, refugees and their way of life are classified as separate and different from 'normal' individuals and 'normal' social life. Thus, refugees become an undifferentiated category with an assumed, universalized 'refugee experience' of trauma, loss, and rootlessness (Malkki 1992, 1995). State-supported measures and legislation tuned to the plight of refugees have varying but related rationales—to control refugees, to keep them separate, to 'normalize' (i.e., integrate) them, to return them to their homelands. The political, historical, social, and cultural contexts in which refugees are created and in which persons experience their lives and their positions as refugees are for the state not the issue (Eastmond 1998; Graham 1999; Long 1993; Shami 1996). Whether one is forcefully displaced or 'chooses' to flee, being classified as a refugee or an asylum-seeker sets processes in motion that have for the different actors uncertain and unpredictable implications and consequences.[1] With the transformation into a refugee, other factors are set in motion that refract on the initial act of leaving and the memory and stories about it. The process of becoming a refugee may be difficult to integrate with one's motives for fleeing and one's sense of being a person.

In 1992, as I was conducting fieldwork in a small Swedish town (Norman 1993, 1994) the National Immigration Bureau opened a refugee reception center or 'camp' there, as in so many other towns and regions at the time.[2] It seemed unwise to ignore this interesting turn of events, and I stayed on, although for various reasons fieldwork took the form of recurrent shorter visits rather than one or two longer stays. The camp was closed a year later, the refugees being moved to different camps or apartments in other towns, and I followed some of them. Thus it went on for the following eight or nine years. One family especially, which I refer to as Fatbardha's family—and its subsequent development into six households—has become central in this ongoing fieldwork, which has recently been concluded.[3] Fatbardha is an Albanian woman from a town in Kosovo. She is the mother of three boys and three girls, the youngest now in his late teens, all the others in their late twenties and early thirties. She came to Sweden in 1991 with her children but without her husband and oldest son. The first three years, they were placed in several different camps, since camps are closed down when the need for them diminishes. Finally, they ended up in two small towns in central Sweden, dividing themselves up into different households. They stayed for some years in these towns after they had received their residence permits at different intervals between 1994 and 1998.[4]

The issue that has concretely concerned me, in a general way, is what the ethnographic material, extended in time, can clarify about the connections between Fatbardha and her family, their notions about 'being Albanian', and Swedish refugee policy. I do not see this as a lineal, one-directional process but as processes of shifts and multi-directional movements. These processes carry strong emotional meanings that continuously take hold of the family dynamics and charge their relationships and activities and their constructions of social meaning. Fieldwork has been open ended, relying heavily on my participation and on the necessity of accepting that most of my plans could not materialize, that my questions were often ill-timed, and that misunderstandings and misinterpretations between us sometimes has made it difficult to keep my bearings.

Early on during my fieldwork, I was informed by a member of the refugee camp staff, and soon heard about it from Fatbardha and her daughters, that the husband/father was in prison, they knew not where. However, during that first year in the camp, they very rarely, if ever, talked about him in my company, and throughout the first several years of fieldwork, I never heard his name mentioned. It was as if he did not exist. I wondered a great deal about this but sensed that I should not ask. Intent on the emotional plight of refugees, I assumed that it was painful for them, that they missed him and were very worried about him. What had happened to this missing father? Who was he? Although the father was seldom directly mentioned during much of my fieldwork, his presence as part of the family history appeared to me significant in revealing the complexity of the family members' positions to each other and as refugees and Albanians in Sweden. In turn, this has had repercussions for their relationship to me and for my own process of getting to know, or not know. For these reasons, the 'missing father' is pivotal in my construction of this case.

It was not until February 1995, some years after I first met her, that Fatbardha began to talk about her husband. We sat in her kitchen, drinking tea, undisturbed by her oldest son, Arben, who was in the living room, struggling with homework for his Swedish language course. She wanted to talk. As so often, she was preoccupied with all her troubles and worries, and with the increasing repression and violence in Kosovo. She grew angry as she talked, and it seemed in the context reasonable to ask a little bit about her husband. She became even angrier, and I was afraid I had pushed her too far. She was very intense, her eyes darkened with remorse. She related that her husband had been imprisoned for a few years in the 1980s and had been badly beaten. This happened again in 1991 and continued until now, though she said with some hesitance, "I don't know, I think so." The police always came in the middle of the night, looking for her husband, she said. Finally, she couldn't stand it. She was afraid for her daughters' safety, since they were in their early and mid teens (alluding to a fear of sexual abuse, as I assumed). So she fled together with them and her two younger sons. Arben, the oldest, went into hiding from the army "somewhere in Macedonia." Arben had recently arrived in Sweden, three years after Fatbardha, and was staying with her, although officially he had been placed in the camp apartment of his married sister, Besa, who had not received a residence permit with the others.[5] Fatbardha was at first happy and relieved that her son was safe with her, but she soon tired of him. During the first few years in Sweden, he was constantly listening to loud Albanian music, smoked incessantly, drank large quantities of beer, and kept nagging her for money. He tried to be bossy, but having managed this far on her own, Fatbardha was not willing to succumb to any male relative. In turn, Arben felt estranged in Sweden. His sisters were much more accomplished than he, and his mother had been transformed into an unkempt-looking woman; nothing was seemingly left of her Albanian female beauty (cf. Norman 1997).

In April of that same year, Marigona, Fatbardha's youngest daughter, had been telling me about her wish to go back to Kosovo for a visit, to see what they had so abruptly left behind. Her Yugoslavian passport was still valid, in contrast to Fatbardha's. Marigona seemed set on trying, and we fantasized about my accompanying her.[6] In that context, I thought it reasonable to ask about her father, given the possible danger upon her return due to her father's political activities and current imprisonment. She said she had not seen him for five years, and then it had been in the prison. Without being able to clarify it in my mind, I could not get the dates straight in relation to his imprisonment, but I did not push the point. I had become aware that the family members were not very exact in noting events in relation to specific dates. "Do you miss him?" I ventured. Yes, she missed him, she said—"But we don't talk about it. Mama doesn't want to." She said that she was very angry with him, though, "for all he cared about was politics, not us." But often there seems to be something admirable and heroic about a person who gives up all for the sake of freedom and justice, for a greater cause. It conjures respect and can effectively prevent probing or seemingly insensitive questioning.

One day in March 1996, we were off to visit some Albanian friends of the family. The issue of marriage arose, and Fatbardha declared that she did not want Marigona to marry without first getting a good education. Marigona, who wanted to quit school since she always felt that she was "stupid" in comparison with her Swedish classmates, had started playing with the idea of getting married. She teased her mother, retorting, "Well, look at you. You interrupted your education and got married." Fatbardha obviously disliked this remark but let it be. Since then, Marigona and her sisters have now and then returned to this point, teasing their mother that she should find herself a man and get married "to a Swede—they're much better!" Fatbardha sometimes laughed, sometimes became annoyed, but gave no answer. The father was not mentioned, and I felt quite bewildered at the time: Are they divorced? Is he dead? What is going on? I wanted to ask but again felt I could not. A few months later, Besa, Marigona's older sister mentioned the father and how angry she and her sisters were with him: "He cared only about politics, putting all our lives in danger." Fatbardha did not want to hear about this. "She loves him and won't hear of any criticism," Besa explained. Used to such statements, I again refrained from any further questions.

In the fall of 1996—I had by then followed this family intermittently for many years—Marigona, no longer in her teens, had become a student at an adult school. She had missed several years of schooling, first through Serbian legislation in the late 1980s to the early 1990s (Kostovicova 2002), subsequently as a refugee in Sweden waiting for a residence permit, and finally after giving up her short-lived attempt to go to regular Swedish secondary school. She and her classmates had recently received an assignment to do some research and write an essay about a well-known Swedish personality of their own choosing. Marigona had chosen to write about a poet, "her favorite," as she said, and had decided to interview one of Sweden's well-known female poets. Marigona had written to her, telling her a little bit about herself, and the elderly poet consented to be interviewed. We decided that I should call the poet to arrange the time and place for their meeting, also confirming that Marigona was a serious and reliable person. The writer lived in another town quite far away, and I promised Marigona that I would take her there. On our way, she was worrying about what to tell this poet about her father, should the woman ask her. I was a little bit surprised. I knew by then that the sisters were very disappointed and angry with their father and his constant engagement in politics, but that was hardly anything she had to tell this poet. "Tell her how it is. Details are not needed," I told her supportively.

Later in the evening, we were driving in my car to Marigona's apartment. She was by then married to a young Albanian man, and they were living on their own. Suddenly, she declared: "My father was here." "What?!?" I could not believe it, or understand it. "When?!?" "A month ago," Marigona replied. "You weren't here. He's living in Switzerland. He's married and has children. Grandma [her father's mother] and all the rest of them knew where he was when you and I were in Kosovo, but no one said anything." Everyone had pretended he was lost, in prison. I knew by then that Fatbardha often concealed things from me, telling me only part of a story. And yet I had often wanted to believe that I was hearing the 'whole story', that I was special and privileged in contrast to other Swedes. Fatbardha had refused to see him when he arrived. The father had spent one night at each of the daughters' places, and they had "talked a lot." He awakened hopes in them, but they were wary, well aware of their mother's staunch rejection. For all his 'charm', he had been a violent man, and they were all afraid that he would return to them and never leave them alone.

Marigona and her sisters and brothers had promised Fatbardha never to tell anyone about the father's visit—"Not even you," Marigona said to me. "You know, Mama actually hasn't really trusted you," she added, peering at me. My disappointment and hurt feelings kept me for some time from considering Fatbardha's possible reasons, something only continued fieldwork could remedy. Marigona declared there in the car that she did not want to keep on lying anymore, that she felt terrible about all those lies. She had said as much to her mother and had told her to say that she is divorced instead. That is acceptable and "no big deal" in Sweden, she had explained to her mother. Marigona preferred to lie 'in Swedish', as it were, for Fatbardha was *not* in fact formally divorced. In Kosovo, divorce occurs, but for women it is usually quite difficult, as most often they lose custody of their children to the father (cf. Reineck 1991). This would especially have been the case with the youngest boy. However, instead of filing for divorce, some men take a second wife or a lover, all the while retaining a claim on their first wife, which appeared to be what Fatbardha's husband was attempting, for the second time. But things had changed for Fatbardha and her family in Sweden. She was now head of her family and was not prepared to comply.

Fatbardha never said anything about all this to me—not then, not later—although she was aware that her daughters wanted to let me know. She concealed, created family confusion, and controlled her daughters, demanding their loyalty. Through their flight and position as refugees without asylum, their dependence on her had increased. A number of times they have said, with both pride and anger, "We always do what she wants, always take her into consideration." This has also been an indirect message to me, a reminder not to push them with my questions but rather to wait. Fatbardha is a capable woman, not lacking in humor and charm. Throughout her stay in Sweden, she has been struggling hard for the well-being of her daughters and sons. She wants her daughters to have a good life, better than hers, she says, but I have never really been sure what she means by 'her life'.

## Besa's Dilemma

The practical everyday activities of this family have not revolved around the absent father, yet recurrently and in (to me) unexpected ways, his presence has made itself felt in the dynamics of their family relations and how these relations have become entangled with refugee policy. Whereas Marigona was the most oppositional and least willing to succumb to 'Albanian ways', an older sister, Besa, had for some years been stuck in a rut. Early on, she married a young Albanian man she had met in one of the refugee centers. Officially, this placed her outside the family, as far as the Immigration Bureau was concerned, and she, together with her husband, was denied a residence permit when the other family members received one. A general amnesty was proclaimed in the spring of 1994 for all those families who had sought asylum before a specific date in 1993 (31 December) and had at that time children under the age of 18. Besa did not fit into this slot. The fact that she had come with her mother and had been under 18 at the time was not taken into account. She and her husband were now a separate family, and their application for an asylum/residence permit was an open issue. This raised a great deal of anxiety and bitterness. Besa felt that she could not 'develop', get an education or a job, 'be something', like her sisters, especially since she soon gave birth to her first child, who in turn was often sick and unhappy.

Throughout these years of waiting and hoping for a permit, Besa often complained about having a malformed ear, saying it looked so ugly and disfigured, and she was sometimes even plagued by tinnitus. She wanted to have plastic surgery. Enviously comparing herself with her sisters, she pestered her young husband about it, and she tried to get me to help her find a good surgeon in Stockholm. Everyone, including myself, tried to convince her that she looked fine, that she was a nice and pretty girl, that one couldn't see much of her ears anyway beneath all her black curls. Having trouble with her hearing was of course something different, something worth examining. But plastic surgery? No one supported it, and who could possibly pay for it? At the time, I never really understood why Besa kept worrying so much about her ear when there were much worse things in her life—such as not having received a residence permit and living in constant fear of being sent back; being forced by the Immigration Bureau to move to different refugee centers; having worries about her little boy, who was very unhappy and easily frightened, often sick and difficult to love.

According to Swedish refugee policy, Besa was no longer considered a part of Fatbardha's family. According to their own classification of family and kin, she would no longer be a part of her mother's family either, since the patrilineal tendency in Albanian notions of family and kinship is quite pronounced. This need not mean that a woman's ties of closeness and association, even solidarity and responsibility, with her parents and siblings are severed. Through the various crises and the new situation of refugeeness, such ties had become very tight, and the family members considered themselves as belonging together, as being 'family'. Since the young husband's family was not living in Sweden, the only family head present to relate to and negotiate with was Fatbardha. A few of the refugee camp staff tried to convince Besa to file for a divorce, as doing so could save her. She would then be returned to her family and would certainly receive a permit, they said. Their insinuation, voiced to me, was that the young man had probably married Besa in order to get a residence permit, anyway. The suggestion of divorce made Besa feel confused and uncertain, and her ambivalence about having married a 'village boy' increased. Yet to leave her husband? Let him be sent back? She could not imagine that. It would be too cruel, and she loved him. He was kind and very good-looking.

What was this? Was Besa's disgust with her ear a way of symbolically concretizing this cruel unfairness, as if she were not good enough, making her feel humiliated and powerless—everything was against her, you could tell by her ugly ear, as it were? At the same time, it seemed to give her some satisfaction because she could annoy others and evoke guilt in them with her complaints. Finally, in early summer of 1998, almost four years after the rest of the family—years that had cost them endless troubles and anxiety, with appeals and visits to lawyers and psychiatrists—Besa and her husband with their (at the time) two children, received residence permits.[7] Safe with her permit, Besa, Marigona, and the oldest sister appeared to feel more freedom to talk openly about their father, especially when their mother was not present. Arben kept out of all these talks, at least in my presence. He disliked that they gossiped about their father or their paternal kin in front of others, or even criticized Albanians in general. As for Fatbardha, she never talked about her husband and his family to me. We have both been pretending that I do not know. Arben has wanted to show his loyalty toward his 'family' and thereby to Kosovo and Albanian culture, whereas Fatbardha's mission has in a sense been the opposite—to secure her own and her children's survival away from the family and Albanian culture.

In 1999, the story about Besa's ear took another turn. Besa underwent ear surgery, but not plastic surgery. Instead, a more realistic attempt was made to see what the trouble was. It turned out that the problem with her ear was not due to vanity, unhappiness, or a hereditary mishap. Rather, it had been caused by some form of direct violence that no fall or child's play alone could have caused, the doctor told her. So what had happened to her as a young child? No one remembered, not Besa herself, not her mother, no one. Could it have been the father? They had several times mentioned his violence. Dared I ask? No, I did not, and the issue was for some time laid to rest.

After these events, the family and their history appeared in fuller view. Perspectives shifted, and other dimensions have been added to Fatbardha's and her daughters' fear and anxiety, their anger over politics, the police in Kosovo, Albanian culture, Swedish refugee policy. And I slowly learned to hold to a more complex, less idealizing view of the trials involved in seeking refuge. As it turns out, Fatbardha had 'fled' before. In Kosovo, she had packed her bags and disappeared a number of times when the children were young, leaving them with her husband's parental family, not telling them where she was going or when she would be back, if at all. She had solved many difficulties in her married life by just abruptly leaving. "Mama wasn't always that much different from our father, you know." The sisters have always stayed very close, looking out for each other, the younger obeying the older. "We sisters became like one body, welded together, always taking care of our younger brothers." Their family life in Kosovo is a long story of abuse, quarrels and fights, and recurring separations: "We fled as much from our father as from the police."

The implications of Fatbardha's story about her flight—how she took her children, telling no one, and just got on a bus without any luggage, bringing only her passports and some photo albums—has slowly emerged in a different light. And I have had to keep revising my sense of the realities, as they have revised theirs.

## The Uncertainty of 'True' Stories

At the time of Fatbardha's flight, the political situation in Kosovo was worsening, the repression setting its mark on all relationships and on people's daily lives. This undeniably had serious repercussions with regard to Fatbardha and her family and so must be part of any story about her. My condensed description of the process of revelation (about the 'missing' father) is not aimed at minimizing the significance of these circumstances. Rather, I seek to highlight other dimensions and dilemmas of the family's transformation into refugees and their subsequent life in exile. These dimensions could only have been grasped through a long-term relationship with them. Layers of secrets and fears have given way, slowly and seemingly haphazardly, throughout these many years. Their fear may seem 'natural' when superficially interpreted in terms of the refugee experience, but their fear must be contextualized through the details of their lives. Fear is not a static condition but rather is connected to specific experiences and situations, just as dishonesty is not a straightforward, acultural moral problem of right and wrong or true and false. In modern state systems, like that in Sweden, refugee bureaucracy strives to create order through regulations and taxonomic constructions but instead contributes to the uncertainty, evasiveness, and subversive acts that it sets out to prevent, as in the case of Fatbardha.

Even the most miserable and dangerous situation and conditions are subjectively experienced and given their particular meaning. Revealing Fatbardha's 'lies' about her husband's whereabouts could seriously have jeopardized her right first to receive and then to be allowed to keep her and her children's residence permit. Swedish refugee policy and the officials working with asylum-seekers are caught up in a rigid opposition between truth and falsehood, adjusted to their classificatory procedures. Interaction between refugees and various immigration bureaucrats, police, and social workers is then marred by the constant worry among such personnel that they are being deceived. Fatbardha and her daughters would not have been able to tell their 'true' story in a way that would have appeased Swedish immigration officials. The 'true' story is also painful, humiliating, full of conflicts and contradictions, and would be difficult to sort out and make credible. She would have had to take stock of her whole life. How do you manage that when being interrogated by immigration officials and police?[8] And how could Fatbardha ever really feel at ease with me, given her share in creating the havoc in this family?

As I briefly mentioned earlier, Marigona returned for a short visit to Kosovo in the mid-1990s, several years after the family's arrival in Sweden. She was set on finding out what they had left behind in such a hurry. I accompanied Marigona on this trip and in doing so had thereby unwittingly distanced myself more than I realized from Fatbardha. She was very reluctant to let Marigona go and not so very reassured by my accompanying her, although I wanted to think so, since I was very keen on going. In retrospect, I have realized that she must have been afraid that I would find out about her husband's whereabouts and, on that account, been worried about the consequences for her and her children. The Immigration Bureau could have canceled their residence permits, if it emerged that they had been issued based on 'false premises'. At the very least, Besa would definitely have been denied a permit. In those years, some refugees who had made false claims of identity were deported or threatened with deportation even after having lived many years in Sweden with a residence permit. Or, from a completely different aspect, the husband/father could have found out where they were—which he finally did. I do not know how or when he found out, since this continued to be more or less a non-topic between Fatbardha and myself.

Fatbardha chose to take a new hold on life, leaving behind what she could not control or change. But she did not choose to be a refugee; her designation as such was rather the result of a political-bureaucratic order that classified her in those terms. The consequence of this transformation was thereafter a constant yet shifting presence in their ongoing lives. For Fatbardha, living in Sweden meant a completely different emphasis in the family relations. There was no longer a husband as head of the family, no mother-in-law, no affinal kin—all obligations and support that such relations imply were gone. She became head of the family. She was responsible for its well-being, and she could not, and would not, return. She must induce and retain respect, keep her good reputation intact in relation to other Albanian refugees, and negotiate her daughters' marriages. In addition, she must handle a completely new set of bureaucratic rules and regulations and the uncertainties they instilled. She created her new reality by withholding information, by associating as little as possible with other Albanians, by appearing drab (from an Albanian perspective) with constant aches and pains, and by leaning heavily on her daughters' loyalty and endurance.

The events of this case are ordered chronologically, year by year, but the sequences of the events overlap and are not clearly bounded.[9] For the family, the story has been there all along, and it emerges in its shifting details as their lives in Sweden change through marriages, childbirths, illnesses, residence permits, surgery, schooling, jobs—circumstances that also form their relationship to me. Quite concretely, the problem of the 'missing' father becomes a problem from my outsider point of view, whereas for the family members, the problem is to conceal that he is instead rejected and kept at a distance. The emergence of these different views and experiences of the father articulate my own misconceptions and uncertain position as an anthropologist in relation to the family. The father is made central in the construction of this case because his absence points both to Yugoslav state repression and the workings of Swedish refugee policy. Since I am a Swede and a researcher, the family cannot know who I really am, or what power I may have over their lives. Fatbardha has been evasive and suspicious from the start, given the complexity of her reasons for her flight. Her daughters have been more prepared to accept me, at times also seeking my help and advice, making me both a gateway into Swedish society and a potential source of danger. The complexity of these experiences and their meanings would have eluded me with a short stay and a preoccupation with questions and answers (Hastrup 1995). However, long-term fieldwork among a small number of persons creates bonds that open up to processes of dependence and misunderstandings, as well as moral dilemmas that may be difficult to see and sort out, becoming a hindrance to critical reflection. My position in the practical and emotional dramas of the family have then been a central source of illusion as well as insight in this study.

## Case 2: Illustrating and Convincing—the Case of a Psychosocial Screening Project

Moving from the case of Fatbardha to this second case is like moving from an experientially uncertain, confusing, and seemingly confused reality to a reality that gives an illusion of order, boundedness, and certainty. The ethnographic material constituting this case is based on a short-term study, undertaken in the spring of 2000, of a psychiatrically oriented institution—a Swedish psychosocial health screening project for Albanian refugees who were evacuated from camps in Macedonia in the spring of 1999 during the war in Kosovo.[10] The case I present is an encounter between a psychiatrist and his refugee patient. As I try to show, the certainty that the psychiatrist attempts to create or manifest resembles a reliance on apt illustrations to bolster an analytical argument.

The screening project was initiated by a number of psychologists and health-care and social workers employed within the child and adult psychiatric care profession in the region. It was designed to contravene the transformation of refugees into psychiatric patients by discovering and treating their traumas in time, before they would run the risk of developing what is labeled PTSD (post-traumatic stress disorder), according to the DSM-IV international classification (American Psychiatric Association 1994). The project team was enthusiastic about developing something they perceived as new. Their proudly stated aim was to break the trend of refugees becoming patients. In the late fall of 1999, I was contacted by the project staff and asked to make an evaluation of their work (which I reformulated as a study). I was intrigued by the seeming efficiency with which they had organized the project, by their radical critique of the Immigration Bureau and government refugee policy, and especially by the increasing medicalization of refugees, all of which I had become acquainted with through my previous fieldwork among refugees. However, as my fieldwork was underway, I was disconcerted by discovering that all activities and interactions organized by staff in relation to the refugees were explicitly or implicitly oriented toward the discovery and/or treatment of trauma and PTSD. In what way would this be articulated in the kind of case I was constructing? Or was it actually more a case of an apt illustration?

The screening interviews, as they were called, followed a set of pre-formulated questions. The focus of the interview was on what refugees had experienced during the war and their subsequent flight. The screening for the adults also included two trauma-oriented questionnaires that the interviewee was to fill in him- or herself. During the screening interview, one of the interviewers took notes, which afterwards were dictated into a tape recorder. Both notes and tape were later handed over to the project secretary, who copied out and catalogued the interview. The interview also included the interviewers' views about the person and recommendations for possible treatment—group thera-peutic activities, psychiatric treatment, somatic treatment, and so on. These recommendations were then to be discussed with the team and followed up. About one-third of the refugees were referred to some form of treatment, many of these to a psychiatrist or to the psychiatric hospital ward.

During a six-month period, I came and went, staying for a few days or at most a week at a time. The ethnographic material consists of observations of a screening interview and the careful reading of the screening documents; par-ticipation in several women's and children's group sessions, a small number of psychiatric sessions, and a few staff meetings and seminars; interviews with most staff members and with the local Immigration Bureau staff; and visits in the homes of a few of the refugee families. I was an observer in most of these situations—listening, watching, taking notes—and my delimitation of the field followed fairly closely the institutional boundaries of the project. This delimita-tion of the field in time and space differs a great deal from that of Fatbardha's case. The project was scheduled for a short period, and I did not have the means or the time to extend my fieldwork. However, this is an unreflexive reason. A more challenging issue in this context is the extent to which my case corresponds to the psychiatric construction of a case, accepting the parameters of the diagnostic event. Fieldwork in bureaucratically institutionalized settings is in a sense seductive: everything is ordered and neatly categorized, people are in place, there is an agenda, open-ended interaction is minimized, and the uncertainties of everyday life are kept out of range.

## The Doctor and His Patient

Dr. Nilsson, a psychiatrist, was hired by the screening program as a consultant and practicing doctor. He also participated in staff meetings and was active in some of the discussions about the planning of the screening project. Dr. Nils-son says that he considers his work with patients as supportive, which also includes some cognitive training, what he also calls positive thinking. This coincides with the main orientation of the women's and children's groups. Dr. Nilsson underlines that his main task, however, is to make a diagnosis and to give suitable medication. He sees his patients about once or twice a month, three or four times in all. I was permitted to attend and to take notes at a few of Dr. Nilsson's sessions with his patients. This I saw as significant since it soon became apparent that a psychiatric perception of refugees had a strong explicit and implicit influence on the screening project. For analytical purposes, the encounter is divided into sequences.

## The Session

Accompanied by his Albanian interpreter, Dr. Nilsson summons Hamit, his patient, to his office, while the man's wife and little boy stay in the waiting room. Hamit keeps his jacket on. He looks tired and harried. Dr. Nilsson briefly introduces me and asks if Hamit accepts my presence. He nods and does not seem to care. Dr. Nilsson is casually dressed; he never wears the white doctor's outfit.

Dr. N: We increased the medication last time. What has happened since then?
H: Nothing has happened. My mouth is dry. I feel sick. I have the same emotional problems as before.
Dr. N: How is your sleep?
H: Still difficult.
Dr. N: Has it become a little better since the medication began?
H: I feel tired, can't sleep, my thoughts are in a turmoil. I have much inner fever.
Dr. N: Have you become just a little calmer?
H: I feel terrible. I don't even dare look at myself in the mirror. I've changed. I don't recognize myself.
Dr. N: So there is not much change?
H: I'm very nervous, too. I go out, come in again. Shut myself in.
Dr. N: I've now read the screening interview with you and it is shattering reading.
H: It's what I've experienced.
Dr. N: It tells about your nightmares, the grenades, the burnt houses, your flight. Have you been beaten and hurt yourself?
H: Yes, I was beaten. [He leans forward and shows the scar on his head.] I've seen corpses. I've been threatened.
Dr. N: Any normal person who has had such experiences would become mentally sick.
H: I've survived, but I don't feel like a normal person.
Dr. N: Well, you're not, but we're going to give you additional medicine. When is your anxiety greatest?
H: When I go to bed. I hear voices, see images. And I'm afraid when I'm outdoors.
Dr. N: That is typical for people who have been through what you have. We have to lower your fear and anxiety. We will give you a complementary medicine to the one you have. (*Sequence one*)

In a brief pause, Dr. Nilsson turns to me and explains that this is a common syndrome—a post-traumatic stress syndrome—and also a depression, together with an anxiety disorder. The serotonin system has been altered and for that psychotherapy is not enough, he says. (*Sequence two*)

Dr. Nilsson then goes on to ask Hamit about his wife.

Dr. N: How is your wife?
H: She is not well. She just cries and cries.
Dr. N: Well, then we will just have give her an additional medicine. What else do you have—support, group therapy? And your wife?
Hamit says that they have really only met him, Dr. Nilsson.
Dr. N: I'm not satisfied. We have to find another medicine and see to it that you get more support. (*Sequence three*)

During a pause after this part of the session, Hamit goes out to the waiting room. Dr. Nilsson says that he will join him shortly. While he is gone, Dr. Nilsson wants to explain to me why he goes "straight to the point, almost being authoritarian," as he says. He has met Hamit three times, the first time four months earlier when he set him on medication. With a Swedish patient, he must discuss, negotiate, ask what do you think? (about treatment suggestions). "But they [the refugees] can't handle it if I'm too hesitant. I've worked with Bosnians and Albanians. I know the culture, the people. This man is educated, but he couldn't handle it." Dr. Nilsson tells me he uses one of the most modern anti-depressive medicines, but it is a medicine that is not yet registered in Sweden, so he does not want me to divulge its name. It is supposed to have few side effects, he says, and it provides good protection against post-traumatic stress disorder, panic anxiety, and social phobia. (*Sequence four*)

While Dr. Nilsson goes out of the room for a while and Hamit is in the waiting room, Besnik, the interpreter, and I sit and wait. Besnik says that Hamit and his family live in very cramped quarters. They have been put up in a very small apartment with only one room and a small kitchenette. He believes that it must make them feel much worse, aggravating their situation, as they can never get away from each other. Besnik has not wanted to say anything about it to Dr. Nilsson and asks me to do it. I am somewhat surprised, since Dr. Nilsson is not unaffected by such information. I tell Besnik I think he should say it himself, but he will not do it, and since I assume that it is a relevant piece of information, I later pass it on to Dr. Nilsson, who takes note of it. (*Sequence five*)

Dr. Nilsson has gone out to the waiting room to Hamit and his wife. Dr. Nilsson is saying to the wife that it is not good for her heart or stomach to be so worried as she obviously is. She says that her whole body is tense, and she feels cold. "I shall give you a prescription. I'll write it in Hamit's name, and you can both take it. If it doesn't help, take a double dose. You can test and see, but no more than three tablets at a time. The medicine is not dangerous. It can make you a bit tired and relaxed, but that can be good for you." Dr. Nilsson says, "We must have close contact," and he tells them to come back to him in two weeks. He reminds them that the nurse is also available and knows about their situation. In addition, someone will come to their home, he says, which seems to be connected with the information he just received from me about their living conditions. (*Sequence six*)

Again Dr. Nilsson turns to Hamit's wife and asks her if there is something she had wanted to ask him today. She says her whole body aches, and Dr. Nilsson is reminded that they stayed out in the woods in Kosovo during the war for several months. He asks her if it hurts when she urinates, and she affirms. She has also had two miscarriages, and it took a long time before she could see a doctor. He tells her to go see the local district doctor. She has already gone to see him, but there was no interpreter there. She has apparently been given medicine, but it does not help and she asks Dr. Nilsson why. He in turn considers which emergency hospital they should turn to, and the nurse informs him. Dr. Nilsson thinks it is too long to wait two days until Monday and suggests calling. "She's been there three times already," the nurse says, "and they say that she has an infection." But Dr. Nilsson still thinks she should go. "We'll write a referral," he decides. The wife says that they cannot pay what it costs. "It's not necessary. It will have to be paid in some other way," Dr. Nilsson assures her. He says, directing himself to me, that he is ashamed of how the refugees are treated, at what bad care they receive: "Things are not followed up. No one finds out what is really ailing the refugee patient." (*Sequence seven*)

### The Logic of the Session

As in the case of Fatbardha, but in a completely different vein, there is something disconcerting about this encounter that I cannot quite grasp. What is happening during this session? What is Dr. Nilsson aiming at? What goes on between him and Hamit?

Dividing the session into sequences is aimed at highlighting their interrelated logic and rationale and at clarifying the interactive process. In line with Don Handelman (personal communication), I would also assume that such sequencing may "shift the aptness of the illustrative example into more of an extended-case modality."

In the first sequence, Dr. Nilsson must finally conclude that no real change in Hamit has occurred, and the central issue of normality soon comes into focus. According to DSM-IV and the screening project, it is normal to react with fear and anxiety to an 'abnormal situation', but if the reaction does not subside after a stipulated period of time (about two months), it is no longer classified as normal. Here Dr. Nilsson is on home ground and decides that Hamit should have more medicine, asking him for some additional affirmation to support the medication.

The second sequence is a brief interlude in which Dr. Nilsson interrupts the ongoing interaction with Hamit to explain to me what the symptoms are about and that medication is the only alternative. His expertise is now ascertained, and in the third sequence, Dr. Nilsson incorporates Hamit's wife, who without further ado will also get more medicine. Yet he announces his dissatisfaction with their lack of other support. In the fourth sequence, there is a pause. When Hamit leaves the room, Dr. Nilsson wants to explain the situation to me, as a Swede and an observer, and be reassured that I understand it as I should. Most importantly, he wants to tell me about the new, efficient medicine he uses. But using an unregistered medicine is not without its professional risks, and his request that I treat this information confidentially connects with our conversation before the session, when he asked me about research ethics (this sequence is omitted in the description here).

In the fifth sequence, Besnik, the interpreter, and I are left alone in the room. A different form of interaction begins, pointing to relationships and obligations that belong outside the session. My special position, Besnik's deference to authority and his dependent position within the project, and, perhaps most importantly, our recently established 'relatedness' (a neighbor and distant relative in Kosovo proved to be related to Fatbardha's husband's family) make him implore me to act on Hamit's behalf, on the behalf of his compatriot. He himself once sought asylum, arriving several years before the war, and was now privileged in relation to these evacuated refugees. I give in to his request, thereby also admittedly succumbing to my feelings of frustration over the session and the sole concentration on medication.

Toward the end of the session, in the sixth sequence, Dr. Nilsson's performance in the waiting room appears more improvised, demonstrating to me and his refugee patients that his authority counts, that his critique of refugee policy is justified, legitimate, and that he has the empathy and the power to do something about it. In the last sequence, Dr. Nilsson ends the session by giving voice to his critique of refugee reception policy and the bad care refugees receive, making a distinction between himself, indirectly including the project, and these other deficient conditions. His last statement, "No one finds out what is really ailing the refugee patient," in a way brings the session full circle. For what has Dr. Nilsson really found out about his refugee patient?

Hamit comes to the appointment feeling very miserable and tries to describe his discouragement and sense of self-estrangement. Dr. Nilsson, on his part, is constructing this particular session with a mission striving toward mastery over the emerging uncertainties. With declared authority and expertise, he tries to set things straight in accordance with his diagnosis, his perception of normality, and his conviction of the necessity to medicate, for which he wants recognition from Hamit. However, his demonstrations and comments on his own actions and decisions are to a large extent for my benefit, with Hamit playing the part of a 'walker-on' in their interaction. Dr. Nilsson is like a captain at sea trying to convince a motley crew that we are on the right course.

In effect, the interactive process ensures the authoritative position of the expert and underlines the legitimacy of the state-controlled taxonomic system on which this expertise is based. In this way, it bears resemblance with Handelman's (1990: 76–77) analysis of the relationship between form and practice in the 'public events' orchestrated by modern states, what he terms "events-that-present." The psychiatrist–refugee patient encounter is not part of a national parade that overtly expresses and celebrates state order, but it is an event with a particular goal, operating within a context that holds to the same goal: the enhancement of the psychiatric-medical mode of classifying human experience. The screening project, within which this encounter takes place, works in relation to two ideological and political structures, psychiatry and its system of classification and the Immigration Bureau and its refugee reception. Both of these structures are respectively bound to state refugee policy and to state health-care policy and the economically and politically highly influential medical industry.

The screening project emanated from a local political crisis and a concomitant critique of government refugee-reception policy and the bureaucratic rules and regulations of the Immigration Bureau and their often detrimental effects on the health of refugees. The screening project was meant to circumvent the otherwise common course of events that transform refugees, during the prolonged waiting period for a residence permit, into patients, especially psychiatric patients (compare the situation of Fatbardha to that of Besa). However, to augment the chances of receiving a residence permit, refugees are frequently encouraged, even by the screening personnel themselves, to 'solve' this problem by becoming patients. In turn, the screening project was caught up in another set of rules and regulations following state health policy and the classifications of the international psychiatric diagnostic system, the DSM-IV, which structures the contacts between 'care-givers' and 'care-takers'. In the process of receiving support from the screening project, the refugees must be classified as patients with a diagnosis. An unsolvable contradiction was built into the project since the orientation was to look for symptoms of trauma. All listening became 'directed', that is, closed and predictive, rather than open-ended and interactionally reflexive. Many of the encounters were reduced to instances of an ideology that pre-defined particular kinds of action. It seems inevitable, then, that staff supported and created, rather than changed, what they had set out to prevent.

## Concluding Remarks

In this essay, the first case (that of Fatbardha) exhibits something of the extended case, whereas the second case (involving Dr. Nilsson) leans toward the apt illustration. Now why is this? The question points in the two directions stated at the beginning of this chapter: first, how a particular social reality impacts on the process of constructing a case, and, second, how the delimitation of a field—as a site and a problem, and the relationships it engenders—contributes to the kind of case one establishes.

In relation to the realities that they are constructed to problematize, these two cases describe different ways of circumscribing a field and forming a unit of analysis. The ethnography in both cases concerns refugee policy in Sweden, but it is seen from very different angles, raising separate sets of problems. The refugees were staying in Sweden through various but related circumstances (war, deportation, state repression, family conflicts). Those involved in the screening project were residing in Sweden temporarily and were embroiled in the intricacies of institutionalized health care and state refugee surveillance. Fatbardha and her family were more on their own, with a hard-won permanent residence permit, but nonetheless they were still 'refugees', caught up in a family and state history precariously interweaving their ongoing lives. So the perspectives in these cases cover differing ranges of vision—outside bureaucracy and inside bureaucracy. Yet the cases intersect in certain ways, primarily through the authorities' power to judge what a 'true' story of refugeeness should amount to and the consequences of such judgments. Both Fatbardha and Hamit must cope with the uncertainty such power relations imply, but in very different settings and sets of relationships. In the case of Hamit, Dr. Nilsson and the screening staff are supportive and reassuring, but only as long as Hamit accepts their interpretations of his situation. In the case of Fatbardha, the process of being accepted and given a residence permit is a more diffuse, prolonged, and unpredictable process.

There are important distinctions to make between the meanings and uses of 'cases' (Mitchell 1983; cf. Holy 1984). In his critique of Malinowski's presentation of cases, Gluckman termed it "the method of apt illustrations" (Gluckman [1967] 1979: xvii; cf. Gluckman 1961). It was not the perceptive and rich ethnographic detail that was wanting, nor the time spent in the field. It was rather the use to which the material was analytically put—primarily to 'appropriately illustrate' specific statements, social events, and relationships. The cases did not connect the relationships and interactions among the same actors over an extended period of time in relation to a specified problem. The extended-case study or situational analysis problematizes the situatedness of actors, following them through various contexts, discovering the contradictions and inconsistencies of their lives (Garbett 1970; Mitchell 1983, 1987; van Velsen [1967] 1979). Following the same persons through a number of different contexts in relation to a specifically defined problem (which in the present context is how the tension between certainty and uncertainty permeates specific, bureaucratically formed social realities and the study of them) is the essential point of the extended-case study, as is "the critical connection between the state system and social lives," how "the state emerges in the processes of daily life" (Kapferer, personal communication; cf. Kapferer 1996). Yet the critique of early uses of case material has been that individuals and activities were set within a structural framework of which they remained expressive rather than dynamically and indeterminately emergent (Kapferer 1987).

In the two cases I have constructed, a number of disconcerting issues take shape. In the case of Dr. Nilsson, I came to feel a predictability in the various group sessions with children and women, as well as other kinds of activities, meetings, conducting interviews, even reading the screening documents. For all their hopes and good intentions, the staff seemed ideologically monitored to value only specific kinds of information and answers from the refugees, focused as they were on symptoms. Although the session between Dr. Nilsson and Hamit has a particular frame and composition in comparison with other activities of the screening project, all activities were closely linked to the ideological logic of the project, celebrating its main stated goal: discovering and remedying early signs of PTSD in accordance with general psychiatric symptomatology and the taxonomic system (cf. Luhrman 2000; Young 1995). The interactional sequences between Dr. Nilsson and his patient Hamit were a central performance of this taxonomic ideology, partly on my behalf. In large measure, agreement reigned among staff as to the symptoms to look for and the possible remedies to be used. Among these remedies was Dr. Nilsson's treatment as shown in his interaction with Hamit. In turn, he made the loop back to the screenings made by staff and their primary classifications and gradations of symptoms. Through such practices, the refugees were reduced to signs of (actual or potential) affliction. Bureaucracies are presentations of certainty, of how the world is or should be ordered and regulated. Reflexivity is not on the agenda. My sense of predictability was engendered by Dr. Nilsson's attempts at being certain and his relating to the experiences of Hamit as if these were a predictable set of symptoms that in turn are reproducible in any refugee (or person) with war experiences. This is a manifestation of the 'good bureaucracy', which adheres to the principle of equality. Everyone has the right to the same treatment—same symptoms, same treatment.[11] From the perspective of different individuals, however, this sameness can instead be experienced as quite repressive.

With Fatbardha's family, it is a different situation. There is no goal-oriented activity. Their lives are not set up according to schedules and bureaucratic procedures in the way of the screening project. Consequently, my practical aim in studying them is more open-ended in the attempt to understand how they construct their lives as these shift and change in relation to a state system that has classified them as asylum-seekers/refugees. I am moved by these complex family members in the different meanings of the term. I come close to what state bureaucracy cannot reach but which its rules and their refugeeness nonetheless contribute to bringing forth—the many-faceted, and misconceived, problem of the 'missing' father upon which the case is focused. Their lives wind their way around rules and conditions to which they are subordinated but which they seek to evade. How such meanings keep shifting, transforming experiences, emerges through a fieldwork that opens up to surprise and the time and space needed for reappraisals.

### Reflexivity and Limits Set by Different Realities

Fieldwork, our main means of creating data, is an open-ended, inexact endeavor that necessarily sets reflections in motion, both in and by the anthropologist as well as the people being studied. In the attempt to know through one's own experiences that which is most elusive—the lived experience of others and their emergent meanings—fieldwork is unpredictable. It is a process of dealing with uncertainties, a balancing act on a boundary between realities (cf. Hastrup 1995; Hastrup and Hervik 1994). It has affinities with 'play', in the terms of Handelman, conceptualizing play not as make-believe or fictiveness, but rather as uncertainty, "identified with the unpredictable play of forces in flux" (Handelman 1990: 63). The reflexive mode tries to lift up to awareness the uncertainties inherent in the attempt at coming to know that which simultaneously shifts and changes during and through the attempt (cf. Bruner 1986).

Even though Gluckman stated that "nowadays it becomes essential to know a great deal more about the way in which the field anthropologist has gone about his task" ([1967] 1979: xxii) and criticized Malinowski for showing, although deeply involved, "little awareness of how [his] involvement might have shaped his analysis" (ibid.: xxiii), situational analysis nonetheless has ascribed less analytical significance to the subjective presence and experience of the anthropologist as a personal, political, and gendered self (Okely 1992). The recent several decades, in particular, have meant more thought-provoking debates about the anthropologist's gaze, position, voice, text, and person, placing the ethnographer's reflexivity more directly on the theoretical and methodological agenda. In also taking into account the ways in which the anthropologist can use and be used by informants, I would argue that this widening of the reflexive scope opens up to the uncertainties of social process and may contribute to giving us some more tools to discover and analyze those uncertainties. The case of Fatbardha, in particular, is an attempt to demonstrate this point.

The study of the screening project was short term and instrumental in its plan. My relationship with the staff and the refugees was dimensioned according to my formal position set within the limits of their organization, which underscored the boundedness and predictability. A sense of such closure is where the ethnographer's reflexivity may come to a standstill. There is only certainty. A longer and more open-ended fieldwork could have brought forth a more complex ethnography, focusing on both parties—staff and refugees—crossing the fault lines between them. For Dr. Nilsson and the screening project, the refugees seemed to be reduced to apt illustrations, as it were. This bureaucratized process of making certain is central to my analysis, but in the construction of this case, the risk has been that the distinction between the bureaucratic construction of a case and my own construction of a case becomes blurred: the screening project is constructed to relate to refugees as apt illustrations, and I construct the case of Dr. Nilsson as an apt illustration of this bureaucratic process.

As for Fatbardha and her family, given the small number of persons and the long time span, I became a part of their everyday life, however problematically. The gist of our relationship has always been unclear and shifting. As a knowing Swede, an outsider, I have the power and position to be a potential threat to their security, while at the same time I am an asset and a confidant. Many times I could not find out the why or the when until after the fact. The family members' vulnerable, and at times demeaning, position in Sweden as asylum-seekers/refugees, their emotionally taxing family relations, their changing everyday experiences in exile have moved me in different ways. In this process, I have then been both a motor and a drag cart. They were holding me in a state of uncertainty, while I was participating in and observing their uncertainty.[12]

Fatbardha has reasons, of which I am at first unaware, to present or exaggerate vagueness and uncertainty, with which I comply, more or less unknowingly. The long-term study makes it possible to discover these shifts, to understand some of the political and historical implications as these emerge, and, no less, to see my own role in these complications. Dr. Nilsson, on the other hand, has reason to do the opposite of Fatbardha. He is certain of his mission and of his position in an institution that has certainty on the agenda. What he is momentarily *not* certain of is his patient, Hamit, and especially of myself. For this reason, a goal of the session is to alleviate and remove any reflexive doubt and uncertainty.

We use the details of our ethnographic data more or less explicitly to demonstrate or illustrate theoretical arguments or, more generally, abstract descriptions. But how can we be certain that the compilation of material is a telling case study rather than an illustrative example? There is an important distinction between demonstrating and illustrating something of which one may not always take note. To demonstrate is to describe the details of events and relations and problematize their seeming connections as these unfold in order to reach a plausible interpretation. To illustrate is to find appropriate material to support a theoretical or descriptive statement. The former is a more reflexive, processual procedure, whereas the latter is a more predictable, exemplifying procedure. In compiling ethnographic texts—or in reading others' texts, for that matter—it is not necessarily such a straightforward matter to grasp where the boundary is to be drawn between the case study and the apt illustration.

In the case of Fatbardha, experiences and relationships in exile are continuously reshaped in relation to the workings of state policies and the presence of the anthropologist. In the screening project, the refugee as an experiencing person is lost from sight, being instead reduced to an apt illustration—at times explicitly demonstrated for the benefit of the ('evaluating') anthropologist. Different realities open up to different means of participation and presence, which in turn influence the anthropologist's reflexive scope. Studying bureaucratically induced and organized institutions creates a dilemma. Institutions—in the sense of bounded, specifically defined and organized settings of relationships, ideas, and interactions, such as the screening project, with its particular agenda—are structured to present coherence, consistency, and predictability, tending to reduce events and relations into apt illustrations. This may induce the researcher to perceive the interactional events as more coherent and predictable, more closely and statically tied to overarching ideologies than they are. However, the sequencing of the material, as demonstrated in this chapter, can bring forth certain processual aspects of the psychiatric-bureaucratic activities and shift the case away from mere illustration and closer to an extended case.

## Acknowledgments

I wish to thank the editors, Terry Evens and Don Handelman, for their valuable and instructive comments and their kind support and patience. I have also received helpful comments from seminar participants in connection with the European Association of Social Anthropologist conference in Copenhagen 2002. Foremost, I want to mention the importance of my husband, Johan Norman, who contributed many clarifying comments to earlier versions before he was taken ill. His untimely death in 2005 was a devastating blow and has made the completion of this essay all the more difficult. During the final stages of this work, Andreas Norman and Ludvig Norman, my sons, gave me perceptive comments when I most needed them, and I thank them warmly. The essay has thereby become a family endeavor. I dedicate it to Johan Norman.

Karin Norman is Associate Professor in the Department of Social Anthropology, Stockholm University. Her main research interests concern issues on displacement and transnational relations, children's lives and processes of socialization, and problems of method. She has conducted fieldwork in Germany, Sweden, and Kosovo (former Yugoslavia), and has published in both Swedish and English. Recent publications include "Equality and Exclusion: 'Racism' in a Swedish Town" (*Ethnos*, 2004) and a contribution in *The Asylum-Seeking Child in Europe* (edited by H. E. Andersson et al., 2005).

## Notes

1. Although the term 'refugee' is generally used in most everyday contexts, it is not straight-forward but rather a political construction differentiated into various sub-categories. A so-called asylum-seeker is a person seeking refuge, asylum, in another country. Until asylum has been formally accorded, that is, with a residence permit, the person is not classified as a refugee. Once asylum has been granted through a residence permit, the person is a refugee but is not necessarily—or rather, is very seldom—considered to be a 'real' refugee (Hammar 1999). At what point a refugee is considered to be an immigrant is an open question.

2. In Sweden, the period of waiting for a residence permit or to be expelled/deported is very long, sometimes several years, and very few persons seeking asylum are accepted as 'real' refugees. Rather, they are given residence permits for 'humanitarian' reasons (Hammar 1999). What counts as a humanitarian reason varies in relation to the pressure put on the Immigration Bureau and the government from other bureaucratic organizations, the medical world, various NGOs, or the media (ibid.). Usually, it relates to the length of time an asylum-seeker has been waiting for a residence permit, especially if the person has become a psychiatric case, which is not uncommon (Eastmond 2005). During the 1990s, there were also a few so-called general amnesties, based on some unaccounted for choice of criteria and time limits. The Immigration Bureau had been unable to process the many applications individually, as is the legal rule. Thousands of mainly Albanian asylum-seekers were waiting in refugee reception centers or camps all over Sweden. They could not be sent back; the Yugoslav regime refused to accept them. In effect, this exception was a relinquishing of contemporary jurisprudence in which all legal cases are to be tried individually.

3. All names of persons and places are fictive. Some dates and other information have also been changed. The whole issue around which Fatbardha's case revolves is sensitive and raises ethical problems that I have found difficult to resolve. Over time, the informants concerned have related differently to my 'knowing' and 'revealing'. The uncertainty we have induced in each other has come to appear central for my understanding of their position as refugees in Sweden, and I have found no other way of ethnographically describing the workings of such uncertainty than by 'revealing'.

4. Their lives in Sweden have revolved around "problems, always new problems, Karina," as Fatbardha often complains to me in Swedish. Over the years, there have been problems with the youngest boy's school and his choice of friends, worries about negotiating her daughters' marriages and subsequently about the husbands they have ended up with, anxiety over one daughter's recurring illnesses, worries about a daughter's residence permit, worries about the grandchildren, and the constant worry about getting a job and having enough money, both for herself and to fulfill a pressing obligation to send money to her sisters in Kosovo. Living on welfare, as she has throughout, attending an endless number of Swedish-language and other courses arranged for refugees and the unemployed, has been detrimental to her sense of well-being. However, in the last few years, at least her daughters and oldest son and their families have managed economically, finishing different kinds of education and finding jobs. And money and favors continue to flow between them in their elaborate ties of reciprocity.

5. The Immigration Bureau regulates the number of rooms or size of living space allowed per asylum-seeker. Accordingly, Besa's family had one room too many, a room they felt they needed, so in practice Arben stayed in his mother's flat.

6. As it turned out, Marigona did go back to Kosovo for a visit that summer, and I accompanied her (see Norman 1997, 2001). Even this trip of a few weeks proved to be significant for the twists and turns in relation to the missing father, but in what way became known first several years later.

7. Even Fatbardha's oldest son, who had come on his own to Sweden two years later than the rest of the family, at that time 21 years old, received a permit. This was because he

then lived together with a Swedish girl long enough to appear to have a steady relationship. They were even expecting a baby (divorcing two years later).

8. Few have the stamina of the old Romanian man being interrogated by the police in the novel by Mircea Eliade, *The Old Man and the General*. Interrogated by the general, the old man stubbornly claims that there are no simple, brief replies to his questions. Everything has its story and is connected to something else. For the general really to understand, he must first learn about the intricacies of previous events and relations. The old man goes on to tell long and fantastic stories, and the general loses his bearings. These stories are not true in any simple way. They are, as life is, difficult to fathom. They do not lead up to any simple conclusion or solution—and they are also intended to confuse the interrogator/power holder.

9. As a reminder, here follows a brief summary of the sequences. The first sequence is at an early stage of the fieldwork. It reveals the father as missing, imprisoned but mentioned only very briefly. With the second sequence, two years have passed. The oldest son has recently arrived. The mother, Fatbardha, who by then has a residence permit, is relieved but very tired of her son's ways and his 'Albanianness'. Her anger and exasperation, as well as her fear of the increasing repression in Kosovo, induces her to talk, and it becomes possible to ask about her husband. But her story trails off into uncertainty. In the third sequence, in the same year, the youngest daughter, who still has a valid Yugoslavian passport, wants to visit Kosovo, to see what they left behind. I consider the danger for her because of her father. There is some confusion as to time, such as when she met him last. I assume she misses him even though she is angry with him for his (laudable) political engagement. The fourth sequence, a year later, concerns the conflict between marriage and education. Fatbardha is being teased by her daughters about her own marriage, that she should find a Swedish husband. Again, their anger about the father's political activities surfaces. I am left in the dark about the circumstances of the father. With the fifth sequence, yet one more year has passed, and the missing father finally makes his appearance, which is revealed in three interwoven stages. In the first, Marigona has a school assignment to interview a poet. She worries about what to tell the poet about her father, which I do not understand. In the second, Marigona announces that her father has visited them, and in the third, I am suddenly made aware of how little I have realized and how much I have been kept at a distance. The sixth sequence overlaps the second through the fifth. Now Besa, one of the daughters, is in focus, denied a residence permit and so separated from the rest of the family through ad hoc refugee legislation. Her preoccupation with her malformed ear increases, and she wants plastic surgery. In the seventh sequence, Besa and her own family finally receive a residence permit, several years after Fatbardha. The father is now a topic of conversation when Fatbardha is not present. In her presence, the pretence of not knowing continues. In the last sequence, Besa has had ear surgery, and it turns out that her ear problem is due to violence against her as a child. No one remembers an occasion from the past that would have resulted in the injury, and the sequence fades out unresolved.

10. The refugees evacuated to Sweden were spread out in different regions where housing was available and accorded a temporary residence permit of 11 months. Beyond this time limit, they would have to be registered as residents, given rights to health care and schooling, and so be on "the same level as you or me and that would cost the state and municipality a lot," as one project member explained. The temporary permit was therefore limited to less than a year.

11. Goals among staff may shift over time and sometimes clash with personal goals and motives, but as for the screening project, such shifts did not in any significant way seem to influence and change the main work and goal of the project. Such personal variations among staff did, however, point to the unavoidable indeterminacies and uncertainties inherent in all social interactions—which actors may sense, and feel disturbed by—in relation to even the most tightly framed institutional activity. The refugees spotted some of the shifts, gaps, and loose ends and attached themselves to certain members of the

staff, hoping for favors and friendship. However, given the structure of bureaucratic administrative policy in which staff were caught up, this appeared to have little impact on the project. Instead, the authority and certainty of the screening project and the well-meaning of the staff members induced many of the refugees to express their hopes, exposing symptoms and making health-care demands in line with the ideology of the project. They learned to use the PTSD label. They participated in the project activities. They asked for medications, ascribing to several staff members increasing power to help them change their situation, perhaps even to help them receive a residence permit.

12. In a different context, Turner refers to Sally Falk Moore's critique of focusing exclusively on regularities and congruences. In an (for my purposes) apt quote, Moore writes: "[I]ndividuals or groups may exaggerate the degree of order or the quality of indeterminacy in their situations for myriad reasons" (in Turner 1977: 78), and Turner (ibid.) goes on to say: "[H]ow they do this, and why, can be ascertained only if the investigator has also become an actor in the field of living relationships" (cf. more recent debates on reflexivity, Hastrup and Hervik 1994; Okely 1992). As Turner (1977: 78) exclaims: "[T]here are risks in not staying aloof, of course, but the acquisition of knowledge has always been beset by dangers, here physical as well as intellectual!"

# References

American Psychiatric Association. 1994. *Diagnostic and Statistical Manual of Mental Disorders*. 4th ed. (DSM-IV). Washington, DC: American Psychiatric Press. (1995 in Swedish: *MINI-D IV, Diagnostiska kriterier enligt DSM-IV*. Stockholm: Pilgrim Press.)

Bruner, E. 1986. "Experience and Its Expression." Pp. 3–30 in *Anthropology of Experience*, ed. V. W. Turner and E. Bruner. Chicago: University of Illinois Press.

Eastmond, M. 1998. "Nationalist Discourses and the Construction of Difference: Bosnian Muslim Refugees in Sweden." *Journal of Refugee Studies* 11, no. 2: 161–181.

———. 2005. "The Disorders of Displacement: Bosnian Refugees and the Reconstitution of Normality." Pp. 149–172 in *Managing Uncertainty: Ethnographic Studies of Illness, Risk and the Struggle for Control*, ed. R. Jenkins, V. Steffen, and H. Jessen. Copenhagen: Museum Tuscalanum Press.

Epstein, A. L., ed. [1967] 1979. *The Craft of Social Anthropology*. Oxford: Pergamon Press.

Garbett, G. K. 1970. "The Analysis of Social Situations." *Man* (n.s.) 5, no. 2: 214–227.

Gluckman, M. 1961. "Ethnographic Data in British Social Anthropology." *Sociological Review* 9: 5–17.

———. [1967] 1979. "Introduction." Pp. xv–xxiv in Epstein [1967] 1979.

Gorfain, P. 1986. "Play and the Problem of Knowing in *Hamlet*: An Excursion into Interpretive Anthropology." Pp. 207–238 in *Anthropology of Experience*, ed. V. W. Turner and E. Bruner. Chicago: University of Illinois Press.

Graham, M. 1999. "Classifications, Person and Policies: Refugees and Swedish Welfare Bureaucracy." PhD diss., Department of Social Anthropology, Stockholm University.

Hammar, T. 1999. "Closing the Doors to the Swedish Welfare State." Pp. 169–201 in *Mechanisms of Immigration Control: A Comparative Analysis of European Regulation Policies*, ed. G. Brochmann and T. Hammar. Oxford and New York: Berg Press.

Handelman, D. 1990. *Models and Mirrors: Towards an Anthropology of Public Events*. Cambridge and New York: Cambridge University Press.

Hastrup, K. 1995. *A Passage to Anthropology: Between Experience and Theory*. London: Routledge.

Hastrup, K., and P. Hervik, eds. 1994. *Social Experience and Anthropological Knowledge*. London: Routledge.

Herzfeld, M. 1992. *The Social Production of Indifference: Exploring the Symbolic Roots of Western Bureaucracy*. Chicago and London: Chicago University Press.

Holy, L. 1984. "Theory, Methodology and the Research Process." Pp. 13–34 in *Ethnographic Research: A Guide to General Conduct*, ed. R. F. Ellen. New York: Academic Press.

Kapferer, B. 1987. "Foreword." Pp. v–xv in *Cities, Society, and Social Perception: A Central African Perspective*, ed. J. C. Mitchell. Oxford: Clarendon Press.

_____. 1996. "Preface to 1996 Edition." Pp. vii–xiii in *Schism and Continuity in an African Society: A Study of Ndembu Village Life*, ed. V. W. Turner. Oxford: Berg.

Kostovicova, D. 2002. "*Shkolla Shqipe* and Nationhood: Albanians in Pursuit of Education in the Native Language in Interwar (1918–41) and Post-Autonomy Kosovo." Pp. 157–171 in *Albanian Identities, Myth and History*, ed. S. Schwandner-Sievers and B. J. Fischer. Bloomington: Indiana University Press.

Long, L. 1993. *Ban Vinai: The Refugee Camp.* New York: Columbia University Press.

Luhrman, T. M. 2000. *Of Two Minds: An Anthropologist Looks at American Psychiatry.* New York: Vintage Books.

Malkki, L. 1992. "National Geographic: The Rooting of Peoples and the Territorialization of National Identity among Scholars and Refugees." *Cultural Anthropology* 7, no. 1: 24–44.

_____. 1995. "Refugees and Exile: From 'Refugee Studies' to the National Order of Things." *Annual Review of Anthropology* 24: 495–523.

Mitchell, J. C. 1983. "Case and Situation Analysis." *Sociological Review* 31, no. 2: 187–211.

_____. 1987. "The Situational Perspective." Pp. 1–33 in *Cities, Society, and Social Perception: A Central African Perspective.* Oxford: Clarendon Press.

Moore, S. F. 1986. *Social Facts and Fabrications: 'Customary' Law on Kilimanjaro 1880–1980.* Cambridge and New York: Cambridge University Press.

Norman, K. 1993. "Controlling a Future by Admiring a Past: An Ecomuseum in Sweden." *Ethnos* 58, no. 1–2: 37–51.

_____. 1994. "The Ironic Body: Obscene Joking among Swedish Working-Class Women." *Ethnos* 59, no. 3–4: 187–211.

_____. 1997. "Young Girls Dressing: Experiences of Exile and Memories of Home among Kosovo Albanian Refugees in Sweden." Pp. 122–145 in *Beyond Boundaries: Selected Papers on Refugees and Immigrants*, vol. 5, ed. Diane Baxter and Ruth Krulfeld. Arlington, VA: American Anthropological Association.

_____. 2001. "Phoning the Field: Meanings of Place and Involvement in Fieldwork at Home." Pp. 120–146 in *Constructing the Field, Ethnographic Fieldwork in the Contemporary World*, ed. V. Amit. London: Routledge.

Okely, J. 1992. "Anthropology and Autobiography: Participatory Experience and Embodied Knowledge." Pp. 1–23 in *Anthropology and Autobiography*, ed. J. Okely and H. Callaway. London: Routledge.

Pieke, F. 2000. "Serendipity: Reflections on Fieldwork in China." Pp. 129–150 in *Anthropologists in a Wider World: Essays on Field Research*, ed. P. Dresch, W. James, and D. Parkin. New York and Oxford: Berghahn Books.

Reineck, J. 1991. "The Past as Refuge: Gender, Migration, and Ideology among the Kosovo Albanians." PhD diss., University of California, Berkeley.

Shami, S. 1996. "Transnationalism and Refugee Studies: Rethinking Forced Migration and Identity in the Middle East." *Journal of Refugee Studies* 9, no. 1: 3–26.

Shweder, R. 1997. "The Surprise of Ethnography." *Ethos* 25, no. 2: 152–163.

Turner, V. W. 1977. "Process, System, and Symbol: A New Anthropological Synthesis." *Daedalus* 106, no. 3: 61–80.

Van Velsen, J. [1967] 1979. "The Extended-Case Method and Situational Analysis." Pp. 129–149 in Epstein [1967] 1979.

Young, A. 1995. *The Harmony of Illusions: Inventing Post-Traumatic Stress Disorder.* Princeton, NJ: Princeton University Press.

*Chapter 9*

# THE VINDICATION OF CHAKA ZULU
Retreat into the Enchantment of the Past

*C. Bawa Yamba*

The title of this chapter might invoke an unintended association with the famous warrior king Chaka Zulu, about whom Gluckman has written in his numerous analyses on Zululand (e.g., Gluckman 1940, 1960, 1974). But the similarity in names is merely coincidental. Of course, the Chaka Zulu of this story, in choosing to call himself by that name, had not only presumed that people would make such an association, but thought he was modeling himself after the more famous historical figure. The name 'Zulu' is now found as a common surname in places as far removed from Zululand as Zambia and Zimbabwe. While many of those who now carry this name might have legitimate historical claims to it, it could also be assumed that some, like the present Chaka Zulu, have appropriated the name because it conveys fear and connotes something of the power and grandeur of the historical Chaka Zulu, who consolidated the Zulu

Notes for this chapter begin on page 269.

kingdom around the nineteenth century (see Taylor 1994). The Chaka of this essay was neither Zulu nor a warrior king; he was an infamous witch hunter whose activities over a brief period of six months left the villagers of Chiawa, in the Zambezi valley of Zambia, mourning and burying 16 local people whom he had accused of witchcraft and put to death. You might well ask about the association with the historical figure. The answer will unfold in the following story, which deals with witchcraft accusations and the fatal poison ordeals in contemporary Africa that conflict with state laws of the country.

Let me proceed by situating the Chaka Zulu of this story in context so as to bring out the relevance of all this to the extended-case method, the theme under consideration. My task is not an easy one. When I was first invited to submit a contribution, I knew that other contributors would include those consciously practiced in the Manchester School of Social Anthropology; indeed, some would even be members of that school, whose heritage would make them more genuine proponents of the method that we are revisiting. What could I contribute here, beyond, perhaps, presenting something that I have, through my training as an anthropologist, acquired by proxy, as it were, from some of those who can trace their pedigree to the Manchester School? It is thus with some humility that I extrapolate any significance from my specific case for the method.

## Casting Out Evil

In June 1994, Chaka Zulu arrived in Chiawa village, where my colleagues and I had been working since the beginning of the 1990s in a Swedish-funded research project on how to prevent and mitigate the impact of HIV/AIDS. Chaka Zulu was a witchfinder of some repute, who had been invited by the local headmen to help them uproot evil. I found out from my informants and some of those who had invited the witchfinder that acts conceptualized as evil had been occurring recently with disastrous consequences. The occurrences were not random, nor did they result from pure chance. They derived from malevolent intentions of malevolent persons and affected particular victims—hence the need to counteract these forces through witchfinders. Witchfinders are, in effect, higher-level witches who possess the power to identify malevolent persons (that is, witches) and to 'diffuse' them, as well as to exact retribution. What, then, did Chiawa people perceive as the manifestations of evil in their community? They enumerated the following: first, a recent increase in mortalities, the ostensible and proximate causes of which, they accepted, were diseases such as malaria, cholera, and undoubtedly HIV/AIDS; and, second, the recent occurrence of a number of fatal disasters in Chiawa and neighboring villages, the most serious of which were a lorry accident, which caused the deaths of a dozen local people, and a capsized boat in the Zambezi, which took nine lives. Even if the people of Chiawa accepted the label 'accident', these events were clear indicators of increased evil in Chiawa. The fact that there could have been other causes or reasons for these disasters was irrelevant. For example, the people would, and in fact did, accept that the principal reason for the high mortality rates could well have been HIV/AIDS, or that the capsizing of the boat might have been an overloaded, ill-maintained dugout. However, more important for them was the interaction of such factors with other factors, which led inexorably to disaster that affected particular individuals. Thus, the fact that Chiawa had all the classic predisposing factors that sometimes conjoin to make an African community susceptible to, for example, HIV/AIDS was somehow of secondary importance. AIDS kills, but it is something that becomes potent when it is harnessed by witches and directed at specific persons. Outsiders concerned with HIV/AIDS prevention may advocate preventive measures at the level of behavior, but local people did not regard this as enough. They went one step further: the need to change sexual behavior would have to be supplemented by addressing the forces that brought about the causal link between the event (sexual contact) and its consequence (HIV infection). For such reasons, the people of Chiawa persuaded their leaders to do something about the situation

Let us take a closer look at the predisposing factors that contributed to the vulnerability of Chiawa. The village was near a commercial farm that employed over 3,000 migrant male laborers who lived in barracks, making it impossible for spouses to live together. Indeed, most of the young men had left their partners behind in their home villages. Chiawa was also only five miles to the Zambia-Zimbabwe border post of Chirundu, where on any given day over 130 lorries would be waiting for customs clearance to enter or leave the country. Sex work emerged as a common occupation in the area around the late 1980s. Quite soon, scores of commercial sex workers could be observed competing aggressively for clients in drinking bars, while itinerant traders moved from one temporary liaison to another. Partly as a result of such conditions, the area turned into a fertile ground for sexually transmitted diseases (STDs, now referred to as STIs, sexually transmitted infections). It was also partly for such reasons that Chiawa became the center of HIV/AIDS prevention activities long before Chaka's arrival in 1994.[1] The principal objective of the AIDS prevention project was to encourage the local people to take some responsibility for the AIDS epidemic—to accept it as their own problem and to partly contribute to strategies for preventing it. This simple but illusive objective was conveyed in the idea of 'capacity building'. The goal was to build local capacity to cope with the impact of the pandemic through the application of different kinds of interactive methods and strategies that highlighted the primacy of AIDS prevention in the minds of the people, as well as made them constantly grapple with solutions that would be effective and, hopefully, sustainable. It might, therefore, be valid to argue that the people of Chiawa, in deciding to invite a witchfinder to help them fight AIDS, were displaying a remarkably high capacity to cope with the local HIV epidemic, even if the promoters of capacity building, of which I was one, had not envisaged bringing in a witchfinder as an appropriate measure. The Swedish AIDS project had, paradoxically, achieved some of its objectives of building capacity, but the consequences entailed in this kind of (enhanced) capacity were unanticipated and certainly unintended.

When he started his work in Chiawa, Chaka Zulu had an attractive solution to the problems of the people. He told them HIV was, until recently, one of a number of defunct diseases that were re-emerging because people had ceased to lead virtuous lives. The main reason for its reappearance was the transgression of traditional norms, such as committing adultery or having sex with a recently widowed woman who had not yet been 'cleansed' or a woman who had recently aborted, and so forth. Chaka gave his explanation a further clever twist by adding that witches thrived in such an environment because they could easily manipulate the prevailing ailments for their own ends. Witches were able to, as it were, harness AIDS and direct it toward particular persons they wished to harm. The epidemiology of HIV/AIDS might suggest that the disease randomly affects those who expose themselves through, for example, unprotected sex, but the reason why it was killing some people—even the exposure to the risk itself—was believed to have been 'caused' by witches. He had a similar explanation for the fatal accidents. Whatever calamity the victims encountered was inevitable; they had been bewitched. Thus, he told the people that crocodiles in the Chiawa stretch of the Zambezi River were eating people because they were controlled by witches. The witches, he assured them, devoured human flesh by proxy, as it were, through the crocodiles. Chaka managed to present an alternative discourse on the aetiology of AIDS in such a manner that Chiawa people believed his claim that he could cure the diseases it produced, as well as exact vengeance on those who made it afflict specific people. Most significant, however, is the fact that he offered the people an explanation for contingent misfortunes that resonated with their own beliefs. The AIDS prevention team stood by helplessly as Chaka accused people of witchcraft and put them through poison ordeals that resulted in the deaths of 16 people.[2]

This present essay is a continuation of the Chaka story, with a focus on how the local community managed the upheavals that followed accusations of neighbors and friends of witchcraft, and the resulting deaths of some of those who refused to confess. More importantly, however, I use the story to illustrate what I perceive as an underlying corollary of the extended-case method: the propensity to regard social events as interrelated and thus as constituting an interconnected whole. No matter how we conceptualize and approach the notion of a social situation in analysis,[3] it is likely to encompass a set of events in the same social context. The events that might be rendered in written documents or in narratives may themselves conflict or resonate when we examine their embeddedness in the wider structure (in this case, that of Chiawa social life). However, by postulating an interconnection, we presume an overarching whole within which the disparate narratives are sub-sets of the system. This means we end up explaining social situations by knitting the disparate narratives into a significant whole. In a sense, therefore, the extended-case method, excellent tool for analysis though it is, might not to be the best methodology for dealing with disruptive conflict. It is therefore not surprising that even though the proponents of the method were to achieve novel insight in the analysis of conflict situations, they ended up illustrating and emphasizing continuity, despite the tension and conflict that might have existed in the societies they studied. Another epistemological consequence of the method, it seems to me, is the problem of delimitation. Social processes, which are the focus of the extended-case method, comprise events that do not begin and end—they shade into each other. And yet the analyst must necessarily, as it were, impose some form of closure to the narrative and the analysis. One of the essential characteristics of the extended-case method, the detailed analysis of an ethnographic case, operates by selective omission, in which some details are included and others excluded from the analysis. This may well be true of ethnographic analysis in general, but I would maintain that it is particularly acute when one applies the extended-case method as a tool. Perhaps that is why Gluckman dispensed some effort to one of the most important problems in any scientific endeavor, that of delimiting the research problem/question theoretically and, for anthropologists, geographically as well (see Devons and Gluckman 1964). I shall return to these points toward the end of this chapter.

Chiawa village is only 150 kilometers away from Lusaka. Geographical proximity to the capital, however, does not mean it is easily accessible. During the rainy seasons, it can take up to eight hours to reach the village in a good four-wheel-drive vehicle. Until 2003, the stretch of road from Chirundu to Chiawa had never been improved. It was regarded as part of the charm of the African bush. Tourists sweated and rocked back and forth in safari trucks as they passed the village on their way to the tourist camps along the Zambezi, where they paid more than US $150 a night to sleep in tents and observe wildlife. One of the tour operators, responding to a chance comment on the need to improve the local roads, replied: "Oh, no. Tourists love potholes and erratic driving. It increases the exotic feeling of being in Africa and the bush." So until 2001, when the government and a consortium of local safari camp owners started to repair the road, trying to get from Chiawa to Chirundu, or to the Catholic Mission Hospital 18 kilometers away, took many hours and cost the lives of many local people who had no access to powerful four-wheel-drive vehicles. The tourists, who love Africa with its potholes and all but capture instant images with advanced contraptions such as digital cameras, while paying substantially to sleep under 'primitive' conditions, very much contributed to heightening the relative deprivation of the local people. Local people were, therefore, not very fond of tourists. They were further dismayed to hear that their own chieftainess had recently become a business partner to two of the safari tour operators. They feared that such an association would entail a divided loyalty between foreign investors and local people.

## The Goba: People of the Valley

Chiawa has about 8,000 inhabitants, a majority of whom speak a Shona dialect and designate themselves as Goba (Shona for 'people of the valley'). They live in an area close to the foot of the Mindwe Hills, in scattered homesteads surrounded by their fields, divided into about 30 villages, each under the authority of a headman. The headmen, in turn, rule their villages on behalf of a traditional tribal leader, to whom most of them are matrilineally related. Chiawa is divided into two wards. Each ward elects a political representative who is addressed as Councilor and represents the ward in the District Council, as well as liaising with the Member of Parliament who represents the area. The role of the district councilor has conflicted, on some occasions, with the position of the traditional headmen, who sometimes belong to different political parties from that of the local councilor.

Officially, Chiawa District was evacuated in 1975 because of the Zimbabwean Liberation War, but this is only a fictive bureaucratic claim. Indeed, a survey at the beginning of our project (Bond and Wallman 1993) indicated that only about 18 percent of the households actually left Chiawa during the war. However, in designating the area as evacuated, the government could consider itself as not responsible for the inhabitants. Those who remained in their homes did so at great peril.[4] Services, whatever few existed, were cut back or simply terminated; the rudimentary but vital health clinic in Chiawa village was closed. In 1981, Chiawa was officially opened up, and its inhabitants began to return. The government resumed responsibility for the area and the provision of services for the populace (Scudder 1995). Returning Chiawians found overgrown fields and fallen houses, as well as roaming bandits who had had easy access to AK-74 rifles, which they used mainly for poaching (for some time, one of the few sources of livelihood). Quite soon the villagers managed to rebuild their homesteads, cultivate their fields, and start producing and reproducing again. They augmented poor harvests and recurrent droughts with riverside gardening, known as *materos*. Keeping livestock, particularly cattle, was not viable because of the presence of tsetse flies. This contributed to the perception not only of the Goba as non-cattle-herding people but also of the Goba environment as being non-conducive to herding. Cattle-herding tribes simply kept out of Goba land. However, this changed when a European Union tsetse fly project, implemented in 1989, succeeded, over the course of less than half a decade, in eradicating the tsetse fly. As a result, some local farmers began to keep cattle and other livestock. The eradication of the tsetse fly offered new ecological opportunities to neighboring groups as well, such as the Tonga, some of whom moved into Chiawa with their herds (Brinn 1996). The new groups brought with them other kinds of social organization and culture, although Goba social structure and systems of social organization remained the dominant ones.

The present traditional ruler is the Chieftainess Chiawa, an articulate, well-educated lady who resides in Lusaka. She has been described in some of the Zambian newspapers as a modern ruler who is struggling to bring her people into the twentieth century. Lest the significance of this statement escape us, she herself has explained that while the rest of the world was moving into the twenty-first century, her people had still not quite entered the twentieth one. She therefore actively sought—and was sometimes instrumental in bringing— development projects to Chiawa to provide jobs for local people, all in an effort to carry her people toward the still elusive twentieth century and modernity. In the course of this kind of endeavor, she had become a business partner to a number of foreign investors who had started various enterprises, such as safari camping, and commercial farming in Chiawa.

Chieftainess Chiawa's efforts to promote an image of herself as a modern and progressive ruler have been tarnished by the witchfinding activities of Chaka in Chiawa. Her role in the whole Chaka affair has been discussed extensively by local people. Was it possible for the witchfinder to enter and operate in Chiawa without the knowledge and approval of the Chieftainess? Since the Chieftainess vehemently denies having anything to do with Chaka Zulu's affairs, the question of who gave Chaka permission to hunt witches in Chiawa—if indeed he needed any formal permission to do so—is difficult to answer. There are those who would appear to agree with the Chieftainess's claim that she had no part in bringing Chaka to Chiawa. Such people see Chaka Zulu's activities as the triumph of the will of the people over the wishes of their chieftainess. The claim here is that it was the ordinary people of Chiawa who demanded the services of a witchfinder to address social problems they believed could be resolved only through traditional remedies and ritual. Others, however, explain the whole affair as the result of a deliberate connivance between the Chieftainess and some of her headmen in an effort to control some difficult subjects. The ultimate purpose of either point of view seems to be to portray the Chieftainess in a negative light. Both points of view claim either that she did not manage to thwart the wishes of her subjects, or that she had actually brought the witchfinder to Chiawa to help her control her subjects. The Chieftainess prefers to describe herself as a benign leader who was unable to prevent her people from engaging in acts derived from 'superstition' because they were not sufficiently educated, a state of affairs for which she thought the government was to blame. Education would have taught her subjects to reject such 'primitive ideas' (Yamba 1997), and Christianity might have made them less likely to follow a witchfinder. Her position on the issue of witchcraft has been quite clear: she finds it unacceptable. Not surprisingly, she appears to have been the main dissenting voice during a debate on witchcraft in the House of Chiefs on a motion to amend the Witchcraft Act to acknowledge the existence of witchcraft as a potent force to be reckoned with in Zambian society.[5] Whatever her actual role in the affair of Chaka's witchfinding might have been, the fact remains that the Chieftainess did not succeed in stopping the witch hunts in Chiawa, even though some of the accused and victims were her own kinsmen.

Chaka Zulu, the witchfinder of Chiawa, achieved some notoriety through newspapers and national television coverage.[6] He was sent to prison in 1996 after protracted trials at various levels of the judicial system in which the families of those he had killed were unable or unwilling to testify against him. It is significant to note that Chaka Zulu commanded absolute fear and respect as a witchfinder in Chiawa. One of the victims, out of only two who survived the poison ordeals, dared to appear in court to testify. Not a single one of the relatives of the victims testified against Chaka, and the authorities would emphasize that none of those connected with the case was willing to give evidence. The fact of the matter is that it was not only fear that made them unable or unwilling to appear in court, even though it must be conceded that fear was certainly a significant factor.[7] I had occasion to interview Chaka in prison. His warders served us with cold beer during my interview and lingered at a considerable distance from us while I talked with him. He spoke flamboyantly and acted toward his jailors more like a prince with minions around him than a convict with guards.[8] One other obvious thing about the court trials, even if it would be impolitic to say so, is the fact that the judges who heard Chaka's case and ruled that there was insufficient evidence to find him guilty of murder were themselves somehow afraid of him. Not surprisingly, they ruled that it could not be proved beyond reasonable doubt that he had murdered people; however, they felt that there was sufficient evidence to show that he had received money under false pretenses. Nonetheless, though found guilty, he was not fined. The time he had spent in custody was considered a sufficient punishment, and he was released

Following Chaka's arrest in January 1995 and his trials, a nationwide television program discussed the case of Chaka Zulu. How could a witchfinder not only exist in modern Zambia but even be able to put people to death with impunity? Chieftainess Chiawa, who took part in one televised discussion, said that the ultimate responsibility lay with the government, which had failed to educate the people to resist such 'primitive' ideas. After the trial, she banned Chaka from entering Chiawa District.

Manifestations of evil in Chiawa, the initial reasons for the witch hunts, have persisted in many forms, for example, through increased AIDS-related mortalities, motor vehicle accidents, and frequent attacks by man-eating crocodiles. The discourse on witchcraft has somehow been revived, and local people have clamored for the return of Chaka Zulu. The rest of my chapter will deal with contesting views on the causes of the disasters and on the increasing demand that the ban on Chaka be lifted and that he be allowed to resume his witch hunts.

## Two Accounts of Contingent Mishaps in Chiawa

On being released from prison, Chaka moved to a village near the Kafue River, which marks the border between Chiawa and Chirundu Districts. A dilapidated ferry carries vehicles and passengers across the river from dawn to dusk, with tourist safari vehicles from Lusaka providing much of the traffic. From Chaka's village, it is easy to spot vehicles that are ferried across the river. Chaka or any of his many supporters could thus easily see the Chieftainess's unmistakable vehicle, with its royal flag, leaving Chiawa for Lusaka. Informants from the villages around the pontoon say that invariably Chaka crossed the river into Chiawa almost as soon as the Chieftainess had left the area. Although barred by the Chieftainess from operating in the area, Chaka still had his in-laws and numerous clients to attend to.

In January 2002, during a visit to Zambia, I decided to find Chaka Zulu in order to continue my interviews with him. I wanted to hear how his life had evolved after the trials and the time in prison. I also wanted to know if he felt any remorse for causing the deaths of so many people. When we met, Chaka was unrepentant; he wished he had been allowed to complete his task of finding witches. He told me that he visited Chiawa regularly to see his in-laws (6 of his 13 wives were from the district), but that he no longer hunted witches. He knew the people of Chiawa were demanding that he be allowed to resume his work of "removing evil" from the area, by which he meant a return to witch hunting. My earlier interviews with him were mainly on belief in witchcraft and traditional healing practices, but as his specialty was hunting and neutralizing witches, I was very keen to know what would happen if the people were to succeed through their headmen in persuading the Chieftainess to allow him to return.

While in Zambia, I heard of an impending community meeting in Chiawa, the purpose of which was to figure out how to get the ban against Chaka Zulu lifted. It was rumored that some local people who supported the witchfinder were going to insist on his being allowed to return to Chiawa. I attended one such meeting and tape-recorded the proceedings. From the choice of venue, it was clear that the most important traditional leaders of the district did not sanction the meeting. It was held under the shade of a large tree instead of in the village square, which was often referred to as "the Royal advisory council meeting place." Nonetheless, about four village headmen were present who, I thought, made unlikely allies of this witchfinder. Two of them had been among the lucky few to survive Chaka's witch hunts six years earlier. Another important person present was Charles Phiri, who a decade earlier had been a research assistant in our AIDS project. Now a respected political party representative in the District Council, Phiri turned out to be the only dissenting voice at the meeting.

The participants sat in a semi-circle facing the three headmen and Phiri. Each speaker looked at the chairperson who nodded his approval, yielding the floor to the person. This meeting was very similar to some of the so-called community participation meetings I had witnessed in the past. I have been unable to ascertain as to whether these meetings were recent creations, which have emerged as a result of the efforts of organizations such as UNICEF or WHO, or whether they were truly traditional examples of participatory decision-making processes in Zambia. Most of the meetings I had attended in the past had focused primarily on STDs and HIV/AIDS prevention. Now, of course, the topic was what to do about the growing evil in the village. There were about 25 men at the meeting, but not a single woman was there.[9]

I recognized among those present several persons whom I had interviewed in the past about traditional healing practices and witchcraft. Much of what they said in their speeches here contradicted their earlier views on witchcraft and witchfinding. In the interviews, they had denied any belief in witchcraft, stating that personal responsibility was paramount in HIV/AIDS causation. In the present context, they perceived witchcraft as all pervasive and an ultimate causal force in their lives.

It is usually the group dynamics in community meetings of this kind that both drives the process in a given direction and determines the achievement of the purpose for which the meeting was convened. Usually, one person emerges as the leading figure. The obvious leader of the group, and the one who also acted as the informal chairperson, was Phiri. No doubt, he commanded some respect by virtue of his position as District Council representative, even though it was obvious he had difficulties converting the crowd to his own point of view. The first speaker was the headman of one of the larger villages, whom I will refer to as Headman of Village X:

The Chieftainess and the big men in Lusaka do no care about us. They took Chaka from away from us. They sent him to prison before he could finish his work. Now the witches are back. They even work in broad daylight. They have no fear. They have no shame. They know nothing can stop them now. We want Chaka back. Even some of those whose relatives died because of Chaka want him back. [It should be noted that this speaker frames an important part of his delivery in the passive sense. He does not say "those Chaka accused of witchcraft and poisoned" but "those whose relatives died."]

Phiri asked Headman of Village X to explain how he could tell the witches were back: "What do you mean by 'They even work in broad daylight'?" Another speaker took over to elaborate:

All our *matero* [riverside gardens] are continuously destroyed by floods or by hippos. The fishermen can no longer go out to fish because of crocodiles. When Chaka was here, the witches were afraid to practice in daylight. Now they do so through these man-eating crocodiles. We all know that one of the people he defused in the past controlled a crocodile, which he used to carry out his evil practices. We cannot take it anymore. Let us appeal to the Chieftainess to allow Chaka to return.

There had been a general murmur of approval at the end of the speech by Headman of Village X, who happened to be a kinsman of the Chieftainess. But this headman had himself barely survived Chaka's poison in the earlier witch hunts (Yamba 1997). In 1995, he had talked to me at some length about his near-fatal encounter with Chaka's poison. I produce his exact words from a recording taped in 1995.

Chaka said my witchcraft allowed me to farm and reap more maize than others in the village. He said that I *caused* [emphasis added] the villagers to weed my plots during the night without their knowledge. That I used witchcraft to water my fields even though there was drought in other people's fields.

I drunk the poison because I thought it was *muchape* [traditionally, a concoction that was used to identify witches]. I don't believe in witchcraft, but over one hundred people were shouting "Make him drink!" "Kill the witch!" Chaka said if I was not a witch, I would survive. If I was a witch, I would die. I do not believe in witchcraft, but I could not refuse to drink. That would have been the same as agreeing I am a witch. But I also feared that if I drunk I would die like many before me who had drunk.

You ask me why I went to the square[10] when Chaka sent for me. I am a headman. The Chieftainess is my relative, but her mother [the queen mother] was seated by Chaka in the square when I was summoned. To have refused to go would have been like to challenge the authority of the Chieftainess's mother ...

The Chieftainess did not do anything to save me, and yet we are the same blood.

This was the very same person who now spoke with great force on the need to bring the witchfinder back to Chiawa. Speaker after speaker gave examples of some incidences they regarded as clearly the work of witches.

Another speaker, Boniface Muyinga, said that although he was a Christian, he too believed in the need for uprooting evil in Chiawa. Since the traditional leaders did not have the power to do so, it was time to allow an outsider like Chaka to do the job for them. He was milder in his speech, although it was clear that he too advocated the resumption of witchfinding in Chiawa. Muyinga called out the names of the villagers who had been recently killed by crocodiles, presumably to remind the crowd of how serious the situation had become. After each name, there were shouts of "Witchcraft!" It was for me even more difficult to reconcile the past of this speaker with his present demands for the return of witch hunts. I return again to tape-recorded interviews with the same man in 1995.

> He [Chaka] said to me "Big man. You are a witch, confess." I have always been a big man. My father was big. He had a big belly because he was a successful man. My grandfather too was tall and big. But now Chaka said I had killed my own grand-daughter. I had sacrificed the child in a feast with other witches— that is why I am big.
>
> I was told that Chaka was planning to get me, so I sent word to the Chieftainess to come and stop all the nonsense. Nothing happened. I was later called to a schoolyard. I went because we all know Chaka could not have practiced in Chiawa without the permission of the Chieftainess. There were about 300 people present. They made me drink. I started purging [diarrhea] after about 40 minutes. The crowd put their hands over their noses and started laughing. My daughter felt sorry for me, so she took a wheelbarrow and tried to carry me home. She is not strong, so after a few yards she stopped and put me under a tree. She went to get me something to drink. I was dead for a week, but, thank God. I survived.
>
> You researchers have no business here if you cannot get the government to stop people like Chaka.

Speaker after speaker returned inevitably to the man-eating crocodiles. They argued that normal crocodiles would run away from people. Chiawa crocodiles were different because they often attacked people in boats. They do so because they are controlled by witches.

Phiri, who had previously allowed each speaker to express his own view, now spoke:

> I don't understand how you can mention bad harvests and floods as examples of witchcraft. Only four years ago we were all happy when Chaka was arrested. Bad harvests and floods are the work of God, they are *ngozi*.[11] There is nothing we can do about it. It is true that in the past man-eating crocodiles were rare. Now there are many, and we worry. We all know that some *musungus* [Europeans] have established crocodile farms along the Zambezi. Last year, for example, the Zambezi dam authorities opened the floodgates without warning. You will remember our gardens were destroyed after each flood. It is not only we, the poor people of Chiawa, who have suffered from the floods. After each flood, the crocodiles and the fish from the farms are washed away. The crocodiles, which are usually fed everyday with red meat, suddenly find themselves in the river.

They have to try to survive, so they become aggressive. How can we consider their attacking men the work of witches? I too believe witches exist. But witches are evil people who wish their fellow humans ill. They cannot hurt us through crocodiles. It is time for us to accept this fact.

I will not dwell on the meeting any longer but wish to say that I was able to verify that the gates of the Kariba Dam were sometimes opened without warning the farmers who had gardens along the Zambezi River. When that happened, the farmers' crops, which were vital for the livelihood of the people, were destroyed. Also located along the riverbank were a number of crocodile farms, and many of the beasts were indeed washed away in the flooding. However, it was not easy to know if the crocodiles did in fact become man-eaters when they found themselves in the wild.

Another issue worth considering is whether Chaka Zulu, if he were granted permission to return, would do so as the charismatic leader he had been several years previously. What his supporters perhaps did not know was that Chaka had recently been released by the local hospital where he had been treated for a number of AIDS-related diseases. Apparently, he had fallen ill, sought medical help, and been diagnosed with HIV. Such information should have been confidential, according to WHO regulations, but the doctor who passed on the information to me in conspiratorial tones saw me as an ally in AIDS prevention, rather than as an anthropologist or an outsider to whom such considerations would apply. The irony of the case was that the very person who had gained some notoriety for being able to cure HIV/AIDS was now himself seeking modern biomedical help for his own condition.

## Undercurrents of Rebellion

Around the same time as the community meeting described above, other meetings were taking place in Chiawa in which Councilor Phiri was playing a prominent role in opposition to the Chieftainess. The commercial farm that had been the largest employer and an unwitting factor in turning the area into a risk arena for HIV spread had gone into liquidation. The farm was taken over by a prominent local white Zambian family. The new owners had their own plans on how to restructure the farm. First and foremost among these was a complete switch from the production of marigold (which had been the favored cash crop of the previous owners) to maize and other locally vital crops. However, this move necessitated a substantial reduction of the workforce. Consequently, most of the farm laborers found themselves out of work. Another plan involved the eviction of some local villagers, a couple hundred families or so, who had resided on a fertile stretch of land—it is claimed by some—for generations. The owners had offered to resettle the villagers at a new location. Unwilling to leave their homes, which they perceived as ancestral, the villagers approached their Chieftainess, expecting her to intervene on their behalf. But the Chieftainess told them that they would have to move in accordance with the law.

She further told them that they should count themselves lucky that they had been offered resettlement. The villagers felt let down and took their case to the newly elected local councilor, who was none other than Phiri. The cause of the evicted villagers became Phiri's other battle. He framed the whole issue as one involving land-owning foreigners (ignoring the fact that the new owners were also Zambian citizens) and their local cronies against poor, helpless villagers. After unsuccessful attempts to meet with the new owners to persuade them to revoke the eviction of the villagers, Phiri summonsed the new owners to the local police station for a meeting to discuss the case. The owners ignored the summons, which, it is worth noting, was not legally binding; there were no legal grounds to compel them to meet Phiri at the local police station.

Phiri then took his case to the Chieftainess, who presumably had already been informed about his campaigns on behalf of the villagers. She agreed to receive him. Accounts of the encounter differ. Phiri claims that the Chieftainess treated him "like a small boy" and refused to listen to what he had to say. Others present say that Phiri was rude and that this angered the Chieftainess. The following is the version of one of the Chieftainess's advisers.

> Phiri asked for an audience with the Chieftainess, and the Chieftainess agreed to see him. Phiri did not know how to behave properly in front of the Chieftainess. He showed no respect. He even raised his voice and did not listen to anyone. The Chieftainess got angry and dismissed him. These modern young men have no sense of history. They don't try to learn about what has happened before, why things are as they are at present. They think they are into politics, and it gives them power. The land belongs to new owners. The villagers have no right to settle there. The new owners are not obliged to resettle the villagers, but they have even offered to build them new homes. Because of people like Phiri, they will become fed up and offended, and the people may get nothing. Phiri has hurt the people he says he wants to support.[12]

Phiri's own version of the event, while not contradicting the above account, expands on other aspects.

> I went to see her [the Chieftainess]. She talked to me like a small boy. She did not even listen to all I had to say. She said I did not understand what I was talking about. Of course, she would say that. She is a good friend of the new owners of the farm. She dines and parties with them all the time. Whenever she crosses the pontoon from Lusaka, the first thing she does is drive straight to the farm house to relax and drink with them before she drives on to her own place to see her own people. She knows that these villagers have lived on the land for generations. It is Goba land. She sold it. She has forgotten her own people. I must take my case to Lusaka. We cannot let these people treat Zambians like this.

Phiri took his case to Lusaka, where he claims to have been received by a Member of Parliament, but not the cabinet minister, who had also promised to look into the case. The Member of Parliament happened to be from Phiri's own party, which is in opposition to the MMD (Movement for Multi-party Democracy), the ruling

party at present. Aligned with Phiri against the Chieftainess in this eviction controversy are the evicted villagers and their families, as well as the jobless former
farm workers. On the issue of the need to return to witchfinding because of man-
eating crocodiles and Phiri's rational, but by no means faultless, explanation as
to why tame crocodiles have become man-eaters, his allies shift and are less
solidly behind him. They find it difficult to accept that tame crocodiles become
man-eaters overnight because they are flushed into the gushing waters of the
Zambezi. It would appear that some of those who support him against the Chieftainess might not be so solidly behind him when it comes to his 'disenchanted'
accounts for contingent events. Furthermore, there is yet a middle group who
are torn between the purported heartlessness of the new owners of Chiawa farm
who plan to evict villagers and the fact that these same (white Zambian) farmers have been the only source of supplying local people with maize during two
recent years of drought and famine in the area.[13]

Thus, the small skirmishes in Chiawa that were carried to the centers of
power in Lusaka do not appear to have resulted in a meaningful response or
to have made any difference to the people of Chiawa. Oddly enough, it is this
kind of inertia that Chaka was so good at dealing with. His witchfindings and
witch hunts shook the very structure of Chiawa life.

## Concluding Remarks

I think beneath the staged orchestration on the pros and cons of fighting
witches, there was a structure of brooding rebellion against the authority of the
Chieftainess. The rebellion was not against the office as such, but against the
incumbent. What the people of Chiawa perceived in their Chieftainess was not
a ruler who shared their hardships and disasters, but one who ruled through
some of her more devoted headmen from the comforts of her Lusaka home.
"She comes from Lusaka with only new rules and regulations and goes away
with her air-conditioned Land Cruiser filled with maize, chickens, and eggs"
was how one of her own advisers once described her.[14]

The Chieftainess's dilemma is partly due to the fact that she had sought to
help her people by attracting foreign investors to the district. Some of these,
such as the commercial farmers, a majority of whom were white, had invested
in farming, thus providing some employment for local people. Other investors
were of the kind whose presence did not lead to visible jobs for any significant
number of people. An example of the latter were those who had built safari
camps and lodges along the Zambezi River, some of whom had thought it pru-
dent to make the Chieftainess their business partner. The Chieftainess was thus
a partner in some of the ventures that the local headmen and her own subjects
often came into conflict with. However, she was also instrumental in bringing
research projects, for example, on HIV/AIDS prevention and tsetse fly eradication, into the district. Such projects did not benefit her as an individual but
helped the community as a whole. She would thus not seem to be only genuinely concerned with lining her own pocket, so to speak. However, her relatively

altruistic activities, such as seeking research projects that would improve life for the people, remain unnoticed and undercommunicated. It would appear, therefore, that to truly lead her people into the new millennium, the Chieftainess has a gigantic task before her. She will have to blend successfully the enchanted perceptions of past situations with—in Weberian terms—'disenchanted' definitions of present reality. This reality is perhaps partly derived from the incursions of modernization as refracted from rich tourist safari camps, which serve delicate dishes of crocodile stew from the selfsame crocodiles that are thought to escape into the wilderness to become man-eaters.

Whether or not the people of Chiawa will be able to bring Chaka Zulu back to hunt witches and remove evil, or whether his own post-modern (Sontag 1988) affliction of AIDS will pre-empt such a possibility, is something that only time will tell.

* * *

I said at the beginning of this essay that I was not quite certain if I had anything to contribute to the extended-case method, and I cannot quite rid myself of this misgiving. I had always thought of the method as something all anthropologists did, without quite knowing the epistemological background to the method or its underlying premises. When I was a student in London, we once had Prof. Clyde Mitchell as a lecturer for one of the pre-fieldwork courses. Although the theme of his lecture was listed as the role of statistics in fieldwork methodology, which he succinctly framed as "simply an issue about whether to count or not to count," he spoke at length on the extended-case method. He mentioned his own *Kalela Dance*, but he particularly talked about another piece as essential reading: Bruce Kapferer's (1969) "Norms and the Manipulation of Relationships in a Work Context." He thought that piece a fine exemplification of the extended-case method. If memory serves me right, he said that the key to a successful extended-case analysis was the demand for great detail. You have to analyze the data until it was "completely exhausted." "Give the theme paper," I quote from my notes. Some of us found this daunting because about the same time some of our tutors were sending us to classes and seminars on the philosophy of science in which we were exposed to what appeared to be another style of analysis: one that dissected the complex and made it seem deceptively simple.[15] The extended-case method, which we were being taught, appeared to advance in the opposite style: one that analyzed anthropological phenomena to arrive at how very complicated and complex it all was. Kapferer's article in the *Social Networks* volume exceeds 160 pages. One might be permitted, therefore, to believe that the limits of analysis in the extended-case method correspond to the limits of the anthropologist's interest—unless constrained, as in the case here, by something that could be compressed into a 20-minute verbal presentation, or by some other consideration.

The question of what to include in an analysis is also pertinent when we consider the notion of process that underlies the analysis of a particular extended case. Processes are events, and events, whether contemporary or historical, are continuous and do not, as Collingwood (1956) once observed, begin and end—they shade into one another. Earlier forms are contained in present (ongoing) forms of the same events, the constitution and combination of which might direct the future course of the same events. In analyzing an event, therefore, the need for closure and the point of closure—'delimitation', in Gluckman's terms—is necessarily arbitrary. It is the anthropologist who decides when to cut off an ongoing process, either because sufficient data have been collected for a complete academic paper, or because what has been collected is enough to provide a fairly adequate understanding of the phenomenon. Given this necessary issue of closure, there is also the matter of the depth of analysis. Is there a stage in the analysis of anthropological phenomena that corresponds to the notion of 'saturation' in focus-group discussions, which canonically inclined writers of method would see as being when one has reached a stage at which nothing new emerges from the discussions? There is no reason to suppose we could ever exhaust the analysis of social phenomenon. Nor is there ever a clear point at which we could execute a clean cut-off. Some constraints would have to determine when we would cut off the analysis, as it were, and I find it difficult to think that this would be decided for scientific reasons alone. Some of the proponents of the extended-case method remind us of Gluckman's advice that we keep on analyzing our data until we exhaust its potentials for extrapolation and interpretation. I have not been able to do so, nor do I see how that might be accomplished.

This is my visit to Manchester, but only as a brief and confused visitor.

## Acknowledgments

I wish to express my gratitude to Terry Evens and Don Handelman for their comments, encouragement, and patience, without which I might not have been able to finish this essay. Particular thanks go to Terry Evens for a thorough reading of an earlier version and for suggesting whither I might fruitfully advance my arguments. Thanks also to Ulla Wagner for many useful comments. I have tried to follow their suggestions but may not have always done so successfully, and must therefore accept responsibility alone for the piece as it is. My research in Chiawa was funded by SIDA/SAREC, Sweden.

---

C. Bawa Yamba is Associate Professor of Anthropology at Diakonhjemmet University College, Oslo. He received his PhD in social anthropology from the University of Stockholm. His principal interests are the study of ritual and moral institutions, traditional epistemologies and world-views, and HIV/AIDS. He is the author of *Permanent Pilgrims: The Role of Pilgrimage in the Lives of West African Muslims in Sudan* (1995); "Some Dilemmas of HIV/AIDS Prevention and Coping in a Zambian Village," *African Sociological Review* (2004); "Loveness and Her Brothers: Trajectories of Life for Children Orphaned by HIV/AIDS in Zambia," *African Journal of AIDS Research* (2005).

## Notes

Fatal attacks by crocodiles in Chiawa have continued and even recently received attention in the national media. Attacks by crocodiles are, however, not only limited to Chiawa, as is clear from the minutes in the *Parliamentary Debates for the Third Session of the Ninth Assembly* from 5 November 2004. Several speakers demanded that something be done about the "menace of man-eating crocodiles." As recently as 6 February 2006, some Zambian newspapers reported one case in which a 70-year-old woman was attacked by a crocodile. Chieftainess Chiawa is said to have appealed to the Zambia Wild Life Authority "to crop the reptiles because they are too many" (www.zana.gov.zm/news/viewnews).

1. I have worked intermittently in Chiawa District in Zambia since 1990, in an HIV/AIDS project funded by SIDA (Swedish International Development Agency).
2. For a full account of the Chiawa witchfindings, see Yamba (1997).
3. Gluckman (1958: 9) defines a social situation as "the behaviour on some occasion of members of a community as such, analysed and compared with their behaviour on other occasions, so that the analysis reveals the underlying system of relationships between the social structure of the community, the parts of the social structure, the physical environment and the physiological life of the community's members."
4. Chiawa people recall how they had to sleep in the bush at night to avoid being interrogated, sexually harassed, or raped by Rhodesian soldiers or by the guerrillas. Some older women claim that it is from this date that a change of sexual behavior took place, particularly among young girls. They are said to have become more daring and promiscuous, meeting the threat of sexual harassment with at brazen attempt to extract 'gifts' from the men. As one woman put it: "They [the young girls] would have sex with freedom fighters for food and clothes and pots from Zimbabwe. They could smoke and drink beer with the soldiers. Before this, girls in Chiawa had respect" (Bond 1995).
5. The *Daily Mail of Zambia* (14 May 2004) reports one speaker, Chief Mubanga of Chinsali District, as proposing that the chiefs be empowered to impose death penalties on people convicted of witchcraft. He was, in effect, asking for the chiefs to be allowed to carry out the work of witchfinders such as Chaka.
6. From January 1995, the *Post of Zambia* carried many stories about the witchfinding in Chiawa.
7. The prosecuting authorities had promised prospective witnesses free transport to the court in the capital, but according to some villagers, no such transport was provided. Most of those who had agreed to come forward as witnesses did not hear back from the police or the prosecuting attorney. And yet the whole episode was portrayed in some newspapers as one in which the villagers were too terrified to face Chaka and give evidence against him in a court of law. We will, of course, not know whether the potential witnesses would have been bold enough to face Chaka in court if transport had been forthcoming.
8. Here I must draw a contrast between my visit to a witchfinder in prison with my visit to a former cabinet minister, also in prison. The witchfinder was in jail for the alleged murder of 16 people. The former minister, a personal friend and an outstanding researcher who left academia to enter politics, was detained under a spurious charge of motor vehicle theft, one of the few crimes for which there was no bail in Zambia. Although the difference in the treatment of these two people may have depended on the situations involved, and the dispositions and personalities of the jailors as well, there was, nonetheless, clearly a more oppressive atmosphere in the way that the former minister was treated than in the way the witchfinder was treated. The jailors were deferential and even obsequious to the witchfinder. They were polite but firm with the former minister, and behaved toward me, the visitor, as though they would lock me up as well, if I was not careful.
9. In most of the community meetings I had attended in the past, women were present, and particularly the older women were usually very vocal. Those meetings, however,

were on HIV/AIDS prevention. Reproductive health issues were thought to be particularly pertinent to women, which might explain why women were active in those meetings. At the community meeting canvassing the return of Chaka, I was unable to get an explanation as to why no women attended the meeting. One participant said, "It is men's business." Another said, "Women are not interested in such politics'. I find neither explanation satisfactory. It is also significant to note that of the people Chaka accused of witchcraft and put through the poison ordeals, about 18 in all, 16 were men and only 2 were women.

10. The square was the spot in the village where Chaka summoned the people he accused. He sometimes used game guards to 'arrest' people he accused. Sometimes, the same game guards were made to restrain and lock up Chaka's prisoners instead of looking for poachers.

11. *Ngozi* is Goba for 'accident', usually an occurrence that does not have a disastrous outcome. *Ngozi* is also sometimes used to denote spirits with various degrees of malevolence.

12. The late Peter Katiyo, until his death on 4 November 2004, was the Chief Adviser to Chieftainess Chiawa. Katiyo kindly gave me his permission to identify him whenever he appeared in anything I wrote about Chiawa. A brave man, he was the principal antagonist of Chaka. See my account (Yamba 1997) of his humiliating encounter with the witchfinder.

13. During 2003 Chiawa suffered from drought and a failed harvest. The Italian government purchased maize from the Chiawa farm and commissioned an NGO to supply the local people with maize flour, the staple of the people, in a 'food-for-work' program. Each household would supply an able-bodied person to perform some communal task, the most common of which was filling potholes. At the end of the day, the household received food rations. While some villagers say that they would not have survived without this food-for-work program, others found it unfair and quite demeaning. There was also the fact that some households, such as those with aged grandparents caring for orphans or people who were ill, could not field a worker, and so did not receive food. I pointed out this important flaw to some of the NGOs administering the food-for-work program, and was told that they had planned for this. They depended on local headmen to identify the "most vulnerable" households, which then received help without fielding a worker. Phiri was prompt to point out that some headmen used this as an opportunity to punish difficult villagers or those they disliked by refusing to identify them as vulnerable. Furthermore, he pointed out that the Italian government had contracted the farm because the new owners were part Italian. This latter point is of course not quite relevant. It does not negate the fact that some people benefited from maize rations, even if one accepts that it might be humiliating to have to work for food.

14. On two occasions I found myself crossing the Kafue River ferry in a vehicle next to the Chieftainess's Land Cruiser, and we exchanged greetings and other pleasantries. I saw enough of her vehicle to ascertain that it did not contain live chickens and sacks of maize. The claim that she comes to her village to replenish an opulent life-style in Lusaka may not be quite true.

15. The seduction of pieces such as John Watkins's 1957 article, "Farewell to the Paradigm Case Argument," or Joseph Agassi's "Tristram Shandy, Pierre Menard, and All That: Comments on Criticism and the Growth of Knowledge" of 1971 was very huge indeed. Some of us saw such pieces as exemplifying a mode of analysis that was quite different from that advanced by the extended-case method. We were, of course, confusing two different academic traditions, as I must now concede.

# References

Bond, Virginia. 1995. "Emotions: What Are Young Women Looking for in Sexual Relationships in and around a Migrant Labour Camp?" Oral presentation, 5th National AIDS Conference, 8–10 May, Lusaka, Zambia. Unpublished typescript.

Bond, V., and S. Wallman. 1993. "Report on the 1991 Survey of Households in Chiawa: Community Capacity to Prevent, Manage and Survive HIV/AIDS." IHCAR/Hull/IAS, Working Paper, no. 5.

Brinn, P. J. 1996. "Cattle in Chiawa, 1994–96: The Results of Three Years of Monitoring." Regional Tsetse and Tryrenosomosis Control Programme (RTCCP). Ministry of Agriculture, Food and Fisheries.

Collingwood, R. G. 1956. *The Idea of History.* London: Oxford University Press.

Devons, Ely, and Max Gluckman. 1964. "Introduction." Pp. 13–19 in *Closed Systems and Open Minds: The Limits of Naïvety in Social Anthropology,* ed. Max Gluckman. Edinburgh: Oliver & Boyd.

Gluckman, Max. 1940. "The Kingdom of the Zulu of Southeast Africa." Pp. 25–55 in *African Political Systems,* ed. M. Fortes and E. E. Evans-Pritchard. London: Oxford University Press.

_____. 1958. *Analysis of a Social Situation in Modern Zululand.* Foreword by J. C. Mitchell. Rhodes-Livingstone Paper, no. 28. (Reprinted articles from *Bantu Studies,* 1940, and *African Studies,* 1942.) Manchester: Manchester University Press for the Rhodes-Livingstone Institute.

_____. 1960. "The Rise of a Zulu Empire." *Scientific American* 202, no. 4: 157–168.

_____. 1974. "The Individual in a Social Framework: The Rise of King Shaka of Zululand." *Journal of African Studies* 1, no. 2: 113–144.

Kapferer, Bruce. 1969. "Norms and the Manipulation of Relationships in a Work Context." Pp. 181–244 in *Social Networks in Urban Situations,* ed. J. Clyde Mitchell. Manchester: Manchester University Press.

Mitchell, J. Clyde. 1956. *The Kalela Dance.* Manchester: Manchester University Press.

Scudder, T. 1995. *A History of Development in the Twentieth Century: The Zambian Portion of the Middle Zambezi Valley and the Lake Kariba Basin.* Institute for Development Anthropology and California Institute of Technology.

Sontag, Susan. 1988. *Illness as Metaphor and AIDS and its Metaphors.* New York: Anchor Books.

Taylor, Stephen. 1994. *Shaka's Children: A History of the Zulu People.* London: Harper Collins.

Yamba, C. Bawa. 1997. "Cosmologies in Turmoil: Witchfinding and AIDS in Chiawa, Zambia." *Africa* 67, no. 2: 200–223.

*Chapter 10*

# THE POLITICS OF ETHNICITY AS AN EXTENDED CASE
## Thoughts on a Chiefly Succession Crisis

*Björn Lindgren*

There seems to have been a renewed interest in the works of the so-called Manchester School during the last decade, not least among anthropologists working in southern Africa (see, e.g., Crehan 1997; Englund 2001; Ferguson 1999). There are good reasons for this. At a time when the traditional ethnographic subject in the form of a pre-defined 'people' situated in a certain place at a certain time has been questioned, the focus on a 'social situation', a 'social field', or, especially, an 'extended case' has become appealing. By focusing on a series of social situations in an extended case, both spatial ('glocal') relations and temporal (past, present, and future) relations may be brought into a more open-ended social analysis.

---

Notes for this chapter begin on page 288.

This also holds for the study of ethnicity, even if it appears to have been somewhat neglected. Fredrik Barth (1969; 1994: 11) acknowledged Erving Goffman's and Edmund Leach's influence on his early works on ethnic identity, as well as that of their respective predecessors within the Chicago School and British 'corporate group theory'. But Barth did not refer to researchers within the Manchester School. Yet Anthony Cohen (1994: 59) has discerned seeds of Barth's social interactionist perspective on ethnicity in two research traditions in Britain—in the works of "some members of the Manchester School and of their unlikely bedfellow Edmund Leach" (see also Eriksen 1993: 36f.; Kapferer 1976; Paine 1974).[1]

In this chapter, I revisit the Manchester School in order to analyze the politics of ethnicity as an extended case. My example, a chiefly succession crisis involving a female chief in southern Zimbabwe, consists of an old topic in a new setting, wherein the media played an important role. Since Barth's writings on ethnicity in the late 1960s, it has almost become a truism to state that ethnic identity, although allegedly deeply rooted, is socially constructed in specific situations and instrumentally used in social boundary-making. But such statements have also been criticized in order to allow for more complex analyses of ethnicity. For the purposes of this essay, three objections are relevant.

Firstly, ethnic identification is not a priori a "basic" identification, as Fredrik Barth (1969: 13) once put it, but rather one of several possible identifications. Ethnic identity should therefore not be analyzed in isolation from other aspects of social life (see Fardon 1999: 74ff.). Whether ethnicity is more important than, for instance, nationality or gender in a given situation is a matter for empirical research. Moreover, ethnic identification may be difficult to separate from other kinds of identification. This makes an analysis of the relation between ethnicity and other categories of belonging highly relevant.

Secondly, if ethnic identifications are socially constructed in certain situations, these identifications and the situations in which they occur must themselves be situated (Verdery 1994: 36). One way of situating identifications is to put them in historical context, and one way of doing that is to study how subsequent state formations have formed subjects by ethnic and other categories over time (e.g., Bayart 2000). Such a study may cover a longer or shorter time span, but with the current theoretical focus within anthropology on twentieth-century colonization, modernity, and globalization, it may be refreshing to also apply a *longue durée* and incorporate pre-colonial state formations (cf. Lindgren 2004).

Thirdly, a focus on the making of social boundaries is important when studying the politics of ethnicity (Barth 1969; 1994; 2000: 30, 32f.), but so is the 'cultural stuff' that Barth and his colleagues once downplayed in their analyses of ethnicity, that is, the shared ideas, experiences, and feelings that people employ when drawing social boundaries (e.g., Burnham 1996; Cohen 2000b, 2000c; Eriksen 1991). Ideas about origin, kinship, and gender are perceived as something real as they pass through concrete ascendant, collateral, and descendant persons in a family (Roosens 1994: 86). In this context, research on memory work is important, whether these memories are based on information from personal experiences or on information distributed via oral and written media.

To a certain degree, the extended-case method may tackle the three weak points of the Barthian perspective on ethnicity. There are historical reasons for this. For many Manchester scholars, the task was not to explore mental or social structures, but rather to analyze how people use social categories, kinship genealogies, and other devices to reach personal and political ends in given settings (e.g., Mitchell 1956; Turner 1957; van Velsen 1964). In opposition to Claude Lévi-Strauss's and Edmund Leach's structuralism, Gluckman and his students emphasized social practice rather than logical system (Gluckman 1961; Kapferer 1987). And in reaction to A. R. Radcliffe-Brown's structural functionalism, they focused on specific individuals causing social change rather than on social persons upholding social structures (van Velsen 1967; Werbner 1984).

In the following, I first introduce the case of Sinqobile Mabhena, that is, the chiefly succession crisis in Zimbabwe, and the socio-cultural environment in which it occurred. Thereafter, I describe some of the events that eventually led to the installation of the female chief, before I turn to how critics of the installation viewed it as being imposed upon the Ndebele. I then nuance this description by relating ethnicity to nationality in the form of how memories of earlier government-controlled violence influenced people's views; to a discussion of the chief's origin; and to the question of gender relations through an analysis of the gender order in southern Zimbabwe. Finally, I return to the usefulness of analyzing ethnicity as an extended case, and how it may improve the three drawbacks of the Barthian perspective.

## The Mabhena Chiefs and the Ndebele Conglomerate

In December 1996, Sinqobile Mabhena was the first woman to be installed as Ndebele chief in Zimbabwe. She had been appointed to rule over the Nswazi area in Umzingwane District by President Robert Mugabe a year earlier, but the installation had been postponed because of protests. When the installation was carried out in spite of the protests, it caused an outcry that was ventilated in two newspapers, the *Chronicle* and the *Sunday News*, based in the city of Bulawayo. To have a woman as chief was against Ndebele culture and tradition, the critics argued. It was unheard of to have a woman rule men.

However, 'Ndebele', the term that is commonly used when referring to the people in southern Zimbabwe, came about due to a nineteenth-century migration from today's South Africa and includes a conglomerate of people of different origins. When the founder of the Ndebele state, Mzilikazi Khumalo, left Shaka Zulu in South Africa and migrated northwards in the 1820s, he was joined by Nguni-speakers like himself. During the migration, Sotho-speakers were incorporated into the kingdom. Still later, when Mzilikazi settled in today's Matabeleland in southern Zimbabwe, yet other people were included, among them those who are today referred to as Shona-speakers (see, e.g., Cobbing 1976).

As a consequence, Ndebele today may be of, for example, Nguni, Sotho, or Shona origin, depending on who their ancestors were at the time of their incorporation into the Ndebele state. Such categories of belonging are constantly used in Matabeleland, often in a hierarchical manner. While the Nguni form a kind of aristocracy, people of Shona origin are more often considered as commoners. People also tend to arrange these and other categories of origin hierarchically according to an older caste-like division. People of Nguni origin are then termed 'Zanzi', the highest caste. People of Sotho origin are referred to as 'Enhla', and those of Shona origin as 'Lozwi' or, pejoratively, 'Holi' (slaves).

In order to control the office as chief, various actors played on ethnic and other categories of belonging before, during, and after the installation. Apart from the use of ethnic categories (Lindgren 2005), people also referred to the internal division of the Ndebele based on origin, and debated different traditions of chiefly succession order. Further, they played on categories based on gender and kinship (Lindgren 2001). Although Sinqobile Mabhena eventually was installed as chief, the debate has continued up the present, and will continue to do so for many years to come.

Like most Ndebele chiefs, Sinqobile Mabhena and her family are of Nguni origin. The Mabhena settled at Umzingwane River together with Mzilikazi Khumalo's *amatshetshe* regiment in the 1840s. This settlement was governed by Sifo Masuku and his male descendants from the 1870s onwards; however, it became too vast to rule. In 1910, Ndamoya Mabhena was asked to take over the Nswazi part of the settlement as the first Mabhena chief.[2] Although Nswazi and Umzingwane District belonged to the Ndebele 'inner state' rather then the 'tributary state' (Cobbing 1976, 1977), its inhabitants were of various origins. In the vocabulary used in Matabeleland today, some were Nguni and some were Sotho, but many were Shona (Karanga and Kalanga) who had inhabited the land long before the Khumalo, Masuku, and Mabhena arrived.

Like other chiefs, Sinqobile Mabhena holds meetings and courts, where she informs Nswazi people about political decisions and tries to solve disputes. In addition to the headman and the kraal heads, she has six advisers who help her.[3] Headmen often try to solve disputes themselves before the matter reaches the chief. The subjects of these disputes include cases of divorce, ownership of cattle, and land conflicts. Both chiefs and headmen are authorized to assess fines. The chief is also a member of the District Council, which is otherwise made up of elected councilors. Ten chiefs also sit in the Parliament. They are sometimes referred to as the House of Chiefs. For their work, both chiefs and headmen receive allowances from the state.[4]

## The Installation of Chief Mabhena

Originally, Sinqobile Mabhena was supposed to have been installed as chief in 1995. The former chief, Howard, died in September 1993, and the Mabhena family recommended to the district administrator (DA) in August 1994 that Howard's eldest daughter, Sinqobile, should be named as his successor. Sinqobile was then 22 years old and the eldest of four sisters. After formal inquires, the DA forwarded this recommendation to the provincial administrator in June

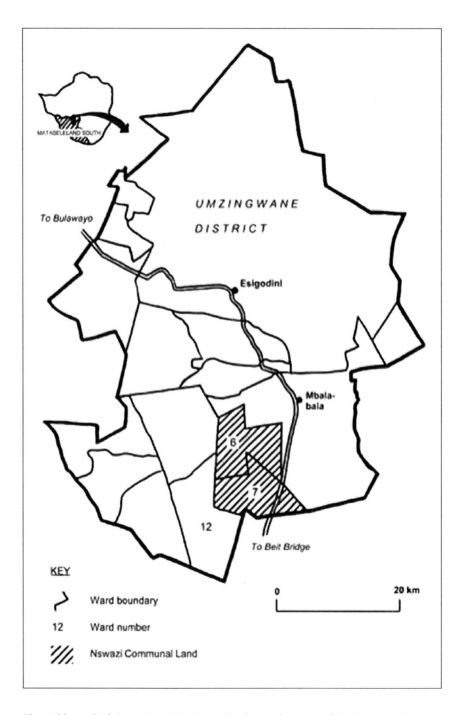

The Mabhena chieftaincy, Nswazi, is situated in the southern part of Umzingwane District, Matabeleland South, in southern Zimbabwe.

1995. The president approved the recommendation the same month, and the official installation was scheduled to be held in November 1995.[5]

At Howard's burial in 1993, Sinqobile, as his first-born, 'stood for' him at his grave. To stand for one's father (*ukuma ubaba whake*) is normally done by the eldest son; that is, the son stands by the head of the deceased with his father's knobkerrie (cane) and other regalia to show that he is now the head of the family. Howard had no son, however, and when Sinqobile stood for her father, this was a clear indication that the Mabhena family had her in mind as Howard's successor. Rather than choosing the late chief's half-brother or another male relative as successor, or reviving the late chief's lineage by arranging the birth of a son, the Mabhena nominated a daughter of the chiefly lineage.[6]

A few weeks before the scheduled installation in 1995, however, several chiefs in southern Zimbabwe protested. A meeting was held at which the chiefs said that in the Nguni sub-tribe, in which they placed the Mabhena clan, there was no history of a female chief. The chiefs argued that instead of Sinqobile, her grandfather's younger half-brothers should be considered for the chieftaincy. The meeting concluded that the Mabhena family should discuss the matter with Chief Augustin Masuku, whose forefather left Nswazi for Gwanda and handed over Nswazi to the first Mabhena chief in 1910, and that Sinqobile should be suspended until they had agreed upon a successor.[7]

However, the DA, John Dhlamini, never suspended Sinqobile. "I don't get instructions from meetings," he explained. "I get instructions from the minister of local government, comrade [John] Nkomo, through the secretary, through the provincial administrator. So I refused." But despite letters to superiors asking how to proceed, Dhlamini received no instructions. The part of the Mabhena family that supported Sinqobile then formed the Mabhena Committee and wrote to the DA, informing him that they still regarded Sinqobile as the rightful successor and complaining that the chiefs were "talking against the people."

In May 1996, the chiefs held a second meeting in Nswazi with some members of the Mabhena family. This meeting agreed that Sinqobile's grandfather's half-brothers, Anderson Mabhena and Kefazi Mabhena, were next in line of succession. Since the Mabhena Committee had been excluded from the meeting, they wrote a letter directly to the minister and complained about the interference of chiefs. The committee also contacted the press, after which several articles were published in the *Chronicle* and the *Sunday News*.[8]

Finally, after three meetings with the chiefs and the Mabhena Committee, Minister Nkomo decided the issue in November 1996. Although a chief walked out in the middle of one of these meetings, and many of the other chiefs were upset, it was decided that Sinqobile Mabhena was to be installed as chief on 21 December 1996. Some thought that with this decision, public debate would come to an end. Discussions were intensified, however, with chiefs and intellectuals protesting louder than ever, both in the daily press and in public forums, including a debate on the issue held at the City Hall in Bulawayo.[9]

Chief Khayisa Ndiweni, the most senior chief in Matabeleland, and several other chiefs stood by their earlier critique that it is against Ndebele culture and tradition to have a woman as chief and did not attend the installation ceremony

(*Chronicle*, 27 December 1996; *Sunday News*, 22 December 1996).[10] Governor Welshman Mabhena of Matabeleland North argued that the case should be taken to the High Court, adding: "As Ndebeles we are not going to allow our culture to be abused by anyone. Whatever has so far taken place is a mockery of our culture, which we will fight to the bitter end" (*Sunday News*, 19 January 1997).[11] Agrippa Ngwenya, secretary-general of the Vukani Mahlabezulu Cultural Society, argued that the installation should be nullified, since it was carried out over the objections of "Ndebele traditional leaders" (*Sunday News*, 26 January 1997).[12]

## President Mugabe and Ndebele Tradition

Many of the chiefs and intellectuals who opposed Sinqobile Mabhena as chief blamed President Mugabe, the Zanu-pf government, and the Shona majority in Zimbabwe for imposing a female chief upon them. Although traditional leaders such as chiefs and headmen may be superior to elected politicians locally, they are subordinated to them nationally since their recommendation of successor travels upwards in the state bureaucracy: first to the district administrator, then to the provincial administrator, then to the minister of local government, and finally to the president, who officially appoints the chief. The critics felt that at one stage or another during this process, senior chiefs should have been consulted about the appropriateness of appointing Sinqobile Mabhena as chief.[13]

When I talked with Chief Khayisa Ndiweni, for instance, he blamed the Zanu-pf government and the Shona in general for imposing a female chief upon the Ndebele: "We have our own rules, which should not be broken by the government. There is a House of Chiefs in this country. Ten of us are in Parliament. If there is something which goes against tradition, we discuss it. Why did they bypass the House of Chiefs? ... Why is it done in Matabeleland when it is not done in Mashonaland? It is not done in Manicaland. We know it is a defeat of the Ndebele people by the Shona people."

The legal principle that the critics cited to justify the chiefs' interference is found in the Chiefs and Headmen Act (1982: 3:1, 2), which is repeated in the Traditional Leaders Act (1998: 3:1, 2). According to this act, "The president shall appoint chiefs to preside over communities." When doing so, however, "the president shall give due consideration to the customary principles of succession, if any, applicable to the community over which such chief is to preside." The critics claimed that such consideration should have been taken, regardless of personal opinion.

Agrippa Ngwenya held: "It is not a matter of what I think, but of what culture says. It is taboo that a woman becomes a chief in our culture. Let's suppose she gets married to a Shona man. That means that the chieftainship would be removed from the Mabhenas and transferred ... to another tribe. But here we are. A woman chief has been imposed against our culture." And Pathisa Nyathi, a locally renowned indigenous historian, claimed: "The tradition according to which the chief is appointed must be stated. Ndebele tradition is very clear on that, whether it is progressive or counter-progressive is neither here nor there. It is always a male line, and even then it is not smooth. There are contentions because the seniority of houses differs."

Ndebele people felt threatened by the installation of Sinqobile Mabhena because President Mugabe and the Zanu-pf government, as well as the Shona, were seen as making crucial decisions without taking into account what Ndebele spokesmen said or did. From the critics' point of view, the president did not "give due consideration to the customary principles of succession," and when Ndebele chiefs and intellectuals tried to put things straight at meetings and in the media, they were ignored. The argument that it is against Ndebele culture and tradition to have a female chief was, in this context, not primarily directed against the Mabhena family's original recommendation of a female chief, but rather against the politicians' decision and the administrators' work to appoint and install her.

## Memories of the Fifth Brigade's Atrocities

A principal reason for the reactions against the president, the government, and the Shona is that people still remember that Mugabe and the Zanu-pf government sent the notorious Fifth Brigade to Matabeleland in the 1980s. Both Robert Mugabe and Joshua Nkomo, as leaders of Zimbabwe liberation organizations, helped bring about an end to colonialism. Zimbabwean nationalism sprang from this struggle for independence. However, after Mugabe and Zanu-pf's victory in the 1980 elections, Ndebele-speakers in southern Zimbabwe were excluded from continuing the national project.

A few years after independence, the Zanu-pf sent the North Korean-trained Fifth Brigade to deal with so-called dissidents in Matabeleland. In reality, they targeted the political opposition, Nkomo's Zapu Party, and its supporters. In this conflict, a politics was conducted in which ethnicity was central (see, e.g., Yap 2001). Shona-speaking soldiers were used against Ndebele-speaking civilians, and thousands of people in Matabeleland were murdered. Joshua Nkomo, who had strong support in Matabeleland, was expelled from the Zimbabwean government and later forced into exile in Britain.

Today, memories of the political violence since independence, and especially of the Fifth Brigade's atrocities in the 1980s, are a strong undercurrent in many people's self-perception as Ndebele. In Umzingwane District, and indeed in other parts of Matabeleland (see, e.g., Alexander, McGregor, and Ranger 2000), many Ndebele-speakers regard the Fifth Brigade's actions as directed not toward the dissidents but toward the Ndebele and Zapu.

Increased self-perception as Ndebele is expressed in several ways, for instance, through the formation of Ndebele movements and political parties. One example is Zapu 2000, a political movement that was dissatisfied with the Zanu-pf government's 'discrimination' against the Ndebele and that unsuccessfully ran as a political party in the parliamentary elections in 2000. Similar expressions exist in the countryside. At a chiefs' meeting in Umzingwane District in 2001, participants gathered money to arrange workshops on Ndebele culture for youth, and in 2002, they planned a cultural festival with visiting chiefs from South Africa.

With this background, the chiefs' and intellectuals' reactions toward the president, the Zanu-pf government, and the Shona is more understandable. Prior to the parliamentary elections in June 2000, people related that the Fifth Brigade "was sent to kill the *amaNdebele*," that Mugabe "wanted one party only," and that the Brigade "came here to kill people only, to destroy their homelands." Such statements were also made by the opposition party, MDC, in its political rhetoric prior to the presidential election in March 2002. In both elections, MDC received many votes in southern Zimbabwe.

Mugabe's and Zanu-pf's political strategy of sending Shona-speaking soldiers to Matabeleland thus provoked a cultural 'resistance', in Caroline Nordstrom's (1997) sense of the word, that led to a re-creation and strengthening of Ndebele ethnicity. This has made the Fifth Brigade's atrocities in 1983 and 1984 constitutive of Ndebele ethnicity today. Men and women in southern Zimbabwe have reorganized the categories 'Shona' and 'Ndebele' and filled them with new meanings, portraying Shonas as perpetrators of violence and Ndebeles as victims (Lindgren 2003).

## Negotiating Origin: Nguni and Sotho Succession

The Mabhena family was not at all inactive during the discussions following their choice of successor. Apart from forming the Mabhena Committee, writing directly to minister John Nkomo, and contacting the press, Sinqobile also paid a visit to the Zhilo Shrine to seek acceptance as chief from the high god Mwali. "It is Mwali who gives chiefs their power," the caretaker of the shrine told me. "No one can contest her after that."

At one point, Sinqobile and some of her relatives even negotiated with their Nguni origin to avoid Nguni succession and marriage rules, which created much debate. As stated, the Mabhena family is of Nguni origin. At least, that was what people had taken for granted until Sinqobile Mabhena answered her critics in the press, saying, "I don't see what their problem is. We are not Nguni but Sutho, and under that culture, women can become chiefs as is the case with Ketso Mathe from Gwanda" (*Chronicle*, 18 May 1996b). If this was true, much of the critique against Sinqobile was misdirected. Since there already was a female Sotho chief in Matabeleland, the Mabhena could claim a different tradition.

The Ndebele succession rule, applied to Nguni chiefs, headmen, and ordinary people, follows the principles of patrilineality and patrilocality. The first-born son inherits his father's position and remains in the area in which he grows up, while daughters are incorporated into their husbands' families and move to their area of living. When a chief, or any other man, has two wives, they are ranked into the first or great house (*indluendala*) and the second or small house (*indluencane*). His successor should come from the first or great house. If he has more than two wives, they are ranked into the third house, and so on.

At this stage of events, Sinqobile Mabhena was not married, and anxieties about whom she might marry circulated wildly. Ndebele of Nguni origin practice clan exogamy. On that ground, Chief Khayisa Ndiweni explained to me, "We cannot allow the woman as chief. With us she can marry anyone." The chieftaincy would then move into another clan. The logic is that if Sinqobile Mabhena gives birth to a son, he would inherit her position as chief, but his father's *isibongo*, ancestral spirits, and cattle. Moreover, since daughters move to their husbands' area, Sinqobile herself might have to leave Nswazi when she marries, if she does not find a husband within her chieftaincy.[14]

However, if Sinqobile Mabhena was an Ndebele of Sotho origin, things would look different. Since Sotho-speakers allow endogamic marriages, the chieftaincy would not have to be transferred to another clan at marriage. In fact, many Ndebele, especially of Nguni origin, claim that Sotho will marry anyone. "I cannot marry a woman of the same totem," Agrippa Ngwenya of the Vukani Mahlabezulu Cultural Society said. "It is not allowed. The Sotho do it … She [Ketso Mathe] can marry another Mathe. It is no problem. That's where the key difference is."[15]

As it turned out, Sinqobile Mabhena's statement in the *Chronicle* was immediately challenged by historian Pathisa Nyathi, who wrote in a debate article: "Sinqobile Mabhena has claimed to be a Sotho. Very convenient indeed! Has she all along been calling herself Sotho? Or is it now convenient to claim to be Sotho in order to avoid an Ndebele custom that disqualifies her? For all I know, the Mabhenas, Mahlangus and the Khumalos are descended from one ancestor—Ndabezitha" (*Sunday News*, 30 June 1996b). Nyathi later told me, "They are not Sotho. The Mabhena are Nguni. They became Sothos only for convenience. I belong to Ketso [Mathe]'s tribe, and we don't have Mabhenas in our tribe." He also argued that there is a vast difference between the people living under Chief Mabhena in Nswazi and those living under Chief Mathe. While the Nswazi area belonged to the pre-colonial Ndebele 'inner state', Chief Mathe's area, toward the border of South Africa, belonged to the 'tributary state' (cf. Cobbing 1976). As a consequence, most people living in Nswazi today, regardless of their origin, speak *isiNdebele* as their first, and sometimes only, language. Most people in Chief Mathe's area, however, speak *seSotho* as their first language, and have to a large degree also maintained their Sotho culture, including the succession order of chiefs.

## Sinqobile Mabhena as an *Indunakazi*

Apart from instigating debate on ethnic versus national belonging and different succession rules depending on origin, the installation of Chief Mabhena also brought to the fore the issue of gender order in southern Zimbabwe. We may focus on three areas when describing this order: power relations, marriage, and division of labor (cf. Connell 1987, 1995, 2000). In Matabeleland, power relations often go hand in hand with marriage and the division of labor. The husband represents the family in public meetings, and the wife is responsible for

### The Succession Order of the Mabhena Chiefs in Nswazi

**Ndamoya** (from 1910)

**Mpetshengwa**

| House 1: | House 2: | House 3: | House 4: |
|---|---|---|---|
| MaMguni | MaNtini | MaTshabangu | Mathobela |
| **Makheyi** (1947) | Mbuzi | Msundwa | Kefazi |
| | (deceased) | (deceased) | |
| **Howard** (1975) | | Shadrek | |
| | | (deceased) | |
| **Sinqobile** (1996) | | Anderson | |

The critics of Sinqobile followed the Mabhena family tree back to find an alternative candidate who was more in line with what, they argued, is Ndebele culture and tradition. Howard's only brother Milton is ill, and their father Makheyi, who lost his position as chief during colonialism, refuses to become chief again. The critics therefore started their search for an appropriate candidate in Makheyi's father Mpetshengwa's polygamous household. His four Nguni wives were then ranked according to marriage sequence into four houses, of which the first is the one to which Makheyi, Howard, and Sinqobile belong. These houses are, first, MaMguni, second, MaNtini, third, MaTshabangu, and fourth, Mathobela. Basing their choice on the rules of seniority, the critics presented their candidates: Anderson was ranked first, followed by Kefazi.

most of the domestic work. Men and boys herd cattle and goats, and women take care of children. Men slaughter cows; women slaughter chickens. Both men and women farm, but women prepare, cook, and serve the food. Men may collect firewood, but this is mainly the woman's task. She also collects water, washes clothes, and does the dishes.

As a female chief, Sinqobile Mabhena did not follow the established gender order in Matabeleland or the gender regime within traditional leadership. Instead, her installation as chief threatened to change both by reversing the structures of power, marriage, and labor. Robert Connell (1987: 91ff.) defines these structures as "patterns of constraint on (individual) practice in specific situations." This definition is a bit narrow, since structures are also used by actors—in this case, chiefs and intellectuals—to achieve personal or political goals. However, from Sinqobile Mabhena's point of view, her installation as chief was indeed a situation in which practice was constrained by these structures.[16]

As in many other rural areas in Matabeleland, the homestead in Nswazi is related to the traditional leadership structure with the man standing above the woman. There is a saying in *isiNdebele* that the man is the head of the household (*Indoda yinhloko yomuzi*). These words are sometimes used by a man when he wants to end a quarrel with his wife by reminding her that she should respect him, and these words were also used by critics opposed to Sinqobile as chief. In the same way as a wife should respect her husband, the head of a homestead should respect the kraal head (*usobhuko*), who in turn should respect the headman (*umlisa*), who in turn should respect the chief (*induna*).

An *induna*, as the term implies, is the most respected man within the traditional leadership structure—but now the *induna* is a woman. This led some of Sinqobile Mabhena's subjects to jokingly claim that the dictionaries must be rewritten. Linguistically, the term *induna* is connected to maleness and men. The adjective *-duna* means 'male', while the prefix *in-* turns it into the noun "chief, officer, captain" (see Pelling 1971). As a chief, they told me, Sinqobile Mabhena is an anomaly, something that does not fit the linguistic categories in *isiNdebele*. A new word with the feminine suffix *-kazi* must therefore to be added to the dictionaries: *indunakazi*, meaning female chief.

How should one behave toward this *indunakazi*? As one would toward a chief or as one would toward a woman? Should one greet her as a superior or as an inferior? Should one eat together with her, normally a great honor if the chief is a man, or should one refuse, since men normally do not eat together with women, at least not in public settings. And what happens if she marries? Is she superior or inferior to her husband? And who will succeed her? In meetings, should one talk after her as her subject, or should one talk before her as a man?

The installation of Sinqobile Mabhena as chief caused a lot of anxieties. It challenged the established gender order in Matabeleland, as well as a gender regime within a traditional leadership structure almost totally controlled by men. When chiefs and intellectuals say that the installation of Sinqobile Mabhena is against Ndebele culture and tradition, that they will take it to the High Court, and that they want to nullify it, they are thus not only criticizing the Zanu-pf government and the Mabhena family. They are simultaneously defending the gender order and regime within traditional leadership. A gender order, however, is always subject to change.

## Changing the Gender Order in Matabeleland

Unlike the many chiefs and intellectuals who were critical of the installation of Sinqobile Mabhena as chief, and contrary to most of what was published in the *Chronicle* and the *Sunday News*, many of the people in Nswazi, both men and women, supported the branch of the Mabhena family that had chosen Sinqobile as chief. This was already obvious in June 1994, when the Mabhena family publicly announced their choice of successor. Sinqobile was accepted as the rightful heir of her father, Howard, at a meeting where she was paraded in front of headman Absalom Ndlovu, 17 kraal heads, and 256 registered subjects.[17]

The reasons given by people in Nswazi for their support were many, dealing with culture and tradition, equal rights, and the capabilities of a chief. In the background, however, was an identification with the Nswazi chieftaincy, and a desire to defend their own chiefly family, which was under attack by other chiefs and outsiders.

Contrary to the claims of Khayisa Ndiweni, Welshman Mabhena, and Agrippa Ngwenya, some Nswazi people argued that culture had indeed been followed by pointing out that "a chief begets a chief" (*induna izala induna*). According to these people, Sinqobile Mabhena is the correct chief since she, like her predecessors, is the first-born within the great house (*indlu endala*). "It's obvious according to Ndebele culture that the heir should come from the first house," said Mrs. Sibanda, a farmer in her fifties. "The second wife is just a girlfriend," she added with reference to Sinqobile's grandfather's half-brothers Anderson and Kefazi. Mark Nyoni, teacher and subsequently adviser to Sinqobile Mabhena, likewise held: "Welshman Mabhena was here and saw our culture taking place: Sinqobile standing at the grave holding a spear. They know that the one who stands at the father's grave according to our culture automatically takes over after him."

Others legitimated Sinqobile Mabhena's chieftaincy not by arguing that culture had been followed but by claiming that culture changes, sometimes comparing her with other female leaders. "These days we are living in a changing world," said Mrs. Hadebe, an elderly woman with beer-brewing as a specialty. "We have headmasters, MPs and governors who are women. There is no problem having a woman chief." Phelani Gumpi, a male farmer, likewise argued: "There are so many things that have changed in our culture ... The women had no rights ... Now we feel we are on the same level ... Queen Elizabeth is a woman. She is leading a whole country. Is it a problem?"

Some people also explicitly referred to equal rights between men and women as a way to legitimize their new chief. A Mrs. Ndlovu said, "Today we have equal rights, and we are now educated." A Mr. Dube commented, "It is a position wanted by men. I think they are power hungry." And a Mrs. Ngwenya held, "The law has given women rights, so it's okay." Mrs. Vainah Ndlovu, a farmer and former teacher in her forties, said: "There are always men, men, men. We women are downtrodden ... Men say chiefs are for men. I don't understand why they stick to it. Is it only my being a man or a woman? Is it not also a question of intelligence, the way I am, the way I listen to people?"

Among the various traditions that were invoked, the issue of succession principles was perhaps the most central. With the proposal of Sinqobile Mabhena as chief, the principle stating that the eldest son takes over after his father was interpreted in two ways, sometimes expressed by citing one of the two, in this instance, contradictory axioms: "The man is the head of the household' (*indoda yinhloko yomuzi*), and "A chief begets a chief" (*induna izala induna*). While the first proverb was referred to by chiefs and intellectuals who accepted the established gender order in Matabeleland and who felt threatened by a female chief, the other proverb was drawn upon by people who did not accept the gender order and who wished to change it.[18]

Who is going to succeed Sinqobile Mabhena is still an open question, but at least some people seem ready to have a second female chief in Nswazi. "When she steps down, the Mabhenas will sit down and choose a boy within the family," explained the elderly kraal head, Pahle Ndlovu, adding: "For myself, I see no problem if they choose another girl." Moreover, Sinqobile Mabhena is young, while Khayisa Ndiweni and the other critics are old. Fifty years from now, things may be different, as Mabhena spokesman Agrippa Ndlovu optimistically argued: "Some people are still very bitter about it. That's why you see all these stories in the newspapers, [but] in any revolutionary situation, once anything starts moving, it doesn't stop ... You can't go the other way. It's like trying to swim against the tide."

Indeed, in October 1997, Sinqobile Mabhena married Regiment Sibanda, a teacher in Nswazi, and in January 1998, she gave birth to their first child—a daughter named Nobulelo. In June 2000, they told me that from their perspective, Nobulelo could very well take over after her mother as chief. In that case, Nobulelo would simply be referred to as Chief Mabhena when acting as such, although she bears her father's *isibongo* Sibanda. However, others are more skeptical about such a development. Pathisa Nyathi, for instance, argued: "The chieftainship was given to a family, the Mabhena family, by the Masukus, and not to a Sibanda family ... It won't be easy at all for her offspring, any of them, to claim it. They have no basis at all, unless we change the laws, the rules, the traditions."

In 2002, Chief Mabhena gave birth to her second child, Sinentokozo, also a girl. This again evoked some discussion on who Chief Mabhena's heir should be. In general, however, people seem to have accepted Sinqobile Mabhena as chief. This also holds for many of the chiefs with whom Sinqobile collaborates. "I haven't met any serious problems," she said in November 2002, "although you never know what people say behind your back." The case, however, is not finished yet. "When I step down or die, the Mabhena family will sit down and decide who will take over," Sinqobile says. Before that, and after, many more events will have occurred.

Chief Sinqobile Mabhena and her daughter Nobulelo, 2000.

## Conclusion: Ethnicity and the Extended Case Revisited

George Marcus (1995: 110) sorts the Manchester School's extended-case method under the 'follow-the-conflict' approach in multi-sited ethnography. Rather than studying ethnicity as a characteristic of a pre-categorized people or in a geographically located village, the enactment of ethnicity may be more fruitfully studied in such a case. Ethnicity is formed and expressed in local and global processes simultaneously. By focusing on a social event or conflict, the study has its focal point in a web of social relations. From there, one may follow the actors participating in the event and, in different ways, depending on who the actors are and the issues that are at stake, end up at the local, national, and global levels.

As stated, this method has the potential to tackle the three weak points inherent in the Barthian social-constructivist perspective on ethnicity. Firstly, it enables the researcher to study ethnicity in relation to other social phenomena. In his research on southern Africa, one of Gluckman's mottoes was to study "the total context of the plural society" (Kuper 1973: 183). From this perspective, it was important to study not tribes as isolated units but rather relations between white and black, urban and rural, colonialist and African (cf. Kapferer 1987).

Kate Crehan (1997: 55ff.), however, has criticized Gluckman (1965) and others at the Rhodes-Livingstone Institute for separating colonizers from colonized and studying tribes as bounded units. Many of the first generation of Manchester scholars did focus on various tribes, and, in that way, were involved in the construction of ethnic groups.[19] However, this kind of critique also distorts some of the early Manchester studies that focused on the social field (cf. Werbner 1984: 159). In fact, with her focus on social relations in two communities, Crehan seems to be pretty close to this branch of the Manchester School. Early Manchester scholars, too, debated and criticized the use of tribes as units of study (see, e.g., Devons and Gluckman 1964: 15; van Velsen 1967: 145), and some did indeed study social relations in specific communities (e.g., Epstein 1958).

Secondly, the extended-case method makes possible the inclusion of an analysis of historical change. Preferably, this is done by paying attention to both social practice in a series of events and to larger historical processes. Attention to the former may pinpoint specific actors and their behavior in a sequence of events, while attention to the latter can put these actors, their behavior, and events into a wider historical context. By thus paying attention to both individual action and societal transformation, specific events may also be judged as typical or atypical in processes of continuity and change. Social interaction in specific events may either follow established patterns of behavior, such as a gender order, or go against and change these patterns.

In his frequently cited essay, "Analysis of a Social Situation in Modern Zululand," Gluckman (1940) initiated what was to become the extended-case method. In this essay, Gluckman analyzed a single day's events at the opening of a bridge in Zululand. Robert Thornton (1996: 151) writes: "Gluckman described boundaries as being at the center of the 'situation', defining interactions between missionaries, Zulu commoners, chiefs and kings, and various agents of the colonial state." Not only did Gluckman describe social interaction, he also put this interaction into the wider historical context of colonialism in southern Africa. Richard Werbner (1984: 162), however, comments: "No attempt was made to account for a micro history of events involving the individuals prior to that day. Nor were the actors' own definitions of the situation taken to be problematic."

Many Manchester scholars were interested not only in historical change as such but also in processes of modernization. James Ferguson has targeted this linear developmental thinking within the school. Several anthropologists at the institute viewed the changing political, economic, and social relations of the time as an African industrial revolution. They also argued that these developmental processes would make Africans full members of a "new world society" (Ferguson 1999: 2, 234). Rather than subscribing to the still widespread notion of development, Ferguson works with non-linear variation-centered models of social transformation, which, again, resonates quite well with the extended-case method. Such variation-centered models pay attention to the possible multiple outcomes of social interaction. The African industrial revolution never came to pass, and many Zambians in the Copperbelt today regard themselves as being globally disconnected rather than as belonging to a new world society.

Thirdly, by studying extended cases over time, we are able to take culture into account in social interaction. At least in his earlier works, Gluckman lacked an analysis of culture in the form of actors' previous experiences, intentions, and definitions of the situation. Here, the work of memory comes into the picture as guiding actors' behavior. Indeed, elaborations of the Manchester School's focus on the social situation have involved such ideas. Don Handelman (2005), for instance, has suggested that we should not only study social practice retrospectively as 'micro history', but that we should also study it prospectively by taking into account the intentions of actors.

In studying the politics of ethnicity as an extended case, the researcher has thus the possibility to relate ethnicity to other social phenomena, to put the use of ethnic and other categories into historical context, and to analyze culture's role in social boundary-making by analyzing the work of memory. If one wants to engage in what Sherry Ortner (1996: 2f.) calls "practice theory," research within the Manchester School may be as good a starting point as Ortner's suggested works by Pierre Bourdieu, Anthony Giddens, and Marshall Sahlins (ibid.: 3). Many Manchester anthropologists focused strongly on social interaction, but they quickly developed analyses of interaction in social situations into analyses of extended cases over time. Research topics and the world itself have changed since then, but the extended-case method revisited may be as valuable as it was half a century ago in tackling old dilemmas in new settings.

Björn Lindgren (1963–2004) received his BA in Journalism from Stockholm University, and his PhD in Cultural Anthropology from Uppsala University in 2002, for his study, "The Politics of Ndebele Ethnicity: Origins, Nationality, and Gender in Southern Zimbabwe." Björn's ongoing fieldwork was done in Matabeleland, Zimbabwe. His major research interests were in politics, ethnicity, gender, and local governance. At the time of his death, Björn held the position of Researcher at the Nordic Africa Institute. Among his publications are: "The Green Bombers of Salisbury: Elections and Political Violence in Zimbabwe" (2003); "The Internal Dynamics of Ethnicity: Clan Names, Origins, and Castes in Southern Zimbabwe" (2004); and "Memories of Violence: Recreation of Ethnicity in Post-Colonial Zimbabwe" (2005).

## Notes

1. See also Kuper (1996: 135ff.) for how similarities in Gluckman's and Leach's otherwise distinct approaches later were merged in the works of Fredrik Barth and others.
2. Umzingwane District's administrative archive, Sinqobile Mabhena, Personal File 5. Julian Cobbing (1974; 1976: 70f.) has briefly described Sifo Masuku and the *amatshetshe* regiment in today's Umzingwane District, and refers to *amatshetshe* as one of the older regiments that originated in Zululand.
3. Normally, chiefs and headmen each have six advisers—elderly men representing different families and areas within the chieftaincy or headmanship. Sinqobile Mabhena, however, has three male and three female advisers.
4. The chiefs' and headmen's allowances were greatly increased by the Zanu-pf government as a result of implementing the Traditional Leaders Act in January 2000, which led to a relative shift of power from elected politicians to traditional leaders at the local level. This has been seen by some as a means for Zanu-pf to buy votes from influential leaders in the rural areas for the general elections held in June 2000.
5. Behind the Mabhena family's recommendation to install Sinqobile as chief was a family conflict in which Sinqobile's grandfather and mother argued strongly that the chieftaincy should remain within the first house of the Mabhena family; that is, the chief should come from the grandfather's line of descent rather than from one of his half-brother's lines of descent. Sinqobile's grandfather, Makheyi, lost his position as chief during the colonial era, and considers himself as too old to take up the position of chief again, even if he were allowed to do so by the present government.
6. See Hughes and van Velsen (1954: 91f.) for succession rules in pre-colonial and colonial Matabeleland, and Gluckman (1950: 182f.) and Vilakazi (1962: 4) for succession rules in Zululand.
7. Umzingwane District's administrative archive, Sinqobile Mabhena, Personal File 5.
8. The *Chronicle* and the *Sunday News* carried a number of articles on the subject, including one in which the local Zanu-pf women's league supported Sinqobile as chief (*Sunday News*, 30 June 1996a). See, e.g., *Chronicle*, 16 May, 24 May, 3 June, 6 June, 9 September 1996, and 18 May 1996a, 1996b; *Sunday News*, 26 May, 24 October 1996, and 30 June 1996a, 1996b.
9. *Chronicle*, 27 December 1996, 21 January, 6 February, 1 March, 5 March, 12 March 1997. *Sunday News*, 22 December 1996, 19 January, 26 January, 2 February 1997.
10. See *Chronicle*, 16 May, 24 May 1996, and 18 May 1996a, and *Sunday News*, 30 June 1996b for reports on the chiefs' critique. The English terms 'culture' and 'tradition' are used synonymously in these articles. In Nswazi, people used the Ndebele term *isiko* (pl. *amasiko*) for both culture and tradition, and explained that *isiko* embraces both these

terms. In J. N. Pelling's (1971) Ndebele dictionary, the term 'culture' is not translated, while *isiko* is translated as "custom, tradition."

11. Welshman Mabhena is a cousin of Sinqobile's grandfather, Makheyi Mabhena.

12. The Vukani Mahlabezulu Cultural Society is based in Bulawayo and has as its general purpose to promote Ndebele culture. The society was formed in 1991. 'Vukani Mahlabezulu' is roughly translated as "Wake up people," with reference to the Ndebele as the people (referred to as the Zulu in the organization's name).

13. See, e.g., Welshman Mabhena in *Sunday News*, 19 January 1997; Agrippa Ngwenya in *Sunday News*, 26 January 1997; and Pathisa Nyathi in *Sunday News*, 30 June 1996b.

14. Some of those within the Mabhena chieftaincy who were against Sinqobile as chief joked that in the worst-case scenario, the chieftaincy might be transferred to a Banda (Malawian) family. There are quite a few Malawian guest-workers in Nswazi, some of whom have settled permanently.

15. See also V. G. J. Sheddick (1953: 28f.), who has described Sotho clans as having totems but being non-exogamous.

16. The installation ceremony itself is structured for installing a man as chief, and the chief's regalia are meant for a man. This is in accordance with the belief in ancestral spirits, in which the paternal line of chiefly spirits is important for the whole community. At the installation ceremony, Sinqobile Mabhena wore, as her predecessors had, the skin of a leopard around her waist, but, as a woman, she also wore a bra. She also received the usual regalia from the government: a British colonial-style helmet, a red robe, and a knobkerrie. Women do not wear helmets, however, and at public meetings Sinqobile wears a scarf around her head.

17. Umzingwane District's administrative archive, Sinqobile Mabhena, Personal File 5.

18. For more examples of Nswazi people who supported Sinqobile Mabhena, see Lindgren (2001, 2005).

19. See, for instance, the Ethnographic Survey of Africa series published by the International African Institute, in which the Rhodes-Livingstone Institute was engaged. In this series, Hilda Kuper, A. J. B. Hughes and Jaap van Velsen (1954) wrote about the Shona and the Ndebele in Southern Rhodesia. On the one hand, Hughes's and van Velsen's focus on the Ndebele is problematic in that the Ndebele as a people are taken for granted as an object of research. On the other hand, they describe the internal stratification among Ndebele in quite a detailed way.

# References

Alexander, J., J. McGregor, and T. Ranger. 2000. *Violence and Memory: One Hundred Years in the Dark Forests of Matabeleland.* Oxford: James Currey; Portsmouth: Heinemann.

Barth, Fredrik. 1969. "Introduction." Pp. 9–38 in *Ethnic Groups and Boundaries: The Social Organization of Culture Difference,* ed. F. Barth. Oslo: University Press.

_____. 1994. "Enduring and Emerging Issues in the Analysis of Ethnicity." Pp. 11–32 in Vermeulen and Govers 1994.

_____. 2000. "Boundaries and Connections." Pp. 15–36 in Cohen 2000a.

Bayart, J.-F. 2000. "Africa in the World: A History of Extraversion." *African Affairs* 99: 217–267.

Burnham, Philip. 1996. *The Politics of Cultural Difference in Northern Cameroon.* London: Edinburgh University Press.

Chiefs and Headmen Act. 1982. The Government of Zimbabwe.

Cobbing, Julian. 1974. "The Evolution of Ndebele Amabhuto." *Journal of African History* 15, no. 4: 607–631.

_____. 1976. "The Ndebele under the Khumalos, 1820–1896." Unpublished thesis. Lancaster University.

_____. 1977. "The Absent Priesthood: Another Look at the Rhodesian Risings of 1986/7." *Journal of African History* 18: 61–84.

Cohen, Anthony. 1994. "Boundaries of Consciousness, Consciousness of Boundaries: Critical Questions for Anthropology." Pp. 59–79 in Vermeulen and Govers 1994.

_____, ed. 2000a. *Signifying Identities: Anthropological Perspectives on Boundaries and Contested Values*. London: Routledge.

_____. 2000b. "Introduction: Discriminating Relations: Identity, Boundary, and Authenticity." Pp. 1–14 in Cohen 2000a.

_____. 2000c. "Peripheral Vision: Nationalism, National Identity and the Objective Correlative in Scotland." Pp. 145–169 in Cohen 2000a.

Connell, Robert. 1987. *Gender and Power*. Cambridge: Polity Press.

_____. 1995. *Masculinities*. Berkeley: University of California Press.

_____. 2000. *The Men and the Boys*. Cambridge: Polity Press.

Crehan, Kate. 1997. *The Fractured Community: Landscapes of Power and Gender in Rural Zambia*. Berkeley: University of California Press.

Devons, Ely, and Max Gluckman. 1964. "Introduction." Pp. 13–19 in *Closed Systems and Open Minds: The Limits of Naïvety in Social Anthropology*, ed. Max Gluckman. Chicago: Aldine.

Englund, Harri. 2001. *From War to Peace on the Mozambique-Malawi Borderline*. Edinburgh: Edinburgh University Press.

Epstein, A. L. 1958. *Politics in an Urban African Community*. Manchester: Manchester University Press.

Eriksen, Thomas Hylland. 1991. "The Cultural Context of Ethnic Differences." *Man* 26, no. 1: 127–144.

_____. 1993. *Ethnicity and Nationalism: Anthropological Perspectives*. London: Pluto Press.

Fardon, Richard. 1999. "Ethnic Pervasion." Pp. 64–81 in *The Media of Conflict: War Reporting and Representations of Ethnic Violence*, ed. T. Allen and S. Jean. London: Zed.

Ferguson, James. 1999. *Expectations of Modernity*. Berkeley: University of California Press.

Gluckman, Max. 1940. "Analysis of a Social Situation in Modern Zululand." *Bantu Studies* 14: 1–30.

_____. 1950. "Kinship and Marriage Among the Lozi of Northern Rhodesia and the Zulu of Natal." Pp. 166–206 in *African Systems of Kinship and Marriage*, ed. A. R. Radcliffe-Brown and D. Forde. London. Oxford University Press.

_____. 1961. "Ethnographic Data in British Social Anthropology." *Sociological Review* 9, no. 1: 5–17.

_____. 1965. *Politics, Law, and Ritual in Tribal Society*. Oxford: Basil Blackwell.

Handelman. Don. 2005. "Microhistorical Anthropology: Toward a Prospective Perspective." Pp. 29–52 in *Critical Junctions: History and Anthropology beyond the Cultural Turn*, ed. D. Kalb and H. Tak. New York: Berghahn Books.

Hughes, A. J. B., and J. van Velsen. 1954. "The Ndebele." Pp. 86–110 in Kuper, Hughes, and van Velsen 1954.

Kapferer, Bruce. 1976. Introduction: Transnational Models Reconsidered. Pp. 1–22 in *Transaction and Meaning: Directions in the Anthropology of Exchange and Symbolic Behavior*, ed. B. Kapferer. Philadelphia: Institute for the Study of Human Issues.

_____. 1987. "The Anthropology of Max Gluckman." *Social Analysis* 22: 3–21.

Kuper, Adam. 1973. *Anthropologists and Anthropology: The British School 1922–72*. London: Allen Lane.

_____. 1996. *Anthropology and Anthropologists: The Modern British School*. London: Routledge.

Kuper, Hilda, A. J. B. Hughes, and Jaap van Velsen. 1954. *The Shona and Ndebele of Southern Rhodesia*. Ethnographic Survey of Africa: Southern Africa. London: International African Institute.

Lindgren, Björn. 2001. "Men Rule, but Blood Speaks: Gender, Identity, and Kinship at the Installation of a Female Chief in Matabeleland, Zimbabwe." Pp. 177–194 in *Changing Men in Southern Africa*, ed. R. Morrell. Pietermaritzburg and London: University of Natal Press, Zed Books.

_____. 2003. "The Green Bombers of Salisbury: Elections and Political Violence in Zimbabwe." *Anthropology Today* 19, no. 2: 6–10.

_____. 2004. "The Internal Dynamics of Ethnicity: Clan Names, Origins, and Castes in Southern Zimbabwe." *Africa* 74, no. 2: 173–193.

_____. 2005. "The Politics of Identity and the Remembrance of Violence: Ethnicity and Gender at the Installation of a Female Chief in Zimbabwe." Pp. 153–172 in *Violence and Belonging: The Quest for Identity in Post-Colonial Africa*. ed. V. Broch-Due. London: Routledge.

Marcus, George. 1995. "Ethnography in/of the World System: The Emergence of Multi-sited Ethnography." *Annual Review of Anthropology* 24: 95–117.

Mitchell, J. Clyde. 1956. *The Kalela Dance: Aspects of Social Relationships among Urban Africans in Northern Rhodesia*. Manchester: Manchester University Press.

Nordstrom, Carolyn. 1997. *A Different Kind of War Story*. Philadelphia: University of Pennsylvania Press.

Ortner, Sherry. 1996. *Making Gender: The Politics and Erotics of Culture*. Boston, MA: Beacon Press.

Paine, Robert. 1974. *Second Thoughts about Barth's Models*. London: The Royal Anthropological Institute.

Pelling, John. 1971. *A Practical Ndebele Dictionary*. Harare: Longman.

Roosens, Eugeen. 1994. "The Primordial Nature of Origins in Migrant Ethnicity." Pp. 81–104 in Vermeulen and Govers, 1994.

Sheddick, V. G. J. 1953. *The Southern Sotho*. Ethnographic Survey of Africa: Southern Africa. London: International African Institute.

Thornton, Robert. 1996. "The Potentials of Boundaries in South Africa: Steps Towards a Theory of the Social Edge." Pp. 136–161 in *Postcolonial Identities in Africa*. ed. R. Werbner and T. Ranger. London: Zed Books.

Traditional Leaders Act. 1998. The Government of Zimbabwe.

Turner, Victor. 1957. *Schism and Continuity in an African Society: A Study of Ndembu Village Life*. Manchester: Manchester University Press.

Van Velsen, Jaap. 1964. *The Politics of Kinship: A Study in Social Manipulation among the Lakeside Tonga of Nyasaland*. Manchester: University of Manchester Press.

_____. 1967. "The Extended-Case Method and Situational Analysis." Pp. 129–149 in *The Craft of Social Anthropology*, ed. A. L. Epstein. London: Tavistock Publications.

Verdery, Katherine. 1994. Ethnicity, Nationalism, and State-Making. Pp. 33–58 in Vermeulen and Govers 1994.

Vermeulen, H., and C. Govers, eds. 1994. *The Anthropology of Ethnicity: Beyond Ethnic Groups and Boundaries*. Amsterdam: Het Spinhuis

Vilakazi, Absalom. 1962. *Zulu Transformations: A Study of the Dynamics of Social Change*. Pietermaritzburg: University of Natal Press.

Werbner, Richard. 1984. "The Manchester School in South-Central Africa." *Annual Review of Anthropology* 13: 157–185.

Yap, Pohjolainen Katri. 2001. "Uprooting the Weeds: Power, Ethnicity and Violence in the Matabeleland Conflict, 1980–1987." PhD diss. Universiteit van Amsterdam.

*Chapter 11*

# FROM TRIBES AND TRADITIONS TO COMPOSITES AND CONJUNCTURES

*Sally Falk Moore*

## Gluckman on Gluckman

To revisit Max Gluckman's ideas about extended-case studies is to risk heaping commentary on commentary. Gluckman (1967) wrote about where he placed himself in the great parade of theoretical regimens, and Jaap van Velsen (1967) added a detailed methodological analysis, referring to the very same method as 'situational analysis'.

Gluckman opened by reviewing a short history of ethnography and by dismissing some of its ancestors. First, he says, there were the "superficial observations" of the late-nineteenth- and early-twentieth-century anthropologists, W. H. Rivers, C. G. Seligman, and A. R. Radcliffe-Brown (Gluckman 1967: xii). Gluckman could afford to dismiss them, for by the time he published this comment, not only were they all dead, but Malinowski, also dead, had initiated intensive fieldwork that was much admired by Gluckman. About Malinowski, Gluckman says that he raised "ethnographic fieldwork to a professional art" (1967: xiii). Gluckman asserts that Malinowski and the next generation of anthropologists, among whom Gluckman counted himself, used cases in two ways. In the first, they began their ethnographic work with classic techniques. We "made a large

References for this chapter are located on page 310.

number of observations on how our subjects actually behaved, we collected genealogies and censuses, made diagrams of villages and gardens, listened to disputes and quarrels … collected texts from informants about customs and rituals," and elicited indigenous commentaries on all of these matters. Having analyzed these data and constructed an outline of the social system and the general organization of the society, he then used selected cases as 'apt illustrations' of the points made. The second use of cases was quite different and proceeded in the opposite order. The case itself was the point of departure. Gluckman cites his famous paper ([1940] 1958) on the dedication of a newly built bridge, which he used to show how Zulu and white colonials were involved in a single social system. This was but a single instance and in no sense extended, but in its time it was a highly unorthodox and original approach. Gluckman did not follow it up, attributing this both to his fieldwork circumstances and to the limitations of analysis in his own generation (1967: xx). In fact, the dedication of the bridge was not an extended case at all. It was called a 'case', yet in the circumstances, it could more appropriately be called an 'event'. I shall be discussing both cases extended over time, and some time-limited events in this chapter.

An extended case consists of connected field observations collected over time in the same social field, while events may be more limited, one-time occasions. But events are not necessarily without an extended time dimension. When historically contextualized, events can be placed in a time frame longer than the moment they were observed in fieldwork. Thus, both extended-case studies and events may be infused with temporal dimensions. Fieldwork is likely to include both kinds of data. Mine certainly did. While I used many extended-case studies in my ethnography of Chagga lineages and villages (see Moore 1986), I have another purpose here.

What I propose to show in this essay is how numbers of quite disparate and seemingly disconnected small-scale events may sometimes be analytically combined to reflect instability and incipient change in a larger social structure, in this case the Tanzanian version of African socialism. Many of these events came my way more or less by chance while I was in Africa. In that sense they were unlike the more systematic study I undertook of local land-holding populations and local affairs in and out of the courts. The events referred to here could be treated as irrelevant to my central project, as random occurrences, as the social equivalent of electronic noise. Instead, I proceed on the postulate that nothing that happens is meaningless. However, what has connections with what is already known, and what has none, is not always clear. The significance of odd events that occur outside the domain of the immediate fieldwork project is not always self-evident. Do these odd events have a common thread? In this instance, abandoning extended-case studies for the moment, I shall argue that what appear to be disconnected occurrences link up with processes on the large scale. They point to locations of disturbance and instability in the practical operations of that supposedly consistently organized social 'system', African socialism.

In his introduction to Epstein's edited volume, *The Craft of Social Anthropology*, Gluckman calls on his successors to do more than take extended cases into account. He calls on them to study process (1967: xiv). In describing what he considers a further elaboration and development of the extended-case method, he says, "This new kind of analysis treats each case as a stage in an on-going process of social relations between specific persons and groups in a social system and culture ... A full analysis would continue to trace the relations within the specific groups involved back in time, and then forward, if possible" (ibid.: xv). With a respectful nod to van Velsen's article in the same volume, Gluckman says, "This kind of approach will greatly alter our view of the working of some institutions, and deepen our understanding of the significance of all custom" (ibid.). Then, disarmingly, Gluckman criticizes his own book, *The Judicial Process Among the Barotse of Northern Rhodesia* (1955), for having treated each case coming before the court as an isolated incident: "Yet each case was obviously but an incident in a long process of social relations ... I had not studied that process of social life ... here lies the next step ... the intensive study of the processes of social control in a limited area of social life viewed over a period of time" (ibid.: xvi).

One might have imagined that this urgent call for studies over time would have ushered in a new era of theoretical construction. Yet even then, in Gluckman's formulation, process was to be studied "in a limited area of social life viewed over a period of time." Gluckman had not completely broken away from his commitment to the analysis of the structure of "a limited area." He had tried to incorporate time into the picture, but still thought of the object of ethnography as a strictly bounded aspect of social life, that which Evens (personal communication) calls Gluckman's "analytical institutionalism."

But Gluckman must have had intimations that process might expand into broader fields. Hints of this are found in his remarks about a change in the relationship between the anthropologist and his informants, the fact that some informants could read what the anthropologist wrote and had definite opinions about being observed and commented on. He also warned (1967: xix): "[W]e are getting into a much less tidy era of research and analysis ... moreover as we appreciate that customs and values are to some extent independent of one another, discrepant, conflicting, contradictory, we shall have to evolve concepts to deal with social life which are less rigid and which can cope ... with the haphazard as well as the systematic."

What my essay will present is a particular example from my own experience in Tanzania of this changed scope of fieldwork analysis. As we shall see, I believe that the "limited area of social life" that Gluckman conceived of as the next step in fieldwork was much more circumscribed than it need have been. In my own fieldwork in Africa, I studied the work of local courts, and to get more of a sense of where the court cases originated, I followed the affairs of several lineages as they proceeded forward over the many years of my contact, reconstructing their past as best I could. But I still found that I had to go much further (Moore 1986). Localized lineages included a full range of households, from those of illiterate farmers to absent bureaucrats who left wives and children behind while they worked in the cities.

Extending my inquiries, I set out to discover what was going on outside the lineage and village on the large scale. The interdigitation of the national, state, and world economies with local systems was patent. I was not following Gluckman's definition of process as "the study of a limited area of social life viewed over a period of time." In fact, having known Gluckman well, I am sure that he would not have held to that definition himself, had the expanded case been put to him. When he made that remark, he was obviously thinking in terms of the anthropological models of tribal life of an earlier time. Yet in his own work he had addressed the effects of the colonial economy, labor migration, and the copper mines on Lozi life.

I moved on, abandoning entirely the notion of an isolated tribal community. I sifted glimpses of the 'state' in action, from colonial times to socialist and post-socialist days. I went beyond the ethnographically observable to seek out what records and interviews might reveal about the way missionaries, international commerce, and politics impinged on local life. Obviously, for example, the price of coffee is not determined in rural East Africa. I explored the dealings of the coffee cooperative and its history, since everyone sold their coffee through the cooperative, a legally decreed monopoly. I followed more than one process in parallel sequences of time, the administrative developments in government, the changes in church policy, the alterations of the judicial system, and the like. Some of this material was politically delicate. There were periods when Tanzania was not friendly to the United States. My fieldwork visits were of several months each, and I made many such visits over many years. It was therefore possible to follow the trails over time, not only by consulting records of the past, but by attending to changes and stabilities observable in the intermittent periods of current contact.

## Events: What Is Their Significance?

Gluckman's proposal that we look at cases over time was a radical departure from the earlier, conventional objective of ethnographic work—the exploration of custom. For the ethnographer today, the temporal perspective must be kept in the foreground, even when what is being observed is perceived to be a reproduction of the past. This has methodological consequences.

Given the fieldwork method, it follows logically that the only thing that can be observed in action is the present state of affairs. To the extent that it can be recovered, the history of the present state of affairs must also be sought. Are elements of the past really being reproduced? Is the context different so that even a fragment of the past is altered by having its contextual place in the scheme of things transformed?

What is being inspected in fieldwork is a moving thing, a society in process, located somewhere between the past and the future. From the perspective of process, events—mundane and extraordinary, local and large scale—are very useful pieces of evidence. Events, to the extent that they are the moving subsegments of process, can illumine parts of its trajectory.

Events that come along early in fieldwork can be used as objects of research, to discover what surrounds them, where they come from, who is involved, what they mean, how they happened to happen, and the like. Late in field-work, one can see events in other terms, as confirming or unsettling broader interpretations or understandings that have been developed. This is particularly useful in the construction of process, in supporting inferences about the connection between micro events observed locally and the understanding of the larger scale. The result is usually a tentative, partially substantiated notion of connections and tendencies and of processes in motion. This essay illustrates these propositions.

The problems with which I began my fieldwork were twofold. First, I wanted to study the impact of imposed, intentional, planned change in a social field. In East Africa I wanted to see how the post-independence policies of the Tanzanian state, referred to as African socialism, affected life on Kilimanjaro. Second, I wanted to examine the dynamics of change being generated in other ways, for example, by shifts in local demography, by pressures and opportunities presented by the world economy, by education, and by divergent and convergent innovations in individual practice. These were all processes in motion.

I considered that law would serve as an entry point for many of these topics. I thought it unlikely that the extended case, as Gluckman described it, would encompass these large-scale dimensions, though it might capture some of the goings-on at the local level. As Gluckman said, cases used to be used as apt illustrations of norms and customs already documented by other techniques. His advance, as he stood at the dedication of the bridge, was to see that event as a reflection of the fact that Africans and whites were part of the same social structure. It was not a processual analysis. It was static. But that event nevertheless constituted a major shakeup of the dominant mode of anthropology of the time, which was to treat African life as a separate, enclosed system. Notice that I use the word 'event' rather than 'case' as the unit to be analyzed. 'Event' has the implication of a time-specific happening. And that emphasis broadens and complicates the category to be examined.

From that point of view, a case extended in time consists of a sequence of events. The boundaries of an event or case are, of course, a function of the analytic purpose at hand; indeed, the selection of cogent events is part of the analysis. There can be reasons to divide the data in a chronicle or to keep them seamless, but time is not the only direction in which an event, or a case, can be extended. The extensions can go in other directions—for example, in social space. It is often interesting to know what is happening in other domains at the same moment. The social meanings of an event can be explored through its context, broadly understood.

In a time-oriented anthropology, events present the riddles of process to the ethnographer. But what Gluckman meant by process was special to his own interests. In The Judicial Process, he was talking about some "repeated unfoldings of events in an institutional context, and in a regular sequence" (Moore [1973] 2000: 43). His thesis was intended to apply beyond the ethnography of the Barotse. He was reaching for universals in judicial reasoning, believing that the same judicial processes occurred in other societies and other cultures. Similarly, Turner's The Ritual Process (1969) also had a generalizing, comparative ambition.

Today, the idea of process is often used as a much more open concept. Questions can be asked without necessarily being confined in advance to particular institutions. What is going on in this quarreling crowd in this market? How did the present state of affairs come about? What events and circumstances have impinged on the situation? If there are any clues, in what direction are matters developing? Is this sequential process repetitive, cyclic, unique?

Added to all the conventional techniques of fieldwork that serve as context, events and event sequences now deserve a foregrounded position. They can give clues to a moment in history that is the present. They hint at what is transitory and what is durable, what is situationally particular and what is general. They give clues to causality, one of the most vexed questions in social science. Events are easy to describe, but they are often much harder to understand.

Marshall Sahlins made his own proposal about how events should be understood and about the nature of process. In *Islands of History* (1985), with much charm and a great story to explain, Marshall Sahlins tried to solve the problem of the relation between events and structure—as he put it, between history and culture (ibid.: x). When and how do events change the content and course of culture? At the base of Sahlins's analytic premises is a Lévi-Straussian and Saussurean conception of culture defined as a set of meaningful categories. He attempts to go beyond those two theorists' static conception of the categories by introducing process and change. He says, "In its global and most powerful representation, structure is processual: a dynamic development of the cultural categories and their relationships" (ibid.: 77).

But the dynamism he postulates is about the use of cultural categories and the way each use, each application in action, becomes part of the baggage of categorical meanings, changes them, and hence rearranges their relation to other categories. He illustrates this process by narrating the misadventures of Captain Cook and the way these were caused by and received by Hawaiians. As is well known, his thesis was that Cook was interpreted at first to be the god Lono, of Hawaiian myth, and that when Cook reappeared on a second occasion, this was mythologically inappropriate, and he was killed. Sahlins says (1985: xiv): "An event becomes such as it is interpreted. Only as it is appropriated in and through the cultural scheme does it acquire an historical *significance.*"

Thus, for Sahlins, events matter because they enter the cultural scheme and modify it. Each practical action using the cultural scheme adds to or changes its meanings. In his lexicon, structure is "the symbolic relations of cultural order" (1985: vii). His interest is in the way each event, each action in practice, contributes to the burden of meaning carried by the cultural categories it refers to or employs. For Sahlins, the fundamental cultural categories of ritual and ceremony can be represented by persons, as was the case with Captain Cook (ibid.: 89). As he says, "And as the given category is revalued in the course of historic reference, so must the relationship between categories change: the structure is transformed" (ibid.: 31).

Sahlins's account of the process of symbolic alteration illuminates that dimension of change convincingly and shows how it is actualized. But Sahlins is playing the explanatory game with a limited number of variables of his own choosing, in which the system of cultural categories has primacy. But what if, as we will see in the case of the cultures of Kilimanjaro, there are multiple clusters of social and symbolic categories, all of them in motion, and some events that do not seem to have any clear reference to any of them. On Kilimanjaro there are a jumble of such 'systems': socialist thought, Lutheran religion, Catholicism, traditional Chagga ideas about everything from patrilineal kinship to supernatural interventions in daily life, and lots more. Could any of these be said to be dominant? Where is the equivalent of the Hawaiian myths on which Captain Cook ran aground?

In Gluckman's thought the fundamental facts are those of social, economic, and political relationships between and among people, not relationships between cultural categories. The closest Gluckman came to attending to cultural categories was in the large place he gave to custom—customary roles, customary behaviors, customary expectations. If the symbolic order is *not* taken to be the primary focus of analysis, and it certainly did not have primacy in Gluckman's thought, one is in a different intellectual domain from Sahlins's analysis of Captain Cook's story.

Events in the socio-political arena vary a great deal in their effects on the course of history. Most are mundane and trivial. Some move in a cumulative direction; others do not. The fieldwork anthropologist preoccupied with process does not necessarily expect to observe a particular transformative moment in which a basic socio-economic or political change is enacted. Such sudden marking events can happen, but they are not usually to be expected. Cumulative processes that are ongoing are more likely to be an accessible part of the fieldwork experience, for example, population increase, the broadening of educational opportunity, soil erosion, an increase in pressures from central government, the alteration of the 'customary', and so forth.

What is a process? I tried to answer this question 30 years ago (Moore [1973] 2000: 42–43). Before proceeding to process, some clarification is needed of related notions of structure (for a summary of the structure/process literature, see Vincent 1986). Structure for Sahlins, and for Lévi-Strauss, is symbolic structure, a symbolic *system*; however, most social anthropologists do not use the term that way. Firth (1964: 45–46), for one, thought of structure as "the persistent and invariant in social life." The processual, he called "social organization" meaning, in his scheme of things, all the decisions and choices that make up daily life, all the dynamic activities in which people engage. Nadel (1957: 97, 138, 153) considered structure to be an analytic abstraction sifted out of relatively ordered, relatively durable arrangements in social life. He pointed out, however, that in practice the orderliness and durability were imperfect.

I use the term 'structure' rather as Nadel does, but for 'process', I have several meanings: "The term is variously used in ethnographies: (1) to describe universal contexts of social contact such as processes of competition, or of cooperation, and the like; (2) to describe series of events that recur again and again in certain institutional contexts, such as political processes, economic processes, educational processes, and so on; and (3) to describe the kinds of circumstances that lead to certain results, such as the process of industrialization, the process of urbanization, the process of segmentation, the process of stratification, and so on" (Moore [1973] 2000: 42–43). In other words, process has more than one meaning in anthropology, but all of its meanings include the idea of social activity that takes place over time. From the start, I decided to take a processual approach to my own fieldwork, to look at everything as an occurrence in a historical moment. The situation on Kilimanjaro required such an approach, or rather, I chose to work on Kilimanjaro because I knew a certain amount of the history of the area was accessible.

## Fieldwork on Mount Kilimanjaro

For those of you who do not know my ethnographic work, I should say a few words of introduction. The fieldwork was on Mount Kilimanjaro in Tanzania, among a people who call themselves Chagga. I visited at many intervals between 1969 and 1993. I arrived with the idea of using the legal dimension as the organizing focus of my research, since many aspects of law were in full view. I was particularly interested in the reorganizing changes of socialism and in what was left of earlier legal arrangements, pre-colonial and colonial. The process of change and the durability of parts of the past were on the front burner of my academic stove. I knew from the missionary literature and some historical works that throughout the century there had been a well-documented conception of Chagga custom (Gutmann 1926). What I was to discover was that there were many old practices that were ongoing, many that were modified, many that were replaced.

The colonial rulers, from the end of the nineteenth century, were German until 1916, then British after World War I until 1961. Both redefined the nature of colonial rule (for pre-colonial fighting between the chiefdoms and competition thereafter, see Stahl 1964; for late administrative developments, see Johnston 1953). New laws and regulations were put in place. But there was never any idea of doing away with all aspects of existing local 'customary' practice. 'Custom' and 'government' were conceived to be co-existing with regard to many matters, the most important of which was land law. The missionaries tried to replace indigenous beliefs with Christianity, but they, too, had to put up with the co-existence of Chagga ideas and practices and Christian teachings. In 1961, at Independence, the socialist government led by Julius Nyerere and the TANU Party took over. Many aspects of customary law continued with official approval, but others were eliminated. Chiefship was abolished. The Chagga, when meeting a chief, would greet him as "ex-chiefu." How much irony was involved, and how much deference, was hard to say.

In theory, title to all land was nationalized, but the paradox is that when the only change made in land tenure is to declare that formal title to land is transferred to the state, possessory control remains untouched. The possessors remain in place, the change in title hardly mattering. That was the Chagga situation. People continued to occupy and claim possessory control of the land where they had always lived and cultivated just as before. For the farmers, there were some administrative reorganizations that came with the socialist regime, but their basic economic and residential arrangements were unchanged, as was most of their way of life.

President Nyerere had planned to institute a total social change in the whole country, affecting everything from the attitudes of individuals to the reorganization of the polity and economy. Yet while Nyerere's African socialism was in place for about 25 years, the program had many problems, and full implementation in the Kilimanjaro region lagged. In fact, not only were there organizational and economic failures in Tanzania as a whole, but even the ideological aspects of the movement more or less petered out in the 1980s. "African socialism failed," declared Nyerere, after he had resigned, in a speech of unusual candor delivered at the London School of Economics. How visible was that failure in the midst of the 1960s, 1970s, and 1980s?

The Chagga acknowledged some obvious changes introduced by African socialism, but they also perceived much continuity in their way of life. They had little regret about the ultimate fading of the government's socialist project. The Chagga are coffee growers whose product involved them in the world economy beginning shortly after the start of the twentieth century. (Their involvement in other long-distance trade existed earlier and was well established by the nineteenth century.) They were, for the most part, converts to Christianity who never gave up a wide array of indigenous beliefs that they maintained as a parallel belief system, which itself was in the process of change. In addition to churches, the missions established schools, dispensaries, and clinics. Until Independence, the churches themselves owned land and grew coffee, with African tenants living on the land and cultivating it. African socialism profoundly affected church properties and institutional influence, but for most independent farmers, socialism was just one more bureaucratic layer of ideas and organizations to which the residents of Kilimanjaro were subject.

Most important, the relation of the Chagga people to the land on which they planted their coffee, banana groves, and other crops was unusual in Africa. They had adequate water, which streamed down the mountainside, and which, as they saw the need, they diverted into narrow irrigation canals. They fertilized their land with the manure of cattle, which they collected by keeping numbers of the cattle stall-fed. Consequently, unlike many peoples in Africa who had to move their settlements periodically because their land was exhausted, the Chagga were able to occupy land continually. They developed a sophisticated land law as a consequence.

But to say that the Chagga could occupy the land without interruption is not to say that for 100 years, all Chagga could be accommodated in the same geographical space. Over the twentieth century, in the presence of enormous demographic increase, they began to suffer land shortage. There were many disputes over land—its inheritance, its boundaries, its transfer. Local settlements spun off their own sub-units, which moved up-mountain and down-mountain as land became scarce. The population grew from a figure estimated at 110,000 by the German government in 1900 to 476,000 in 1967. The population has continued to climb precipitously as more recent census figures attest. (The boundaries of the present census area are different from the one used in earlier counts, so precise comparability is in question, but figures of over 700,000 are often used.)

While in principle the Chagga resided in localized patrilineages, kinsmen and their families were, in effect, often irregularly distributed around the countryside. Land shortage and population increase often forced them to settle away from their kin. Though kinship remained a major factor in their lives, many other elements have to be taken into account to understand Chagga affairs today. Off-farm employment is one such factor. To envision household life on the mountain as a practical matter, one should realize that most Chagga still live without electricity and do not have piped running water in their houses.

It is obvious that fieldwork contact can be made with only a small segment of such a large population, even over many years of intermittent visits. Taking into account the immense diversity of persons was—and remains—a difficult task. Some Chagga are literate. (In the 1970s, I advised a Chagga graduate student in political science while he was preparing his PhD thesis at Yale. I know of other instances of such unusual achievements.) But on the mountain, too, some speak Kichagga, Swahili, and English, some only Kichagga and Kiswahili. Many are not literate, and some few speak only Kichagga. Some Chagga have salaries, being employed in schools, dispensaries, government offices, and the like. Some men have gone to the cities and work there, coming home only for occasional weekends and holidays. But most people do not have such paying jobs. They depend for cash entirely on the money that their small coffee-holdings bring and on occasional work, wherever it can be picked up. It is a varied scene, not the imaginary homogeneous culture of anthropological legend. It was an ideal opportunity for methodological experiment.

This is a brief sketch of the general situation. Thinking about local, observed relationships in a national, regional, and international world was clearly important. Placing them in that larger context was mandatory, but neither the extended case of the 1960s, nor the conception of process "in a limited area of social life" was capacious enough to accommodate that much contextual breadth (Gluckman 1967: xvi). Worse, on that scale, trying to judge the momentum of any long-term transformational process was at best a matter of informed conjecture. How long would African socialism last? What would the effect of AIDS be on Tanzania? Would the market for coffee hold up? What effect would Nyerere's educational reforms have in the long run?

There were ways of obtaining a retrospective body of data on the large scale. I collected tax records, court records, records of the coffee-selling cooperative, church records, and other documents from five sub-villages, and obtained court and administrative records from the town of Moshi, the seat of regional government. Over the years, I worked intensively in three sub-villages. There I came to know families and their affairs, who was born and who died, who borrowed money from whom, who claimed land, who made witchcraft accusations. Piecing together the documentary material, and combining it with the genealogies, the variations within and between the lineages, and the news from different villages, I was able to see where some of the individual instances fit into a larger history. It was important to know that there were people suing each other for bridewealth and accusing family members of witchcraft at the same time that some of the younger generation were off in foreign schools studying medicine and pharmacy and others were in cities learning to be auto mechanics.

From this massive accumulation of diverse information, I have selected a set of events. They have to do with the activities and machinations of the elite, and illustrate the ways in which such materials can speak to the anthropologist. The events noted were supplemented by bits of unsolicited information that I could piece together from a variety of encounters. The account would have been unpublishable at the time the events occurred, as it did not reflect favorably on socialism in action, nor on some Kilimanjaro bigwigs. Disclosing the facts, which were politically controversial then, would have prevented me from obtaining a renewal of my research permit. Knowing about them augmented the fear that at any moment the foreign anthropologist could be used as the tool of someone's political purposes. However, today the whole story reads like a mediocre vaudeville comedy.

## Skullduggery: A Tourist Hotel

A century of social history can be traced in the way a once important piece of property, a now seedy hotel on Kilimanjaro, was originally established and how it changed hands. I witnessed the most dramatic moment of this tale. An elderly German lady who was then the proprietor was carted off to jail by a bunch of rough and self-righteous Tanzanians in the name of the law. But the whole story can be extended deep into the past and continued forward beyond that frightening moment of her forcible removal.

This event occurred in 1970 during the high period of Tanzanian socialism, when ideals of unselfishness, fairness, uprightness, and politically correct behavior on the part of all community leaders and public officials were being extolled from every pulpit, broadcast from every radio station, and restated at every public meeting. Those who were fingered as not conforming were punished. On Kilimanjaro, confiscations of land were taking place, some people were being denounced as exploiters and parasites, the black market was thriving, and the well-off tried to remain so, or to improve their lot—but they had to take pains to conceal what they had, lest it be taken away. There was no freedom of assembly. Large lineages could not convene their members without permission, and a party representative had to be present. There was much fear. An anthropology that cannot take account of such matters seems to me sadly self-censored.

The Kibo Hotel, which I have alluded to, was where I lived. It was a shabby, very old climbers' lodge high up on a hill, at the end of the macadam road to the towns of Himo and Moshi. That road had been paved in the 1950s, while dirt roads and dirt paths served as modes of access for much of the rest of the mountain. Beyond the grand building of the Kibo Hotel and around it on all sides are small Chagga gardens full of banana plants and coffee bushes that hide small tin-roofed Chagga dwellings like those all over the mountain.

The hotel has a long and colorful past. The original building was there in German colonial times, before 1900, when it was part of a warehouse and trading post owned by a German settler named Forster. Forster married the daughter of the famous Lutheran missionary, Gutmann, who lived on the mountain for many years and was the first ethnographer of the Chagga. Eventually, as tourism increased because Europeans wanted to climb the great mountain, the warehouse was made into a guest house, and wings and outbuildings were added to the original core structure. In time, it ceased to be a warehouse and became entirely a hotel.

By the time I stayed there, intermittently from 1969, it was owned and managed by a plump, bossy, German woman, a Mrs. Bruhl. I first supposed she was a leftover from German times, but it turned out that her story was quite different. She had come to East Africa in the 1930s because her Jewish husband, foreseeing Nazi disasters, had fled from Germany. They managed to establish themselves as hotel keepers in Tanga on the coast. Later they bought the broken-down Kibo and moved to Kilimanjaro where the husband died. Mrs. Bruhl carried on alone, not without complaining about the burden involved.

By the late 1960s and 1970s, the Kibo Hotel was a place where, in season, tourists came, often by the busload, to climb the mountain. They arrived, stayed overnight, got themselves equipped with boots and other gear, met their guides and porters, and set out for the three days' climb and the two-day descent. All this was arranged by Mrs. Bruhl, who stood in the front hall beside a huge scale on which the porters' loads were weighed. She was there to see that the large boxes of provisions they carried did not exceed the allowed limit, and indeed to make sure they carried as much as was allowed. If a box was slightly underweight, she could be seen running to tuck in some extra socks or a roll of toilet paper. Five days later, the tourists would reappear, exhausted, dirty, and happy. After a meal, a bath, and a night's sleep, they would leave, and the next group of tourists would appear.

But the Kibo was not only a place for foreign tourists. It was also a place where African politicians occasionally came and freeloaded. They expected to be fed and feted with their entourage. It would not have been wise to try to charge them. The Kibo was also a place where visiting African officials stayed when they had business on Kilimanjaro. In the evenings, elite Africans from the neighborhood occasionally came to have a beer.

It was there that I met General Sarakikia, then head of the Tanzanian army, who visited annually to climb the mountain. In an expansive mood, he asked me how I happened to be there. One thing led to another, and I asked him what the army did with itself in a peaceful place like Tanzania. He replied that Tanzania had no enemies. The army did not have to prepare to defend the country from attack, and had no wish to attack others. "In a country like this, the function of the army," he said, no doubt thinking of the earlier attempted coup in 1964, "the function of the army is to keep the government in power." A few years later, I read that he was removed from his army post and made minister of culture and sport, not an inappropriate assignment for a regular climber of Kilimanjaro, though perhaps a comedown for a general.

Some years later I came to know another Kibo Hotel regular, ex-Chief Petro Itosi Marealle, who after his retirement from a government position in Dar es Salaam had resumed living in his Kilimanjaro house not far from the hotel. He was a descendant of the Chief Marealle who had been of enormous help to the German colonial government in its early days, and had been rewarded by the Germans by being made chief of much of the mountain. That large domain of Marealle the First lasted for only a short time, and the mountain soon reverted to being an area of multiple chiefdoms, reduced to 17 under the British administration. One of those chiefdoms was that of Marangu, where the Kibo Hotel was located and where, until Independence, Marealle's descendants continued to reign as local chiefs.

Petro Itosi Marealle was such a descendant. He had been a very important official under the British—not only the local chief of Marangu, but a super-chief, head of a British-designed geographical division, with many local chiefs under his authority (Johnston 1953). I was surprised to hear from him that he knew what an anthropologist was. In fact, it was a measure of his importance that Malinowski had contacted him when he visited the mountain. They later corresponded, and Chief Petro showed me the Malinowski letters he had saved. Petro Itosi (1947) also had enough interest in ethnology and in the traditions of his people to write a little book about them.

When Julius Nyerere came to power in 1961 and abolished chiefship in all of Tanzania, he was mindful of the local popularity of some of those he had ousted. He must have decided that they might be useful—and certainly less dangerous—to his government if he moved them out of their home constituencies and into government posts in Dar es Salaam. Thus was Petro Itosi Marealle's period as a British colonial super-chief closed. He became, instead, an important official in Nyerere's socialist government. After many years in Dar, he retired and came back to Kilimanjaro. From time to time, he came to the hotel to drink beer and receive visitors in the late afternoons and early evenings. When he would go home, he often took three extra bottles of beer with him, one for his current wife and one each for his former wives, who lived nearby. Most Chagga beer is home-brewed stuff made of rotted bananas, but at the hotel, cold bottled beer, a considerable luxury, was the order of the day. I had met Petro Itosi at the hotel, but I later visited him at his house.

The hotel was strategically located and had some singular advantages. Not only was it at the end of a paved road, but also it had a generator, so sometimes there were a few hours of feeble electric power in the evenings. And it had one telephone, which sometimes worked. Sizable meetings could be held in its public rooms, but these were seldom used. The hotel was filled with noisy, lively guests during the climbing season, but it was quite cold and empty during the rains. I was there for months in both seasons.

By the 1970s, Mrs. Bruhl, the hotel owner, was also in her seventies. She had long been a Tanzanian citizen, so she owned the hotel legally. But feeling her age, she worried about what would become of the hotel when she died. She had no children nor any close relatives to whom to leave it. She was not the only person interested in this question. One day a group of scowling African officials drove up, entered the hotel and strode aggressively to the front desk. Saying that they were from the Game Department, they demanded to see Mrs. Bruhl immediately. She came to the desk, and they explained that they had come to arrest her. She said, "What for?" They explained that there were fur blankets on the beds in the hotel that were not marked with Game Department stamps, and this showed that she had obtained them illegally.

There is a small rodent on the mountain, the hyrax, out of which some Chagga made fur blankets, both for themselves, since it can be very cold at night, and to sell. In fact, the moth-eaten, much-mended hyrax blankets in the hotel had been on the beds when the Bruhls had bought it, decades earlier—they were anything but new. The Game Department and the rules about stamps had only just been established. The stamps were necessary to show that the skins had been obtained with official permission and that the hunter had been licensed by the Game Department. The Game Department men did not care to discuss the age of the blankets. Several of them bullied a Chagga employee into unlocking all the rooms. They pulled the blankets off of the beds in the presence of startled guests and carried them down to their vehicles as 'evidence'.

Mrs. Bruhl was generally a calm lady, but when indignant, she boiled like a steaming tea kettle. She was outraged by the accusations of the Game Department men. She said, "I know what you want. You want me to bribe you. Well, you will not get anything from me. I have a pistol in my room, and I will go and get it. You get out of here." The Game Department men did not leave and did not care for such talk. They wanted her to come with them.

My husband persuaded Mrs. Bruhl not to get her pistol and to go with the men. They bundled her off in one of their cars to go to the police station in Moshi, the nearest town, 25 miles away. My husband and I followed in our car. When we arrived at the courthouse, she refused to get out. The Game Department people carried her in to jail. We contacted a lawyer for her, rather against her wishes. "I have no need for a lawyer. I have done nothing wrong." Mrs. Bruhl was held in jail overnight and released the next day. Some months later, when I was no longer on the mountain, there was a trial and she was exonerated.

However, the next year when I returned, she was still much exercised over what she thought was the scenario behind this unpleasant interlude. She said there were several rich Chagga who wanted her hotel, and one in particular, a Chagga lawyer with wide political connections (characterized by the Marealle family as a crook), had made her an offer. When she refused, he had become threatening. She was sure he had used his influence to put the Game Department people up to this escapade, to make her look disreputable and to make it possible for the party to confiscate her hotel, at which point he might be in a position to take it over, given his party connections.

Not long after this incident, tired and discouraged by the hostility she imagined to be around her, Mrs. Bruhl decided to retire to Germany. A succession of dreadful hotel managers followed. Chief Marealle died. Mrs. Bruhl died. I was told that she had willed the hotel to the Catholic Church so that it might be Africanized under auspices that she trusted. Whatever her wishes were in this matter, there must have been some interesting subsequent transactions about which I do not know. What I *do* know is that when I was last on Kilimanjaro in the 1990s, the hotel was owned by George Marealle, a businessman, who is one of the current prominent members of the local chiefly lineage.

A full circle had been closed. Land in the Marangu chiefdom that had been appropriated by the Germans in the 1890s had found its way back into the hands of the chiefly family a century later. Now, though, it was owned as a business proposition, not controlled as a chiefly political prerogative. This is an interesting manifestation of transformation and continuity in combination, a phenomenon familiar to historians. For anthropologists addressing the social processes at work before their eyes, these hybrids of change are of crucial interest.

It is not difficult to use this series of incidents to talk about continuities of power. On Kilimanjaro, certain lineages have maintained their importance from generation to generation in radically altered circumstances. There are unsuccessful members, of course, poor relatives. But the successful members manage to shift their occupations in tandem with the times. The businessman is not the only example of ongoing Marealle success. Another member of the family, a son of Petro Itosi and an ex-army colonel, was once sent into exile because he was thought to be plotting a coup against Nyerere with some of his fellow officers. He spent his exile in China, Japan, and London. It cannot have been too painful a period of exile. Petro Itosi told me that his son had managed to send him a Japanese car that was technically in the diplomatic pouch so that no import duty was paid on it. Petro Itosi occasionally drove around the mountain roads in this splendid vehicle.

It was generous of Nyerere not to imprison the colonel, but Nyerere was mindful of the family power. There was some talk of the colonel being in the weapons business "but only on the side of freedom fighters," said his father. I do not know the truth of this. The colonel was allowed back on the mountain in the 1980s. His wife had cultivated their plot of land to ensure that it would not be confiscated, that is, to secure legitimate socialist ownership. By 1993, the colonel was transmogrified and appeared as a prominent organizer of one of the new national political parties. The United States considered multiple parties a sure sign of democracy, so the ex-colonel tried to become a facilitator of that new politics.

This tale is not the simple playing out of traditional chiefly prerogatives. Nor is it a simple matter of property controlling politics. Nor is it exclusively about the advantage of having old, extensive political and property networks. It is all of those things together, fueled by the talents of particular individuals for repositioning themselves as the ground shifts.

But what does this set of incidents tell us about the socialist time in Tanzania? By itself, it is not enough to indicate much. Sarakikiya's comments on the function of the army suggest the insecurity of the state in the early years, and the need that a civilian government had for the support of its army. Colonel Marealle's exile suggests the same, and his return and political activity tells much about later changes in the political wind.

As for the hotel story, in one dimension it is one more instance of the legitimacy of Africanization, the taking over by Africans of property and positions that were once held by whites. But what is one to make of the peculiar, violent intervention of the Game Department? As a piece of evidence, it is like the instance of a single bribe, an overreaching of power by low-level officials, probably at the behest of a more powerful individual behind the scenes. But combined with many other local instances, the Game Department's behavior shows that Nyerere's wonderful ideals and the legislation that was supposed to implement them miscarried egregiously on the ground. The poor farmers I knew, and with whom I spent most of my time, were all extremely cynical about the doings of the state and of the elite. They assumed that such people were making deals all the time, with agencies of the state, with each other, and with them, the unprivileged. How did they know? Part of it was local gossip. But they also knew because on a much smaller scale, those poor farmers were also fiddling with the rules—legal, customary, administrative, religious. And whenever they could, they mobilized organizations or organizational representatives on their behalf. They knew what the elite were up to because they were doing the same thing. Socialism does not succeed in doing away with the universality of cheating for gain. Any tourist who made friendly overtures to a particular elderly waiter in the hotel could obtain a hyrax blanket for himself at a price. The new blanket would not have Game Department stamps. The "I can fix a deal for you" spirit is widespread on the mountain, but the speaker has to be sure he is not dealing with an agent provocateur.

To return to Gluckman and the extended case, or the situational analysis of van Velsen, is this hotel tale an extended case? Or, in my terms, is it a series of events used for diagnostic purposes in the context of ethnographic work? Surely Clifford (1988: 13) is right: "Ethnography, a hybrid activity,... appears as writing, as collecting, as modernist collage, as imperial power, as subversive critique."

Because I was interested in what most people were doing and thinking, the largest part of my research was carried out among persons of far less political importance than the Marealles. My lineage and village data are very detailed, carried on over a period of many years in several villages. I could easily have used mundane events selected from that material to make other ethnographic points. The unusual events presented here simply dramatize some of the methodological implications of using events themselves as diagnostic tools (Moore 1987).

It is obvious that I have taken liberties with the idea of the extension of a case history. I have extended it in many directions, not just over time. I have chosen some accidentally encountered small-scale fieldwork experiences and pasted them together. The combination of these events, chosen for their political implications, confirms clues about what I knew about what was going on on the larger scale.

I have used the history of a piece of property and bits of information about the people who were directly or tangentially involved with it to say something about the unfolding of a century of history on Kilimanjaro. Given that the witnessed encounters were played out in the second decade of Tanzania's socialist period, they have implications regarding the limited effectiveness of party and government control over the countryside. By no means does this give a full picture of the processes under way at that level, but it does provide exceptionally indicative, though fragmentary, clues.

Anthropological observations can be used to contribute detailed underpinning for conjectures about processes taking place on a larger scale. The miscellany of micro happenings described here makes larger-scale sense because it is selectively presented toward the uncovering of an overarching theme. The uncovering is incomplete. The political flow can only be hinted at. What is shown is only partially shown. Background material has been added that glues the pieces together. In other words, using events like these for diagnostic purposes is not a story that tells itself.

I have had a strong hand in organizing the facts to provide a glimpse of a historical process, from the original appropriation of the property by colonial interests to the reclaiming of the property by Africans a century later, with some ups and downs for the elite and some frightening political behavior along the way. Not all accounts of events require as much handling and interpretation, but I think it is time to acknowledge that manipulation of the presentation process in anthropology is not unusual. Telling it like it is does not guarantee an unedited product. There is no such thing in human affairs as a simple description.

I chose among myriad other events certain examples through which multiple political and property interests were manifest. To the actors, myriad ideas and relationships appeared momentarily urgent to them and were pressed. Whatever longer historical processes of which these were a part had no conscious immediacy, no great importance in the particular confrontations and interactions that took place. But the events, and the commentaries embedded in them, are of interest because they contribute to a partial understanding. What emerges is somewhat more than a conjecture about where the fragments of rather theatrical action fit in the composition of a being-shaped present and future.

I chose these events, among other reasons, because they suggested cracks and strains in the socialist program. They hinted at elements that might dismantle the grand, orderly plans for social change so much touted by the government. These events suggested fault lines that might make the socialist structure tremble a little, even perhaps eventually quake and fall down.

The events also indicated some of the other transformations experienced over the past decades. The hotel property provided a unifying historical thread and a spatial focus. But these incidents did not constitute an extended case in Gluckman's sense. The boundaries he seems to have had in mind for the extended case were institutional boundaries. I could have, of course described the long-term relations inside a large lineage and the machinations of some individuals to bring about the fission of the lineage into two parts. I could have written about the courts and the transformations of the judicial system, about a village and its vagaries, or addressed any other such bounded entities about which I have gathered field material. Those, too, would have told much about ongoing affairs on the mountain. However, I deliberately chose to report the events described here because they were not enclosed within the frame of a social institution. I wanted to show that even such seemingly disconnected goings-on could be seen to be part of the jumbled story of larger-scale, longer-term processes.

This brings us to Clifford Geertz's recent reflections on his anthropological career in *After the Fact: Two Countries, Four Decades, One Anthropologist* (1995) and his comments on large-scale process. He frames his review of his long ethnographic experience in terms of the issues of modernization and modernity, saying, "The way we live now is a stage in a vast historical proceeding with an intrinsic dynamic, a settled direction, and a determinate form" (1995: 137). He continues, saying "that modernization (and thus modernity, its goal and product) is a general phenomenon unevenly realized" (ibid.). Geertz emphasizes that the anthropologist striving to do a local study cannot escape the "currents and cross-currents of world-scale politics" (ibid.: 94). "You may set out to isolate yourself from cosmopolitan concerns and contain your interests within hermetical contexts. But the concerns follow you. The contexts explode" (ibid.: 95).

But what if one does not set out to isolate oneself? What if one begins, as many anthropologists do today, with the idea that some emanations from world-scale politics are bound to be visible in any ethnographic field? And what if the exploration of that dimension is a central interest? Surely, the quest today is often for an understanding of local life within that larger context. The present chapter argues that spontaneous events, even unusual ones, may be an excellent way to illuminate that connection without abandoning for a moment the detailed study of the local milieu.

---

Sally Falk Moore is Professor of Anthropology (Emerita) at Harvard University. She received a BA from Barnard College, a PhD in Anthropology at Columbia University, and an LLB from Columbia Law School. A specialist in legal and political anthropology, she has done fieldwork in East Africa visiting at intervals from 1969 to 1993. She has also done consulting in West Africa. She came to Harvard in 1981, where she taught regularly in the Faculty of Arts and Sciences and intermittently at Harvard Law School. From 1985 to 1989, she was Dean of the Graduate School at Harvard, and was Master of Dunster House. Her books include *Law as Process* (1978, 2nd ed. 2000), *Social Facts and Fabrications: "Customary" Law on Kilimanjaro 1880–1980* (1986), *Anthropology and Africa* (1994), *Law and Anthropology: A Reader* (2005).

# References

Clifford, James. 1988. *The Predicament of Culture*. Cambridge, MA: Harvard University Press.

Epstein, A. L., ed. 1967. *The Craft of Social Anthropology*. London: Tavistock Publications.

Firth, Raymond. 1964. *Essays on Social Organization and Values*. London: Athlone Press.

Geertz, Clifford. 1995. *After the Fact*. Cambridge, MA: Harvard University Press.

Gluckman, Max. [1940] 1958. *Analysis of a Social Situation in Modern Zululand*. Rhodes-Livingstone Paper, no. 28. Manchester: Manchester University Press for the Rhodes-Livingstone Institute. (Originally published in *Bantu Studies*.)

_____. 1955. *The Judicial Process Among the Barotse of Northern Rhodesia*. Manchester, Manchester University Press.

_____. 1967. "Introduction." Pp. xi–xx in Epstein 1967.

Gutmann, Bruno. 1926. *Das Recht der Dschagga*. Munich: C. H. Beck.

Johnston, P. H. 1953. "Chagga Constitutional Development." *Journal of African Administration* 5, no. 3: 134–140.

Marealle, Petro Itosi. 1947. *Maisha ya Mchagga hapa duniani na ahera* [The Life of a Mchagga Here on Earth and After Death]. Kimetungwa na Petro Itoshi Marealle. Dar es Salaam: Mkuki na Nyota Publishers.

Moore, Sally Falk. [1973] 2000. *Law as Process*. Oxford: James Currey.

_____. 1986. *Social Facts and Fabrications: "Customary Law" on Kilimanjaro 1880–1980*. Cambridge: Cambridge University Press.

_____. 1987. "Explaining the Present: Theoretical Dilemmas in Processual Ethnography." *American Ethnologist* 14, no. 4: 727–736.

Nadel, S. F. 1957. *The Theory of Social Structure*. London: Cohen and West.

Sahlins, Marshall. 1985. *Islands of History*. Chicago: University of Chicago Press.

Stahl, K. 1964. *History of the Chagga People of Kilimanjaro*. The Hague: Mouton.

Turner, Victor. 1969. *The Ritual Process*. Chicago: Aldine Press.

Van Velsen, Jaap. 1967. "The Extended-Case Method and Situational Analysis." Pp. 129–149 in Epstein 1967.

Vincent, Joan. 1986. "System and Process, 1974–1985." *Annual Review of Anthropology* 15: 99–119.

# CODA
## Recollections and Refutations

*Bruce Kapferer*

I find this collection a Proustian experience. It excites memories regarding events and significant others who for some of us writing here continue to be poignantly influential in the different courses that we have taken in the constantly forming subject of anthropology. Most of us who were involved with Gluckman's Manchester circle have different recollections of what it was and the scope of its influence, such recollections (or imaginings of the past) gathering their import through our different standpoints and projections in a moving present. In this regard, I find the two historical essays (Mills, Kempny) useful for the general confirmation that they give to a large amount of received opinion in this volume and elsewhere. Frankenberg's essay imparts a strong sense of the spirit of the main period of Manchester and reminds us of important emissaries of ideas that had their source in the department during Gluckman's time. There is a difficulty with collections such as this for they always run the risk of excluding scholars who were influential (and there are many who were at Manchester at the time who possibly have received insufficient mention). Here I stress that the Manchester of Gluckman's idea was very much a collective event. Gluckman may have stamped his personality on things, but there was, I think, a powerful notion that those gathered at Manchester—and earlier at the RLI—were participating in the exploration of new possibilities for the then still very young discipline of anthropology. In both settings, Gluckman grouped around him scholars with diverse intellectual interests and skills, and he strove to exploit this synergy.

Perhaps those scholars who joined forces with Gluckman at Manchester are better characterized as a circle than as a school, if by the term 'school' is meant some kind of theoretically coherent, narrowly conformist group. They were far from this, no matter how hard Gluckman may have tried to impose his will or labored to establish some kind of collective conscience. Gluckman certainly reacted when a few tried to stray from what he considered the line, and I think he felt saddened when Victor Turner left the fold. The label

'Manchester School' was more a spillover effect of the fact that Gluckman's anthropology took shape in the shadow of the already famous Manchester School of Economics. There were many divisions within Gluckman's circle of Manchester anthropologists, which undoubtedly contributed to its profusion of ideas and the several directions its participants took. An undercurrent of resistance was always apparent in reaction to Gluckman's routine effort—in a series of introductions to books, collected volumes, and position articles—to present a semblance of agreement and coherence. Most of all, Gluckman's Manchester circle was defined by its opposition to what were seen then as conventionalist, conservative, even primitivist directions in social anthropology in Britain and abroad (perhaps most stridently voiced by Mitchell, who would inveigh increasingly against what he would refer to as "bare bollocks anthropology").

If Manchester can be regarded as a school, this was so in Thomas Kuhn's sense. It identified a collection of scholars concerned overridingly with social and political practice among whom the ideas of situational analysis and the extended-case method were of some unifying importance. I say some importance because many of those who identified with Manchester anthropology did not apply the method; rather, they pursued what can be called its spirit as it was set out primarily in Gluckman's essay known as "The Bridge." That is, scholars were directed to open up fields for analysis that largely had not been addressed hitherto by anthropologists, especially those of modernity. Situational analysis describes an attitude, an orientation to the understanding of social life quite as much as an actual methodology, the main direction of the essays in this volume.

At this point, I would like to stress the problem-centered emphasis behind the situational idea for Gluckman's RLI and Manchester anthropologists. They were not interested in description for description or for mere ethnography's sake. The vital thing was to focus on a particular problem and open it up to reveal its complexities. The journal of the Rhodes-Livingstone Institute was entitled *Human Problems in British Central Africa*. Its aim was to pinpoint issues or problematics that emerged in social and political practice and to pursue them rigorously in an effort to find explanations—resolutions, even. The concentration on situations and events was key to such an investigation. Furthermore, Gluckman and his colleagues were concerned to link theoretical issues to pragmatics. If theory could not produce an understanding of issues arising from concrete practices, then it was little better than musing in the void. The whole tenor of the Manchester seminar was issue and problem directed. If no clear issue was at stake in a presentation, Gluckman and his colleagues would struggle to find one. General ethnographic statements that glossed what they more often conceived of as the messiness of reality would be thrown into question, as too would neat theoretical or perspectival pronouncements or assessments. Theoretical understanding was not an objective in itself; rather, the goal was identifying theory that was emergent from and attached to particular ethnographically related problematics and specifics. Elizabeth Colson, so central in the early days of the RLI and Manchester and whose work is continuing, represents much of the pragmatic, problem-centered orientation of the Gluckman and Manchester intervention in the formation of anthropology.

Overall, the point of the situational and extended-case method was not to use events and practices as mere illustrations. That is, they were not to be engaged simply to exemplify already established analytical or theoretical positions or general, descriptive opinions. Ideally, events and practices were to be intertwined with analysis in such a way that the assumptions engaged to the analysis (those of the anthropologist as well as those of the subjects of the inquiry) were apparent in the process of the construction of the event and in the description of practice. The procedures underlying the descriptions were, as far as possible, to be revealed in this process. Situational analysis was directed to the very problematics of ethnographic construction. Furthermore, theory and the development of abstract formulations were to be from a ground-up rather than sky-down perspective. Data and analysis or theory were not to be separated (as in common presentations of case material) but rather to be dialectically interrelated so that they emerged or developed more directly, and evidently, out of each other. Of course, analytical, theoretical, and ideological assumptions are always embedded in the action of description (vital in the very acts of ethnographic selection, choice, and construction of event, etc.), but Gluckman's RLI and Manchester perspective attempted to confront this fact. It was designed to reveal the very process of construction and explanation. For this reason, the situational and extended-case method was also known as 'processual analysis', and not simply because it studied processes, a simplification of the methodological point.

The most important motivation behind the situational approach concerned the authority and standing of anthropology and the findings based in its defining ethnographic method in the knowledge communities (the sciences, the humanities, and those reliant more pragmatically on their findings). Gluckman and his colleagues would openly voice uncertainties that most anthropologists and others outside the discipline routinely ask of qualitative materials. What checks are there on the accuracy of anthropological ethnography? Are the findings of an ethnographically based anthropology to be taken on faith and trust alone? In such a discipline, in which the replication of the ethnography is impossible (after all, social life is in constant flux) and the materials are dependent on the deeply subjective work of a single individual (whose competence and imagination may be limited), how can others, let alone the anthropologist, have confidence in the results?

I think these uncertainties gathered force in the ethos of social anthropology, especially in the early days of its establishment, because it often used its ethnographic method to challenge largely metropolitan conceptions and theories (Malinowski is the example). This was given additional impetus as a result of the broad political orientation of the Manchester anthropologists, who were directed to question, or intervene within, official conceptions of reality.

Situational or processual analysis aimed to connect dialectically ethnographic description with analysis so that they were in continual and mutually reflexive critical, problematizing, and questioning relation to each other. Through this process, ethnographic work was to have its own method of verification. Assumptions and ideas derived from action in one set of situated practices were authenticated or reassessed under the conditions of another set of situated practices elsewhere that were in some way connected by persons, context, or temporal sequence. The objective was to develop a method for the production of theory and its confirmation that was specific to the centrality of ethnography in anthropology. This was intended to gain appropriate recognition for the results of anthropological inquiry among the already established sciences and humanities. In other words, anthropology through the method was to have its own means of verification equivalent to those in history or the laboratory sciences yet distinct from them. The method of verification was integral to the pivotal position of ethnographic fieldwork in anthropology. Gluckman, I think, wanted anthropology and the method he inspired to carry social anthropology beyond a certain debunking role of which he sometimes accused Malinowski (but of which he himself was far from innocent).

Yamba asks the challenging question concerning the innovation of situational analysis as a method, which he in part answers. Of course, it is an extension within the ethnographic fieldwork conception of anthropology recommended by Malinowski, among others, causing Yamba, wittily citing Molière, to admit to a certain sense of *déjà vu*. But, I hope, my short repetition of the raison d'être of situational analysis (aspects of which are pursued in many essays in this volume) indicates some of the key developments and, therefore, the relative innovation of the method. Yamba's other and important challenge (pertaining in Norman's essay, too) relates to the key position of events in situational analysis and their constructed nature. I think this is an enduring issue that is probably impossible to resolve entirely satisfactorily, either theoretically or pragmatically. Norman's reflexive essay demonstrates that cases, events, or encounters are not natural sites, as it were, for the application of situational analysis.

The four major ethnographically based essays (Norman, Yamba, Lindgren, Moore) highlight other problems with situational analysis, most of all the divergence between methodological ideal and reality, at least in terms of my outlining of some of the aims. In the main, these essays engage ethnography to illustrate arguments and theories rather than deriving these in a dialectical process whereby analysis is developmentally articulated with the formation of ethnographic description. But I acknowledge that this is likely to be difficult in many instances. It may also be especially cumbersome these days, given publication restrictions and market demands. In my view, situational analysis—as it was initially developed and in terms of its overall aims—is most appropriate to monographic rather than article presentation. The method generates ethnographic detail, is thirsty for it, and this detail can be overwhelming, especially if the analytical or emerging theoretical points are not constantly at the forefront. Even in the essays presented here there is a tendency to lose sight of the point. Lindgren's essay, most of all of the ethnographic presentations, points up the situational analysis commitment to the notions that analytical point or theoretical assertion must emerge through the ethnography and not proceed, as far as is possible, from pre-given theoretical assumptions. The theory is in the practice, as it were. He demonstrates some of the advantage of the approach over the transactionalist perspective of Barth (1969) to ethnicity. This is grounded in untested and largely untestable universalizing assumptions, often of a kind that the Manchester situational perspective questioned over 10 years before.

Moore's essay raises the issue of whether Gluckman's Manchester approach continues its relevance into contemporary times. However, surprisingly, I think, she seriously misconceives the perspective. Nevertheless, she provides a useful case in point for underlining some of the key directions of the situational analysis perspective, and I will address her essay at greater length as a means of doing this. As a broad observation, the event she discusses is engaged to illustrate larger Tanzanian political processes. This is a common approach with the general anthropological analysis of events. Moore essentially maintains the very kind of perspective that Gluckman and Manchester were arguing against.

Moore's concluding comments suggest that the Manchester perspective has passed its 'use by' date largely because of current globalizing realities. The changes in scale brought about by global political trends, she asserts, reduce the relevance of the situational perspective. This may well be so, but not for the reasons she presents, as I will explain. Moore indicates that the Gluckman orientation is too bounded, perhaps single sited. But the situational approach, as other essays in this volume demonstrate, stresses situational and situated diversity in an open field or horizon. Many of the early Manchester anthropologists located themselves more or less in one spot, but this does not mean that the approach is not easily adaptable to contemporary global conditions (see Kapferer 2000). Moreover, aligning herself with some recent trends in North American anthropological post-modernism, Moore opts for a kind of happenstance, haphazard form of ethnography and analysis. But in my opinion, at least with regard to her particular flirtation with post-modernism, there is the danger of retreating from the significance of anthropological ethnography and its potential in larger knowledge discourses. Like it or not, anthropology is in the explanation game, and this fact has to be positively confronted. This is of course not foreign to many post-modernist and post-structuralist positions (e.g., Derridean deconstruction, discourse analysis), which involve a serious interrogation of forms of description and analysis in order to better establish the ground of understanding. Without overinflating Gluckman or the early Manchester orientation, situational or processual analysis was taking a path in this direction.

Moore is at risk of establishing a humanistic type of opposition to the Gluckman and Manchester approach. Gluckman, by the way, did not overlook humanistic and literary perspectives but (well aware of the narrative and biographical properties of situational analysis) strove to incorporate them into the situational method to their mutual advantage. Turner is outstanding in this regard. I note his concern in *Schism and Continuity* (Turner 1957) to imbue the central figure, Sandombu, with the proportions of a character in Greek tragedy and the mutual insight emergent from his juxtaposition of the *chihamba* rite with critical themes in Melville's *Moby Dick*. Gluckman and some of those in his Manchester circle were to take advantage of the intuitive and imaginative quality of literary and poetic approaches and, by marrying these to situational and extended-case analysis, to expand their possibilities, extending as well as verifying their insights with regard to other practices. Jane Austen was a special literary favorite of Gluckman. Through the fine grain of her observations, she brilliantly critiqued English bourgeois society, and Gluckman would hold her work up as a model of the close, insightful description and interpretation that guided his situational orientation. (It is a major point of reference for Gluckman's article "Gossip and Scandal" [1963].)

I mention Austen because a strong implication in the situational approach is that there is no necessary opposition between large-scale processes and analysis of the fine grain. Handelman, in his more abstract essay, makes the point excellently. He effectively criticizes Gluckman for not seeing the implications of his situational perspective more thoroughly, for cursorily dismissing some possibilities. Handelman engages the work of Goffman, whom Gluckman had invited to Manchester. Goffman appealed to Gluckman precisely because he saw an Austen-esque, deft quality in Goffman's ethnography, which led to theoretical understandings that could inform Gluckman's broader institutional concerns (see also, Sansom [1980], another participant in the Manchester collective). Nonetheless, Gluckman was suspicious of Goffman's interactionism, although he would stress Goffman's own self-reference that he was an ethnographer rather than a theoretician. Handelman concentrates on themes of micro history and emergence (the latter concept further subverting the notion of the case as illustration or representation), but he also shows how micro/macro, large-scale/small-scale oppositions can be overcome and ultimately miss the point. Micro processes, everyday interactional encounters, are the lifeblood of apparently bigger dynamics. They not only embody what is identified in the large scale—they are also integral in its production, a point of much post-modern analysis that might have better informed Moore.

Moore asserts that she uses situational and extended-case analysis in a diagnostic sense, an interesting medical metaphor in the context of her ethnographic discussion of the Tanzanian political context. But how exactly? She seems to be using it to demonstrate previously established and very loosely formulated opinions (symptoms) that are already integral to her diagnostic method. This was a difficulty also with Gluckman's early attempt in the bridge article, a reflexive critique that Gluckman offered of himself (and why he advocated the further development of extended-case analysis). Mitchell made similar complaints about his own analyses, impelling him (along with Turner and later van Velsen) to attempt new ways of achieving the situational methodological ideal. Moore returns to a position even before Gluckman in "The Bridge," sidestepping the issues and effectively abandoning the situational project.

There is the suggestion in Moore that Gluckman's orientation is static, repeating a common misrepresentation of his equilibrium concept. Applying his understanding of the notion of statics in physics, Gluckman conceived of equilibrium as a dynamic process. In Gluckman's usage, the notion of equilibrium was part of his problematization of change—that it might be but a moment within the *longue durée*, a process contributing to a repetitive cycle of the long run. Moore's repeating of a mistaken criticism of Gluckman's equilibrium concept seems to be connected to her implication that processual or situational analysis is less relevant to contemporary realities. But she ignores the fact that the approach was invented precisely to deal with a world in flux, with realities of major social, political, technological, rapidly urbanizing, even cosmopolitan (re)formation. The most apparently conventional (even tribal) of Manchester studies, Turner's ethnography of the Ndembu, which brought the extended-case method to fruition, was explicitly directed to understanding major structural shifts of a political-economic character, a factor that probably encouraged Turner's refinement and usage of the extended-case method.

But I add that situational analysis was not necessarily directed to the study of change or process as such. Change or process was the condition of its development and not the point or object of its analysis per se. It was devised as a means to conduct intensive fieldwork in realities where the then accepted circumstances and conventions of anthropological ethnography did not apply; where the social world was not delimited or neatly physically circumscribed; where the boundaries of the tribe, community, and village had been breached, and the small scale, the large scale, the local, and the global intermeshed. Moreover, the situational and extended-case method involved a shift in anthropological attitude. The objective was not the description of forms of life of a people in the island-like way. This had more or less become routine for anthropology in which the issue or the problem, in the Manchester sense, was little more than the act of description itself, and often unreflexively so. Prone to exoticism, such an orientation was challenged by Gluckman and his colleagues. If they continued to work in what appeared to be the expected units of anthropological analysis, of tribe, community, and village—and many were encouraged not to do so—this was to be so because the specific locus gave access to a particular problematic of human practice that resonated with potential general theoretical implications, with larger matters of wider human significance. An anthropological concern to etch out progressively a global map of social and cultural difference was far from the objective and was, in fact, rejected. In Gluckman's view and in that of his peers, these shifts in direction maintained the value of anthropological ethnographic fieldwork in contemporary realities outside the areas of more conventional anthropological work, intensifying the importance of ethnography in the anthropological project. I might add here that situational analysis facilitates the breaking of the anthropological bond with fixed and circumscribed locations. To a degree, the advantages of ethnographic work in the one location are shifted to the method itself, as is apparent at least in my interpretation in this volume of the significance of Gluckman's *Analysis of a Social Situation* ([1940] 1958).

Situational analysis was the method that Gluckman and his Manchester circle invented to expand the relevance of anthropology in a world that was no longer—if it ever had been—the closed-off, isolated sets of realities of the anthropological imagination at the heart of the discipline's beginnings. Furthermore, situational or processual analysis is/was a method for constructing and opening up space into complexity, holding aspects of the fluidity of reality in momentary abeyance, catching the world at the vital problematic moments of its formation in a way that enabled anthropologists to practice their craft, to realize more fully possibilities of the role of ethnography in their work.

I stress that in my view situational analysis is a way to theoretical conceptualization, not a worked-out theoretical position in itself. Numerous theoretical positions may be attached to it, but in a sense the method is outside theory. This does not mean that the method is free of what Evens explores as the ontological commitments of the social sciences as these have been constituted mainly in the historical circumstances of Northern Europe and the United States over the last 150 years or so. The ontology that Evens discusses is evident in a variety of dualisms (individual/society, part/whole, agency/structure, freedom/determinism, reduction/abstraction) that appear to operate at the core of much social science, spinning its conundrums and motivating its questions. These are seemingly irresolute, trapped in a dialectic from which many, influenced by numerous philosophies (e.g., Nietzsche, Deleuze), are trying to break free, usually unsuccessfully. In anthropology, ontological dualism of an irresolute kind is apparent in a slew of overarching perspectives, from functionalist through to post-structural and post-modern paradigms. The individual/society problematic is ontologically central in the situational and processual approach itself and governs many of its difficulties. The method attempts to overcome individualist/societal/structural oppositions but perhaps inevitably falls into the chasm that it tries to bridge, thereby often negating its objectives.

Gluckman's method is imprisoned—for the foreseeable future, I think, but is far from alone in this—in a conundrum of ontological proportions. For example, Gluckman and others among his colleagues expressed ambivalence toward, as well as fascination with, various individualist and interactionist perspectives, especially as developed in the United States. Their occasional frustration with them, and a reluctance to take them more fully on board, relates to what is tantamount to a balancing act born of the ontological roots of their own method. This is a factor opening up pitfalls in the method, tendencies to reduction as well as over-abstraction, shifts to transactional individualism, or an emphasis on the fundamental strategic nature of human action, all of which tend to contradict the broad ideals and objective of situational and processual analysis. In this regard, I find Handelman's essay interesting in his critical readdressing of Goffman's interactionism. He does so in the situationalist spirit of challenging theoretical conceptualization in an effort to develop a new direction. Handelman's essay, as I see it, attempts to overcome Gluckman's unconsciously realized ontological frustration with interactionist perspectives, potentially achieving a resolution (a new synthesis?) that attempts to combat some of the difficulties in Goffman and the situational perspective but is, nonetheless, consistent with their aims and potential.

Here I want to comment briefly on connections between the Manchester processual, situational method and what appear to be similar moves in the Chicago School of sociology, especially noted by the historians of Manchester in this volume and elsewhere. I believe that these were largely independent developments and that Chicago sociology was not as influential as is sometimes implied. The two approaches had rather different intellectual trajectories, motivated in divergent political commitments and arising from distinct socio-political contexts. Certainly, Mitchell was drawn to the Chicago ethnographies but quite critically so in his formative period. Wirth and Robert Redfield offered approaches with which Mitchell strongly disagreed. Chicago was influential in the sense of permitting a Manchester distinction; there was an association in topic but not in analytical perspective. The Chicago studies pursued arguments of adaptation, assimilation, ecological determinism, social and historical evolution, and devolution, etc. Such orientations were anathema to Mitchell and Gluckman, and were effectively contested by them. Mitchell was interested in Park and Burgess's urban ecology and in Thomas and Znaniecki's study of the Polish peasant because of their concerns with urbanism and transnational migration, but otherwise they were poles apart in perspective. It is said that Mitchell applies reference group theory in *The Kalela Dance* (1959), but this is so only to a degree, for in Mitchell's view it is not sensitive enough to variation. His situational approach is concerned to show that identity and ethnicity achieve diversity of import under a variety of differently situated structural circumstances. Pursuing a line derived from Evans-Pritchard, he demonstrates that apparently different and opposed constructions of identity can co-exist in the practices of the same members of the population, coming into and out of usage according to the parameters of the situation. The essay by Glaeser in this volume is oriented to the study of identity, but Glaeser's stance is sharply different from that of Mitchell, who stresses the nature of identity as not just a historical construct or a socially organizing idiom, but as assuming diverse formation and effect in varying situated circumstances. It is very much later in the piece that Chicago and American sociology begins to have a strong impact. The Manchester circle were interested in Chicago sociology (the symbolic interactionists especially) because it seemed to confirm an orientation that had already been formulated and methodologically developed by them. Anselm Strauss was invited to Manchester in its latter days and formed a friendship with Mitchell. The relationship, I consider, was initiated by the publication of Glazer and Strauss's *The Discovery of Grounded Theory* (1967), which essayed an idea that was already the point of situational analysis—the revelation of theoretical understanding from the intensive investigation of grounded practice.

In some ways, the processual or situational approach is antithetical to theorizing or conceptual/theoretical schematizing. These risk a totalizing that the method is inherently oriented against. In this perspective, theory is continually relative. Suggested by the study of practices in the historical flux of existence, the theories that are produced must themselves be limited by such flux and conditioned by a myriad of cross-cutting structural variations. There is a degree of parallel with the notion of singularity in post-structuralist orientations (see Agamben 1993; Deleuze and Guattari 1994)—that no theory can fully embrace the complexities that are engaged in human action and causation, that particular human actions constitute a unique complexity and conjunction of processes. Aspects of this notion are implicit in the work of Gluckman (e.g., *Closed Systems and Open Minds*), as is his concern to define carefully the nature of the problem and the kinds of process that might be amenable to the production of anthropological theoretical knowledge. But the whole situational idea insists on the situatedness of theory, on its enduring relativity to the situation, which in itself is irreducible and ultimately resistant to abstract conceptualizations and categories. To be open to the phenomena in question, to realize a degree of theoretical potential, the situational idea is continually subject to contingency. In this, situational analysis, the notion of the situation, is geared for a kind of anthropological surprise (or as Handelman comments, a Peircean surprise) or Husserlian astonishment. In other words, the idea of the situation and of situational analysis supplants the earlier anthropological notion of the exotic and breaks with its primordialist and evolutionist implications.

Processual or situational analysis leads *to* theory rather than extends *from* theory or its schematic formalizations. It is through and through empirical in this sense, a further reason why its potential is risked if it becomes merely a method of illustration. For this reason, I am a little wary of Glaeser's setting out of a conceptual scheme, for all its interest, into which situational analysis might be slotted and find a direction. It threatens the entire point of the Manchester approach, which was to discover conceptual and theoretical possibility in the ground of practice itself. What human realities are or how sociality is achieved, or even what social ontologies are in play, is an empirical matter in the Manchester orientation. Max Weber once stated that sociology is forever young; that is, it must constantly be concerned with reinventing itself as new issues and problems arise in the flux that is history. Programmatic statements for an anthropology or sociology of the kind that Glaeser essays here, for all its interest, risk stultification if applied to the Manchester idea.

One final observation. Situational analysis and the extended-case method saw their beginnings in Gluckman's analysis of a bridge opening—in the study of a particular event or case. Events or cases usually constitute a particular conjunction or concentration of forces that act as a prism through which to enter and encounter the varying complexity of ongoing social realities. But as I (and Handelman, this volume) have tried to indicate, the method is not to be restricted as merely a way to study events or to illustrate the larger processes of which they are a part. The method that began with the study of events is potentially of broader methodological importance. This is why I prefer the term 'processual analysis', which I think better communicates its larger significance as an approach to the understanding of the diversities of human action through practices.

My aim here has been to clarify what I consider to be a few of the critical directions implicated in the invention of situational or processual analysis as outlined by the essays in this volume. In my view, situational analysis was and still is a method in progress to which the essays here contribute. Most of all, I have tried to underline that situational analysis is thoroughly continuous with that which inspired the development of the once young discipline of anthropology. It offers a way in which anthropologists can engage their ethnographic method to the study of contemporary issues. Anthropology was once relatively alone in its championing of ethnography, but this is no longer the case. There is currently an apotheosis of the ethnographic in all forms and styles. However, the idea of situational and processual analysis is one way in which ethnographic fieldwork as initially imagined in anthropology can continue to play a role in the production of knowledge in ongoing human realities. Through it, the anthropologist can transcend his or her own intuition or poetic imagination as well as the imagination spawned in the human realities that the anthropologist encounters and to which situational analysis is intensely sensitive.

## References

Agamben, Giorgio. 1993. *The Coming Community.* Trans. Michael Hardt. London and Minneapolis: University of Minneapolis Press.

Barth, Fredrik, ed. 1969. *Ethnic Groups and Boundaries.* London: George Allen and Unwin.

Deleuze, Gilles, and Felix Guattari. 1994. *What Is Philosophy?* Trans. Hugh Tomlinson and Graham Burchell. New York: Columbia University Press.

Glazer, Barney G., and Anslem L. Strauss. 1967. *The Discovery of Grounded Theory.* Chicago: Aldine.

Gluckman, Max. [1940] 1958. *Analysis of a Social Situation in Modern Zululand.* Manchester: Manchester University Press for Rhodes-Livingstone Institute.

_____. 1963. "Gossip and Scandal." *Current Anthropology* 4, no. 3: 307–316.

_____, ed. 1964. *Closed Systems and Open Minds: The Limits of Naïvety in Social Anthropology.* Chicago: Aldine.

Kapferer, Bruce. 2000. "Star Wars: About Anthropology, Culture and Globalization." *Australian Journal of Anthropology* 11, no. 2: 174–198.

Mitchell, J. Clyde. 1959. *The Kalela Dance.* Manchester: Manchester University Press.

Sansom, B. L. 1980. *The Camp at Wallaby Creek.* Canberra: Australian Institute of Aboriginal Studies.

Turner, Victor W. 1957. *Schism and Continuity in an African Society.* Manchester: University of Manchester Press.

# INDEX

Abbott, Andrew, 172
abduction, 97, 99, 162, 224. *See also* Peirce;
    surprise
Aberle, David, 214
action, 65, 67, 69, 73–74, 87n5
action-reaction, 67, 69–71, 75, 80–81, 85–86,
    87n5
action-reaction-effect, 66-67, 69–70, 73, 74,
    77, 80. *See also* Glaeser
actors, 6, 26, 68, 69
    collective, 75
Adam and Eve, 56
African socialism, 225, 293, 296, 300, 301.
    *See also* Moore; Nyerere
agency, 5, 53, 68, 69, 76, 141, 195–96
    vs. determinism, 130
    of individuals, 99, 127, 145
Alexander, Rae, 211
alienation, 62n6
Allan, W. M., 211
Allcorn, D., 189, 199n16
Althusser, Louis, 215
ambiguity, 57, 58, 60, 62n2, 128
American academia, corporate managerial
    model of, 161
American Anthropological Association, 6,
    121–22
American anthropology, 5–6, 7, 122, 160
    cultural, 7, 130, 146
    disavowal of Manchester anthropology, 7
    dominance of global anthropology, 7
    post-modernism in, 122, 151n22, 315
American lit-crit hit mob, 161, 223
American sociology, 72, 166, 174, 198n5,
    218n14
    network concept, 72
    "quantitative/qualitative, humanistic/
        scientific controversy," 172
analytical languages, 206–7
Anderson, Benedict, 74

anthropology
    and colonialism, 78, 79, 119, 122, 130,
        148n6, 150n16, 207, 214
    and crises in world history, 118–19, 123
    of globalization, 273
    historical, 79, 87n4
    legal, 3, 176, 223
    of modernity, 119, 273, 312
    political, 195
    reflexive turn in, 8, 225
apartheid, 98, 128
apt illustration, 1, 20, 21, 25, 28, 50, 98–99,
    134, 140, 176, 225, 238, 244–45,
    247. *See also* extended-case method;
    Gluckman; Malinowski; situational
    analysis
Ardener, Edwin, 206
Aristotle, 4
Aronoff, Myron J., 7, 188
Association of Social Anthropologists, 165
auditory perception, 139
Austen, Jane, 316
auto-anthropology, 206, 208

Bailey, F. G., 186, 188, 189, 216
Balandier, Georges, 181
bare life, 59
Barnes, John A., 20, 24, 172, 188, 205, 216
    networks, 72, 145, 210
    at Rhodes-Livingstone Institute of Social
        Studies, 168, 184
    statistical data collection and analysis,
        20, 169
Barth, Fredrik, 6, 152n28, 225, 315
    ethnicity, 273–74, 286, 315
Barton, Roy F., 15
Bateson, Gregory, 113n6
Becker, H. S., 40n6
Beckett, Samuel, 58
Being-in-the-world (Heidegger), 54, 56

Lightning Source UK Ltd.
Milton Keynes UK
09 July 2010

156790UK00009B/173/P